## The Art of Law in the International Community

International law evolved to end and prevent armed conflict as much as for any other reason. Yet, the law against war appears weaker today than ever in its long history, evidenced by raging armed conflicts in which people are killed, injured, and forcibly displaced; the environment is devastated, and the planet impoverished. These consequences can be traced to the dominant ideology of Realism. In 1946, Hersch Lauterpacht challenged that ideology by contrasting it with the idea of international law, composed of natural law, positive law, and process theory. *The Art of Law in the International Community* revives his vision, rebuilding the understanding of why international law binds, what its norms require, and how courts are the ideal substitutes for war. The secret to the renewal of international law lies in revitalizing the moral foundation of natural law through drawing on aesthetic philosophy and the arts.

MARY ELLEN O'CONNELL is the Robert and Marion Short Professor of Law and Research Professor of International Dispute Resolution at the Kroc Institute, University of Notre Dame, where she devotes her research to strengthening international law in the interest of peace. In 2018, Professor O'Connell was a Fulbright Fellow at the Norwegian Nobel Institute. From 2005–2010, she chaired the International Law Association's Committee on the Use of Force, followed by two years as a vice president of the American Society of International Law. She has been a professional military educator for the United States Department of Defense and a practicing attorney.

**Recent Books in the Hersch Lauterpacht Memorial Lecture Series**

Mary Ellen O'Connell *The Art of Law in the International Community*

Yuval Shany *Questions of Jurisdiction and Admissibility before International Courts*

W. Michael Reisman and Christina Parajon Skinner *Fraudulent Evidence before Public International Tribunals: The Dirty Stories of International Law*

Andrés Rigo Sureda *Investment Treaty Arbitration: Judging Under Uncertainty*

Ralph Zacklin *The United Nations Secretariat and the Use of Force in a Unipolar World: Power v. Principle*

John H. Jackson *Sovereignty, the WTO, and Changing Fundamentals of International Law*

Jan Paulsson *Denial of Justice in International Law*

Francisco Orrego Vicuña *International Dispute Settlement in an Evolving Global Society: Constitutionalization, Accessibility, Privatization*

Martti Koskenniemi *The Gentle Civilizer of Nations: The Rise and Fall of International Law 1870–1960*

Thomas M. Franck *Recourse to Force: State Action against Threats and Armed Attacks*

Mohamed Shahabuddeen *Precedent in the World Court*

Antonio Cassese *Self-Determination of Peoples: A Legal Reappraisal*

# The Art of Law in the International Community

MARY ELLEN O'CONNELL
*University of Notre Dame*

CAMBRIDGE
UNIVERSITY PRESS

**CAMBRIDGE**
**UNIVERSITY PRESS**

University Printing House, Cambridge CB2 8BS, United Kingdom

One Liberty Plaza, 20th Floor, New York, NY 10006, USA

477 Williamstown Road, Port Melbourne, VIC 3207, Australia

314–321, 3rd Floor, Plot 3, Splendor Forum, Jasola District Centre, New Delhi – 110025, India

79 Anson Road, #06–04/06, Singapore 079906

Cambridge University Press is part of the University of Cambridge.

It furthers the University's mission by disseminating knowledge in the pursuit of education, learning, and research at the highest international levels of excellence.

www.cambridge.org
Information on this title: www.cambridge.org/9781108426664
DOI: 10.1017/9781108551144



First published 2019

Printed and bound in Great Britain by Clays Ltd, Elcograf S.p.A.

*A catalogue record for this publication is available from the British Library.*

*Library of Congress Cataloging-in-Publication Data*
Names: O'Connell, Mary Ellen, 1958– author.
Title: The art of law in the international community / Mary Ellen O'Connell.
Other titles: International law and the art of peace
Description: Cambridge, United Kingdom ; New York, NY, USA : Cambridge University Press, 2019. | Series: Hersch Lauterpacht memorial lectures ; 23 | "The book began as the 2014 Sir Hersch Lauterpacht Memorial Lectures, titled, International Law and the Art of Peace". | Includes bibliographical references and index.
Identifiers: LCCN 2018059145 | ISBN 9781108426664 (hardback)
Subjects: LCSH: International law.
Classification: LCC KZ3410 .O23 2019 | DDC 341–dc23
LC record available at https://lccn.loc.gov/2018059145

ISBN 978-1-108-42666-4 Hardback

*For*
Philip Allott

# *Contents*

# *Acknowledgements*

This book developed through the efforts and support of so many people, too many to thank here. It has been a pleasure and a privilege to discuss the importance of art to law with audiences, classes, at dinners and during chance meetings. The footnotes reflect the contribution of numerous colleagues. Various institutions provided opportunities and environments for creative thinking, especially the Lauterpacht Centre for International Law, the Center of Theological Inquiry and the Program in Law and Public Affairs of Princeton University, and the Norwegian Nobel Institute. Research assistants were collaborators in the ideas, the research, and the drafting, especially Felicia Caponigri, Marie-Claire Klassen, Zachary Stackhouse, and Sawyer White. My editor at Cambridge University Press, Finola O'Sullivan, gave me confidence. My husband, Peter Bauer, a former United States Army interrogator, a photographer, and a Photoshop expert, provided the original inspiration, as well as constant love, encouragement, and support.

# Introduction

Humanity faces extraordinary challenges of major violence, environmental decline, human rights abuse, and economic deprivation. International law is one of the few tools for responding to these problems, a fact long motivating efforts to improve the effectiveness of international law.[1] This book is one of those efforts. It offers a distinctive approach, drawing on the arts and aesthetic philosophy.[2] These are largely untapped sources in responding to the persistent doubts that hinder confidence and participation in international law, weakening its support of flourishing around the globe.

The book began as the 2014 Sir Hersch Lauterpacht Memorial Lectures, titled, 'International Law and the Art of Peace'.[3] The lectures were inspired by two of Lauterpacht's own celebrated

[1] For past proposals aimed improving compliance, see A. Chayes and A. Handler Chayes, 'On Compliance', *International Organization*, 47 (1993), 175–205; T. M. Franck, *The Power of Legitimacy among Nations* (Oxford: Oxford University Press, 1990) and R. Fisher, *Improving Compliance with International Law* (Charlottesville, VA: University of Virginia Press, 1981).

[2] Aesthetic philosophy 'employs the term "aesthetic" to circumscribe' the following:

> The experiences that we have when we listen to music, read poetry and look at paintings or scenes in nature, have a distinctive immediate, emotional and contemplative character, and lead us to describe what we experience in a special vocabulary, and to use terms such as beautiful, exquisite, inspiring, moving and so on.

S. Gardner, 'Aesthetics', in N. Bunnin and E. P. Tsui-James (eds.), *The Blackwell Companion to Philosophy* 2nd edn (Oxford: Blackwell Publishing, 2003), 231–56, 231. See also Chapter 1.

[3] M. E. O'Connell, 'International Law and the Art of Peace', 17–19 February 2014, available at https://itunes.apple.com/us/itunes-u/lcil-international-law-seminar-series/id472214191?mt=10 (nos. 105–7).

publications: his 1933 book *The Function of Law in the International Community*[4] and his 1946 article 'The Grotian Tradition in International Law'.[5] In *The Function of Law,* Lauterpacht identifies the 'reign of law' as an essential condition in securing and preserving the ultimate good for which law is instituted, the attainment of peace.[6] Lauterpacht argued that courts are the best available means of incorporating international law into the life of the international community. Courts can uniquely mandate change while maintaining stability in ordering society through law.[7] He particularly advocated for international courts to have the compulsory jurisdiction typical of national courts.[8] Lauterpacht saw compulsory adjudication to be the *sine qua non* of a legal system.[9]

After World War II, during which he lost most of his family in the Holocaust, Lauterpacht wrote his inspirational article 'The Grotian Tradition'. He wrote to restore confidence in international law and to respond to the proponents of Realism who were blaming weak international law and institutions and the failure of military readiness for the outbreak of the war.[10] Lauterpacht provided a very different assessment. He described international law as built on the view of the seventeenth-century Dutch jurist, diplomat, and theologian Hugo Grotius that human beings are social, other-oriented, and thus willing and able to make the sacrifices of self-interest needed to live in peaceful community under law. Grotius saw people as 'intrinsically moved by a desire for social life, endowed with an ample measure of goodness, altruism, and morality, and capable of acting on general principle and of learning from experience'.[11]

[4] Sir Hersch Lauterpacht, *The Function of Law in the International Community* (Oxford: Oxford University Press, 1933).

[5] Sir Hersch Lauterpacht, 'The Grotian Tradition in International Law', *British Yearbook of International Law,* 23 (1946), 1–53, 1.

[6] Lauterpacht, *The Function of Law* 1933 (n. 4), 346. [7] Ibid., 346.

[8] On the life of Sir Hersch Lauterpacht, see E. Lauterpacht, *The Life of Hersch Lauterpacht,* (Cambridge: Cambridge University Press, 2010) and P. Sands, *East West Street* (New York: Vintage Books, 2016).

[9] Lauterpacht, *The Function of Law* 1933 (n. 4), 438.

[10] See, e.g., E. H. Carr, *The Twenty Years' Crisis 1919–1939* (New York: Macmillan & Co, 1939) and H. J. Morgenthau, 'Positivism, Functionalism, and International Law', *American Journal of International Law,* 34 (1940), 260–84.

[11] Lauterpacht, 'The Grotian Tradition' 1946 (n. 5), 24.

By contrast, Grotius's contemporary, the British political commentator Thomas Hobbes, saw human beings as unable to act other than in self-interest unless coerced. Hobbes saw human beings as 'essentially selfish, anti-social, and unable to learn from experience ... the basis of political obligation is interest pure and simple; the idea of a sense of moral duty rising supreme over desire and passion is a figment of imagination ...'.[12] For Hobbes, law is impossible at the international level, beyond a national government's coercive reach. It is this Hobbesian world view that is imbedded in the theory of political Realism and gives rise to Realism's greater respect for military power in relations among states than law.

Lauterpacht linked the noted Realist Hans Morgenthau to Hobbes and Hobbes's exclusion of international law from a role in restraining the use of force. Morgenthau similarly viewed military affairs as beyond the capacity of international legal influence. For Morgenthau, military matters raise non-justiciable political questions that must be resolved by national executives, not judges. He also saw executives as having a duty to amass and use military assets to maintain the freedom that comes with the ability to coerce others. This, he argued, is the national leader's higher moral duty, certainly higher than compliance with international law.[13] He encouraged this position by pointing out that, in his view, international law has no sanctions sufficient to compel a leader to take principles on the use of force seriously.

Lauterpacht pushed back against arguments he found to be 'the work of international lawyers anxious to give legal expression to the State's claim to be independent of law'.[14] He objected to arguments on the use of force that depicted legal restrictions as illusory.[15] He also rejected self-serving arguments designed to avoid resort to binding dispute resolution, arguments like Morgenthau's that some disputes are too important, grave, political, or military in nature to be proper subjects of dispute resolution. For Lauterpacht, it was 'the refusal of the State to submit the dispute to judicial settlement, and not the intrinsic

[12] Ibid., 24–5.
[13] Hans Morgenthau deserves credit as an originator of the theory of political Realism. See H. J. Morgenthau, *Politics Among Nations, The Struggle for Power and Peace* (New York, NY: Alfred A. Knopf, 1948). See, also, Chapter 1.
[14] Lauterpacht, *The Function of Law* 1933 (n. 4), 6. [15] Ibid., 180.

nature of the controversy, which makes it political'.[16] No activity is strictly either legal or political. Judges and lawyers are capable of focusing on the legal aspects of questions, even those considered to be issues of sovereignty or security.

Lauterpacht could take these strong, principled positions in support of the rule of law over the will of sovereign states because he was a natural lawyer. Other international lawyers of his time were losing the ability to argue that the promotion of law is the superior moral activity to amassing and projecting military force. They were relying not on natural law but positivism alone. Positivism requires material proof of state acceptance, whether express or tacit.[17] It lacks a normative hierarchy or moral basis for law beyond consent.[18] Because consent may be withdrawn, positive law can be seen as inferior to the sovereign state's will. Positivism is thus consistent with Realist political theory holding that the only actual fetter on state action is coercive power, especially an opponent's superior military strength.

Positivists could hardly argue otherwise than Morgenthau – if state will is the source of law and states prefer to be free of legal restraint in military affairs, their will is determinative. For Lauterpacht, however, 'the will of States cannot be the exclusive

[16] Ibid., 164. See also, M. Koskenniemi, 'Introduction', in H. Lauterpacht, *The Function of Law in the International Community* (Oxford: Oxford University Press, 2011), 30.

[17] Lauterpacht, *The Function of Law* 1933 (n. 4), 3.

Positive law is the law that emerges from the voluntary or consensual sources of law, whether national legislation, treaty, or practice. It involves action that can be confirmed with material evidence. For two views of positivist theory relevant to the sources of international law, see D. Lefkowitz, 'Sources in Legal Positivist Theories: Law as Necessarily Posited and the Challenge of Customary Law Creation', in S. Besson and J. d'Aspremont (eds.), *The Oxford Handbook of the Sources of International Law* (Oxford: Oxford University Press, 2017), 323–42 and J. Kammerhofer, 'Sources in Legal Positivist Theories: The Pure Theory's Structural Analysis of the Law', in S. Besson and J. d'Aspremont (eds.), *The Oxford Handbook of the Sources of International Law* (Oxford: Oxford University Press, 2017), 343–63.

The two main forms of positive international law are treaties, international agreements that bind on the basis of consent, and customary international law, principles that reflect general practice undertaken out of a sense of legal obligation. See Statute of the International Court of Justice, Art. 38(1)(a) & (b), icj-cij.org.

[18] For a comparison of positive law rules to the rules of a game, see J. Gardner, 'Legal Positivism: 5½ Myths', *American Journal of Jurisprudence*, 46 (1) 1 January 2001, 199–227.

For more on the limits of positivism as a comprehensive theory of law, see Chapters 1 and 2.

or even, in the last resort, the decisive source' of international law.[19] He accepted the essential role of positive law and positive law theory but within a more complete theoretical concept of law that included natural law and the legal process. Lauterpacht understood that all law consists of mostly positive law within a frame of natural law but argued that while this fact could be merely assumed with national legal systems, it had to be openly acknowledged in the case of international law. International law lacks the government institutions for lawmaking that exist in national systems. How law is made without them needs explaining. Natural law theory does in fact explain that some norms remain binding with or without consent. Lauterpacht looked to natural law as the 'ever-present source for supplementing the voluntary (consent-based) law of nations'.[20]

He said little more in 'The Grotian Tradition' about natural law.[21] Positivism was already dominant by the 1930s,[22] but he could assume lingering understanding of what natural law entailed as the basis for his appeal for confidence in world law. More than three generations later, knowledge of natural law has all but disappeared.[23] To understand law beyond positivism, to find law once again, as Lauterpacht did, superior to the consent of states and their will to military power and avoidance of international courts, is to understand natural law. Natural law is needed for concepts such as universality and equality to have a solid place in international relations. Natural law supports the search for what Philip Allott has called 'a revival of the ancient idea of the essential unity of humanity'.[24]

[19] Lauterpacht, 'The Grotian Tradition' 1946 (n. 5), 22. [20] Ibid., 21–2.

[21] Koskenniemi surmises that Lauterpacht had no well-developed theory of natural law. Koskenniemi, 'Introduction', (n. 16), 27.

[22] Ibid.

[23] Interest in natural law is again on the increase, however, see, e.g., M. Koskenniemi, 'Transformations of Natural Law, Germany 1648–1815', in A. Orford and F. Hoffmann (eds.), *The Oxford Handbook of the Theory of International Law* (Oxford: Oxford University Press, 2016), 59–81; A. Augusto Cançado Trindade, *International Law for Humankind: Towards a New* Jus Gentium 2nd edn (Leiden: Martinus Nijhoff, 2013), 139 and C. G. Weeramantry, *Universalizing International Law* (Leiden: Martinus Nijhoff, 2004). See also M. E. O'Connell and C. Day, 'Sources and the Legality and Validity of International Law: Natural Law as Source of Extra-Positive Norms', in S. Besson and J. d'Aspremont (eds.), *The Oxford Handbook of the Sources of International Law* (Oxford: Oxford University Press, 2017), 562–80.

[24] P. Allott, 'Towards Utopia – Rethinking International Law' *German Yearbook of International' Law*, 60 (2017), 269–312.

Positivism lacks a universal perspective that considers the whole of the international community.[25] Chapter 1 provides a detailed discussion of the limits of positivism and the need for natural law explanations of why law binds sovereign states, even when leaders find a rule not in their nation's interest.

The theory of international legal process is also in need of renewal. The situation has been transformed since Lauterpacht assessed it in 1933. From the few international courts and tribunals in existence when *The Function of Law* was written, today there are dozens. Yet, international law still lacks courts with general compulsory jurisdiction, which Lauterpacht considered essential.[26] States still resist judicial settlement. More remarkably, the global popular movement that once promoted courts and legal mechanisms of dispute resolution to serve as a substitute for war has all but vanished.[27] The success of Realist thinking has helped create a world with greater confidence in military force than in mechanisms for the peaceful settlement of disputes. A contemporary response is needed that can re-ignite the appeal of international legal process for peace with a new emphasis on the International Court of Justice and compulsory jurisdiction.[28]

[25] '[I]n the nineteenth century, the law of nations, which had been universal in the sixteenth, seventeenth and eighteenth centuries, abandoned the centuries-old universalist tradition based on natural law theory and "narrowed" [itself] to a regional (purely European) legal system.' C. H. Alexandrowicz, *An Introduction to the History of the Law of Nations of the East Indies (16th, 17th, and 18th Centuries)* (Oxford: Clarendon Press, 1967), 2.

[26] Lauterpacht, *The Function of Law*, 1933 (n. 4), 437–8.

[27] See Chapter 6.

[28] The International Court of Justice (ICJ) is the 'principal judicial organ of the United Nations'. United Nations Charter, Art. 92, un.org. The ICJ is the only permanent adjudicative body with authority to hear cases on any subject of international law brought between any states that are members of the United Nations. See also, the Statute of the International Court of Justice, icj-cij.org; V. Lowe and M. Fitzmaurice (eds.), *Fifty Years of the International Court of Justice, Essays in Honour of Sir Robert Jennings* (Cambridge: Cambridge University Press, 1996); A. Zimmerman, C. Tomuschat and K. Oellers-Frahm (eds.), *The Statute of the International Court of Justice, A Commentary* 2nd edn (Oxford: Oxford University Press, 2012), and G. I. Hernández, *The International Court of Justice and the Judicial Function* (Oxford: Oxford University Press, 2014). For a comparison of the ICJ and other courts for the settlement of interstate disputes, see S. D. Murphy, 'International Judicial Bodies for Solving Disputes Between States', in C. P. R. Romano, K. J. Alter, and Y. Shany (eds.), *The Oxford Handbook of International Adjudication* (Oxford: Oxford University Press, 2014), 181–204.

*The Art of Law* takes *jus cogens* status seriously and provides a thorough assessment of the prohibition on force from that perspective. For example, the doctrine of *jus cogens* forbids derogation. It is not possible, therefore, for new rules of customary law to develop that conflict with an established peremptory norm. Any contrary state practice violates these norms; it does not change them.[48] Equally, *jus cogens* norms must be interpreted strictly to avoid derogation. Courts may discern over time that peremptory norms reach more conduct; they may not be interpreted to reach less.[49]

The prohibition on the use of force incorporates two components long identified as exceptions; one concerns the United Nations Security Council's right to authorize force and the other concerns the right of self-defence, the topics of Chapters 3 and 4. Under standard rules of interpretation these exceptions need to be interpreted narrowly.[50] The case for narrow interpretation is even stronger when the norm is *jus cogens.* Some uses of force will meet the exceptions but will still be unlawful unless they meet additional restrictions in the form of certain general principles that are also explained by natural law. Principles such as necessity, proportionality, attribution, consent, and equality are reviewed in Chapters 2–4. These principles significantly restrict the right to resort to armed force by any international actor. They may only use force when no alternatives exist and the use has a high likelihood of accomplishing the legitimate military objective without disproportionate cost.[51]

[48] United Nations Convention on the Law of Treaties, 23 May 1969, 1155 UNTS 331, *reprinted in* 8 ILM. 679 (1969), Arts. 53 and 64.

[49] Chapter 2.

[50] It is 'desirable' to interpret Article 2(4) 'widely enough to ensure that any significant use of military force is banned and to give the acknowledged exception created by Art. 51 a correspondingly narrow meaning'. B. V. A. Röling, 'The Ban on the Use of Force and the UN Charter', in A. Cassese (ed.), *The Current Legal Regulation of the Use of Force* (Dordrecht: Martinus Nijhoff, 1986), 3–8, 4–5. See also, common legal maxims derived from Roman Law, such as *singularia non sunt extendenda,* which can be translated as exceptions should not be applied extensively, and *quae communi legi derogant stricte interpretantur,* derogations from the common law should be interpreted narrowly. W. E. Lattin, 'Legal Maxims, and Their Use in Statutory Interpretations', *Georgetown Law Journal,* 26 (1938), 1–16, 7–8.

[51] The ICJ Statute includes general principles among the sources of international law. See Statute of the International Court of Justice, Art. 38(1)(c), icj-cij.org.

These legal hurdles to resort to force tend to be overlooked due to the widespread confidence in military force that has resulted from the pervasive influence of Realist theory. This confidence has yielded far more than the failure to take the peremptory status of norms seriously. It explains why proponents of using military force resort to moral and ethical arguments to add weight to the thin evidence of legality in positive law. The moral claims have included assertions that certain norms are superior to and therefore trump the prohibition on force or that immoral or undemocratic governments lose the legal protections enjoyed by their states. The quixotic assertion is even made that the prohibition on force is somehow an unjust law if it prevents righteous actors from using force in causes they deem good. The argument is that unjust law is not law – *lex iniusta non est lex* – and, therefore, not binding. Law violation in the pursuit of higher moral principles or values is claimed to be justified or excused.[52]

Scholars and government officials are using such arguments to claim rights of military intervention either on behalf of a government or on behalf of a government's opponents seeking regime change or secession.[53] Advocates for broader rights to resort to force attempt to argue that international law does not apply to intervention with a state's or rebel movement's consent. Human rights law may apply but nothing more. Chapter 5 reaches a different conclusion. The case is made there that the prohibition may well apply to both situations. The prohibition on force of natural law is not restricted to the interstate use of force by UN member states. The first use of major armed force by any state or non-state actor is prohibited unless authorized by the UN Security Council.[54]

Moral arguments do not alter this conclusion. Arguments using moral justification omit the fact that the prohibition on the use of force is itself *jus cogens*, a higher ethical norm. The prohibition in Article 2(4) has equal status to the prohibition on genocide. It has

For the general principles at issue here see, J. Gardam, *Necessity and Proportionality*, (Cambridge: Cambridge University Press, 2004), 4–5 and B. Cheng, *General Principles of Law as Applied by International Courts and Tribunals* (London: Stevens and Sons, 1953), 70–7, 71, 74.

52 For several of these arguments, see H. H. Koh, 'The War Powers and Humanitarian Intervention', *Houston Law Review*, 53 (2016) 971–1033, 1004–15. See also Chapter 5.

53 O. Corten, 'La Rebéllion et le Droit International: Le Principe de Neutralité en Tension', *Hague Recueil des Cours*, 374 (2015), 53–312.

54 Chapter 5.

a higher status than other human rights. There is no justification for violating a peremptory norm, not even in the interest of trying to get compliance with another norm of equal status.

The moral arguments generally tend to be special pleading, attempting to privilege a particular state not all subjects of international law equally.[55] The arguments are invalid for this and many other reasons, including that in international law states have equal status before the law. Non-state actors also have equal rights and duties to others within their category. What sets international law apart, what makes it the law of an international community, is the absence of an imperial power with superior rights and privileges. As will be discussed in Chapter 3, critics often remark that the Permanent Members of the UN Security Council have the privilege of exercising the veto over decisions of peace and security. The veto represents authority within the UN to exercise deliberative judgment on behalf of UN members. It provides no higher status as states to these five members. It does, however, obligate the five to act in the promotion of peace.[56]

The Permanent Members have the duty to lead in promoting peace through law. Instead, all five take exceptionalist positions with respect to the prohibition on the use of force and the duty of peaceful settlement of disputes. Permanent Members are obligated not only to respect the negative obligations to refrain from resort to force but to model law compliance.[57] Only the United Kingdom still accepts the ICJ's compulsory jurisdiction, and its acceptance is hemmed in with reservations.[58] All five frequently resort to unlawful military force. To illustrate this central structural and political challenge to the law of peace, each chapter begins with a significant failure by a Permanent Member to comply with the law on the use of force or the peaceful settlement of disputes. Their conduct undermines the very source of prestige they value by remaining a P5 member.

[55] Cf. Lauterpacht, *The Function of Law* 1933 (n. 4), 6.

[56] See UN Charter, Chap. IV.

[57] M. E. O'Connell, 'Peace Through Law and the Security Council: Modelling Law Compliance', in J. Farrall and H. Charlesworth (eds.), *Strengthening the Rule of Law Through the UN Security Council* (New York: Routledge, 2016) 255–69.

[58] In 2018, only the United Kingdom continued to accept ICJ compulsory jurisdiction but with extensive reservations. The UK amended its acceptance again on 22 February 2017. The USA and France withdrew in 1984 and 1974 respectively. Russia and China never accepted compulsory jurisdiction. ICJ, 'Declarations Accepting the Jurisdiction of the Court as Compulsory', https://www.icj-cij.org/en/declarations.

The approach to these case studies of failure by the Permanent Members follows the classic international law analytic method of applying the law to concrete cases. International law is the legal category perhaps most open to philosophical reflection but rarely are these reflections abstract.[59] To see the importance of the natural law, peremptory norms, and general principles restricting resort to force is to apply them in real-world situations. International law relies as much as any law on informed public opinion. Analysis of the law violations by the Permanent Members in North Korea, Syria, Ukraine, Mali, and the South China Sea not only demonstrates the law of greatest concern in this book – the law of peace – but legal analysis of these cases also serves to inform the international community about non-compliance by actors with the highest duty to lead. It shows how far they stand from the ideal envisioned by Lauterpacht at the end of World War II.

The cases also underscore the limited utility of resort to military force. They contradict the promises of Realism. An armed conflict continuing for decades can only be assessed a failure.[60] The tragedy of such failure is all the greater given the available alternatives to the use of force. International law supports a variety of means for peaceful settlement of disputes, each with a better record of success than military force. Yet, through a confluence of factors, military force has achieved a dominant place in intellectual life on all continents but Antarctica.[61] Confidence in military force supports the

[59] M. Koskenniemi, 'International Law in the World of Ideas', in J. Crawford and M. Koskenniemi, *The Cambridge Companion to International Law* (Cambridge: Cambridge University Press, 2012), 47–63, 47.

[60] For just two examples, see, C. J. Chivers, 'Wars Without End', *New York Times* (8 August 2018), available at www.nytimes.com/2018/08/08/magazine/war-afghanistan-iraq-soldiers.html ('The Pentagon's failed campaigns in Iraq and Afghanistan left a generation of soldiers with little to fight for but one another.' Ibid.) And, 'Democratic Republic of Congo profile – Timeline', *BBC* (1 August 2018), available at www.bbc.com/news/world-africa-13286306. Ongoing conflict in the Democratic Republic of the Congo (formerly Zaire) began in 1996.

[61] At time of writing, civil war looms in Venezuela and Nicaragua but the long civil war in Colombia is being ended through a model peace process. 'The Spector of Civil War in Venezuela', *Washington Post* (3 August 2017), https://www.washingtonpost.com/opinions/the-specter-of-civil-war-in-venezuela/2017/08/13/aaa07852-7ecd-11e7-a669-b400c5c7e1cc_story.html?utm_term=.e0acd112c2a9 and O. J. Pérez, 'Can Nicaragua's Military Prevent a Civil War?', *Foreign Policy* (3 July 2018), https://foreignpolicy.com/2018/07/03/can-nicaraguas-military-prevent-a-civil-war/. On Colombia's peace process, including agreements

vast spending on armed conflict and weapons technology, which, in turn, builds an industry with a profit motive to lobby for the purchase, use, and replacement of their products. A major effort is underway to create computers that select and destroy without human intervention in the 'kill' decision.[62] Resources are devoted to 'slaughterbots' rather than controlling greenhouse gases, a truly existential threat to the planet. Investment choices are driven by ideas. Ideas that can change.

Regenerating interest in the idea of prohibiting force through law and substituting peaceful dispute resolution requires persistence, creativity, and vision. Long-separated from the transcendent ideas that gave rise to them, interest in alternatives to war has declined dramatically. Peaceful settlement through international legal process is no longer promoted as a cause. The driving force behind the proliferation of courts and tribunals in the late twentieth and early twenty-first century has been interest in specific substantive areas. Arguments are no longer made in favour of the compulsory jurisdiction of the ICJ. Advocates do not pursue expanding the ICJ's jurisdiction or the scope of Article 2(4).

Lauterpacht wrote passionately of the ideas of transcendence integral to international law.[63] He invited the international community to embrace those ideas in the wake of world war. The international community is currently experiencing a 'piecemeal' World War III.[64] To exit this war requires, once again, a renewal of confidence in the law of peace. Philip Allott sees the possibility of at last making 'a world without war'.[65] This book contributes to his vision by restoring the ideas of transcendence at the heart of international law. It responds to what Allott

reached between the government and principal opposition groups, see http://colombiapeace.org/.

62 On the basic facts and ethical challenges of lethal autonomous weapons systems, see D. Amaroso and G. Tamburrini, 'The Ethical and Legal Case Against Autonomy in Weapons Systems', *Global Jurist*, (2017), available at https://www.degruyter.com/view/j/gj.ahead-of-print/gj-2017-0012/gj-2017-0012.xml and R. Sparrow, 'Robots and Respect: Assessing the Case Against Autonomous Weapons Systems', *Journal of Ethics and International Affairs*, 30 (2016) 93–116.

63 'A stable law is rooted in passion, and does not transcend it.' P. Gewirtz, 'Aeschylus' Law', *Harvard Law Review*, 101 (1988), 1043–55, 1047.

64 'Pope Francis Warns on "Piecemeal World War III,"' *BBC* (13 September 2014), bbc.com/news/world-europe-29190890.

65 Allott, 'Towards Utopia', 2017 (n. 24).

calls 'the sordid justifications of war [that] persist and, in the 21st century, are being strengthened by the emerging of new forms of old atavisms'.[66] These justifications rely on international law but do so erroneously. The chapters that follow explain why.

Law is more art than science; it is composed of theory, substance, and process, and draws on all sources of human knowledge – the rational, the emotional, and the spiritual. Promoting compliance requires understanding, coercive means of enforcement,[67] positive benefits,[68] and the conviction that compliance is a moral good, that it is doing the right thing. Revitalized natural law, supported by the insights of aesthetic philosophy, reveal the morality of law, the good of law compliance, non-violence, and peaceful settlement. Hersch Lauterpacht encouraged just such a holistic approach when he extolled Grotius's appeal 'to the law of love, the law of charity, . . . and of goodness'[69] on behalf of the international community.

66 Ibid.

67 On the means of coercive enforcement in international law and their essential role in distinguishing law from other order systems, see M. E. O'Connell, *The Power and Purpose of International Law, Insights from the Theory and Practice of Enforcement* (New York: Oxford University Press, 2008).

68 On the benefits of law compliance, see L. Henkin, *How Nations Behave* 2nd edn (New York: Columbia University Press, 1974).

69 Lauterpacht, 'The Grotian Tradition' 1946 (n. 5), 25.

# 1

# Revitalizing the Theory of International Law Compliance

As modern international law emerged with the rise of the state system, the theory of natural law was fading.[1] As it did, international law lost the source of answers to fundamental questions. Natural law held the explanation of why law compliance is a moral good. Natural law explained why some law binds even in the absence of consent, and why some norms are superior to others. Without natural law, positivism alone remains as an explanatory source, but positivism explains only the law based on consent.[2] Positivism cannot explain non-consent-based concepts, norms, and principles, referred to sometimes here as the 'extra-positive' aspects of the law. Natural law theory as the only other source of explanation besides positivism is needed for these extra-positive aspects. This chapter offers a revitalized theory of natural law, one well suited to a contemporary explanation of why any actor should comply with law that is not in its self-interest. The chapter also lays the groundwork for a revitalized understanding of natural law as the basis for the superior or *jus cogens* status of the prohibition on the use of force and adjunct general principles of necessity, proportionality, equality, attribution, and consent.[3] Aesthetic philosophy and the

[1] See, in this chapter, notes 7–21 and accompanying text.

[2] Positive law is the law that emerges from the voluntary or consensual sources of law, whether national legislation, treaty, or practice. It involves action that can be confirmed with material evidence. See Introduction, note 17 and accompanying text. 'The term "positive law" was put into wide philosophical circulation first by Aquinas.' J. Finnis, 'Natural Law Theories', in E. N. Zalta (ed.), *The Stanford Encyclopedia of Philosophy* (Winter 2016), 1, available at https://plato.stanford.edu/archives/win2016/entries/natural-law-theories/.

[3] The modified understanding of natural law presented in this chapter was introduced in M. E. O'Connell and C. Day, 'Sources and the Legality and Validity of

study of beauty provide a secular alternative to the religious elements of traditional natural law.[4] The alternative is compatible with religious teaching but also has universal appeal.

It was, in fact, the religious elements that led international lawyers away from natural law despite its importance to international legal theory. Eighteenth- and nineteenth-century lawyers deemed non-material features of law to be suspect in the new world of scientific method.[5] Natural law lacked material proof and was consequently suppressed. Yet, no adequate alternative to natural law emerged in its place. Much of the discussion below concerns the search for a substitute that has ranged from treating law as a branch of science, something like botany, to treating it as a branch of market economics. Scientists stopped restricting their own search for knowledge to material sources long ago, indicating it is safe for international law scholars to do so once again as well. Beauty and the arts inspire discovery in a wide range of disciplines from mathematics to physics to psychology. Theologians have long considered aesthetics and are renewing their own use of this source for non-cognitive, transcendent knowledge.[6]

Traditional natural lawyers discern answers to questions about law through the use of reason applied to observations of nature and

International Law: Natural Law as Source of Extra-Positive Norms', in S. Besson and J. d'Aspremont (eds.), *The Oxford Handbook of the Sources of International Law* (Oxford: Oxford University Press, 2017), 562–80.

[4] S. Gardner, 'Aesthetics', in N. Bunnin and E. P. Tsui-James (eds.), *The Blackwell Companion to Philosophy* 2nd edn (Oxford: Blackwell Publishing, 2003), 231–56, 231. For reflections on beauty as a source of knowledge in mathematics, the sciences, the humanities, theology, and law, see V. Hösle (ed.), *The Many Faces of Beauty* (Notre Dame, IN: University of Notre Dame Press, 2013).

[5] This historical account is confirmed in many places, see, e.g., B. S. Gregory, *The Unintended Reformation* (Cambridge, MA: Harvard University Press, 2012); C. Taylor, *A Secular Age,* (Cambridge, MA: Belknap Press of Harvard University Press, 2007); T. Asad, *Formations of the Secular: Christianity, Islam, Modernity* (Stanford: Stanford University Press, 2003); H. J. Berman, *Law and Revolution, The Formation of the Western Legal Tradition* (Cambridge, MA: Harvard University Press, 1985); M. Brown, *Restoration of Reason: The Eclipse and Recovery of Truth, Goodness, and Beauty* (Grand Rapids, MI: Baker Academic, 2006), 25, and other sources in notes 7–21 of this chapter.

[6] For Cyril O'Regan, 'beauty might be regarded as the proper object of theology, that is, God.' C. O'Regan, 'Theology, Art, and Beauty', in V. Hösle (ed.), *The Many Faces of Beauty* (Notre Dame, IN: University of Notre Dame Press, 2013), 445–71, 455. See also G. Thiessen, *Theological Aesthetics: A Reader* (Grand Rapids, MI; Wm. B. Eerdmans Publishing, 2004) and the references to beauty as an aspect of most religious and spiritual traditions, note 140.

perception of divine will or command.[7] Insight into divine will came from the study of holy texts, revelation, and prayer. Aesthetic philosophy relies on contemplation of beauty in the natural world and the arts. The insight from such contemplation serves well as a substitute or supplement to discerning divine command in natural law, as will be explained below.

The alternative version of natural law introduced in this chapter will be used to explain the authority of international law to command compliance. In Chapter 2 it will be used to explain *jus cogens*, the category of superior norms to which the prohibition on the use of force belongs. Revitalized natural law theory will also be used in Chapter 2 to explain the general principles that are associated with the prohibition on the use of force, including equality, necessity, and proportionality.

## I Legal Authority and Natural Law

Legal authority in the context of international law means 'international law's "right to rule"; the exercise of which binds its subjects by imposing duties of obedience'.[8]

Inherent in the concept of law is the understanding that its principles bind. Legal principles are more than good ideas, policy, standards, courtesies, or moral guidelines. No matter how precise a rule is or how clear, regardless of its origin in a parliament or treaty, arguing for compliance assumes recognition that a rule is binding. When modern international law first emerged, theologians, drawing on scripture and revelation, taught that God ordained obedience to law. Complying with law leads 'men and women to virtue' and promotes the common good.[9]

No one needs to tell a person to comply with the law in her own self-interest or when punishment is sure to follow a failure to

[7] T. Aquinas, *Summa Theologica*, I-II, qs. 90–108, and on Hugo Grotius's view of the natural law, see J. Miller, 'Hugo Grotius', in E. N. Zalta (ed.), *The Stanford Encyclopedia of Philosophy* (Spring 2014) sec. 3, https://plato.stanford.edu/entries/grotius/. See also, O'Connell and Day, 'Natural Law as Source of Extra-Positive Norms', (n. 3).

[8] S. Besson, 'The Authority of International Law – Lifting the Veil', *Sydney Law Review*, 31 (2009), 343–80, 344 and 345 note 2.

[9] M. C. Kaveny, *Law's Virtues, Fostering Autonomy and Solidarity in American Society* (Washington, DC: Georgetown University Press, 2012), 29, citing Aquinas, *Summa Theologica*, I-II, q. 91, art. 4.

comply. It is compliance with law when doing so seems to provide no benefit or detriment, law wholly for the good of others, that needs the invocation of divine command. Compliance with such law may require an attitude of openness to self-sacrifice, empathy, altruism, and love. Religions teach such openness, but with the separation of law and religion and the decline of theology in matters of public, intellectual debate, the search has been on for a persuasive reason to obey law for the good of others.

### A *The Fading of Natural Law*

In the seventeenth century, positive law was understood as part of natural law, the larger part. Positive law filled a frame consisting of natural law derived from the use of reason, the observation of nature, and openness to inspiration in discerning divine command.[10] Natural law was the source of the authority for positive law as well as the higher moral and general principles that the positive law may not transgress.[11] Hugo Grotius expressed the importance of the natural law frame when he said, 'What God has shown to be his Will, that is law.'[12] Yet, to persuade Protestant and Catholic leaders to agree to the same version of international law, Grotius famously removed discernment of divine command when he wrote in the *Prolegomena* to the *Law of War and Peace* in 1625, 'What we have been saying [about law] would have a degree of validity even if we should concede that which cannot be conceded without the utmost wickedness, that there is no God, or that the affairs of men are of no concern to him.'[13]

[10] 'Transcendence' refers to '[e]xistence or experience beyond the normal or physical level'. *Oxford Dictionaries*, www.oxforddictionaries.com/us/definition/english/transcendence.

[11] O'Connell and Day, 'Natural Law as Source of Extra-Positive Norms', (n. 3).

[12] H. Grotius, *Commentary on the Law of Prize and Booty* (1603), chap. II, available online, http://oll.libertyfund.org/titles/grotius-commentary-on-the-law-of-prize-and-booty.

[13] H. Grotius (trans. F. W. Kelsey), De Jure Belli ac Pacis (*The Law of War and Peace*) (1995 edn [1625]), 'Prolegomena'. For a discussion of earlier thinkers preparing the way for Grotius's hypothetical, see Gregory's discussion of John Duns Scotus (1266–1308) and William of Occam (1285–1348), among others. Gregory, *The Unintended Reformation* 2012 (n. 5), 36–68. See also the influence of the Spanish Scholastics, discussed in S. Neff, *Justice Among Nations: A History of International Law* (Cambridge, MA: Harvard University Press, 2014), 153–8.

Grotius avoided theological disputes in winning adherents in the short term. He followed Aquinas and Suarez in applying a body of positive law, the *jus gentium*, to inter-state relations, explaining that this law incorporated concepts beyond positive law in only limited ways.[14] Grotius taught that the *jus gentium* was needed for its detail and that it should be interpreted in the light of natural law. In other words, the positive law contains the principles and rules that guide daily life. Natural law remains for its explanation of why positive law has authority to bind and what the moral limits of positive law are. Grotius's efforts led to the first 'detailed body of specific rules' in international law.[15]

Two schools emerged to challenge the Grotian conception. Seeking to derive positive law more directly from nature, rather than human conduct or practice, 'naturalists' rejected the extension of the *jus gentium* into the interstate realm. For followers of the English philosopher Thomas Hobbes, it was not possible to ground international law in nature because nature does not provide the coercive structures that are necessary to keep man's tendency toward violence and competition in check. They believed a global, coercive governmental authority was necessary to keep these harmful tendencies under control.[16] Hobbes had declared in his book *Leviathan* (1651) that outside of nation states ruled by governments is the state of nature, where people are prone to engage in constant war – wars of all against all. Hobbes considered the selfish, antisocial side of human nature to be the dominant characteristic. It remains the basis of the Realist ideology that continues as the predominant explanatory theory of international relations. A clear tenet of Realists is that little if any international law actually exists.[17]

Other naturalists who distinguished themselves from Grotius included the German legal scholar Samuel von Pufendorf (1632–1694). Pufendorf believed natural law could yield a detailed body of international law without reliance on the *jus*

[14] Neff, *Justice Among Nations* 2014 (n. 13), 156–7. [15] Ibid., 141.
[16] Ibid., 173–8.
[17] Hans Morgenthau, the founder of political science Realism, who wrote his doctoral thesis on international law, opined that international law exists for purposes such as regulating diplomacy and trade. He did not perceive international law as regulating the use of force, however, since it lacked the means to coerce states into compliance. See *Politics Among Nations: The Struggle for Power and Peace* (New York: Alfred A. Knopf, 1948), 211. See also the Introduction in this Volume.

*gentium* and saw natural law as a 'solid science' alongside the incipient natural sciences.[18] While Grotius has remained more influential than Pufendorf, throughout the eighteenth and nineteenth centuries a great deal of effort was poured into attempting to characterize international law as science free of metaphysics. Emmerich de Vattel (1714–67), second in stature only to Grotius, participated in the effort to secularize international law by looking for material evidence or positive proof of law. One of Vattel's principal conclusions was that no sovereign could sit in judgment of another.[19] He helped give rise to the legal theory of positivism and claims of sovereign state absolutism to the exclusion of the natural law understanding of law as superior to sovereigns.

The theologian Gordon Graham has written of the loss of religious faith in the face of the scientific revolution and the effect of this loss, saying that 'without theological underpinnings morality is no more than convention [tradition] and ethics just a kind of etiquette[;] one would expect the more heroic moral ideas to fall away and the role of positive law as a means of social regulation to grow'.[20] Yet, it stands to reason that over time even law, separated from its source of authority, may prove increasingly less persuasive in influencing thought and action, especially when that reason continues to be the subject of criticism.[21]

### *B The Substitutes for Natural Law*

For centuries scholars have offered a variety of alternatives for the theological reason of divine command to obey the law. The answers have involved consent of the governed, coercion or punishment,

[18] J. Porter, *Nature as Reason: A Thomistic Theory of the Natural Law* (Grand Rapids, MI: Wm. B. Eerdmans Publishing, 2004), 27–8. See also, M. Koskenniemi, 'Transformations of Natural Law, Germany 1648–1815', in A. Orford and F. Hoffmann (eds.), *The Oxford Handbook of the Theory of International Law* (Oxford: Oxford University Press, 2016), 59–81.

[19] P. Allott, *The Health of Nations: Society and Law beyond the State* (Cambridge: Cambridge University Press, 2002), 56–62. J. von Elbe, 'The Evolution of the Just War in International Law', *The American Journal of International Law*, 33 (1939) 665, 682–3.

[20] G. Graham, *The Re-enchantment of the World: Art versus Religion* (Oxford: Oxford University Press, 2007), 44.

[21] Compare Jeffrey Stout's analysis of tradition in underpinning American democracy. J. Stout, *Democracy and Tradition* (Princeton, NJ: Princeton University Press, 2004).

self-interest, acceptance, and the 'law habit'.[22] Each comes up short. Consent, for example, is largely a hypothetical construct that lacks an answer to what happens when a state or other actor withdraws consent. Similarly, coercion does not explain why international actors obey rules even when there is little or no prospect of forceful enforcement or punishment for violations. Self-interest, the basis of economic theories of law compliance, does not explain cases of compliance in the absence of any benefit to the self. Acceptance, participation, and the 'law habit' beg the questions of why and how international actors come to accept the law, to see the importance of participation, and to get into the habit of law compliance. Current answers do not explain what happens should acceptance cease or the habit change.

Further, the explanations just listed rest on a premise that is rarely acknowledged. Each incorporates a view that it is 'right', 'good', or 'just' to obey the law.[23] Some scholars find it sufficient to rely on intuition that law is good, but given the challenge of persuading the powerful to comply as well as the challenge of improving compliance with international law in general, intuition needs supplementation. Intuition is influenced by education, religion, philosophy, the arts and culture. Indeed, when it comes to law, religion has and continues to play a major role in our deep understanding of why law is a social good,[24] despite the emergence

[22] Some might add pluralism as a theory of legal authority. In Roth's impressive discussion of pluralism as an approach to resolving disputes within international law, however, he assumes consent is the basis of legal authority, not pluralism. B. R. Roth, *Sovereign Equality and Moral Disagreement: Premises of a Pluralist International Legal Order* (Oxford: Oxford University Press, 2011), 8.

[23] Social values continue to be shaped by religious and ethical commitments. 'Although people may decide to follow legal rules either from fear of punishment ... or as a result of reasoning about the purpose of rules ... most adults ... have learned the value of following rules for their own sake ... This image differs strikingly from that of self-interest models which dominate current thinking in law, psychology, political science, sociology, and organizational theory ...' T. R. Tyler, *Why People Obey Law* (Princeton, NJ: Princeton University Press, 2006), 177–8. See also M. Greenberg, 'The Moral Impact Theory of Law', *Yale Law Journal*, 123 (2014), 1288–342, 1288.

[24] There is, however, evidence of attempts to revive the law–religion connection. In promoting law against graft, the Chinese Communist Party is referencing religious concepts. See *Bloomberg News*, 'China Party Keeps Grip on Power in Plan to Boost Rule of Law', 28 October 2014, http://web.archive.org/web/20141031055931/http://www.bloomberg.com:80/news/20141028/china

of science with its critique of religious answers and chilling effect on religion in intellectual life. Economics has followed becoming the 'science' of today most often invoked to answer theoretical legal issues. Yet, when it comes to explaining why one should obey law, economics has limits.[25]

Another response to the perceived inadequacy of religion and religious answers for law has been the turn to history. Historic accounts seem as prominent in international law today as economics. Scholarship on international legal history has uncovered the role religion played in the development of contemporary law and in acceptance of law as good. Looking to history may be sufficient to answer the question of why law was once regarded as good and imbued with authority. To the extent past reasons no longer persuade, the revelations of history may only speed the decline in respect for international law.

If economics and history or tradition are inadequate, another answer is to return to religion proper.[26] Religion currently plays little or no part in prominent explanations for why legal principles bind, such as that of H. L. A. Hart in his now-classic 1961 book *The Concept of Law*. Hart relied on widespread, voluntary acceptance of law as the basis of legal authority. He argued that acceptance is more important than coercion in understanding the authority of law.[27] Like Hart, Hans Kelsen, one of the foremost legal theorists of the twentieth century, developed a view that the law depends on social acceptance. Kelsen explained that while consent can be easily

detailsplantoshoreuplawwhilekeepingpartysgrip.html. This approach is consistent with research revealing that religious beliefs are positively correlated with respect for law in a study of over 207 states and other political communities. C. North, W. Orman, and C. North, 'Religion, Corruption, and the Rule of Law', *Journal of Money, Credit, and Banking*, 45 (August 2013), 757–79.

25 See notes 41–66 and accompanying text.

26 For recent scholarly invocations of religion in interpreting contemporary legal theory, see J. Waldron, *One Another's Equals: The Basis of Human Equality*, Gifford Lectures 2014–2015, University of Edinburgh, 26, 27, 29 January and 2, 3, 5 February 2015, available online at www.ed.ac.uk/humanities-soc-sci/news-events/lectures/gifford-lectures/archive/2014-2015/jeremy-waldron, now available as a book, J. Waldron, *One Another's Equals, The Basis of Human Equality* (Cambridge, MA: Harvard University Press, 2017), and J. Porter, *Ministers of the Law: A Natural Law Theory of Legal Authority* (Grand Rapids, MI: Eerdmans, 2010).

27 H. L. A. Hart, *The Concept of Law* (Oxford: Oxford University Press, 1961), 227. See Lon Fuller's critique of *The Concept of Law* for its attempt to omit a moral basis of positive law. L. L. Fuller, 'Positivism and Fidelity to Law: A Reply to Professor Hart', *Harvard Law Review*, 71 (1957), 630–72.

withdrawn, acceptance is more durable, relying as it does on something other than a voluntary act.[28] Thomas Franck described the validity of international law as based on manifestations of acceptance or belief.[29]

In a more recent formulation, Samantha Besson, too, concludes that consent is not the basis of international legal authority. '[I]nternational law may have legitimate authority whether or not its subjects think it does and whether or not they have consented to its authority.'[30] Besson adds that acceptance is demonstrated by participation in lawmaking processes.[31] Participation does provide useful evidence of acceptance. It does not, however, answer the question, why those subject to law are drawn to participate.

Acceptance was once promoted by religious and theological teaching. Graham suggests, theology has been suppressed in public life, leaving only positive law stripped of essential explanations in its place.[32] Positive law did grow while theology and religion continued to decline as systems for social peace in the West. In more recent times we see law, including international law, even spoken of as a substitute for religious belief. Martti Koskenniemi has written: 'Moral pathos and religion frequently fail as vocabularies of engagement, providers of "empty signifiers" for expressing commitment and solidarity.' They could hardly succeed in the face of non-belief. People look instead to such ideas as international law for a 'vocabulary with a horizon of transcendence ... a kind of secular faith'.[33]

International law has a transcendent vocabulary because of its association with religious faith. And Graham may not see that law, while a later development than religion, is also founded on belief that has faded. Commitment to international law is hardly robust. For many decades, the European conception of law, exported through colonialism and other means throughout the world, has continued to benefit from the centuries of association with divine

28 H. Kelsen, *Pure Theory of Law* (M. Knight, trans.) 2nd German edn (Berkeley and Los Angeles, CA: University of California Press, 1967), 136. See also O. Schachter, 'Towards a Theory of International Obligation', *Virginia Journal of International Law*, 8 (1967–8), 300–22.

29 T. Franck, *The Power of Legitimacy among Nations* (New York: Oxford University Press, 1990), 21.

30 Besson, 'The Authority of International Law' 2014 (n. 8) 368.

31 Ibid.

32 Graham, *The Re-enchantment of the World* 2007 (n. 20), 44.

33 M. Koskenniemi, 'The Fate of Public International Law: Between Technique and Politics', *Modern Law Review*, 70 (2007), 1–30, 30.

authority.[34] Yet, by 2004, Stephen Smith presented evidence of growing scepticism about the authority of law in national systems. He reviewed the various theories of legal authority from consent to law and economics and concluded that none is adequate because they fail to replace the historic source of authority for law in the West.[35] Smith reminds us that belief in law's authority is an inheritance from an age when legal scholars believed in God and in the ability to apply reason to understand what God ordained in the form of law. Great jurists were 'heirs of a worldview that assumed God was real – more real than anything else ... This view had important implications for the nature of law.'[36] Tradition can account to some extent for continuing belief in law. Still, Smith may well have been right to sound the alarm about declining respect for legal authority when scholars are unable to explain why to obey. Smith admits to having no remedy for the fading of tradition. What continues to fill the belief gap for many legal scholars is science, no longer the natural sciences but economics.

### *C The Limits of Economics*

Throughout the eighteenth and nineteenth centuries Western legal scholars sought to show that in law, as in other fields, 'interrelated, fundamental and logically demonstrable principles of science' govern.[37] American law schools famously adopted 'the case method' in the 1870s to educate lawyers in a way analogous to the education of

34 Gregory underscores that attempts to remove religion from politics and law were in response to the 'religio-political conflicts between Catholics and magisterial Protestants from the early sixteenth through the mid-seventeenth century'. Gregory, *The Unintended Reformation* 2012 (n. 5), 21.

'The solution eventually adopted in all modern, liberal Western states was to privatize religion and to distinguish it from public life, ideologically as well as institutionally, through politically protected rights to individual religious freedom. Not subjective faith but objective reason, in science and modern philosophy, could be the basis of public life. But modern states continued to rely on citizens' behaviors that depended on beliefs rooted in Christianity (such as individual rights) even as other cross-confessionally embraced behaviors (such as material acquisitiveness) were antithetical to its teachings.' Ibid.

35 S. D. Smith, *Law's Quandary* (Cambridge, MA: Harvard University Press, 2004), 46–7. Concern for the rule of law and democracy has risen steadily in the 2000s, driven by developments in many countries, including Russia, China, the USA, Poland, Hungary, and Brazil, among others.

36 Ibid.

37 N. Duxbury, *Patterns of American Jurisprudence* (Oxford: Clarendon Press, 1995), 10.

scientists. Law students were – and still are – taught to look at the evidence in a judicial opinion to discover the rule, much as a botanist would study a plant to learn the laws of nature. A great effort at classifying rules followed.[38] This was occurring at the same time that another field was developing, namely economics, sometimes called 'the dismal science'. By the middle of the twentieth century, scholars looking beyond simpler notions of 'legal science' began attempting to ground law in economics. Today, law and economics and its variants, such as rational choice, public choice, and behavioural economics, are a widely taught explanation for how law works. Other social sciences such as sociology, psychology, and anthropology are influential in law as well, but arguably not to the extent of economics.

The move to economics was impelled by the plain fact that law is not a science like botany. Indeed, proponents of legal Realism, a critical approach which emerged in the late nineteenth century, viewed law as anything but science. A leading Realist, Justice Oliver Wendell Holmes famously said, 'Law is what the courts say it is.' Some in the legal Realist movement, however, saw certain linkages between law and 'social' science, if not the natural sciences of biology, chemistry, and physics. Julius Stone, beginning in the 1930s, sought to bring the new interest in social science to international law.[39] Social science data provided a basis for a judge's decision beyond his own subjective views. While Stone was promoting his sociological approach to international law, a number of legal scholars concerned with US law and its regulation of the capitalist market economy were already using economics in legal analysis.[40]

Scholars first used economics as a tool for understanding the law aimed directly at market regulation. Economists provided useful insights into how law could impact monopoly behaviour, the securities market, insurance, and the like. Ronald Coase, a British economist, made a significant contribution to widening the scope of

[38] P. Schlag, 'The Aesthetics of American Law', *Harvard Law Review*, 115 (2002), 1047–118. 1062–5.

[39] See J. Stone, *Quest for Survival: Role of Law and Foreign Policy* (Cambridge, MA: Harvard University Press, 1961), 40–56. For a more recent work on sociology and international law, see M. Hirsch, *Invitation to the Sociology of International Law* (Oxford: Oxford University Press, 2015).

[40] E. Kitch, 'The Fire of Truth: A Remembrance of Law and Economics at Chicago, 1932–1970', in F. Parisi and C. K. Rowley (eds.), *The Origins of Law and Economics: Essays by the Founding Fathers* (Cheltenham: Edward Elgar, 2005), 54.

economic analysis of law. He, along with his University of Chicago colleague Judge Richard Posner, argued that economic analysis of law provides 'the analytical rigor necessary for the study of the vast body of legal rules present in a modern legal system. This intellectual revolution came . . . when legal academia was actively searching for a tool that permitted critical appraisal of the law, rather than merely strengthening . . . dogmatic consistencies . . .'[41]

What Coase and Posner also accomplished was an extension deep into the law of a particular view of human nature held by Scottish Enlightenment thinkers David Hume (1711–1776) and his friend Adam Smith (1723–1790). Hume and Smith, building on Hobbes as well as the French *philosophes*,[42] believed that a person's will is orientated naturally to act in her own self-interest in the face of scarcity, and, thus, law needs to be based on self-interest to attract voluntary obedience. Hume decided that a person's self-interest consists in what gives her pleasure. He looked to the natural world and was, thus, also a naturalist, who used the method of science and aesthetics – observing with his eyes and using his other senses in reflecting on his personal experience of pleasure to develop the 'pleasure principle'. This idea is still used to explain human conduct in the market and beyond – conduct aimed at maximizing a person's wealth – and thus pleasure. It is through wealth that Hume opined we could obtain the commodities that give pleasure: food, wine, clothes, shelter.[43]

[41] F. Parisi, 'Methodological Debates in Law and Economics: The Changing Contours of a Discipline', in F. Parisi and C. K. Rowley (eds.), *The Origins of Law and Economics: Essays by the Founding Fathers* (Cheltenham: Edward Elgar, 2005), 35.

[42] 'Hobbes's influence is especially apparent in book 3 of Hume's *Treatise of Human Nature*, where the basic organizing principles of commercial society are analyzed. There we find that the problem of enforcing rules about property, contract performance, and collective action requires government involvement and, indeed, that it is the intervention of ministers and politicians that transforms rules first adopted for convenience and expediency into rules that promote both prosperity and moral virtue in large prospering societies.' L. S. Moss, 'Thomas Hobbes' Influence on David Hume: The Emergence of a Public Choice Tradition', *American Journal of Economics and Society*, 69 (2010), 398 (footnotes omitted).

[43] R. Cohon, 'Hume's Moral Philosophy', in E. N. Zalta (ed.), *The Stanford Encyclopedia of Philosophy* (Fall 2010 Edition), http://plato.stanford.edu/archives/fall2010/entries/hume-moral/; G. Graham, 'Aesthetics as a Normative Science', *Royal Institute of Philosophy Supplement*, 75 (2014) 249–64, and D. M. Johnston, *The Foundations of World Order: The Tower and the Arena* (Leiden, NE: Martinus Nijhof, 2008), 423.

Jeremy Bentham (1748–1832) promoted a similar idea. The good, Bentham argued, is what makes people happy, and, like Hume, he linked happiness to self-interested pleasure. For him, seeking pleasure and avoiding pain basically account for human conduct, and Bentham developed his philosophy of 'utilitarianism' out of these beliefs. Deeming utilitarianism to be based on science, Bentham nevertheless had some intuition that took him beyond basing his approach to law and government on individual self-interest alone. 'Bentham's moral imperative, which has greatly influenced the methodological debate in law and economics, is that policymakers have an obligation to select rules that give "the greatest happiness to the greatest number."'[44] This concept was further developed by Vilfredo Pareto (1848–1923), who argued that law as a normative matter should support a person in gaining greater wealth if the gain can be realized without making another person economically worse off.[45] Pareto also strove to counter the popular appeal of Marxism, which favoured the general welfare of the masses over individual wealth maximization. Economists have been concerned with the good of the many ever since.

Nicholas Kaldor and John Hicks, for example, writing in the 1930s and 1940s, developed something of a middle way between Marx and Pareto respecting the welfare of general society. Kaldor and Hicks argued that a particular situation is preferable if reaching it means 'those who gain from the move ... gain enough to compensate those who lose'.[46] This is a principle promoted by Posner as well,[47] who believes, 'Wealth maximization combines elements of utilitarianism and individualism, and in so doing comes closer to being a consensus political philosophy in our contentiously pluralistic society than any other overarching political principle'.[48] His impact on American legal education has

[44] Parisi, 'Methodological Debates' 2005 (n. 41), 35.

[45] C. K. Rowley, 'An Intellectual History of Law and Economics, 1739–2003', in F. Parisi and C. K. Rowley (eds.), *The Origins of Law and Economics: Essays by the Founding Fathers* (Cheltenham: Edward Elgar, 2005), 3, 19.

[46] Parisi, 'Methodological Debates' 2005 (n. 41), 42.

[47] Rowley, 'An Intellectual History' 2005 (n. 45), 21. Posner published the ninth edition in 2014. R. A. Posner, *Economic Analysis of Law* (New York, NY: Walters, Kluwer Law & Business, 2014).

[48] R. Posner, 'Wealth Maximization Revisited', *Notre Dame Journal of Law, Ethics and Public Policy*, 2 (1985) 85–105, 104.

been profound.[49] Posner argues for wealth maximization alone as the standard against which to judge legal rules. He relies on the assumption that the market captures 'subjective values and preferences' so that wealth maximization is an objective measurable standard for evaluating law. He distinguishes unmeasurable 'happiness', the goal of utilitarianism, with wealth maximization, the measurable goal of law and economics. Wealth maximization promotes the work ethic and 'encourages traditional capacities, such as intelligence, and traditional virtues, such as honesty'.[50] Francesco Parisi, too, argues that in the absence of clear moral or ethical theories of justice 'efficiency provides the most appropriate criterion for allocating limited resources among competing claims'.[51]

Legal theorists with less confidence in the market to determine how to distribute pay-offs to those who bear the costs of wealth maximizing have tried to develop additional theories of distributive fairness. Interestingly, John Rawls's *Theory of Justice* is a popular choice.[52] Rawls, however, relied largely on intuition to figure out guidance for developing principles of a just society. Intuition returns us to the conundrum of tradition, discussed above. Behavioural psychology has enhanced the ability of economists to understand the impact of law on society but the choice of goals remains a challenge for economics.[53] In the end, it seems that law and economics theory helps to identify the best means to reach certain ends, but not how best to identify the ends:

> Law and economics is an eclectic set of rationalist analytical tools that may be used to describe and evaluate whether a particular law or institution achieves the ends of its individual participants. These ends include not only the basest consumption needs, but also the noblest aspirations of the human spirit: for justice, compassion and beauty.[54]

At the international level, economic concepts of 'public goods' and 'global public goods' are being used to tackle common global challenges. For the World Bank, these challenges include

[49] But has it, as Rowley suggests, changed 'mainstream American common law jurisprudence'? See Rowley, 'An Intellectual History' 2005 (n. 45), 24.

[50] Ibid., 21. [51] Parisi, 'Methodological Debates' 2005 (n. 41), 47.

[52] Ibid., 43.

[53] A. Van Aaken, 'Behavioral International Law and Economics', 8 November 2013, available online at: http://www.esil-sedi.eu/node/446.

[54] J. Dunoff and J. Trachtman, 'The Law and Economics of Humanitarian Law Violations in Internal Conflict', *American Journal of International Law*, 93 (1999), 407.

'the environmental commons (including ... climate change and biodiversity), communicable diseases (including HIV/AIDS, tuberculosis, malaria, and avian influenza), international trade, international financial architecture, and global knowledge for development'.[55] Incentive structures to protect the commons, fight disease, and create a more just economy apparently do not exist. This conclusion brings even the newer analytic perspective of global public goods back to the Hobbes-Hume view of human nature. Without benefit to self-interest, human beings apparently are reluctant to act. 'Free-riding' is identified as the problem, where a single actor need not contribute to the global public good but can still benefit from the efforts of others. From an individual perspective, free-riding is a good to be sought. At the national level, government is seen as the institution that can overcome free-riding and other barriers to ensuring public goods are produced adequately and equitably. Without government at the global level, international law is the best available tool for coordination to realize common interests.[56]

In theory, for something to be a global public good, the good must attract agreement over its desirability. That aspect alone, however, does not guarantee that the good meets any normative standard, and there will inevitably be contests over what should actually be funded: 'Different actors will have different preferences about which norm to choose'.[57]

Many of these questions are familiar, under different terminology, to international law scholars.[58] Daniel Bodansky, for example, points to how international law was used to change incentives and thus better support the coordinated effort to protect the ozone layer.[59] Because economic analysis is able to identify obstacles to action on issues of common interest, it can guide the use of international law methods of resolution.[60] Where self-interested incentives are absent,

[55] World Bank, *What Are Global Public Goods?* (2008) http://go.worldbank.org/JKZLIHR2B0. See also F. Cafaggi and D. Caron, 'Global Public Goods amidst a Plurality of Legal Orders: A Symposium', *European Journal of International* Law, 23 (2012), 643.

[56] D. Bodansky, 'What's in a Concept? Global Public Goods, International Law, and Legitimacy', *European Journal International Law*, 23 (2012), 651.

[57] Ibid., 655–6. [58] Cafaggi and Caron, 'Global Public Goods' 2012 (n. 55), 644.

[59] Bodansky, 'What's in a Concept?' 2012 (n. 56), 659–60.

[60] D. Morrow, 'Why Geoengineering Is a Public Good, Even If It Is Bad', *Climate Change*, 23 (2014), 95.

however, regardless of the importance of the good at issue, global public goods analysis offers little. Another limitation is that the analysis relies on property concepts. Economists are good at 'propertizing' many things but not everything. Even where property does exist or can be seen to exist, economic analysis has been shown wanting in providing persuasive normative answers, such as to the questions of fair distribution of wealth.[61]

Consider the problem of reducing greenhouse gas emissions. This goal raises clear collective action issues, and international law has a definite role to play in creating standards and incentives. Reducing emissions also reveals the costs or externalities involved in action that involves no interdependence to move toward the goal. One actor, a 'weak link', can refuse to support the goal, negating the benefit to everyone. Another problem is deciding on responses, such as when to commonly support a state lacking financial resources as a barrier to compliance and when to apply coercion against states deemed able but unwilling to comply.

Separating out types of problems associated with various global public goods permits evaluation of different systems or institutions that produce such goods.[62] More centralized authority through constitutional principles for the international community may be effective for aggregate effort problems, although this type of authority also raises legitimacy issues. Comparing systems, institutions, and mechanisms can be useful for generating information.[63] In the end, however, the basis for selecting goals and the best means of achieving them is not apparent even in this newer area of law and economic analysis.

Francesco Francioni, by moving beyond the limits of self-interest and property, offers new thinking on these fundamental issues. He describes the global common interest in art and cultural heritage and argues that this interest has the potential to generate shared understandings of law's social goals and acceptable means of achieving them. 'In the infinite variety of their expressions, art and heritage reflect the variety of collective inclinations and social

[61] F. Cafaggi, 'Transnational Private Regulation and the Production of Global Public Goods and Private "Bads"', *European Journal of International Law*, 23 (2012), 695.

[62] G. Shaffer, 'International Law and Global Public Goods in a Legal Pluralist World', *European Journal of International Law*, 23 (2012), 669.

[63] G. Shaffer, 'Comparative Institutional Analysis and a New Legal Realism', *Wisconsin Law Review*, 2(2) (2013) 607.

organizations of the communities that have produced and maintained them ... we could say *ubi societas ibi ars et jus.*'[64] Legal orders consist of 'individual and collective beliefs, practices, and shared inclinations of members of the society and the material organization that is the reflection of such practices and inclinations'.[65] This insight into what humanity shares indicates a way of thinking about the gaps left by economic analysis. Economics can help predict the impact of law and judicial decisions on the achievement of public goods. Economics does not explain what makes something 'a good' so that it should be supported by the law. Theology once played that role. Aesthetic philosophy can do so today. It justifies altruism in support of the environment, human rights, the meaning of fairness in wealth distribution, and the imperative of peace.

## II Natural Law and Beauty

Since antiquity, aesthetic philosophers have found in the human reaction to beauty an argument that people have the capacity to act wholly for the good of others. Philosophers use the universal experience of pleasure in contemplation of beauty in nature and the arts to show that people are moved to act not only in their own interest but in the interest of others. Aesthetic philosophy challenges economic analysis that is narrowly premised on the view that human beings act only in self-interest. The aesthetic counterpoint thus provides a secular supplement to, or substitute for, divine command in justifying compliance with law that requires self-sacrifice. This line of reasoning leads to a persuasive theoretical explanation in support of extra-positive norms in a diverse world.[66]

The pleasure human beings experience in the contemplation of beauty is different from the pleasure imparted by food and other

[64] '[W]here a society is, there is art and law.' F. Francioni, 'Public and Private in the International Protection of Global Cultural Goods', *European Journal of International Law*, 23 (2012), 720.

[65] Ibid., 720.

[66] Aesthetics is useful in other respects from guiding interpretation of text to understanding the impact of architecture on the administration of justice to legal criticism. See, e.g., on interpretation J. B. White, *The Legal Imagination* (Chicago: University of Chicago Press, 1973); on architecture, J. Resnik and D. Curtis, *Representing Justice: Invention, Controversy, and Rights In City-states and Democratic Courtrooms* (Published with assistance of the Yale Library Fund, 2011), and on criticism, A. Geary, *Law and Aesthetics* (Oxford: Hart Publishers, 2001).

useful commodities, things that people need. The beauty of a sunset is not something we need, and, yet, it fills us with a kind of happiness that we understand all people share. When we judge something to be beautiful it is based on the sense that others make the same judgment. We are thinking beyond self when experiencing the pleasure of beauty. Beauty takes us out of ourselves and away from our narrow striving to survive. It supplies a common, non-competitive bond with others.

### A *Beauty and the Good of Others*

The insight from beauty into the altruistic aspect of human nature is found in Plato, Aquinas, and Kant, as well as twentieth-century philosophers Iris Murdoch and Hannah Arendt. All have used the study of beauty to show that selflessness is as inherent to humanity as self-interest. It will be argued here that this capacity for selflessness provides an argument for law compliance even in the absence of personal advantage or coercion. Striving for self-interest can hardly support such principles as equality or fairness – the treatment of like cases alike without preference for the wealthy, the well-connected, or the politically or militarily powerful. The capacity for selflessness does support these principles and, thereby, law in general.

Arendt and Murdoch find proof of selflessness, counter-arguments to the philosophy of self-interest, principally in the writing of Immanuel Kant (1724–1804) and in Kant's last major work, *Critique of Judgment.* In a section called 'Analytic of the Beautiful', Kant gives a decidedly different account of human nature and human capacity than that promoted by Hobbes and Hume. Kant was led through contemplation of nature to a profound insight into the experience of disinterested pleasure. Instead of Hume's pleasure from possessions, Kant wrote of the pleasure we experience when reflecting on what has no utility. The reality that we experience pleasure in contemplating sunsets – actual or imagined – regardless of utility is because of the beauty of the sunset. The pleasure is a very different experience than the pleasure of a fine wine, high on Hume's personal list of pleasure-imparting things. Building on Kant, Murdoch invites us to think of moments of self-concern, moments when we are focused on a perceived slight or blow to our self-esteem.[67] In the midst of self-absorbed anger, we look out the window and see a colourful bird, dancing along a tree branch. We experience pleasure triggered by a small example of beauty that does nothing practical for us. Such an experience of pleasure takes us out of ourselves – it is a disinterested pleasure, distinguishable from the pleasure of good food, wine, clothes, or a large, comfortable house.

Arendt, too, finds in *Critique of Judgment* evidence of at least the basis of a political theory that seems even better suited to be a theory of law.[68] Arendt presented her case in a series of lectures at the New School for Social Research in New York in 1970. She created her own justification for orderly social life through politics by focusing on what Kant says about beauty.[69] Kant taught that a human being's happiness does not depend on experiencing pleasure alone. The very ability to know pleasure depends on its contrast with displeasure. Arendt found in Kant 'only one exception to this rule, and that is the pleasure we feel when confronted with beauty'.[70] In judging something beautiful, we experience a disinterested pleasure not dependent on any contrast. We perceive beauty and experience pleasure in the perception instinctually. 'The fact that man is affected by the sheer beauty of nature proves that he is made for and fits into this world . . .'[71] It creates the opposite sense to that of alienation from the world,[72] and is, therefore, a proof of our ability to live with and for others.

Arendt's real interest in Kant's thinking on beauty is what it says about life in society. She focused on what our reaction to beauty tells us about 'disinterest' or interest in the other. Many beautiful things exist solely for their beauty and not because they have any usefulness for us. Thus, the pleasure is owing to the thing's mere existence and not for any gain. Arendt tells us that Kant wrote in a notebook, '"the Beautiful teaches us to love without self-interest"'.[73] The beautiful and the pleasure experienced are intrinsically connected with the sense that others will in fact share the judgment. Judging something beautiful is an internal dialogue with others in

[67] I. Murdoch, *The Sovereignty of Good* (London: Routledge & Kegan Paul, 1970).
[68] H. Arendt, *Lectures on Kant's Political Philosophy*, R. Beiner (ed.), (Chicago: University of Chicago Press, 1989).
[69] Arendt, *Lectures on Kant's Political Philosophy* 1989 (n. 68) 30. [70] Ibid.
[71] Ibid., citing Kant, 'Reflexion zur Logik', in *Gesammelte Schriften*, 16 (1820), 127.
[72] S. Swift, *Hannah Arendt* (Abingdon: Routledge: 2008), 75. [73] Ibid., 73.

mind.[74] This dialogue or communication requires the ability to stand in the shoes of another, to have the enlarged mentality to think not only about our own views but those of others. It is a cosmopolitan perspective that reaches to the consideration of all of humanity. The judgment of beauty and the awareness of others lead us outside ourselves. It is this being with others, 'sociability', that is for Arendt our 'highest end'.[75] Her conclusion is consistent with Grotius's theologically based belief in humanity's social nature and attraction to orderly life in society.

Beyond the disinterested pleasure of beauty, Kant also taught that human beings appreciate beauty most purely through the 'free play of imagination'.[76] Imagination allows experiences of beauty in unexpected ways. For example, imagination helps find beauty in the ugly. Imagination helps us to escape the 'confines' of 'selfhood, and to think from the point of view of others'.[77] Thus, imagination allows the making of judgments of beauty by allowing us to expand our thinking to imagine how others might regard the same object. As Kant puts it, 'we must renounce ourselves in favour of others'. Kant claims that in the activity of judging beauty 'egoism is overcome'.[78] Imagining communication about the beauty of an object 'allows us to overcome what is most private and incommunicable about our experience of the world – that is, the experience of the world that comes to us from our bodily senses . . .'.[79]

Judging something beautiful goes beyond finding it simply agreeable or interesting.[80] Beauty is perceived as such by all. It is not something unique to an individual's personal taste.[81] '*Beautiful* is what pleases universally without a concept.'[82] When we call something beautiful we think that everyone must recognize it as such,

[74] Ibid., 76. [75] Ibid., 76.

[76] I. Kant, *Critique of the Power of Judgment*, P. Guyer (ed.), E. Matthews and P. Guyer (trans.) (Abingdon: Routledge, 2000), 103.

[77] Swift, *Hannah Arendt* 2008 (n. 72), 59. [78] Ibid. [79] Ibid.

[80] Kant, *Critique of the Power of Judgment* 2000 (n. 76), 97–8.

[81] 'With the beautiful it is entirely different. It would be ridiculous . . . if someone who prided himself on his taste thought to justify himself thus: "This object . . . is beautiful for me." For he must not call it beautiful if it please merely him.' Ibid.

[82] I. Kant, *Critique of the Power of Judgment*, (n. 76), 104 (emphasis in the original). See also, D. Wandschneider, 'Beauty in Nature Both in Its Laws and Its Entities', in V. Hösle (ed.), *The Many Faces of Beauty* (Notre Dame, IN: University of Notre Dame Press, 2013), 114.

that everyone must agree with us. Judging something to be beautiful 'carries with it an aesthetic quality of universality'.[83] As Terry Eagleton explains, 'we can experience our shared humanity with all the immediacy of our response to a fine painting or a magnificent symphony. Paradoxically, it is in the apparently most private, frail and intangible aspects of our lives that we blend most harmoniously with one another.'[84] Humanity shares the sense that the beautiful exists.[85] Kant finds 'that judgments about beauty tend simultaneously to exemplify and reinforce collective social judgments even when they do not overtly appear to do so'.[86] This observation brings us back to beauty as evidence of our social nature.

Humanity's shared experience of beauty, and Arendt's extension of that phenomenon to the inclination to communicate about it, is at the foundation of social life for her, and, therefore, also, politics, which is a necessary part of maintaining life in society. One result of politics is law, the tool through which societies control violence and support social peace, harmony, and order. Arendt quotes Kant but uses as many of her own words in saying, 'if everyone expects and requires from everyone else this reference to general communication [of pleasure, of disinterested delight, then we have reached a point where it is as if there existed] an original compact, dictated by mankind itself'.[87]

This proof of humanity's social nature evidenced by the experience of pleasure in beauty is supported by the fact the experience is common and that it is linked to the desire to communicate. For Arendt the aesthetic of beauty is 'common sense'.[88] All human beings experience this pleasure, which has no apparent purpose. The sightless experience beauty through music, touch, or imagination. Pointless pleasure in beauty is a pure aspect of our common humanity, which supplies a far more tangible basis for empathy, for

[83] Ibid., 101.

[84] T. Eagleton, *The Ideology of the Aesthetic* (Cambridge, MA: Basil Blackwell, 1990), 76.

[85] Swift, *Hannah Arendt* 2008 (n. 72), 80.

[86] M. Canuel, *Justice, Dissent, and the Sublime* (Baltimore, MD: Johns Hopkins University Press, 2012), 30.

[87] Arendt, *Lectures on Kant's Political Philosophy*, 1989 (n. 68), 74, citing Kant, *Critique of Judgment*, sec. 41.

[88] Canuel, *Justice, Dissent, and the Sublime*, 2012 (n. 86), 51.

seeing the other as ourselves, than even the concept of human dignity, the existence of a soul, or the fact of common needs or emotions. The pleasure in experiencing beauty is a universal, harmonious, and non-competitive aspect of humanity.

Founding social life on Hume's pleasure principle is far more challenging than building on Kant's insight given the zero-sum nature of the commodities that supply self-interested pleasure. People compete for wealth and what it provides. Common needs, which so often form the content of theories of the common good, require sacrifice to fulfil. People need food, water, accommodation, even love and play.[89] We certainly see commonality in these needs that can lead to empathy, but we also see that the acquisition of these things by me means less for you. Kant's categorical imperative to do unto others as you would have done unto you is self-referential. It is attempting to induce empathy by evoking what the actor would like. Even love, which is associated with altruism, is deficient for Murdoch in that 'human love is normally too profoundly possessive and also too "mechanical" to be a place of vision'.[90]

The great economic and social theories have tried to overcome the essential competitive aspect of human need. Communism and Christianity teach from each according to her ability to each according to his need. Capitalism teaches to each according to ability and more will be created for all. The emphasis on ability in these creeds is a focus on a human characteristic that is differentiated and that inspires hierarchy and competition. In contrast, people can have

[89] See, e.g., J. Finnis, *Natural Law and Natural Rights*, 2nd edn(Oxford: Oxford University Press, 1980). For an argument that Finnis and other New Natural Lawyers have omitted the religious aspect of natural law theory essential to its completeness, see J. Porter, 'A Tradition of Civility: The Natural Law as a Tradition of Moral Inquiry', *Scottish Journal of Theology*, 56 (01) 2003, 27–48, 29. Finnis provided the following comment to the author on whether his views of natural law coincide with the classic tradition, especially as to the element of divine command in obedience to law: 'I have expressed in various places over the years frustration or regret at the misunderstandings caused by the phrase "natural law", ... [and] did not demur when you suggested ... that "Practical Reason and Law" would be an alternative title' to *Natural Law and Natural Rights* (email exchange of 17 January 2018, on file with the author.) See also Chapter 2.

[90] Murdoch, *The Sovereignty of Good* 1970 (n. 67), 75. There are other concepts of love, however, that are other-orientated, such as Martin Buber's, eloquently described in *I and Thou*, (R. G. Smith (trans.) (Edinburgh: T. and T. Clark, 1937).

a common experience of pleasure in a shimmering pond, a Mozart concerto, or a Japanese inkwash landscape. In Hume's theory a person theoretically needs no social life. Arendt sees in the perception of beauty the truth of social life as integral to human existence. Why else have the experience of beauty?

We have largely lost this vocabulary and understanding from our political and jurisprudential thought. The loss fosters scepticism as to whether there really is a common experience of beauty (is not 'beauty is in the eye of the beholder'?), or if there is such a common experience is it really adequate as the basis of a theory of politics or law? The doubts result from an understandable misunderstanding. While it is true that *taste* differs among people, the common experience of pleasure in something judged beautiful does not differ. Someone credited with 'good taste' often has a combination of talent and training and may have a more profound experience of beauty. The intensity of the experience differs. That fact does not, however, diminish the common ability of all people to experience some level of disinterested pleasure in beauty. Pointless pleasure is an extraordinary thing to have in common, and for those still sceptical, there is a wealth of scientific evidence to support what Plato, Aristotle, and Aquinas concluded without brain scans or surveys.[91]

The experience of beauty is something all people share. This universal aspect is more important than any common perception of what *is* beautiful. Nevertheless, since Aristotle, Western thinkers have associated beauty with certain characteristics or qualities. Thomas Aquinas associated beauty with three qualities: proportion, integrity, and clarity. Comparing two roses, the one with greater proportion or symmetry, integrity, and clarity or colour will be judged more beautiful. Some aspects of nature that attract our gaze, such as a calm lake stretching to the horizon, have the quality of complete proportion. Kant apparently believed that only the experience of beauty was common and that people made differing judgments of what they considered beautiful. For him, the experience of disinterested pleasure was the important thing. Yet, findings

[91] See, e.g., G. Gómez-Puerto, *et al*, 'Preference for Curved Contours Across Cultures', *Journal of Psychology of Aesthetics, Creativity and the Arts*, 12 (2018), 432–9, www.apa.org/pubs/journals/aca/. ('We conclude that preference for curved-contour objects is common across cultures and conjecture that it is a constituent of a natural propensity for aesthetics.' Ibid., 432.)

from the sciences and social sciences indicate the earlier philosophers held the more accurate understanding. People tend to agree as to what is beautiful, judging on the basis of the qualities Aquinas described. Most are familiar with the concept of the 'elegant' mathematical formula. The astrophysicist Mario Livio explains the aesthetic 'measure' of an object is higher the more 'order' it possess.[92] 'Order' is generally determined by the symmetries of the object, underscoring the importance of symmetry in perceptions of beauty. Portrait photographers and painters have known since the dawn of their media that people prefer the natural, symmetrical face. Psychological studies across cultures find that, comparatively, people perceive symmetrical faces to be more beautiful, regardless of skin colour, eye shape, and other ethnic or cultural distinctions. Thus, beauty is perceivable to all, appealing to our 'common sense'.[93]

Popular impressions and assumptions are at odds with these statement about beauty, which is a fact that helps account for why aesthetics is currently rarely a part of legal theory. Not only do people assume beauty is in the eye of the beholder, they also associate the beautiful with passivity and loss of control. The aesthetics of the ugly and the sublime are preferred in our times as promoting a sense of power and mastery. Cultural critic Wendy Steiner argues in her book *Venus in Exile* how such fears led eventually to the suppression of beauty even in the arts. Writing in 2001, Steiner predicted that the time had 'come for a change, and the sudden, widespread fascination with beauty in our day indicates a cultural readiness to move on'.[94] She may have underestimated the strength of certain factors that foster a preference for the overpowering, ugly, and even shocking work of art. The artist aims to trigger a response in the viewer, to move her. Unlike the beautiful, however, people become inured to the ugly so that artists strain to find new ways to shock.[95] Beauty affects us quite differently. We may

[92] M. Livio, 'Symmetry: From Perception to the Laws of Nature', in V. Hösle (ed.), *The Many Faces of Beauty* (Notre Dame, IN: University of Notre Dame Press, 2013), 79–112.

[93] Ibid. Mannequins and other artificially created faces that reflect high symmetry do not create the same reaction as faces that are naturally symmetrical. See also n. 91.

[94] W. Steiner, *Venus in Exile, The Rejection of Beauty in 20th-Century Art* (Chicago: University of Chicago Press, 2001), xxv.

[95] M. Philips, 'The Ugly Truth', 28 January 2005, available online at www.theguardian.com/books/2005/jan/29/history.highereducation.

become tired of the merely pretty or decorative, but the truly beautiful does not fatigue. Our positive reaction to beauty is so strong as to lead us in viewing the ugly to repair it in our imagination, smoothing out asymmetries.

These more accurate insights regarding beauty have yet to impact legal theory. Obstacles exist even beyond popular assumptions and the need to learn from another discipline. Some also worry that valuing beauty leads toward, not away from competition in society and can be used for purposes of control. Even if such dangers exist, they can be avoided if beauty is not treated as a commodity but rather as a path to understanding 'our deepest human nature'.[96]

Still, the study of beauty presents the uncontrollable in life. The three qualities of beauty found in a rose in first bloom will soon be lost – the rose's colour will fade; brown spots will appear; the petals will curl and drop off, leaving a lopsided memory of what was. The beauty of the new rose imparts disinterested pleasure but also the certainty its beauty will not last. 'Here we can grasp why beauty unsettles us in a way we often seek to avoid: we flee from beauty as we flee from the thought of death. And this is indeed not only the experience of individuals, but also of humankind and of whole epochs . . .',[97] including our own.

Until more work is done linking legal theory and the study of beauty, doubts will remain. David Nowak, for example, in a chapter on Jewish natural law writes, 'Th[e] active discovery of authentic human nature and its requirements comes when practical or moral reason is properly exercised. It is not discovered by contemplation of the beauty of the external world . . .'.[98] Practical reason is an important tool, but it leads to rational knowledge, which is only one form. Knowledge gained through the senses, memory, and the emotions is also valuable. Knowledge from the contemplation of beauty uniquely reveals our fitness for orderly social life brought about in part by adherence to the rule of law, including law that requires selflessness.

Aesthetic philosophy supports the binding nature of law even when not in self-interest. The importance of this conclusion will

[96] Steiner, *Venus in Exile* 2001 (n. 94), xviii.

[97] B. Forte, *The Portal of Beauty, Towards a Theology of Aesthetics* P. D. Glenday (trans.) (Grand Rapids, MI: Eerdman's, 2008), 114–15.

[98] A. M. Emon, M. Levering, and D. Novak, *Natural Law: A Jewish, Christian, and Muslim Trialogue* (Oxford: Oxford University Press, 2014), 8.

be seen in Chapter 2, which focuses on the prohibition on the use of force. Today the prohibition is being challenged as almost never before by militarily powerful states interested in using force in their percieved national interest, regardless of the law. Morgenthau's notion that without coercion this law does not really bind when not in self-interest is discredited by the attraction to compliance with law solely for the good of the community. The argument from aesthetics for law compliance regardless of self-interest provides a response. Before reaching that further discussion of what aesthetics offers law, this chapter will conclude with additional considerations as to why an area so promising for legal theory has been largely overlooked and how to remedy the oversight.

### *B Recovering Beauty in the Law*

The challenges to creating a role for beauty in legal theory are plain. Yet, beauty was once deeply integrated in jurisprudence and can be again. Costas Douzinas explains that the connection between beauty and law was once well understood. The legacy of that time is the attractive statue of justice, a woman holding a sword in one hand and a balance in the other. The 'inner relationship between the beautiful and the good', and 'the link between law, order, and harmony, or between justice and beauty form[ed] a consistent theme in the writings of the humanist lawyers both in England and continental Europe'.[99]

The disappearance of this theme can be traced to Reformation-era developments, including the preference for the sublime aesthetic over the beautiful. The Reformation, science, and subsequently the Enlightenment shifted the West from a transcendental world view to a material one.[100] By the time Grotius wrote about international law as separate from religion, Protestant iconoclasm had already

99 C. Douzinas, 'Prosopon and Antiprosopon: Prolegomena for a Legal Iconology', in C. Douzinas and L. Nead (eds.), *Law and the Image: The Authority of Art and the Aesthetics of Law* (Chicago: University of Chicago Press, 1999), 53.

100 Brown, *Restoration of Reason* (n. 5). For more on transcendence and international law, see, P. Allott, 'Europe and the Idea of the Transcendental, Human Rights and Other Imagined Entities', Conference on *The Crisis of Eurocentrism and the Future of the European Humanism: Historical, Cultural, Religious, Legal and Socio-Economic Perspectives,* Università Cattolica del Sacro Cuore, Milan (16 April 2016). See also Chapter 2.

dismissed the idea of beauty in art and nature being a path to God. Understanding from inner reason was the order of the day, and it was inner reason alone, not reasoning from the perspective of others. The shift was to the individual and his personal interpretation of scripture and to the material evidence of historical truth. Grotius was part of this shift as a Protestant theologian as were most of his prominent successors. Samuel von Pufendorf and Emmerich de Vattel, for example, were sons of Protestant ministers.[101] Kant, too, was a Protcstant as well as someone 'deeply interested in the relationship between the law and the prohibition on imagery' in Protestant theology.[102] He considered the Old Testament condemnation of 'graven images' as 'sublime'.[103] The final section of Kant's *Critique of Judgment*, the one following 'Analytic of the Beautiful', is devoted to the sublime. It was a concept that coincided with the mid-nineteenth-century understanding of international law as a phenomenon of strict positivism supporting sovereign absolutism. Both fit more easily the aesthetic of the sublime in contrast to the beautiful:

> At the end of the eighteenth century, writers such as Kant and Burke subdivided the aesthetic realm (which had previously been inclusively called beauty) into two realms, the sublime and the beautiful. ... In the newly subdivided aesthetic realm, the sublime is male and the beautiful is female. The sublime is English, Spanish, and German; the beautiful is French and Italian. The sublime resides in mountains, Milton's Hell, and tall oaks in a sacred grove; the beautiful resides in flowers and Elysian meadows. The sublime is night, the beautiful day. 'The sublime *moves*' ... 'Beauty *charms*.' ... The sublime is principled, noble, righteous; the beautiful is compassionate and good-hearted.[104]

Kant understood the sublime as the equivalent of ideas of power and power as strength, violence, pain, and terror.[105] The New Historicist literary critics underscore the association of the sublime

[101] Johnston, *The Tower and the Arena* 2008 (n. 43), 415, 417.
[102] Douzinas, 'Prosopon and Antiprosopon' 1999 (n. 99), 51–2.
[103] Canuel, *Justice, Dissent, and the Sublime* 2012 (n. 86), 47.
[104] E. Scarry, *On Beauty and Being Just* (Princeton, NJ: Princeton University Press, 1999), 83, citing I. Kant, *Observations on the Feeling of the Beautiful and Sublime* 9 J. T. Goldthwait (trans.) (1960); see also Douzinas, 'Prosopon and Antiprosopon' 1999 (n. 99), 57 and Steiner, *Venus in Exile* 2001 (n. 94), 35.
[105] Canuel, *Justice, Dissent, and the Sublime* 2012 (n. 86), 43, citing E. Burke, *A Philosophical Enquiry into the Origin of Our Ideas of the Sublime and Beautiful* (1757).

'with violent and asocial power, theoretical abstraction, and traditional notions of masculinity'.[106]

Two nineteenth-century thinkers helped foster the preference for the sublime at the expense of beauty, perhaps unintentionally. Søren Kirkegaard, a Protestant theologian, writing in the first half of the nineteenth century warned that contemplation of art, particularly the idealistic art of the Danish Golden Age, could lead the viewer to embrace a reflection of beauty back to the viewer rather than moving her outside herself to the world and the transcendent.[107] Art can serve as icon or idol. Kierkegaard chides his era 'for its embrace of reflection – its tendency to reject authority and tradition in favour of a mindset critical of everything but the individual's self-interest'.[108] His concern led to the further separation of aesthetics from theology and other disciplines,[109] a process that began with the Reformation and Luther, who had 'surrendered beauty'.[110]

Friedrich Nietzsche, in the second half of the nineteenth century, wrote a detailed treatment of aesthetics in his first book, *The Birth of Tragedy*. His subsequent writing incorporates a clearly sublime and seductive aesthetic that famously declared that 'God is dead' and extolled the individual's 'will to power' and man as 'superman'.[111] Nietzsche advised substituting art for religious practice to evoke feelings of ecstasy and empowerment. He particularly emphasized dance.

Noted followers of Nietzsche, including his sister, would go on to promote some of the worst features of fascist ideology, astutely incorporating the sublime aesthetic to attract adherence. Two prominent observers of twentieth-century Europe commented

106 Ibid., 31.
107 C. B. Barnett, *From Despair to Faith: The Spirituality of Søren Kirkegaard* (Minneapolis, MN: Fortress Press, 2014), chap. 3.
108 Ibid., 65.
109 See G. Pattison, 'Art in an Age of Reflection', in A. Hannay and G. D. Marino (eds.), *The Cambridge Companion to Kierkegaard* (Cambridge: Cambridge University Press, 1998). But see Barnett, *From Despair to Faith* 2014 (n. 107), 68. The Catholic theologian Hans Urs Von Balthasar deserves credit for launching the renewal of theological aesthetics.
110 C. O'Regan, 'Theology, Art and Beauty' 2012 (n. 6), 455.
111 See P. Guyer, 'The German Sublime after Kant', in T. M. Costelloe (ed.), *The Sublime, From Antiquity to the Present* (Cambridge: Cambridge University Press, 2012), 102–17.

specifically on the connection between Nietzsche's and fascism's aesthetics, mistakenly characterizing it as an aesthetic of beauty, rather than the sublime. Max Weber credited Nietzsche with separating the beautiful and the good: 'Since Nietzsche we realize that something can be beautiful, not only in spite of the aspect of which it is not good, but rather in that very aspect.'[112] Walter Benjamin also linked fascism to the beautiful, pointing to the fascist understanding that 'war is beautiful' and the 'Nazi propaganda-machine, with its choreographed torch-lit marches and rallies, iconic posters and statues, and films such as *Triumph of the Will*'.[113] These were uses of the sublime aesthetic, however, not the beautiful. They are also additional proof of the impact of aesthetics on human sensibilities.

A counter-aesthetic of beauty might have diffused some of the appeal of the fascist sublime, but Weber and Benjamin helped taint beauty in that role. Beauty has been suppressed in legal philosophy to a far greater extent than the sublime. The sublime aesthetic is found today in the language, approaches, and priorities of law. It is a particularly problematic mindset in the area of law of greatest concern to this book – the law restricting resort to military force. Carl Schmitt and Hans Morgenthau, both devotees of Nietzsche as well as scholars of international law, have had significant influence on contemporary international political and legal theory on military force.[114] Both promoted an understanding of international law consistent with the sublime and inconsistent with the promotion of peace through law. Schmitt argued in the interwar period that Germany should not allow itself to be dominated by other states through accepting their interpretations of what international law meant and required of Germany in the exercise, for example, of self-defence.[115]

Morgenthau, a follower of Schmitt, is the originator of political Realism, which assumes a Hobbesian view of human nature. Realism

[112] M. Weber, *From Max Weber: Essays in Sociology* (H. H. Gert and C. W. Mills (trans.) (eds.) New York: Oxford University Press, 1946), 148.

[113] A. Robinson, 'Walter Benjamin: Fascism and Crisis', https://ceasefiremagazine.co.uk/walter-benjamin-fascism-crisis/ citing W. Benjamin, *The Work of Art in the Age of Mechanical Reproduction* (1936).

[114] D. Bell, *Political Thought and International Relations: Variations on a Realist Theme* (Oxford: Oxford University Press, 2006), 42.

[115] C. Schmitt, *Positionen und Begriffe im Kampf mit Weimar-Genf-Versailles 1923–1939*, (Berlin: Duncker & Humblot, 1940, reissued 1988), 176–80.

generally dismisses the international law that restricts the resort to military force.[116] Every leader, Morgenthau argued, has a duty to amass military strength. This simple idea now drives the foreign and security policies of many states and non-state armed actors today. Realism equates national self-interest with national security, not international peace.[117] Great effort is poured into expanding the legal right to resort to force in order to add the power of law to the force of weapons. Metaphor and analogy draw inspiration from the category of the sublime. States assert the right to use 'Predator', 'Reaper', and 'Avenger' drones on little more legal authority than their sublime names. The culture is saturated with glorification of military force from computer games to campaign rhetoric.

The pursuit of military superiority for national security translates into pressure to buy weapons and other commodities of war. The defence industry adds to this pressure in the pursuit of profit, so that nuclear weapons states purchase the absurd ability to destroy the world many times over. The actual waging of war creates new demand through the destruction of war materiel and infrastructure. War also diverts populations from demanding a fairer share of profits and other indicia of a just society. War channels mass movements and intense emotions, without challenging the property system or political control. It gives people 'a chance to express themselves', as a substitute for real participation.[118] The constant condition of war around the globe,[119] is hardly questioned. The ability to settle disputes peacefully declines, as the failed attempts to end the Syrian, Congo, Libyan, Afghanistan, and other civil wars demonstrate so clearly.[120]

As a source of inspiration, the sublime aesthetic is so deeply and powerfully embedded in Western law it is hardly noticed, its

116 Morgenthau, *Politics Among Nations* 1948 (n. 17), 232. See also N. Guilhot, *After the Enlightenment: Political Realism and International Relations in the Mid-Twentieth Century* (Cambridge: Cambridge University Press, 2017).

117 O. Ben Naftali, *et al.*, *The ABC of the OPT: A Legal Lexicon of the Occupation of the Palestinian Territory* (Cambridge: Cambridge University Press, 2018), 475, citing Y. Berda, 'The Security Risk as a Security Risk: Notes on the Classification and Practices of the Israeli Security Services', in A. Baker and A. Matar (eds.), *Threat: Palestinian Political Prisoners in Israel* (2011), 44–55.

118 Robinson, 'Walter Benjamin: Fascism and Crisis,' (n. 113), 95.

119 'Pope Francis Warns on "Piecemeal World War III,"' *BBC*, 13 September 2014, bbc.com/news/world-europe-29190890.

120 R. Hinnebusch and I. W. Zartman, *UN Mediation in the Syrian Conflict, From Kofi Annan to Lakhdar Brahimi* (International Peace Institute Report, 2016).

negative influence unappreciated. The sublime inspires the seeking of power against competitors. It promotes '*non*-recognition of the self in the Other, for the Other is inhuman, chaotic, annihilating'.[121] The sublime gives the illusion of power, including power over death. Singular appreciation of the sublime, without the ameliorating message of beauty, encourages self-centeredness. While people have the capacity for selflessness, the inclination to self-centeredness is reinforced in cultures devoted to materialism. For this reason, Murdoch built a moral philosophy around antidotes to selfishness, including a central role for beauty in fostering altruism.[122] The most obvious 'occasion for "unselfing"' she finds is beauty.[123] The good life is the unselfish life. This is known through the unselfish pleasure experienced in the contemplation of beauty, especially in nature. 'The self, the place where we live, is a place of illusion. Goodness is connected with the attempt to see the unself, to see and to respond to the real world in the light of a virtuous consciousness.'[124] Murdoch offers a gloss on Kant's experience of disinterested pleasure in contemplation of the beautiful, finding the experience may be produced through contemplation of good art as well as nature.[125] The surer object for the experience of unselfish pleasure, however, is nature: '[W]e take a self-forgetful pleasure in the sheer alien pointless independent existence of animals, birds, stones and trees. "Not how the world is, but that it is is the mystical."'[126]

Scarry, too, argues that these insights must be taught. She advocates education as a 'ladder' to beauty.[127] Coase and Posner have followed such an approach with extraordinary success in the promotion of an economic orientation to law. Recall that Coase's first influential article was written only in 1960. The arts are another path to restoring the alternative of beauty. Theodor Adorno explored the arts for raising consciousness, for inviting people to fully engage their capacities to be aware of the world around them and their role in it.[128] Through education and the arts the recovery of beauty in Western, secular intellectual life is attainable.

[121] Steiner, *Venus in Exile* 2001 (n. 94), xxiv (emphasis in the original).
[122] Murdoch, *The Sovereignty of Good* 1970 (n. 67), 78. [123] Ibid., 84. [124] Ibid.
[125] Ibid. [126] Ibid., 85. [127] Scarry, *On Beauty and Being Just* 1999 (n. 104), 7.
[128] For Theodor Adorno 'art aims for something that can be grasped only in a spiritual way – a "transcendence" of the reality, an ideal'. Wandschneider, 'Beauty in Nature', 2013 (n. 82), 129.

Beauty leads to understanding as to why we should live with one another in peace through recognizing the equality of all others to ourselves. Scarry also draws on Plato, as well as Dante and Simone Weil, to explain how the contemplation of one beautiful thing leads us to the general and the universal. Care for, caring about, something beautiful opens us to care and concern for the world.[129] Empathy is engendered by being drawn outside of ourselves to the world by its beauty, as understood through a single beautiful thing.[130] Scarry links this concern beyond self directly to law, in particular to the fundamental and interrelated legal principles of justice, equality, and fairness. As Aristotle taught, fairness is the equal application of the law. Justice is defined in the same way. The pervasive understanding of the value of treating people equally before the law is an understanding supported by our instinctual interest in or empathy for the other. In different words, the proof of the importance of fairness, equality, and justice as integral aims of law is found in our reaction to beauty and not in our fear of pain or interest in gain.

Scarry sees even more direct linkages between beauty and the reasons for law. She reminds us that 'beauty' and 'fairness' are terms once used interchangeably. Equality, proportion, and symmetry are at the heart of what we understand as beauty. Aquinas's clarity, integrity, and proportion are found in the rose in first bloom – an ancient symbol of beauty. Beauty in its proportion and symmetry exerts 'pressure' toward valuing and seeking equality.[131] Beauty thus persuades us instinctually of the rightness of achieving justice through the fair application of law by treating like cases alike.

Beauty does more than provide the rationale for law in general and the explanation for its core principles. It also inspires action, including action toward justice, which is, again, toward equality of treatment.[132] Scarry is one of the scholars who see 'that beauty's emphasis on symmetry, communicability, and shared emotion provides a model for ideal social relations, relations described in terms of justice or mutuality'.[133] Inspiration to achieve justice is found in our shared experience and sense of commonality. Philip Allott also finds inspiration to act in contemplation of the ideal, which can also

[129] Scarry, *On Beauty and Being Just* 1999 (n. 104), 82.

[130] Psychological studies in behavioural economics are another tool to understand humanity's relationship with beauty.

[131] Scarry, *On Beauty and Being Just* 1999 (n. 104), 109.

[132] Ibid., at 115.

[133] Canuel, *Justice, Dissent, and the Sublime* 2012 (n. 86), 5.

be termed 'excellence'[134] or 'the beautiful': ' ... [T]he mind contains a particular kind of idea – the ideal – a powerful form of mental energy that leads us to make a *better* reality caused by the magnetic attraction of ideas such as justice, the good, the true, the beautiful, the ideal ... '[135]

Insights from the study of beauty must be taught, just as the theological reasons for obedience to law were once taught and the self-interest in complying with some law is taught today. The role of beauty in understanding the reason for law in the interest of others will need to be relearned, and the sublime aesthetic resisted to do so successfully. At this moment in history there seems no better alternative, certainly not one that so appeals to the imagination.

## Conclusion

The human capacity for altruism makes us able to live in society, to live harmoniously with others, to consider another's welfare beyond our own. The ability to truly care about others beyond ourselves provides a reason to comply with law beyond the promise of gain or avoidance of pain. Law functions through common principles that at times support a person's self-interest but at others requires sacrifice for the good of another and the community. All religions teach self-sacrifice for the good of others; so does beauty. Not all people believe in God; everyone believes in beauty.

Protestant theologians are returning to the study of beauty, a path other Christians, especially the Orthodox, as well as other faiths, never abandoned.[136] Theology is being renewed 'in the light of and

[134] Graham, 'Aesthetics as a Normative Science' 2014 (n. 43).

[135] P. Allott, 'The Idealist's Dilemma: Re-Imagining International Society', May 23 2014, available online at www.ejiltalk.org/the-idealists-dilemma-re-imagining-international-society/.

[136] For reflections on beauty in Orthodox Christianity, see A. Schmemann, *For the Life of the World* (Yonkers, NY: St. Vladimir's Seminary Press, 1973); in Buddhism, C. Su, 'Beauty in Buddhism', in Y. K. Greenburg, *Encyclopedia of Love in World Religions*, Vol. 1 (Santa Barbara, CA: ABC-CLIO, 2008), 68; in Islam, S. H. Nasr, 'Religious Art, Traditional Art, Sacred Art, Some Reflections and Definitions', *The Essential Sophia* (Bloomington, IN: World Wisdom, Inc, 2006); in Judaism, Z. Braiterman, 'Aesthetics and Judaism, Art and Revelation', *Jewish Studies Quarterly* 11 (2004), 366–7, 381; and in Navajo teaching, W. Mathews, 'The Night Change: A Navajo Ceremony', in J. Bierhorst (ed.), *Four Master Works of American Indian Literature* (Tuscon, AZ: University of Arizona Press, 1974), 353.

perceived through sense knowledge (sensation, feeling, imagination), through beauty, and the arts'.[137] Graham argues for aesthetics to step in to be the basis of a philosophical understanding of the morally good life, following the exclusion of religion from that role.[138] If for the religious person divine command explains the reason to obey the law for the good of others, beauty conveys the same understanding.

Chapter 2 relies on aesthetic reasoning to answer the challenge from legal advisers in major military states for law that permits greater resort to the use of force. The prohibition on the use of force is found in United Nations Charter Article 2(4), a treaty, but the prohibition is also a natural law norm. As natural law, it permits of no derogation. Reference to natural law, however, is rare in discussions of law today because of its reliance on theological interpretation of divine will. Drawing on the insights of aesthetic philosophy provided in this chapter, Chapter 2 will indicate how beauty can also substitute for theology in discerning natural principles, such as the prohibition on force and the related requirement to settle disputes peacefully. Beauty reveals why these are enduring norms binding on all for the good of all.

137 Thiessen, *Theological Aesthetics* 2004 (n. 6), 1.

138 Graham, *The Re-enchantment of the World* 2007 (n. 20), 94. O'Regan, 'Theology, Art and Beauty' 2013 (n. 6). More recent work in theology seems to be following developments in literary theory. After a return to beauty, criticism in favour of the sublime is again appearing. See Canuel, *Justice, Dissent, and the Sublime* 2012 (n. 86). In theology, see R. Theimann, *The Humble Sublime* (London: IB Tauris & Co, 2014).

# 2

# Prohibiting Force through Peremptory Norms

On 2 September 2017, North Korea tested a nuclear weapon for the sixth time. It may have been a hydrogen bomb yielding 100 kilotonnes. The atomic bombs dropped by the United States on Hiroshima and Nagasaki, Japan, during World War II yielded ten to fifteen kilotonnes.[1] On 11 September 2017, the United Nations (UN) Security Council unanimously condemned North Korea's test, which violated a number of Council resolutions.[2] On 19 September 2017, United States President Donald Trump in a speech to the UN General Assembly said: 'We must reject threats to sovereignty, from the Ukraine to the South China Sea. We must uphold respect for law, respect for borders, and respect for culture, and the peaceful engagement these allow . . .' He added in reference to North Korea's bomb test that if the United States is 'forced to defend itself or its allies, we will have no choice but to totally destroy North Korea'.[3] Following President Trump's speech, a retired United States Army General with long experience in Korea predicted the aftermath of a war between

[1] I. Sample, 'Did North Korea Just Test a Hydrogen Bomb?', *The Guardian*, 3 September 2017, www.theguardian.com/world/2017/sep/03/did-north-korea-just-test-a-hydrogen-bomb.

[2] UN SC Res. 2375 (11 September 2017). The resolution incorporates eleven prior Security Council resolutions. North Korea is thought to possess 'less than 20' nuclear bombs. U. Friedman, 'Can America Live with a Nuclear North Korea?', *The Atlantic*, 14 September 2017, www.theatlantic.com/international/archive/2017/09/north-korea-nuclear-deterrence/539205/.

[3] Remarks by President Donald Trump to the 72nd Session of the United Nations General Assembly, 19 September 2017, www.whitehouse.gov/the-press-office/2017/09/19/remarks-president-trump-72nd-session-united-nations-general-assembly.

the United States and North Korea: 'What impact would a war have? Devastation of Seoul, the unravelling of world order, and China on the other side with "enemy" status. And if the United States and China are belligerents, everything is up for grabs.'[4]

Events threatening world order, threatening violation of the most basic norm of world order – the prohibition on the use of force – occur as if the norm did not exist. Indeed, the prohibition on the use of force 'is under greater assault today than it has been in seven decades'.[5]

Countervailing examples do exist of commitment to the peaceful resolution of disputes and the rejection of war. South Korea has long demonstrated patience and forbearance in the face of violent North Korean provocation.[6] South Korea took creative steps during the 2018 Winter Olympics to open a dialogue with North Korea.[7] The International Criminal Court (ICC), too, has sought to create greater commitment to peace and human rights through holding individuals accountable at the international level for law violations. On 14 December 2017, the 123-member Assembly of States Parties to the Rome Statute of the International Criminal Court met at the UN to activate the ICC's jurisdiction over the crime of aggression.[8] Aggression is defined in a United Nations resolution discussed below as any serious violation of the prohibition on the use of

[4] R. Wright, 'What Would War with North Korea Look Like?', *The New Yorker*, 6 September 2017, www.newyorker.com/news/news-desk/what-would-war-with-north-korea-look-like, quoting US General (retired) James Marks.

[5] O. A. Hathaway and S. J. Shapiro, *The Internationalists: How a Radical Plan to Outlaw War Remade the World* (New York: Simon and Schuster, 2017), 417–18. See also, C. Gray, *International Law and the Use of Force* 4th edn (Oxford: Oxford University Press, 2018), 1.

[6] One of the most serious incidents occurred when North Korea apparently sank a South Korean warship with the loss of forty-six sailors. C. Sang-Hun, 'North Korea Denies Role in Sinking of Warship', *New York Times*, 18 April 2010, A8. South Korea reported to the Security Council its suspicions that linked the sinking to a South Korean report to the Security Council on possible North Korean violations of Security Council mandates respecting the North's nuclear programme. See Letter dated 6 April 2009 from the Permanent Representative of the Republic of Korea to the United Nations addressed to the President of the Security Council, UN Doc S/2009/186 (7 April 2009) referring to UN SC Res. 1718. South Korea did not retaliate militarily.

[7] 'Winter Olympics 2018: North Korea Invites South President to Pyongyang', *BBC*, 10 February 2018, www.bbc.com/news/world-asia-43014269.

[8] Activation of the Jurisdiction of the Court over the Crime of Aggression, Res. ICC-ASP/16/Res.5 (14 December 2017).

force. Activating ICC jurisdiction over individuals accused of aggression signals a measure of new support for the legal ban on resort to armed conflict. The ultimate crime against the peace is under the jurisdiction of an international criminal court for the first time since the Nuremberg and Tokyo tribunals.[9]

In general, however, since the end of the Cold War, the stronger trend among certain governments and academic specialists has been toward relaxing the prohibition of the use of force. Just at the moment when chances for global cooperation to advance the peaceful resolution of disputes were higher than in the previous three decades, new confidence in military force burst forth as well. During the Cold War, when the Soviet Union and the United States dominated international politics, a certain amount of competitive compliance with the prohibition existed. The two superpowers often manipulated facts relevant to a lawful use of force;[10] they rarely attempted to manipulate the law.[11] Since the end of the Cold War, efforts to expand the legal right to use military force have been persistent. Interest in the art of negotiation, mediation, and interstate adjudication has noticeably declined.[12] Apparently, with the end of superpower rivalry, the sense in the United States and some of its allies became one of holding a superior status in the international system owing to success in the decades-long

[9] See generally C. McDougall, *The Crime of Aggression under the Rome Statute of the International Criminal Court* (Cambridge: Cambridge University Press, 2013).

[10] See, e.g., an account of the USA's acquisition of an invitation to invade from the Governor General of the Caribbean Island of Grenada after the invasion in C. C. Joyner, 'Reflections on the Lawfulness of Invasion', *American Journal of International Law*, 78 (1984), 131; or the Soviet acquisition of an invitation to invade Afghanistan by assassinating the Afghan leader and installing someone amenable to the Soviets, M. E. O'Connell, 'Soviet Prisoners in the Afghan Conflict', *Columbia Journal of Transnational Law*, 23 (1985), 483. Similar events occurred during the Prague Spring of 1968, the Hungarian Revolution of 1956, and the Vietnam War.

[11] The superpowers tended to offer legal arguments as justifications for actual uses of force. Some members of US administrations, however, did attempt to get new interpretations in favour of greater rights to use force through publishing academic articles or in lectures or discussions. See, e.g., Judge Abram Sofaer, Legal Adviser to the US State Department during the presidency of George H. W. Bush, who attempted to argue for greater rights to use force in the context of terrorism. A. D. Sofaer, 'Sixth Annual Waldemar A. Solf Lecture in International Law: Terrorism, the Law, and the National Defense', *Military Law Review*, 126 (1989), 89–123, 93.

[12] See Chapter 6.

struggle.[13] Technological developments with respect to weapons have helped boost this sense of superiority. New interpretations of the law have emerged to provide legal justifications for resort to force.[14] These post-Cold War attempts to expand the right to resort to force have reached the point where leaders like Trump and Kim Jong-un fail to acknowledge any legal constraint.[15]

Some see these events as evidence that the prohibition on the use of force no longer binds as it once did. They are mistaken. The prohibition is no simple rule of positive law. The failure to acknowledge and respect it does not pose the same existential threat that would face rules of customary international law or treaties in the same circumstances. As will be discussed in this chapter, the prohibition is a peremptory norm, meaning it is one from which no derogation is permitted. As such it is durable. It may expand but never contract. It governs the conduct of all states regardless of the size of their military or the nature of their system of government. The prohibition is one of the oldest principles of international

[13] An adviser to the former UK Prime Minister Tony Blair demonstrated the new sense of privilege when he said: 'The challenge . . . is to get used to the idea of double standards. Among ourselves, we operate on the basis of laws . . . But when dealing with more old-fashioned kinds of states . . . we need to revert to the rougher methods of an earlier era – force, preemptive attack, deception.' R. Cooper, 'The Post Modern State', in M. Leonard (ed.), *Reordering the World: The Long-term Implications of September 11th* (London: Foreign Policy Centre, 2002), cited in G. Simpson, 'Humanity, Law, Force', in J. Farrall and H. Charlesworth (eds.), *Strengthening the Rule of Law Through the UN Security Council* (New York: Routledge 2016), 85, note 51.

[14] WikiLeaks has revealed a campaign by the US State Department to expand the right to use force on the territory of foreign states. V. Kattan, 'Furthering the "War on Terrorism" through International Law: How the United States and the United Kingdom Resurrected the Bush Doctrine on Using Preventive Military Force to Combat Terrorism', *Journal on the Use of Force and International Law*, 23 (2017), 1–48, 24–6, note 110. See also J. Brunée and S. J. Toope, 'Self-Defence Against Non-State Actors: Are Powerful States Willing but Unable to Change International Law?', *International and Comparative Law Quarterly*, 67 (2017), 263–86 and notes 79–81 and accompanying text.

[15] In addition to threats to annihilate North Korea, Trump has ordered unlawful reprisal attacks on Syria and greatly expanded drone strikes outside areas of armed conflict hostilities involving the USA. Each such strike is a first use of force that violates the prohibition of aggression. On the Syria reprisal attack, see, M. E. O'Connell, 'The Unlawful but Popular Armed Reprisal', *Ohio Northern Law Review* 44 (2018), 325–350; and on targeted killing with drones, see, also C. Gray, 'Targeted Killings: Recent US Attempts to Create a Legal Framework', *Current Legal Problems*, 66 (2013), 259–288.

law.[16] Empirical evidence indicates that it has had real success in virtually ending the acquisition of territory by conquest.[17] Without it, the international legal system makes little practical or moral sense. Law exists essentially as an alternative to unregulated force in ordering human affairs. International law exists for this purpose and with greatest impact at the global level.

After a generation of scholarship and policy moving away from the international legal prohibition on the use of force, it is time to return. This chapter investigates the peremptory status of the prohibition and considers general principles of international law intrinsic to it, such as equality, necessity, and proportionality. Like peremptory norms, principles such as these are essential to legal systems and are, therefore, durable and impervious to dilution through the procedures of positive law change.[18] The aim here is to deepen understanding of these extra-positive aspects of international law, while pursuing the main purpose of laying out the meaning of the international legal prohibition on the use of force.

The research undertaken for both purposes shows that natural law theory is essential to explaining extra-positive norms. Natural law incorporates insights and knowledge gained from extra-positive sources, as will be set out in detail below. As already discussed in the Introduction and Chapter 1, the scientific revolution and other developments led to natural law theory becoming a controversial area of jurisprudence in the West.[19] In the case of the prohibition on the use of force, its codification in positive law has led lawyers to overlook its natural law foundations. This omission might have had

[16] See notes 167–82 and accompanying text.

[17] At time of writing, only one state in the world, Russia, holds territory taken through military force claimed by another member of the United Nations. See M. E. O'Connell, 'The Crisis in Ukraine–2014', in T. Ruys, O. Corten, and A. Hofer (eds.), *The Use of Force in International Law: A Case-Based Approach* (Oxford: Oxford University Press, 2018), 855–72. See also, Hathaway and Shapiro, *The Internationalists* 2017 (n. 5), chap. 13.

[18] See notes 66–80 and accompanying text.

[19] See, e.g., Weisburd, who dismisses natural law on the view it is impractical to apply to legal problems. A. M. Weisburd, *The Failings of the International Court of Justice* (Oxford: Oxford University Press, 2016), 59. On the other hand, Weisburd felt the need to mention natural law, which indicates growing interest in this vital area of legal theory. Not long ago he would likely have deemed it not worth mentioning. As for how impractical natural law actually is, one of the purposes of this chapter is to respond to just such a concern.

little impact, however, if governments had embraced a rigorous application of the positive law version of the prohibition. Indeed, the conclusions of this chapter clash only with the advocacy for weakening the prohibition, whether natural law or positive law.[20]

The chapter builds on the foundation laid in Chapter 1 as to international law's source of authority and theory of compliance. Chapter 1 pointed to extra-positive features of law for an understanding of why human beings have a duty to obey the law in general. Those same extra-positive features are integral to natural law. The introduction to natural law in Chapter 1 will be developed more fully here after first setting out the standard understanding of the prohibition based on positive law. The discussion will then consider natural law in general and specific insights from natural law as to the unique characteristics of peremptory norms and inherent general principles. These insights are supported by the intellectual history of the prohibition on the use of force, which was until the rise of science based solely on natural law theory. The chapter's final section will apply the prohibition to counter a variety of arguments introduced in the post-Cold War period to expand the right to use force. Chapter 3 will then move on to the institutional setting of the UN and the UN Security Council as the body charged with primary responsibility for preserving global peace and security.

## I Prohibiting Force in Positive Law

The place to begin any discussion of the prohibition on the use of force is the United Nations Charter.[21] The Charter is a treaty and, therefore, a manifestation of positive law. The introduction to this chapter stated that the prohibition on the use of force is a principle of extra-positive law. These points are not inconsistent. Natural law is a hybrid of positive law and extra-positive principles. Extra-positive principles may be expressed in positive law form, such as

[20] For an expansive argument promoting the legality of military force to counter terrorism, see D. Bethlehem, 'Self-Defense Against an Imminent or Actual Armed Attack by Nonstate Actors', *American Journal of International Law,* 106 (2012), 770–7. For an expansive argument promoting the legality of military intervention for humanitarian purposes, see, International Commission on Intervention and State Sovereignty, *The Responsibility to Protect* (2001).

[21] Gray, *International Law and the Use of Force* 2018 (n. 5), 9.

a treaty. This is the ideal for practical purposes, and most peremptory norms, from the prohibition on genocide to the prohibition on torture, are found in treaties. The dual location of certain norms, however, also helps to explain why some scholars find that positivism alone suffices to explain the law. This section will draw on the positive law doctrine of sources, but will also indicate where positivism is insufficient to fully explain the meaning of the prohibition on the use of force and related general principles. The discussion will serve as a prelude to analysing the prohibition as natural law.

Beginning with positive law is also important to set a baseline understanding for the purpose of assessing derogation from or expansion beyond the peremptory norm. As explained above, peremptory norms permit no derogation. They may reach more conduct but interpreting them to reach less is a form of derogation.[22]

Following a review of the Charter, the section turns to general principles of law related to the prohibition on the use of force, including necessity, proportionality, attribution, and equality. These principles exist outside treaties, and while they are sometimes described as principles of customary international law, as will be discussed below, they lack the elements of custom. They are better categorized as general principles of law essential to functioning legal systems and, thus, they too are natural law norms.

### *A The Charter*

The prohibition on the use of force was codified in the UN Charter, a multilateral treaty adopted at the end of World War II. From the Charter preamble, with its commitment to 'save succeeding generations from the scourge of war', to the empowerment of the Secretary-General to bring any matter of peace and security to the Security Council,[23] the Charter is devoted to ending war and supplanting it with peaceful methods of dispute resolution.[24] The most direct statement of the prohibition within the Charter is Article 2(4): 'All members shall refrain in their international relations from the threat or use of force against the territorial integrity or political independence of any state, or in any other manner inconsistent with the purposes of the United Nations.' Article 2(4) was

[22] See notes 73–84 and accompanying text. [23] UN Charter, Art. 99.
[24] See, e.g., UN Charter Chap. VI.

designed to render unlawful all uses of force by states above a minimal level.

Article 2(4) has only two express limitations in the Charter, both of which are found in Chapter VII. Articles 39–42 limit the prohibition when the Security Council has authorized force to restore international peace and security.[25] Article 51 further limits it in cases of individual and collective self-defence by a state if an armed attack occurs.[26] The Charter does not provide directly for civil war. No mention is made of whether an outside state may intervene in civil wars.[27] Given that the greater number of conflicts since the adoption of the Charter have been civil wars involving outside state intervention, these conflicts deserve a chapter of their own. It will be argued

[25] UN Charter Art. 39: 'The Security Council shall determine the existence of any threat to the peace, breach of the peace, or act of aggression and shall make recommendations, or decide what measures shall be taken in accordance with Arts 41 and 42, to maintain or restore international peace and security.'

Art. 40: 'In order to prevent an aggravation of the situation, the Security Council may, before making the recommendations or deciding upon the measures provided for in Article 39, call upon the parties concerned to comply with such provisional measures as it deems necessary or desirable. Such provisional measures shall be without prejudice to the rights, claims, or position of the parties concerned. The Security Council shall duly take account of failure to comply with such provisional measures.'

Art. 41: 'The Security Council may decide what measures not involving the use of armed force are to be employed to give effect to its decisions, and it may call upon the Members of the United Nations to apply such measures. These may include complete or partial interruption of economic relations and of rail, sea, air, postal, telegraphic, radio, and other means of communication, and the severance of diplomatic relations.'

Art. 42: 'Should the Security Council consider that measures provided for in Article 41 would be inadequate or have proved to be inadequate, it may take such action by air, sea, or land forces as may be necessary to maintain or restore international peace and security. Such action may include demonstrations, blockade, and other operations by air, sea, or land forces of Members of the United Nations.'

[26] Art. 51: 'Nothing in the present Charter shall impair the inherent right of individual or collective self-defence if an armed attack occurs against a Member of the United Nations, until the Security Council has taken measures necessary to maintain international peace and security. Measures taken by Members in the exercise of this right of self-defence shall be immediately reported to the Security Council and shall not in any way affect the authority and responsibility of the Security Council under the present Charter to take at any time such action as it deems necessary in order to maintain or restore international peace and security.'

[27] The choice of the term 'civil war' over alternatives such as 'non-international armed conflict' is explained in Chapter 6.

in Chapter 5 that the full scope of the prohibition on the use of force has yet to be fully appreciated. Evidence will be offered that the prohibition does limit the right to engage in civil war.

The Charter version of the prohibition was agreed to in June 1945, when US President Harry Truman oversaw a conference of fifty national delegations in San Francisco to negotiate the final text of the Charter. The delegations set out the purpose of the organization in the Charter preamble: 'We the peoples of the United Nations determined to save succeeding generations from the scourge of war ... have agreed to the present Charter of the United Nations and do hereby establish an international organization to be known as the United Nations.' The Charter incorporates three approaches to fulfilling the aim of ending war. First, it includes the general substantive legal obligation not to resort to the use of force. Then it establishes the procedural mechanisms of the Security Council for dealing with 'threats to the peace, breaches of the peace, or acts of aggression' and of other organs for conflict prevention, and, finally, the Charter addresses the causes of conflict by supporting human rights and economic development.[28]

The prohibition on the use of force is the most direct measure for assuring the peace. It is the reason the UN was established. The negotiating history from San Francisco confirms that the delegates intended Article 2(4) to prohibit all armed force of any significance.[29] The references to 'territorial integrity', 'political independence', and, especially 'in any other manner inconsistent with the Purposes of the United Nations', support the broad reach of Article 2(4). A member of the US delegation responded to a question by the Brazilian delegation on the intended scope of Article 2(4) by saying: '[T]he intention of the authors of the original text was to state in the broadest terms an absolute all-inclusive prohibition; the phrase "or in any other manner" was designed to insure that there should be no loopholes.'[30]

[28] UN Charter Art. 39.

[29] For a discussion of what level of force is outlawed by Art. 2(4), see ICJ, *Military and Paramilitary Activities in and against Nicaragua* (*Nicaragua* v. *United States*), Merits, Judgment of 27 June 1986, ICJ Reports 1986, 14, paras. 201, 210, 247–8, and 257.

[30] 'United Nations Conference on International Organization', vol. 6, (San Francisco, 25 April 1945), 334–5. See also I. Brownlie, *International Law and the Use of Force by States* (Oxford: Clarendon Press, 1963), 275.

This understanding of the prohibition is further supported by other Charter articles. The prohibition on force is an obligation on members, not the UN Security Council, which has power to authorize the use of force to enforce the prohibition.[31] Similarly, the right of self-defence in Article 51 is an aspect of the prohibition.[32] It indicates the outer limits of the ban. States acting in emergency response to an armed attack may do so in individual or collective self-defence but only until the Security Council acts. It is a narrow, temporary exception to the prohibition.[33] The rest of the Charter is devoted to peaceful alternatives to force as well as preventing and ending conflict.

Between 1945 and 2008, the world witnessed over 300 armed conflicts.[34] This statistic may make it difficult to believe the drafters of the Charter seriously intended to end war. After the catastrophe of World War II, however, that was the intent, a point essential to take into account in construing the Charter's terms under positive law rules. The Vienna Convention on the Law of Treaties stresses that interpretation of treaty texts must honour the objects and purposes of the treaty.[35] Negotiating history may be cited to confirm the plain meaning of words.[36] Article 2(4) prohibits the use of force, a meaning confirmed by the negotiating history. The long history of violations of Article 2(4) have no effect on its meaning. Subsequent practice may be consulted when the practice indicates agreement of the treaty parties as to how a term is to be

[31] Chapter 3 concerns the Security Council's authority, including limits on that authority found within the general principles of law.

[32] See n. 26. [33] Chapter 4.

[34] M. C. Bassiouni (ed.), *The Pursuit of International Criminal Justice: A World Study on Conflicts, Victimization, and Post-Conflict Justice* (Cambridge: Intersentia, 2010), 75–9.

[35] Vienna Convention on the Law of Treaties, Vienna, 23 May 1969, 1155 UNTS 331 (hereinafter the VCLT), Art. 31. 'General rule of interpretation (1) A treaty shall be interpreted in good faith in accordance with the ordinary meaning to be given to the terms of the treaty in their context and in the light of its object and purpose.'

[36] Art. 32 VCLT. 'Supplementary means of interpretation, Recourse may be had to supplementary means of interpretation, including the preparatory work of the treaty and the circumstances of its conclusion, in order to confirm the meaning resulting from the application of article 31, or to determine the meaning when the interpretation according to article 31:

(a) leaves the meaning ambiguous or obscure; or
(b) leads to a result which is manifestly absurd or unreasonable.'

interpreted.[37] Practice that violates the treaty can have no role in interpretation as it does not indicate an agreement on how to interpret the treaty's rule but rather its negation. The Vienna Convention also requires that treaties be interpreted as consistent with other rules of international law.[38] The most important 'other rule' with respect to Article 2(4) is the rule that derogation from a peremptory norm is prohibited. Derogation following a reinterpretation is no different from derogation following the adoption of a new or modified treaty provision.

The purpose of the UN is to end the scourge of war. This purpose must inform the reading of all the Charter's provisions. The argument that the Charter somehow provides permission to go to war is a misreading of the objects and purposes of the Charter.[39] On the other hand, the Charter does not seek to end all forms of conflict or violence – an unachievable task. The drafters set forth an ambitious goal, but one they believed they could accomplish through substantive law and legal process. Thus, Article 2(4) bans armed force but not every form of coercion.[40]

[37] Art. 31(3) VCLT. 'There shall be taken into account, together with the context: . . .

(b) any subsequent practice in the application of the treaty which establishes the agreement of the parties regarding its interpretation; . . .'

[38] Art. 31(3) VCLT. 'There shall be taken into account, together with the context: . . .

(c) any relevant rules of international law applicable in the relations between the parties . . .'

[39] For an argument by a political scientist that the Charter creates a regime permitting the use of force, see I. Hurd, 'The Permissive Power of the Ban on War', *European Journal of International Security*, 2 (2017), 1–18.

[40] UN Information Organization, 'Documents of the United Nations Conference on International Organization' (25–6 April 1945), 334 (discussing the rejection of a proposal by Brazil to extend the prohibition on force to economic coercion). The Simma commentary points to paragraph seven of the preamble of the Charter – which states that 'armed force shall not be used, save in the common interest' – and to Art. 44 of the Charter – which refers to 'armed force' for instances wherein the Security Council decides to use force – to support the view that the general prohibition on the use of force under Art. 2(4) refers solely to military force. B. Simma *et al.* (eds.), *The Charter of the United Nations, A Commentary* 2nd edn (Oxford: Oxford University Press, 2002), 118.

Some forms of coercion, such as economic sanctions, may be lawful when used as a countermeasure.[41] Even when those forms of coercion are unlawful, other rules of international law apply, such as the principle of non-intervention.[42] Nor does Article 2(4) reach minimal uses of armed force such as shooting across the bow of a ship to arrest it. The same reasoning applies. Some of these minimal uses, such as in law enforcement, are lawful as police measures or justified as countermeasures. If they are unlawful they fall under other prohibitions, including the principle of non-intervention or the restriction on the excessive use of force by police.[43] Article 2(4) has a practical, specific focus on the UN's goal of ending the significant use of armed force in international relations. The drafters did not attempt to do everything and thereby nothing.

In the years following the adoption of the Charter, the UN General Assembly reflected these understandings of the prohibition in various resolutions, most importantly, the Declaration on Friendly Relations,[44] the Definition of Aggression,[45] and the Declaration on Non-Intervention.[46] The International Court of Justice concurs in the General Assembly's understanding, as seen in a series of decisions that will be discussed below.[47]

Nevertheless, outside the UN, efforts began soon after the Charter was adopted toward reinterpreting Article 2(4) to allow states a greater right to use force. Perhaps the best-known early scholar advocating a broader right to resort to force was the University of Sydney's Julius Stone. Stone, born in the UK in 1907,

[41] ILC Articles on the Responsibility of States for Internationally Wrongful Acts, GAOR, 56th Sess., Suppl. 10, 43 *et seq.*, Arts. 22, 49–54.

[42] Declaration on the Inadmissibility of Intervention and Interference in the Internal Affairs of States, GA Res. 36/103 of 9 December 1981 (hereinafter the Declaration on Non-intervention).

[43] M. E. O'Connell, 'The True Meaning of Force', *AJIL Unbound* (4 August 2014), www.asil.org/blogs/true-meaning-force, replying to T. Ruys, 'The Meaning of "Force" and the Boundaries of the Jus Ad Bellum: Are "Minimal" Uses of Force Excluded from UN Charter Article 2(4)?', *American Journal of International Law*, 108 (2014) 159–210, 159.

[44] Declaration on Principles of International Law concerning Friendly Relations and Co-operation among States in accordance with the Charter of the United Nations, GA Res. 2625 (XXV) of 24 October 1970.

[45] Definition of Aggression, GA Res. 3314 (XXIX) of 14 December 1974.

[46] Declaration on Non-intervention (n. 42).

[47] See notes 73–80 and accompanying text.

was from a Russian Jewish family that had fled brutal persecution in Russia for asylum in the UK.[48] Stone studied law at Oxford and Harvard but failed to secure teaching positions at these prestigious universities, owing, in his view, to anti-Semitism.[49] Stone left the UK for Australia, where he remained a harsh critic of the UN, writing an opinion piece in 1950 about the new organization, titled 'A Mad Hatter's World Tea Party'.[50] Soon after the op-ed, he put forward an interpretation of Article 2(4) that functionally eliminated its restrictions on a state's right to use force.[51] In 1958, Stone published a book defending Israel's attack on Egypt during the Suez Crisis, asserting that Article 2(4) only restricted the use of force by a state that intended to interfere with the target state's territorial integrity or political independence.[52]

Stone took as his starting place, not Article 2(4) but Article 51, casting it as a permissive right, a tool to seek justice, rather than as an exception to a general prohibition.[53] Stone plainly wanted to expand the right for some states to use military force irrespective of the Charter's terms and took no account of the objects and purposes of the Charter, its negotiating history,[54] or the status of Article 2(4) as *jus cogens*. He attempted to undermine the legitimacy of the Charter restrictions on the use of force by tainting them as mere concessions to great power demands.[55] He was a pioneer in the field of sociology and the law and believed that the law should be interpreted in such a way that it accomplished important social ends, especially his own view of what 'justice' entailed.[56]

48 L. Star, *Julius Stone: An Intellectual Life* (Oxford: Oxford University Press in association with Sydney University Press, 1992).
49 Ibid.
50 J. Stone, 'A Mad Hatter's World Tea Party', *The Argus*, 7 December 1950, 2, http://trove.nla.gov.au/newspaper/article/23032557.
51 J. Stone, 'Force and the Charter in the Seventies', *Syracuse Journal of International Law and Commerce*, 2 (1974), 1–17. Stone comments on page 6 of this article that he developed his interpretation in the early 1950s. See also J. Stone, *Quest for Survival: The Role of Law and Foreign Policy* (Cambridge, MA: Harvard University Press, 1961), 40–56.
52 J. Stone, *Aggression and World Order: A Critique of United Nations Theories of Aggression* (Clark, New Jersey: The Lawbook Exchange, 1958), 100–103.
53 Ibid., 43, 95, 181–3. See also, B. V. A. Röling, 'The Ban on the Use of Force and the U.N. Charter', in A. Cassese (ed.), *The Current Legal Regulation of the Use of Force* (Dordrecht: Martinus Nijhoff, 1986), 3–8, 4–5.
54 Arts. 31 and 32 VCLT.
55 Stone, 'Force and the Charter in the Seventies' 1974 (n. 51), 13.
56 Star, *Julius Stone* 1992 (n. 48).

Louis Sohn responded to Stone that Article 2(4) must be understood as a prohibition on the use of force, read in the light of the Charter as a whole.[57] Sohn spoke from a position of extraordinary authority. He, too, was from an Eastern European Jewish family and had personally escaped the Holocaust when he left Poland in 1939 on the last ship to leave before the Germans invaded.[58] Sohn, too, went to study law in Harvard. There he became the student of and assistant to Judge Manley O. Hudson. Sohn went with Hudson in the US delegation to the San Francisco conference to negotiate the UN Charter and helped draft Article 51.[59] In 1946, he joined the Harvard Law faculty where he taught United Nations law. He succeeded Hudson in 1961 in the Bemis Chair.[60] In opposition to Stone, he emphasized the requirements of Article 1(1) of the Charter, which calls on states to settle disputes peacefully and comply with international law. Rather than meet Sohn's point that Article 2(4) must be interpreted in the context of the UN Charter and international law as a whole, Stone shifted from standard text analysis – as laid out in the Vienna Convention – to an argument based on his preferred policy justification for using force. That policy required a more permissive Charter regime:[61]

> What, for example, if a wrongdoer is so outrageous and so intransigent, that you cannot bring about settlement of the dispute in accordance with justice and international law, except by resort to threat or use of force? I suppose that the Sohn type of view might say that you have to presume everything for the best and that since we must exclude the use of force, we have to read Article 1(1) as incorporated in Article 2(4) to mean that a State must settle its grievance with the wrongdoer by peaceful means or simply reconcile itself to suffering the wrong.[62]

57 Sohn's critique is detailed in Stone, 'Force and the Charter in the Seventies' 1974 (n. 51), 6, 8, without a source citation beyond mentioning that Sohn raised these points vigorously in the 1950s when Stone first developed his interpretation of Art. 2(4).

58 T. Buergenthal, 'Louis B. Sohn (1914–2006)', *American Journal of International Law*, 100 (2006), 623–8, 623. Sohn was born in Lviv, now in Ukraine. Interestingly, two other accomplished international lawyers of the post-war period were also from Lviv, Sir Hersch Lauterpacht and Rafael Lemkin. See P. Sands, *East-West Street: On the Origins of 'Genocide' and 'Crimes Against Humanity'* (New York: Alfred A. Knopf, 2016).

59 Buergenthal, 'Louis B. Sohn' 2006 (n. 58), 624. 60 Ibid.

61 Arts. 31–3 VCLT (n. 35).

62 Stone, 'Force and the Charter in the Seventies' 1974 (n. 51), 8.

Stone called himself a 'realist-traditionalist'[63] and those from Sohn's camp 'idealist-restrictionists'.[64] This distinction continues to characterize international law scholars working in the area of use of force, with some modification of terms. Today, those interpreting the Charter strictly are still referred to as 'restrictionists', but those arguing for a more relaxed view of the Charter's rules are often labelled 'broad interpreters' or 'expansionists'.[65] 'Expansionists' do not want to expand the Charter's reach. They wish to expand the right to use force. They typically ignore the prohibition's status as *jus cogens*.

### *B General Principles*

The Charter's prohibition on the use of force is part of a regime of international law, the *jus ad bellum*, that includes further restrictions on resort to force. These additional restrictions are found among the general principles of law, including the principles of equality, necessity, and proportionality, as well as principles of attribution, which operate much as *jus cogens* norms do.[66] Like *jus cogens*, general principles of this type may not be negated through treaty, contrary state practice, or interpretation. Given their durable, progressive quality, these principles are discerned, rather than created through positive law method. They will be referred to here as 'inherent' general principles to distinguish them from the other category of general principles found through comparing provisions of national law.[67] Like *jus cogens*, inherent general principles require a theoretical explanation other than the one used to explain the existence and operation of the positive law. Again, they require natural law theory, returned to again in the next section below. The remainder of this section concerns the content of the most

63 Ibid., 11. 64 Ibid., 8.

65 C. Kress, 'Time for Decision: Some Thoughts on the Immediate Future of the Crime of Aggression: A Reply to Andreas Paulus', *European Journal of International Law*, 20 (2009), 1129–46, 1140.

66 For more on general principles, see B. Cheng, *General Principles of Law: As Applied by International Courts and Tribunals* (London: Stevens & Sons, 1953) and Chapter 1.

67 See, e.g., the method used by the International Court of Justice in its search for the nationality of corporations in ICJ, *Barcelona Traction, Light and Power Co, Ltd (Belgium* v. *Spain)*, Judgment of 5 February 1970, ICJ Reports 3, paras. 50–1.

important of the general principles relative to the prohibition on the use of force, beginning with necessity.

The principle of necessity appears throughout international law as a limit on coercive action by states. It is found in the *jus ad bellum,* which is the focus here, as well as the *jus in bello,*[68] and in the peacetime law of state responsibility as a circumstance precluding wrongfulness.[69] As part of the *jus ad bellum,* necessity limits the use of force by mandating that no peaceful alternatives exist prior to a resort to force. Force must be a 'last resort after all peaceful means have failed'.[70] In addition to the requirement of last resort, the principle of necessity requires that the party resorting to force must calculate that there is a high likelihood of success, meaning that force will likely accomplish the legitimate objective.[71]

Proportionality is typically mentioned only in combination with necessity. It is distinctive, however. Proportionality requires that any lawful use of force not be excessive in relation to the injury to which it responds. Gardam finds that proportionality requires a 'balance' between the injury perpetrated by the initial unlawful use of force and the destruction imposed in response to it. The party using force lawfully aims to avoid a disproportionate response. Yet, proportionality may require not so much an assessment of legitimate aims as an assessment of the initial injury endured. The response must be no worse than the initial unlawful action. This conclusion is tied to a careful assessment of what the party using force lawfully intends to achieve through military force.[72] It is the same consideration that must be taken into account respecting the principle of necessity.

The International Court of Justice (ICJ) has found that despite the lack of express provision in the Charter, the principles of necessity, proportionality, and other general principles apply to

[68] See the *jus in bello* targeting rule incorporating a concept of military necessity in Protocol Additional to the Geneva Conventions of 12 August 1949, and relating to the Protection of Victims of International Armed Conflicts of 8 June 1977, 1125 UNTS 3, Art. 53.

[69] See Protocol Additional to the Geneva Conventions of 1949 and J. Gardam, *Necessity, Proportionality and the Use of Military Force by States* (Cambridge: Cambridge University Press, 2004).

[70] Gardam, *Necessity, Proportionality* 2004 (n. 69), 5.

[71] On likelihood of success, see S. Lazar, 'War', in E. N. Zalta (ed.), *The Stanford Encyclopedia of Philosophy* (Summer 2016 edn), para. 2.5, http://plato.stanford.edu/archives/sum2016/entries/war/.

[72] Gardam, *Necessity, Proportionality* 2004 (n. 69), 156.

restrict resort to force. The court treats the Charter as providing the lawful bases for resort to force, then looks to necessity and other principles for the conditions on the lawful exercise of force. The ICJ has consistently mentioned the obligation to comply with the principles of necessity and proportionality in cases involving the *jus ad bellum*. The ICJ explained in the *Nicaragua* case that the principles of necessity and proportionality were part of the law on self-defence prior to the adoption of the Charter in 1945.[73] The Charter's reference to the 'inherent right of self-defence' in Article 51 is a reference to such principles of general law that the Charter did not amend and could not amend, given their status as inherent to the law. In the *Nuclear Weapons* advisory opinion, the court said:

> '[T]here is a specific rule whereby self-defence would warrant only measures which are proportional to the armed attack and necessary to respond to it, a rule well established in customary international law'. This dual condition applies equally to Article 51 of the Charter, whatever the means of force employed.[74]

The court's formulation of necessity indicates two meanings of the principle. A state resorting to force must both assess the likelihood a military operation will succeed in accomplishing the legitimate military objective and it must be a last resort. The responsive action must be a 'way' to accomplish a legitimate end, meaning an effective way, and that no non-violent alternative exists. Commentary on the *jus in bello* tends to contain more references to the likelihood of success. The *jus ad bellum* has more on last resort.

After necessity and proportionality, attribution is the next of the important general principles related to the prohibition on the use of force. The lawful exercise of force must be against a state bearing legal responsibility for the wrong that formed the basis of the justified resort to force in the first place. Once the commission of a wrong is established, responsibility for that wrong is assigned through principles of attribution. As secondary or process rules of

[73] ICJ, *Military and Paramilitary Activities* (n. 29), para. 176.

[74] See *Legality of the Threat or Use of Nuclear Weapons* Advisory Opinion of 8 July 1996, ICJ Reports 1996, 226, 245 (quoting *Military and Paramilitary Activities* (n. 29), para. 94). The ICJ refers to necessity and proportionality in Nicaragua as customary international law rather than as general principles, an erroneous categorization not critical to the court's opinion. See also *Oil Platforms (Islamic Republic of Iran v. United States of America)* Judgment of 6 November 2003 ICJ Reports 2003, 161, 198.

fundamental importance, the law of attribution belongs with the general principles of necessity and proportionality.[75] The ICJ emphasized the importance of links of responsibility in the *Nicaragua, Congo,* and *Bosnia* v. *Serbia* judgments.[76] The court emphasized in *Congo* and *Oil Platforms* the importance of establishing responsibility for an unlawful armed attack.[77]

The International Law Commission (ILC) has set out in detail when action is attributable to a state in its work known as the Draft Articles on State Responsibility, accepted by the UN General Assembly in 2001.[78] The Articles say little about why attribution must be made, perhaps because the point is so widely accepted as basic fairness and common sense – concepts most people understand instinctually. Yet, with respect to the use of force, arguments are being made that ignore attribution principles, ostensibly with the aim of creating broader rights to use force on the territory of states bearing no legal responsibility for wrongdoing.[79] Attribution is the law, however. Attacking a state bearing no legal responsibility violates the prohibition on the use of force. The contrary view appears connected to the belief that greater security can be won through greater resort to force.[80] Removing legal obstacles will

[75] N. Melzer, *Targeted Killing in International Law* (Oxford: Oxford University Press, 2008), 294.

[76] ICJ, *Military and Paramilitary Activities* (n. 29), paras. 64–5; ICJ, *Armed Activities in the Territory of the Congo* (*Democratic Republic of Congo* v. *Uganda*), Judgment of 19 December 2005, ICJ Reports 2005; Application of the Genocide Convention (*Bosnia and Herzegovina* v. *Serbia and Montenegro*) Judgment of 26 February 2007, ICJ Reports 2007, para. 391.

[77] ICJ, *Armed Activities,* (n. 76) paras. 146, 301; *Oil Platforms* (n. 74) paras. 43 and 76 and *Nuclear Weapons* (n. 74), para. 41. See also J. T. Gathii, 'Irregular Forces and Self-Defence Under the UN Charter', in M. E. O'Connell (ed.), *What is War? An Investigation in the Wake of 9/11* (Leiden: Martinus Nijhof, 2012), 91, 97.

[78] ILC Articles on the Responsibility of States (n. 41), chap. II.

[79] See, e.g., the campaign for substituting a concept that a state is 'unwilling' or 'unable' to control terrorism on its territory as a substitute for principles of attribution as sufficient to exercise force in self-defence on the territory of the 'unwilling/unable' state. See, in particular, Bethlehem, 'Self-Defense Against an Imminent or Actual Armed Attack' 2012 (n. 20), 770–7 and commentary on the campaign in Kattan, 'Furthering the "War on Terrorism"' 2017 (n. 14), 24–6 n. 110 and Brunée and Toope, 'Self-Defence Against Non-State Actors' 2017 (n. 14), 263–86.

[80] For an incisive look at this phenomenon, see, O. B. Naftali, M. Sfard, and H. Viterbo, *The ABC of the OPT: A Legal Lexicon of the Occupation of the Palestinian Territory* (Cambridge: Cambridge University Press, 2017), chap. X, 475, citing Y. Berda, 'The Security Risk as a Security Risk: Notes on the

enhance security. The contradictions inherent in this perspective are discussed below.[81]

In sum, the prohibition on the use of force bans states from the first use of more than minimal armed force. The UN Security Council may authorize the use of force, and a state may exercise individual or collective self-defence if a significant armed attack occurs. In the case of both of these exceptions the force used must be necessary, proportional, and aimed at a state responsible for the armed attack or violation of Article 2(4). This restatement of the prohibition forms the baseline from which to determine derogation, whether in the form of new rules or new interpretations. As a peremptory norm, international law forbids derogation. This section has answered the question, derogation from what?

## II Prohibiting Force in Extra-Positive Law

Abundant evidence exists that the prohibition on the use of force is *jus cogens*, and that *jus cogens* is a category of extra-positive law. Evidence also exists that inherent general principles, while not *jus cogens*, are also durable aspects of law, and, thus, also part of extra-positive law. Far less contemporary evidence ties *jus cogens* and inherent general principles to natural law. A case can be made, however. It is strongest when linked to the historical development of these norms.

### A *The Extra-Positive Status of the Prohibition*

The case for using natural law theory to explain *jus cogens* and inherent general principles relies on both affirmative and negative

Classification and Practices of the Israeli Security Services', in A. Baker and A. Matar (eds.), *Threat: Palestinian Political Prisoners in Israel* (London: Pluto Press, 2011), 44–55; N. Shalhoub-Kevorkian, *Security Theology, Surveillance and the Politics of Fear* (Cambridge: Cambridge University Press, 2015), 16–20. Bethlehem charges 'restrictionist' academics with failing to 'address effectively the realities of contemporary threats' and thus rendering the law a mere shibboleth. He, therefore, has rewritten the rules to reverse the restrictions, though he also asserts that his proposals 'are not intended to be enabling of the use of force. They are intended to work with the grain of the UN Charter as well as customary international law ...' D. Bethlehem, 'Self-Defense Against an Imminent or Actual Armed Attack by Nonstate Actors', *American Journal of International Law*, 106 (2012), 770–7.

81 See note 14 and accompanying text.

evidence. States have argued before the ICJ that the prohibition is *jus cogens.* Scholars generally take this position. While some scholars still maintain that no such category as *jus cogens* exists, even those who cannot explain *jus cogens* accept that the prohibition is properly classified as *jus cogens.* Since the 2010 ICJ decision *Jurisdictional Immunities of the State,*[82] which acknowledges *jus cogens,* few contrary views are to be found.

The ILC's Commentary on the drafting of the 1968 Vienna Convention lists examples of *jus cogens,* including 'the law of the Charter concerning the prohibition of the use of force'.[83] In 1986, the ICJ first mentioned *jus cogens.* In its judgment finding the United States in violation of the prohibition on the use of force, the court observed:

> Article 2, paragraph 4, of the Charter of the United Nations ... is frequently referred to in statements by State representatives as being not only a principle of customary international law but also a fundamental or cardinal principle of such law. The International Law Commission, ... expressed the view that 'the law of the Charter concerning the prohibition of the use of force in itself constitutes a conspicuous example of a rule in international law having the character of *jus cogens*' ... The United States, in its Counter-Memorial on the questions of jurisdiction and admissibility, found it material to quote the views of scholars that this principle is a 'universal norm', a 'universal international law', a 'universally recognized principle of international law', and a 'principle of *jus cogens*'.[84]

A few years later, plaintiffs sought to have the *Nicaragua* judgment enforced in a US court. The judge cited the *American Law Institute's Restatement (Third) of Foreign Relations Law* for the proposition that the prohibition on the use of force is *jus cogens.* 'The ... *Restatement* acknowledges two categories of [*jus cogens*] norms: "the principles of the United Nations Charter prohibiting the use of force," ... and

[82] ICJ, *Jurisdictional Immunities of the State* (*Germany* v. *Italy*: Greece intervening), Judgment of 3 February 2012, 2012 ICJ Reports 99, 92. ('Assuming for this purpose that the rules of the law of armed conflict which prohibit the murder of civilians in occupied territory, the deportation of civilian inhabitants to slave labour and the deportation of prisoners of war to slave labour are rules of *jus cogens,* there is no conflict between those rules and the rules on State immunity.')

[83] International Law Commission, Draft Articles on the Law of Treaties with Commentaries, Article 50 – Commentary, ILC Yearbook, 1966, Vol. II, 247.

[84] ICJ, *Military and Paramilitary Activities* (n. 29), para. 190.

fundamental human rights law that prohibits genocide, slavery, murder, torture, prolonged arbitrary detention, and racial discrimination ...'[85] Louis Henkin was the chief reporter of the *Restatement.* He argued in other writing that the prohibition 'is the principal norm of international law of this century'.[86] In an individual opinion in the ICJ's *Wall* advisory case, Judge Elaraby wrote that '[t]he prohibition of the use of force .... is universally recognized as a *jus cogens* principle, a peremptory norm from which no derogation is permitted'.[87] Orakhelashvili reflects the widely held view in saying, 'The prohibition of the use of force by States undoubtedly forms part of *jus cogens.*'[88]

James Green has collected extensive evidence of the *jus cogens* status of the prohibition.[89] Nevertheless, Green raises two important caveats. First, he points to scholars who believe there is a contradiction between Article 2(4) as *jus cogens*, a norm from which no derogation is permitted, and the exceptions for self-defence and Security Council authorization.[90] Exceptions are not, however, derogations. They are aspects of the norm. Self-defence is part of what constitutes the prohibition on the use of force, as is the Security Council's power to authorize force. A police officer is permitted to kill in the line of duty in circumstances that would constitute murder if carried out by a civilian. Orakhelashvili also includes Articles 51 and 39–42 along with Article 2(4) in the peremptory norm, but he goes further and asserts that the whole *jus ad*

85 *Committee of US Citizens* v. *Reagan*, 859 *Federal Reporter 2d* (District Court of the District of Columbia 1988), 929, 939–42.

86 L. Henkin, 'The Use of Force: Law and US Policy', in L. Henkin *et al.*, *Right v. Might: International Law and the Use of Force* (New York: Council on Foreign Relations Press, 1991), 37–70, 69. See also, O. Schachter, 'In Defence of International Rules on the Use of Force', *University of Chicago Law* Review, 53 (1986), 113, 129.

87 ICJ, *Legal Consequences of the Construction of a Wall in the Occupied Palestinian Territory*, Advisory Opinion of 9 July 2004, 2004 ICJ Rep paras. 136, 254 (Separate Opinion of Judge Elaraby).

88 A. Orakhelashvili, *Peremptory Norms in International Law* (Oxford: Oxford University Press, 2006), 50 and L. Hannikainen, *Peremptory Norms (Jus Cogens) in International Law: Historical Development, Criteria, Present Status* (Helsinki: Finnish Lawyer's Publishing Company, 1988) 323, 356.

89 J. A. Green, 'Questioning the Peremptory Status of the Prohibition of the Use of Force', *Michigan Journal of International Law*, 39 (2011), 215–57.

90 Ibid., 221 *et seq.*

*bellum* is *jus cogens.*[91] This may go too far. As explained above, necessity and proportionality are part of the *jus ad bellum* but are general principles of law, related to but not the same as the *jus cogens* prohibition on the use of force. General principles are also non-derogable but lack the substantive moral content of peremptory norms.[92]

Green points to another seeming contradiction in emphasizing that *jus cogens* norms must be strictly construed.[93] He questions whether a wide consensus truly exists that Article 2(4) is *jus cogens* given all the scholarly efforts to limit Article 2(4)'s reach. Rather than strictly construe Articles 2(4) and 51, the trend among scholars is to find loopholes and policy reasons that permit more force for humanitarian purposes, self-defence, arms control, and other reasons that just a few decades ago would not have been contemplated as permitted under the prohibition. As Chapter 4 will detail, a persistent effort has been underway since the Suez Crisis of 1956 to relax the prohibition on the use of force to expand the right of self-defence. The answer to Green is to acknowledge the contradiction but explain it is irrelevant to *jus cogens* status. Scholars who both acknowledge Article 2(4) is a peremptory norm, then seek to limit its reach may fail to understand what *jus cogens* means. It means no derogation from Article 2(4) is permitted. Peremptory norms are durable and universal; they reflect moral commitments. They do not exist because of the views of scholars. The views of scholars are simply helpful in providing evidence of their existence.

Regardless of the amount of evidence supporting the categorization of Article 2(4) as *jus cogens,* legal systems invariably contain durable norms not changeable by consent-based processes. Most law is made through positive action, whether legislation, contracts, treaties, common law, or customary international law, and is unmade using the same process. Some norms, reflecting important moral principles, are not subject to change through consent. Similarly, the fact that legal systems bind the subjects of law, is not changeable through consent. These norms and principles are discerned, rather than created through positive law method. Natural law theory explains the method. Yet, despite the essential role

[91] Orakhelashvili, *Peremptory Norms* 2006 (n. 88), 51.
[92] See discussion at notes 66–81.
[93] Green, 'Questioning the Peremptory Status' 2011 (n. 89).

played by extra-positive aspects of law and the need to explain them, the study of natural law theory has been in decline for well over a century. International law scholars are returning to natural law,[94] but to date the body of contemporary scholarship remains small. Resistance to natural law continues.[95]

Natural law thinking was much in evidence in the development of the 1968 Vienna Convention on the Law of Treaties and the decision to include two articles on *jus cogens* in it.[96] The articles mandate that treaty terms in conflict with *jus cogens* are void.[97] In other words, a *jus cogens* norm is superior to any contrary provision in a treaty. In a book on the Vienna Convention and *jus cogens*, Jerzy Sztucki discusses that wide understanding that *jus cogens* are part of natural law:

> In a number, if not a majority, of writings supporting the category of an international *jus cogens*, this category is understood – explicitly or implicitly – as one of natural rather than of positive law. True enough, the classical natural law school did not use the term *jus cogens* but spoke of 'necessary norms'. However, the essential meaning may be well understood and interpreted in both cases in the same way.[98]

He continues by explaining that contemporary authors refer to 'necessary norms' as *jus cogens*.[99]

Despite the link between *jus cogens* and natural law, already in 1968 delegates to the Vienna Convention negotiations were mostly disinclined to expressly mention natural law. As Sztucki explains, the reluctance could be traced 'to the fact [that] "having religious

94 See, e.g., M. E. O'Connell and C. Day, 'Sources and the Legality and Validity of International Law: Natural Law as Source of Extra-Positive Norms', in S. Besson and J. d'Aspremont (eds.), *The Oxford Handbook of the Sources of International Law* (Oxford: Oxford University Press, 2017), 562–80; M. Koskenniemi, 'Transformations of Natural Law, Germany 1648–1815', in A. Orford and F. Hoffmann (eds.), *The Oxford Handbook of the Theory of International Law* (Oxford: Oxford University Press, 2016), 59–81; A. A. Cançado Trindade, *International Law for Humankind: Towards a New Jus Gentium* 2nd edn (Leiden: Martinus Nijhoff, 2013), 139 and C. G. Weeramantry, *Universalizing International Law* (Leiden: Martinus Nijhoff, 2004).

95 See, e.g., Weisburd, *The Failings of the International Court* 2016 (n. 19).

96 Arts. 53 and 64 VCLT (n. 35).

97 Art. 53 VCLT (n. 35). See also American Law Institute, *Restatement (Third) of the Foreign Relations Law of the United States* (1987) § 102, cmt. k.

98 J. Sztucki, *Jus Cogens and the Vienna Convention on the Law of Treaties, A Critical Appraisal* (Vienna: Springer, 1974), 59 (footnotes omitted).

99 Ibid.

overtones and being incapable of verification, the theory is suspect in a scientific and secular age"'.[100] This reluctance continues today even among those who see that law does not consist of positive law alone. One task for new natural lawyers will be to recover the connection between *jus cogens* and natural law, which has mostly been lost. Great interest has been shown in *jus cogens* but mostly for its impact on positive law. Despite the well-understood distinction between *jus cogens* and positive law, scholars writing on the nature of *jus cogens* tend to use the same positivist explanation employed for customary international law.[101]

Alexander Orakhelashvili, for example, argues that peremptory norms can be considered a special case of customary law. Principles of customary international law are found through amassing evidence of a general practice followed owing to the sense it is required by law (*opinio juris*). Orakhelashvili supplements the standard approach to finding customary international law with the additional requirement that in the case of *jus cogens* the practice must be stronger than for a standard rule, and the *opinio juris* must relate to the status of *jus cogens*. He relies for this conclusion on Article 53 of the Vienna Convention on the Law of Treaties, which says *jus cogens* must reflect 'acceptance and recognition by the international community as a whole'.[102] Orakhelashvili's explanation is insufficient. Not only is it clear that natural law – extra-positive concepts and not customary international law – influenced the adoption of the Vienna Convention's Article 53,[103] the reference to 'acceptance' by the 'community as a whole' is something different than the 'stronger' evidence of state practice and different version of *opinio juris* of his formula.

[100] Ibid., 61, quoting M. Akehurst, *A Modern Introduction to International Law* (1970), 25. chap. 1.

[101] H. Charlesworth, 'Law-making and sources' in J. Crawford and M. Koskenniemi (eds.), *Cambridge Companion to International Law,* (New York: Cambridge University Press, 2012), 187–202. See also, A. de Hoogh, *Obligations Erga Omnes and International Crimes* (Hague: Kluwer Law International, 1996), 44–8; R. Y. Jennings and A. Watts (eds.), *Oppenheim's International Law* (Oxford: Oxford University Press, 1992), 7–8; A. Orakhelashvili, 'Changing *Jus Cogens* Through State Practice? – The Case of the Prohibition of the Use of Force and Its Exceptions' in M. Weller (ed.), *The Oxford Handbook of the Use of Force in International Law* (Oxford: Oxford University Press, 2015), 157–78, 165.

[102] Orakhelashvili, 'Changing *Jus Cogens* Through State Practice?' 2015 (n. 101), 165.

[103] Sztucki, *Jus Cogens* 1974 (n. 98).

Positive law method by definition cannot explain *jus cogens*. *Jus cogens* norms are superior to positive law and as such they cannot be part of positive law. Nor do the characteristics of *jus cogens* align with customary international law. State practice is an essential element of custom. It is not an essential element of *jus cogens*. State practice may be a useful indicator of a peremptory norm, but it is not essential. The international community should as a normative matter work to incorporate into positive law the peremptory norms. It is an ongoing effort. Slavery, for examplc, was once widely practised. It would have been difficult to argue that any ban on it existed in customary international law prior to the twentieth century.[104] Under natural law, however, the case can be made that regardless of state practice slavery was always immoral and unlawful. Communities failed to discern this for hundreds of years, but that does not mean that *jus cogens* properly understood did not include a ban on slavery.

So, too, with respect to the use of force. The use of force has been restricted in natural law since antiquity.[105] It eventually emerged in positive law, first as a treaty principle, then, as the ICJ found in the *Nicaragua* case, it was identified as part of customary international law.[106] Even if UN members amend the UN Charter or the practice relied on by the ICJ loses its place as a general practice, the *jus cogens* norm remains. This is a fact that contradicts not only the attempt to fit *jus cogens* in the positive law category but also the claims by expansionists that the prohibition on the use of force now allows for more exceptions owing to changing state practice and *opinio juris*.[107]

The more interesting part of Orakhelashvili's formula is his reference to the *opinio juris* element of customary international law. He finds that the *opinio juris* needed to establish *jus cogens* must indicate a legal opinion beyond the mere binding nature of

[104] See, e.g., J. Allain, *Slavery in International Law: Of Human Exploitation and Trafficking* (Dordrecht: Martinus Nijhof, 2012).

[105] See Chapter 1.

[106] ICJ, *Military and Paramilitary Activities* (n. 29), paras. 187–94.

[107] Certain expansionists not only believe it is possible for the customary international law on the use of force to weaken in the face of changing state practice and *opinio juris*, they go further to argue they can actually set out to affirmatively change a rule by inviting contrary statements of *opinio juris* and characterizing law violations as examples of changing practice. As attempts to change the law respecting the use of force, these efforts have been critiqued as involving a few states only and not a general practice, as well as purporting to change the UN Charter, a treaty with wide adherence. See notes 14 and 122.

the practice. It must relate to the *jus cogens* status of the principle. Implicit in his view is the admission that finding *jus cogens* requires searching for evidence of something different than customary law principles. With customary principles, the search is for opinion that a practice is mandated by legal obligation. The search with respect to *jus cogens* is for acceptance of a norm as being *jus cogens.* This requires evidence qualitatively different from the content of the *opinio juris* of a customary law practice. Seeking *jus cogens* starts with recognizing that the principles in the category have a character distinctive from other international law rules. Recognition of the category indicates that states and other relevant actors understand the special character of the norms within the category. They are superior to law created through positive acts. Their status as superior is seen historically as derived from morality and concepts of transcendence, which are in turn derived from theology and moral philosophy. Such norms are widely accepted even in the face of contrary practice and doubt about their existence in positive law.

The distinctions between positive law and peremptory norms can be seen in the writing of scholars in the 1960s who still incorporated natural law in their work. The prominent Austrian international law scholar Alfred von Verdross published an article in the *American Journal of International Law* in 1966, titled, '*Jus Dispositivum* and *Jus Cogens* in International Law'.[108] 'Von Verdross wrote in an older natural law tradition that based constraints on the power of states to contract on concepts of reason and morality.'[109] In other words, he used elements of natural law method. Sir Gerald Fitzmaurice, a rapporteur on the law of treaties for the ILC, based the principle that treaties are binding, *pacta sunt servanda,* on natural law.[110] He also described law as containing two general categories, consisting of principles:

> which are mandatory and imperative in all circumstances (*jus cogens*) and those (*jus dispositivum*) which merely furnish a rule for application in the

[108] A. von Verdross, 'Jus Dispositivum and Jus Cogens in International Law', *American Journal of International Law,* 60 (1966), 55–63.

[109] See, e.g., P. B. Stephan, 'The Political Economy of Jus Cogens', *Vanderbilt Journal of International Law,* 44 (2011), 1072–104, 1081 note 23.

[110] Sir Gerald Fitzmaurice, 'The Law and Procedure of the International Court of Justice 1954–1959', *British Yearbook of International Law,* 35 (1959), 183–216, 195.

absence of any other agreed regime, or, more correctly, those the variation or modification of which under an agreed regime is permissible, provided the position and rights of third States are not affected.[111]

Fitzmaurice included inherent general principles, such as *pacta sunt servanda* in the *jus cogens* category. As discussed above, respecting necessity and proportionality, the understanding here is that while inherent general principles are explainable only through natural law, they are not *jus cogens*. They lack the substantive moral content of the prohibitions on slavery, the use of force, genocide and the rest. General principles are essential to the reality of fair systems of law in positing, for example, equality of states or human beings before the law, but they are secondary rules – procedural law – distinctive from *jus cogens*.[112]

'Peremptory norms prevail not because the States involved have so decided but because they are intrinsically superior and cannot be dispensed with through standard inter-State transactions.'[113] Peremptory norms form a barrier to action but do not compel action. To the extent that *jus cogens* norms are similar to rights, they are more like negative rights, such as the right to be free of torture. They do not establish positive obligations that might require the expenditure of resources. They do entail the affirmative duty of respect attaching to all legal prohibitions. *Jus cogens* norms work like principles of public policy or *ordre public* but are, again, as with customary international law, distinctive from public policy.[114] Public policy gives a judge a basis to decline to enforce private law

[111] Third Report on the Law of Treaties, II Ybk Int'l L Comm (1958) at 40.

[112] M. E. O'Connell, 'Jus Cogens: International Law's Higher Ethical Norms', in D. E. Childress III (ed.), *The Role of Ethics in International Law* (Cambridge: Cambridge University Press, 2011), 78.

[113] Orakhelashvili, *Peremptory Norms* 2006 (n. 88), 8.

[114] Robert Kolb defines peremptory norms as the equivalent of public policy for international law. R. Kolb, *Peremptory International Law,* Jus Cogens, *A General Inventory* (Oxford: Hart Publishing, 2015). Again, as discussed above, while some delegates to the Vienna Convention negotiation considered *jus cogens* to be the equivalent to public policy, the reference to public policy was dropped in favour of *jus cogens* and thereby linked the provisions to natural law. Peremptory norms include at least the prohibitions on the use of force, genocide, torture, slavery, apartheid, widespread government-authorized extra-judicial killing, and, according to the ICJ, very likely also the principles protecting civilians in time of armed conflict, especially intentional targeting. ICJ, *Jurisdictional Immunities of the State* (*Germany* v. *Italy,* Greece intervening), Merits, Judgment of 3 February 2012, ICJ Reports 99, para 93.

agreements, or contracts, when she believes to do so will offend public mores. It is a quite limited exception of a procedural nature that is silent as to the specific content of a contract that might offend public order. It provides a ground for a judge to refuse to enforce an agreement when the contract is not clearly illegal. Peremptory norms ban specific conduct. A judge could look to the *jus cogens* norms for guidance as to public policy. The two are, however, distinctive.

As Fitzmaurice held respecting *pacta sunt servanda*, inherent general principles, like *jus cogens*, are best explained using natural law theory. These principles are discerned much as peremptory norms are and will be discussed in more detail below.[115] The general principles of necessity, proportionality, and attribution are essential components of the lawful resort to force.[116] To have the right to resort to force without any limitation based on necessity and proportionality would undermine the prohibition on force. Judith Gardam and Bin Cheng both classify necessity and proportionality as general principles, despite the ICJ's classification of them as rules of customary international law in the *Nuclear Weapons* case.[117] The court provided no basis for this categorization. It cited no state practice or *opinio juris*.

Within the two categories of extra-positive norms, principles are of equal status. No state could excuse the use of torture, for example, to advance the prohibition of genocide. The same is true of the prohibition on the use of force.[118] Arguments to the contrary are rare. More common are attempts to justify resort to force on grounds of national security, necessity, or for arms control. These arguments may have rhetorical appeal, especially in their use of legal terminology. They are inadequate as a matter of law.

[115] See notes 66–80 and accompanying text.

[116] Cheng, *General Principles* 1953 (n. 66) and Gardam, *Necessity, Proportionality*, 2004 (n. 69).

[117] ICJ, *Nuclear Weapons* (n. 74).

[118] The United Kingdom attempted almost such an argument in asserting that air strikes on Syria on 14 April 2018 were a justified response to an alleged use of chemical weapons by the Syrian regime. 'Syria Air Strikes: The UK Government's Position in Full', *BBC*, (14 April 2018) www.bbc.com/news/uk-43768145. Chemical weapons are banned but in distinction to the principle that civilians must never be intentionally targeted in armed conflict, it is difficult to say that the chemical weapons ban is a *jus cogens* norm. Even if it were, that status entails no exception to the prohibition on the use of force or other peremptory norms.

The key to accurate argumentation is to employ the proper approach to interpreting *jus cogens*. Expansionists attempt to use state practice to show that the Charter provisions have changed and are weaker, posing less limitation on state use of force.[119] Indeed, much of the standard work on self-defence looks to state practice, such as the use of force against non-state actors beyond armed conflict zones or the use of force without a territorial state's express consent, to argue that these law violations are capable of diluting the restrictions in Article 51. Given the nature of peremptory prohibitions, however, valid interpretation must not result in a weaker norm. Logically, peremptory norms are to be strictly construed because they admit no derogation.

Diluting the reach of a *jus cogens* prohibition through interpretation is indistinguishable from derogation through creating a new treaty or claiming a new rule of customary international law. When peremptory norms are newly discerned, the discovery may lead to invalidating existing treaties and rules of custom.[120] Similarly, interpretation can lead to greater restrictions where aggression, genocide, torture, or another peremptory prohibition is concerned, not lesser. In any case of doubt as to a prohibition's reach, the presumption favours treating more conduct as restricted, not less. This means, for example, not reading Article 51 as though the armed attack requirement did not exist, as certain authors discussed in Chapter 4 attempt to do.

If Article 2(4) were just a treaty principle or rule of customary international law, standard interpretation rules would include subsequent practice as a guide to meaning, even to some extent meaning that changes over time.[121] As *jus cogens*, however, meaning is stable, and contrary state practice is of little relevance. While this point is widely acknowledged, it is an often overlooked interpretation of state practice.[122] To avoid diluting Article 2(4), Article 51, as

[119] Note that Article 2(4) does not refer directly to internal armed conflict or civil war. These have constituted the larger number of actual armed conflicts since 1945 and are the topic of Chapter 5.

[120] Art 64 VCLT (n. 35).

[121] Arts. 31–2 VCLT (n. 35); ICJ, *Dispute Regarding Navigational and Related Rights* (*Costa Rica* v. *Nicaragua*), Merits, Judgment of 13 July 2009, 2009 ICJ Reports, 213.

[122] For an example see R. van Steenberghe, 'State Practice and the Evolution of the Law of Self-Defence: Clarifying the Methodological Debate', *Journal on International Law and the Use of Force*, 2 (2015), 81–96; and T. Reinold, 'State Weakness, Irregular Warfare, and the Right to Self-Defense Post-9/11',

well as Articles 39–42, must be interpreted in a way that avoids weakening the general prohibition. State practice indicating discernment toward a rule with wider reach is consistent with the 'no derogation' requirement. Practice toward creating a wider exception is a breach. The same is true of general principles such as necessity and proportionality that are part of the prohibition on the use of force. These principles do not operate according to positivist doctrine and require basic understanding of natural law theory – the next topic of this chapter.

### *B Natural Law Theory in Understanding Extra-Positive Law*

The most concrete fact about natural law is that it does not rely on material evidence, in particular, material evidence of consent. As a result, natural law is truly more art and less science than positive law. Whether it counts as real law or is a mere fiction, however, is re-emerging as an issue after some decades of having been settled for the most part in favour of fiction. Verdross, one of the last to hold out in international law in support of natural law, describes the basic positions for and against:

> The question of whether law is simply a product of human will, imposed by a law-giver whose legitimation is derived only from his power to legislate, so that any effective legal order must be regarded as 'law' and obeyed because of its effectiveness, or whether law must, at least to a certain extent, conform to the natural needs of man, society, and mankind at large, has been debated since antiquity. Those who support the second position argue that it is not just order that man longs for, but an order permeated with justice ... their tradition is unbroken from the time of the ancient Greeks to the present.[123]

While natural law went almost completely out of fashion by the 1990s, certainly in the West, it was for so long a part of legal philosophy that it has deeply influenced the law of today. In terms of the contemporary debate, the pro- and anti-natural law sides are

*American Journal of International Law*, 105 (2011), 244–86, arguing that uses of force by the US, Russia, Turkey, Colombia, Israel, and Uganda against weaker opponents has altered Article 51.

123 A. Verdross and H. Franz Koeck, 'Natural Law: The Tradition of Universal Reason and Authority', in R. St. J. Macdonald and D. M. Johnston (eds.), *The Structure and Process of International Law: Essays in Legal Philosophy Doctrine and Theory* (Dordrecht: Martinus Nijhoff, 1983) 18–50, 18.

not so much completely in favour or completely against. Instead, the divide is more along a continuum of those who acknowledge that important legal concepts are dependent on natural law theory, and those who see natural law as always essential but in need of extensive new study. As discussed in Chapter 1, the natural law tradition is embedded in all aspects of law. The principle of justice is not based on consent but is undeniably an essential feature of law. Equally undeniable is the decline in scholarship that can explain a norm such as justice.[124] The point of this section is to provide a preliminary practical guide to re-incorporating natural law theory into mainstream thinking.

At least three judges of the ICJ have considered how to apply natural law in adjudicating disputes. The drafters of the Vienna Convention on the Law of Treaties also foresaw the need for and ability of the ICJ to use law beyond the positive sources of treaty and custom. The drafters assigned to the court the special task of resolving any dispute that might arise over the existence or non-existence of a peremptory norm. In this way, they sought to overcome with a process solution the standard criticism of natural law that without material evidence to limit its content, almost any type of claim could be justified by invoking it. The Vienna Convention provides in only one instance for compulsory ICJ jurisdiction over treaty disputes, the case of a dispute over *jus cogens*. Should parties to a treaty remain unable to resolve such a dispute after twelve months,

> . . . the following procedures shall be followed:
> (*a*) any one of the parties to a dispute concerning the application or the interpretation of article 53 or 64 may, by a written application, submit it to the International Court of Justice for a decision unless the parties by common consent agree to submit the dispute to arbitration . . .[125]

The court has never had such a question and as discussed already has only mentioned peremptory norms in indirect and tentative ways. Still, the evidence is sufficient to reject the view that natural law is no more than the wholly impractical and subjective ideas of a time long past.[126]

[124] Interest is growing once again. See Introduction and Chapter 1.
[125] Art. 66 VCLT (n. 35).
[126] For this view, see, Weisburd, *The Failings of the International Court* 2016 (n. 19).

It is, nevertheless, in the past where the inquiry needs to begin. As with so many topics, classical Greek philosophers are credited with the first conceptual thinking with respect to natural law. We look to them for the basic distinction between the natural and the manmade. Natural law belongs in the first category; positive law is manmade.[127] Aristotle conceived of natural law as related to human nature and the human aspiration for fulfilment. Natural law supports human striving.[128] The principles of peace and those in support of orderly society are specific examples of what we strive for, and, because they are connected to human nature, these principles are common to all humanity, making natural law universal law and supportive of the truly common good.

Neff writes that until the development of natural law theories, international law was not possible. He acknowledges that antecedents existed in the form of collections of principles to govern interstate relations, such as those developed in 'China during the Warring States era before 221 BCE'.[129] Only natural law, however, could support a 'systematic body of principles covering *all* aspects of international relations'.[130]

Among the earliest authors of complete natural law theories are the Roman philosopher, lawyer, and statesman Cicero and the Hellenistic Jewish philosopher Philo of Alexandria. Both saw natural law applying universally and contrasted it with positive law.[131] Both influenced the reception of natural law into Christianity. St Paul is known to have been familiar with contemporary Hellenistic thought and is considered to be referring to natural law in Romans 2:5–16 when he says that non-Jews, 'who do not possess the law, [can] do instinctively [*physei,* by nature] what the law requires', as it is 'written on their hearts' and consciences. After the Bible, Philo is apparently the most important source for early Christian natural law theorists,

127 *Politics*, 1253a and S. Pope, 'Reason and Natural Law', in G. Meilaender and W. Werpehowski (eds.), *The Oxford Handbook of Theological Ethics* (New York: Oxford University Press, 2007) 148–67, 149.
128 Aristotle, *Nichomachean Ethics*, V. ch. 7, 1134b; and Verdross and Koeck, 'Natural Law' (n. 123) note 13.
129 S. Neff, *Justice Among Nations: A History of International Law* (Cambridge, MA: Harvard University Press, 2014), 17–25 (emphasis in the original).
130 Ibid., 7–8. 131 Pope, 'Reason and Natural Law', (n. 127), 150.

accounting for the introduction of biblical concepts, such as the Golden Rule, in subsequent natural law jurisprudence.[132]

Christian natural law thinking flourished in the Middle Ages as the Holy Roman Empire, the papacy, and natural law created three 'forces of unity' in Western Europe.[133] The Scholastic theologians, most notably Aquinas, Vitoria, and Suárez, found support for a system of legal order through rational reflection upon nature and scripture.[134] They saw the existence of the natural world, the use of human reason, and divine revelation as inextricably intertwined.[135] Reason is necessary for interpreting both divine meaning for humanity as well as the lessons of nature. The three strands are discursive. Reason is a God-given capacity for undertaking interpretation. Nature is a gift from God that in its order, chaos, beauty, and sublimity provides evidence of the divine and divine will. The blessed have received scripture and other forms of divine revelation. This three-strand approach balanced individual and interior use of reason and personal observations of nature. Contemplation of nature and revelation takes the thinker out of herself to consider the world from the exterior perspective, which includes the perspective of another person, the community, natural world, and the divine.

This approach is consistent with what is perhaps the most common conclusion about human beings within the natural law tradition. The Scholastics accepted with Aristotle that human beings are naturally social.[136] It is a point almost all natural law scholars affirm.[137] Human sociability leads to a second line of argument in favour of the institution of law. Not only does law support conditions of peace that permit human striving for fulfilment, it allows people to live together in communities, mutually supporting each other. International law is the law that supports the possibility of the community of communities.[138] Most law for the Scholastics is in the

132 R. A. Horsley, 'The Law of Nature in Philo and Cicero', *The Harvard Theological Review*, 71 (1/2) (1978), 35–59, 36, 58–9.
133 Neff, *Justice Among Nations* 2014 (n. 129), 52–3.
134 T. Aquinas, *Summa Theologica*, I-II, q. 94, Arts. 4, 6 and Chapter 1.
135 Pope, 'Reason and Natural Law', (n. 127), 150.
136 Neff, *Justice Among Nations* 2014 (n. 129), 62.
137 One notable exception is Thomas Hobbes in the seventeenth century. Chapter 1.
138 Neff, *Justice Among Nations* 2014 (n. 129), 74, 78. See also, A. Adeno, 'Imagining the International Community', *Human Rights Quarterly*, 31 (2009), 145–50.

form of positive law made through various human institutions of lawmaking. Natural law provides a framework with reasons beyond consent as to why law binds. Within natural law are limits on positive law rules when they conflict with the norms discerned through natural law processes. These are the more basic norms, including the limitation on the use of force and violence against another individual or community. The natural law places the peaceful resolution of disputes over any positive law preference for 'might over right'.

The three strands of natural law are evident in Hugo Grotius's conception of law. He held that human beings are by nature social and that this characteristic is the 'mother of the law of nature'.[139] He understood natural law as 'a dictate of right reason which points out that an act is or is not in conformity with rational nature'.[140] In addition, he looked to sacred texts of the world's prominent religions as a check on positive law. Grotius drew on Judaism, Christianity, Islam, Hinduism, and Confucian ethics as evidence of divine wisdom.[141] Grotius, it will be recalled from Chapter 1, asked his readers to imagine law without God.[142] He put to one side the incendiary issue of whether international law was Catholic or Protestant. He borrowed from the Roman *jus gentium* for answers to many of the everyday questions of law between communities,[143] but he emphasized that rules drawn from *jus gentium* must be 'in harmony with nature', not contradicting or annulling natural law.[144]

In the decades after Grotius, such thinkers as Samuel Pufendorf attempted to complete Grotius's move away from religion.[145] Pufendorf, though a professing Protestant, found theological ideas clashed too profoundly with scientific theory, leaving international law scholars concerned that their discipline would be dismissed as superstition. Pufendorf tried to incorporate scientific

[139] H. Grotius, *De Jure Belli ac Pacis* (*The Law of War and Peace*), F. W. Kelsey (trans.) (Buffalo NY: Liberal Arts Press, 1995) (1625), 'Prolegomena'.
[140] Ibid. [141] Ibid., *passim*. [142] Ibid.
[143] Neff, *Justice Among Nations* 2014 (n. 129), 141. [144] Ibid., 156–7.
[145] J. Porter, *Nature as Reason: A Thomistic Theory of the Natural Law* (Grand Rapids: Wm. B. Eerdmans Publishing Co, 2004), 28–30; J. D'Aspremont and J. Kammerhofer, 'Introduction', in S. Besson and J. d'Aspremont (eds.), *The Oxford Handbook of the Sources of International Law* (Oxford: Oxford University Press, 2017), 1–14, 12–13.

method, relying on reason and observation alone to demonstrate that international law is a '"solid science" alongside the natural sciences'.[146] He attempted in fact to base international law only on nature, excising the Roman *jus gentium*.[147] Without the positive law mechanisms of contract and custom, however, treaties and rules of customary international law were relegated in the Pufendorfian world to a category something like comity.[148]

Pufendorf's views did not take hold. The next trend was rather in the opposite direction. Emerich de Vattel, for example, extolled treaties and other acts of sovereigns as the more important part of international law. He still counselled sovereigns to listen to their consciences with respect to international law, but further counselled that no sovereign was superior to any other. Discussion of a source of law higher than worldly kings faded away. Vattel and his positivist successors left international law without a theory of why law is ever superior to the will of sovereigns. No answer emerged separate from natural law theory. For this reason, natural law answers are still seen in the scholarship of twentieth-century giants of international law theory, Kelsen, Lauterpacht, Franck, and others.[149]

In 1946, Sir Hersch Lauterpacht published *The Grotian Tradition*, in which he, too, re-presented law as a hybrid system of positive and natural law.[150] Lauterpacht understood all law to consist of both forms, but that while this fact could be merely assumed respecting national legal systems, it had to be openly acknowledged in the case of international law. International law has a unique role in regulating relations in a system of diverse nations and cultures lacking regular governmental institutions of courts, legislature, and executive. At the international level, 'the function of natural law, whatever may be its form, must approximate more closely to that of a direct source of law'.[151] Lauterpacht did not provide any developed explanation of what natural law is exactly. He did point to certain 'features' of natural law that he considered essential to international

[146] Pufendorf, quoted in Porter, *Nature as Reason* (n. 145), 27–8.
[147] Verdross and Koeck, 'Natural Law' 1983 (n. 123), 31.
[148] Ibid.; see also Koskenniemi, 'Transformations of Natural Law' (n. 94).
[149] Chapter 1.
[150] H. Lauterpacht, 'The Grotian Tradition in International Law', *British Yearbook of International Law*, 23 (1946), 22–3.
[151] Ibid.

law, including the comprehension of law as superior to 'the totality of international relations'. He credited Grotius with endowing international law with 'unprecedented dignity and authority by making it part not only of a general system of jurisprudence but also of a universal moral code'.[152]

Nevertheless, the references to natural law are ever briefer and the discussions of how it can work in practice limited to a very few. Perhaps the scholar most responsible for preventing the complete disappearance of natural law from the English-speaking legal world is John Finnis. Finnis has done so, however, by emphasizing, once again, human reason over the other strands of the classic three-part synthesis.[153] Finnis's work reflects the power and importance of human reason, but as he himself acknowledges, his work is distinctive from classic natural law.[154] Part of the aim of this book is to offer a secular approach to incorporating wisdom or transcendent ideas to balance the tendency to self-interested thought that results from rationalism alone.

The challenge of incorporating transcendence in the process of identifying extra-positive or natural law norms was apparent to the members of the ILC charged with drafting the Vienna Convention on the Law of Treaties:

152 Ibid., at 51.

153 For Finnis, reason dictates that law concern the following human needs: knowledge, procreation, beauty, excellence, peace, and connection to God or 'some more-than-human source of meaning and value'. J. Finnis, *Natural Law and Natural Rights* 2nd edn (Oxford: Oxford University Press, 1980). See also, G. Grisez, J. Boyle, and J. Finnis, 'Practical Principles, Moral Truth, and Ultimate Ends', *American Journal of Jurisprudence*, 32 (1987) 99–151, 106–8.

154 Finnis responded to a suggestion that his book *Natural Law, Natural Rights* might have been better titled *Practical Reason and Law*:

> *Practical Reason and Law* would indeed be a possible alternative, though countless people would misunderstand it as announcing a subscription to Kant. So there are no ideal titles, or titles that are not from some point of view or in some respects misleading. 'Natural Law and Natural Rights' was the title assigned to me [by H. L. A. Hart] and if Hart had assigned something else the book would doubtless have been significantly different.
>
> It would be fair to say . . . that I have expressed in various places over the years frustration or regret at the misunderstandings caused by the phrase 'natural law', and that I did not demur when you suggested . . . that 'Practical Reason and Law' would be an alternative title.

Email to the author from John Finnis, 17 January 2018 (on file with the author).

The discussion in the Commission indicated such varying viewpoints on what constituted *jus cogens* that the categories were dropped. A comment regarding the resulting draft is pertinent: 'Mr. Bartos explained that the drafting committee had been compelled to refrain from giving any definition of *jus cogens* whatever, because two-thirds of the Commission had been opposed to each formula proposed.' The position in the conference reflected the position in the Commission. There was no substantial attack made upon the concept of *jus cogens*. ... The real problem was how to define the test for recognizing a rule of *jus cogens*.[155]

The drafters did what legislatures do when they cannot agree on substance, namely turn to process. The ILC designated the ICJ as the determiner of *jus cogens*.

While no case turning on an express argument invoking natural law has been decided by the ICJ, several ICJ judges have written specifically on the practical application of natural law. The view most closely aligned with the traditional approach outlined here is that of Judge Kōtarō Tanaka of Japan. In the infamous 1966 *South-West Africa* cases, the ICJ found Ethiopia and Liberia had no standing to challenge South Africa's imposition of apartheid in the territory South-West Africa, which South Africa governed as a United Nations trust territory.[156] In seeking to establish that that the principle of equality is a principle of natural law, Tanaka looked to the sources of international law listed in Article 38 of the ICJ Statute and observed that Article 38 incorporates 'natural law elements' by extending the sources of international law 'beyond the limit of legal positivism', and by indicating that the general principles of Article 38(1)(c) are binding on all states, even those that do not recognize them.[157] He explained how this conclusion could be reached looking to Stoic and Christian teaching, human nature, and the common human capacity to reason.[158] Some law is binding regardless of consent. International law, he concluded, needs natural law to achieve 'its supra-national and supra-positive character'.[159]

ICJ Judge Antônio Augusto Cançado Trindade of Brazil equally sees natural law as an integral part of international law. He argues

[155] R. D. Kearney and R. E. Dalton, 'The Treaty on Treaties', *American Journal of International Law*, 64 (1970), 495, 535.
[156] ICJ, *South West Africa Cases* (*Ethiopia* v. *South Africa*) (*Liberia* v. *South Africa*), Judgment of 18 July 1966, Dissenting opinion, Judge Tanaka, 1966 ICJ Reports, 285–315.
[157] Ibid., 298–9. [158] Ibid., 304–5, quoting Hersch Lauterpacht. [159] Ibid., 298.

that the sole reliance on positivism has denied to international law inspiration from 'beliefs, values, ethics, ideas, and human aspirations'.[160] He argues that human conscience is a 'source' of international law, referring to human conscience as the *recta ratio* or right reason of international law.[161] Conscience is not a feature of individuals alone but is also shared by the members of a community, including the global community, in its 'universal juridical conscience'.[162] The Martens Clause,[163] which calls for new means and methods of warfare to be subject to the dictates of human conscience, is evidence this concept exists. Judge Cançado Trindade, however, has applied his conception beyond the classic understanding of the role of natural law and its limited set of norms. Peremptory norms operate, as discussed above, like *ordre public* to ensure positive law does not violate deeply-held legal and moral norms. General principles ensure that the operation of the law remains consistent with ideals of legality, such as equality and fairness. These norms cannot substitute for positive law that can govern conduct in a detailed way. Natural law cannot establish programmes, organize funding, and the like. Its role is limited but essential.

Former ICJ Judge Christopher Weeramantry also questions why international law has lost the benefit of the teaching of the world's religions, philosophies, arts, and culture. He advocates bringing these sources of human wisdom into the process of legal interpretation.[164] Verdross and Koeck follow a process of deduction from positive law. They look to the positive law and deduce from it directly principles of natural law, '*deductio ex principiis*', or find principles that are near the positive law, 'nearer determination (*determinatiio principiorum*)'.[165] Using their method of deduction and 'near determination' but adding a wider set of considerations beyond the positive law could well re-introduce natural law in a practical and appropriate way.

160 A. A. Cançado Trindade, *International Law for Humankind: Towards a New Jus Gentium* 2nd edn (Leiden: Martinus Nijhoff, 2013), 139.

161 Ibid., 141. 162 Ibid., 143–5.

163 See the Preamble of the Hague Convention II with Respect to the Laws and Customs of War on Land and its Annex: Regulations Respecting the Laws and Customs of War on Land (The Hague, 29 July 1899, 32 Stat 1803).

164 Weeramantry, *Universalizing International Law* 2004 (n. 94).

165 Verdross and Koeck, *Natural Law* 1983 (n. 123).

Reason can be used to deduce natural law norms from positive law, as Verdross recommended. Observation of nature or reference to the arts are openings to beauty and the transcendent. Awareness of the transcendent guides reason in the discernment of natural law and its principles superior to the positive law. Courts use this method today, citing fiction, poetry, essays. Rather than think of such references as supplementary, the natural law method proposed here supports them as integral to interpreting certain aspects of the law. The method results in principles that support community. The long history of the international legal prohibition on the use of force demonstrates natural law method in action.

### *C The Evidence of History*

As international law took its modern form with the rise of the European state, it included a set of principles limiting resort to war to a few causes that could be advanced consistently with necessity and proportionality. This *jus ad bellum*, which was really a *jus contra bellum*, came to international law through the Christian Just War doctrine, a major component of the acknowledged body of natural law.

Early Christians understood their faith to embrace radical pacifism. It was so radical many would not defend themselves from attack, a belief St. Augustine worked to change. He extolled peace but argued self-defence can be conceived of as a necessary component of peace. Building on the earlier work of St Ambrose and others, Augustine wrote:

> Peace should be the object of your desire; war should be waged only as a necessity and waged only that God may by it deliver men from the necessity and preserve them peace. For peace is not sought in order to [be] the kindling of war, but war is waged in order that peace may be obtained.[166]

From this modest start the arguments for war grew, so that Aquinas and the later Scholastics developed a full legal code for resort to military force to guide Christian leaders. Still, the Just War doctrine was a code restricting war, not licensing it. A just and, therefore,

[166] L. Friedman (ed.), *The Law of War: A Documentary History* (New York: Random House, 1972), 7.

lawful war is waged when a person with the legal authority to declare war does so in one of the few just causes of war. The undisputed just cause is self-defence. Even then, the person declaring war must have the intention of fighting for the just cause and not some ulterior motive.[167] Further, a war is only just if resort to it is a last resort to achieve the cause and is proportionate to the wrongdoing that triggered it.

With the end of the Thirty Years' War, imposing religion was no longer considered a just cause of war among Europeans. In the treaties known as the Peace of Westphalia of 1648, the parties pledged not to intervene to impose one version of Christianity or another on a population. Disputes on other topics were to be settled by arbitration. Breach of these principles would be met by collective enforcement action of the other parties.[168] The treaties effectively ended the cycle of religious war in Western Europe.

Hugo Grotius should receive some credit for the success at Westphalia. His book *The Law of War and Peace* was an inspirational code supporting a community of states in place of the Holy Roman Empire.[169] He recognized only three lawful causes of war: self-defence, punishment of wrongs, and recovery of property. He supported the other traditional principles of just and limited war as well, including that it may be waged by legal authorities only and only when the principles of necessity and proportionality can be met. These principles persisted even as natural law declined as a theory of law.[170]

Restrictions on war made their way into positive law in the nineteenth century, often as a result of the advocacy of peace activists motivated by religious belief. The Paris Declaration on Maritime Law of 1856 had provisions regulating the conduct of maritime warfare, including outlawing privateering.[171]

By 1899 the First Hague Peace Conference had been held and multilateral treaties requiring the use of methods of peaceful

[167] J. von Elbe, 'The Evolution of the Concept of the Just War in International Law', *American Journal of International Law*, 33 (1939) 665–88, 669 and Brownlie, *Use of Force* (n. 30), 6.
[168] Reproduced in Friedman, *The Law of War* 1972 (n. 166).
[169] Grotius, *De Jure Belli* 1995 (n. 139).
[170] Elbe, 'The Evolution of the Concept of the Just War' 1939 (n. 167), 684.
[171] A. Nussbaum, *A Concise History of the Law of Nations* rev. edn (New York: MacMillan, 1962), 192.

settlement of disputes be used prior to any use of force. The developments, however, were not all in a positive direction, as European international law scholars sought to justify the use of military force for conquest of non-European territories. According to Alexandrowicz, 'in the nineteenth century, the law of nations, which had been universal in the sixteenth, seventeenth and eighteenth centuries, abandoned the centuries-old universalist tradition based on natural law theory and "narrowed" [itself] to a regional (purely European) legal system'.[172]

Still, in the early twentieth century, the future Whewell Professor of Public International Law in Cambridge Lassa Oppenheim had to continue campaigning for the suppression of any natural law role in thinking about international law.[173] '[O]ne of his objections to natural law approaches was that their practitioners could not agree among themselves on the most basic questions about international law, let alone convince others.'[174] Yet, they always agreed that the natural law limited resort to war.

At the Second Hague Peace Conference of 1907, states adopted the first multilateral treaty that outlawed a certain category of war – armed conflict to collect contract debts.[175] Resort to war was further restricted in the Treaty of Versailles and the Covenant of the League of Nations adopted in 1919,[176] and in the 1928 Kellogg-Briand Pact.[177] Hans Kelsen found the Just War doctrine reflected in the Treaty of Versailles, the League Covenant, and the Kellogg-Briand Pact. He cited Augustine, Aquinas, and Grotius as the founders of the doctrine and blamed nineteenth-century political theories of absolute state sovereignty as responsible for its decline. Kelsen

[172] W. G. Grewe, *The Epochs of International Law* (Berlin: De Gruyter, 2000): 466, citing C. H. Alexandrowicz, *An Introduction to the Law of Nations in the East Indies* (Oxford: Clarendon Press, 1967).

[173] L. Oppenheim, *International Law, A Treatise* (London: Longmans, Green, and Co, 1905), 92. 'We know nowadays that a real Law of Nature does not exist ... Only a positive Law of Nations can be a branch of the science of law.' Ibid.

[174] B. Kingsbury, 'Legal Positivism as Normative Politics: International Society, Balance of Power and Lassa Oppenheim's Positive International Law', *European Journal of International Law*, 13 (2002) 401, 433.

[175] Convention of 1907 Respecting the Limitation of the Employment of Force for the Recovery of Contract Debts, 1907 Stat 36: 2241, Malloy's TS 2:2248.

[176] The Covenant of the League of Nations of 1919 can be found at http://avalon.law.yale.edu/20th_century/leagcov.asp#art12.

[177] The Treaty Providing for the Renunciation of War of 1928 can be found at www.yale.edu/lawweb/avalon/imt/kbpact.htm.

argued against absolute state sovereignty as destructive not only of the Just War doctrine's limitations on war but of all of international law.

The first significant attempt to hold an individual accountable for unlawful resort to major military force occurred after World War I. The Versailles Treaty of 1919 provided in Article 227 for a special tribunal to try the German Kaiser for 'a supreme offense against international morality and the sanctity of treaties'.[178] The Covenant of the League of Nations, concluded as part of the Versailles Treaty, expressly committed states for the first time to protect and preserve other states from 'external aggression'.[179]

The catastrophe of World War II led to the agreement to prohibit war in the United Nations Charter as well as the establishment of the UN system to enforce the prohibition and deal with the causes of conflict. Like the Kellogg-Briand Pact, the Charter's prohibition of war is clearly linked to the Just War doctrine. Following the war, natural law more generally made a return. Gustav Radbuch made the case that positive law, shorn of any connection to natural law, had played a significant role in the Third Reich.[180] Law adopted by the legislature, no matter how immoral, was considered valid and applicable by courts and the executive. The prosecution of German and Japanese leaders had to confront this fact. According to Luban and two co-authors:

> ... Article 8 of the Nuremberg Charter specifically provided that '[t]he fact that the defendant acted pursuant to an order of his government or a superior shall not free him from responsibility.' ... The natural law argument that unjust laws lose their obligatory character provides a straightforward philosophical justification for Article 8.... [N]atural law ... form[s] the most obvious justification for criminalizing 'murder, extermination, enslavement, deportation, and other inhumane acts ... whether or not in violation of domestic law ...'. Such crimes against humanity are radically inconsistent with the common good, and any domestic legal system that permits them must violate natural law.[181]

178 The Treaty of Versailles of 1919 can be found at http://www.yale.edu/lawweb/avalon/imt/kbpact.htm.

179 Covenant of the League of Nations (n. 176).

180 See the discussion of Radbuch in L. L. Fuller, 'Positivism and Fidelity to Law – A Reply to Professor Hart', *Harvard Law Review,* 71 (1957), 630–72.

181 D. Luban, *et al.*, 'Moral Responsibility in the Age of Bureaucracy', *Michigan Law Review,* (1992) 2348–2392, 2352 (footnotes omitted).

The count encompassing 'crimes against the peace' prosecuted in Nuremberg and Tokyo consisted of violations of the Kellogg-Briand Pact, the League Covenant, the Treaty of Versailles, and other treaties. 'Aggression' was declared to be the 'supreme international crime'.[182]

Among the first projects of the United Nations was the drafting of treaties and other positive law instruments on some of the important, immediate post-war legal developments. The Universal Declaration on Human Rights became two treaties, the International Covenant on Civil and Political Rights and the International Covenant on Economic, Social and Cultural Rights. Work began toward establishing a code of international crimes and a permanent international criminal court. That work would only reach completion in 1998 with the adoption of the Rome Statute of the International Criminal Court. Most relevant to this chapter, in 1974, the General Assembly adopted a Definition of Aggression. It is in the form of a resolution and states in the Preamble that 'aggression is the most serious and dangerous form of the illegal use of force'. Article 1 is based on UN Charter Article 2(4) and provides that aggression is 'the use of armed force by a State against the sovereignty, territorial integrity or political independence of another State, or in any other manner inconsistent with the Charter of the United Nations ...'. Article 2 provides that any first use of force in violation of the UN Charter is *prima facie* evidence of an act of aggression. Article 3 is an illustrative list of acts of aggression.[183]

182 'International Military Tribunal (Nuremberg), Judgment and Sentences, 1 October 1946', reprinted in *American Journal of International Law*, 41 (1947), 186.

183 Art. 3 lists: (a) the invasion, attack, military occupation or annexation by the armed forces of one State of the territory of another State; (b) bombardment or the use of any weapons by a State against the territory of another State; (c) blockade of the ports or coasts of a State by the armed forces of another State; (d) an attack by the armed forces of a State on the land, sea or air forces, or marine and air fleets of another State; (e) the use of armed forces of one State which are within the territory of another State with the agreement of the receiving State, in contravention of the conditions provided for in the agreement or any extension of their presence in such territory beyond the termination of the agreement; (f) the action of a State in allowing its territory, which it has placed at the disposal of another State, to be used by that other State for perpetrating an act of aggression against a third State; (g) the sending by or on behalf of a State of armed bands, groups, irregulars or mercenaries, which carry out acts of armed force against another State of such gravity as to amount to the acts listed above, or its substantial involvement therein.

In 2010, at the review conference for the ICC in Kampala, Uganda, the states parties to the ICC finally added the crime of aggression to the Rome Statute. It is a new definition that significantly departs from the UN resolution. The ICC crime is far narrower than the resolution's, a result of considerable lobbying by a non-party to the court, the United States. The US delegation was led by Harold Koh, a legal adviser to US President Bill Clinton during NATO's bombing campaign of Serbia in 1999. The ICC definition would make prosecution of individuals connected to any future use of force like NATO's difficult if not impossible.[184] State parties activated the court's jurisdiction over the crime of aggression in December 2017.

The inclusion of a limited form of aggression in the ICC Statute is a recognition of the importance of individual criminal responsibility for this most serious of all international law violations. The limits placed on the definition of the crime, however, indicate lack of commitment to the peremptory norm. It is an aspect of the assault on the prohibition on the use of force mentioned at the outset of the chapter.

Proponents of force for humanitarian goals, to counter terrorism, for arms control, and other goods, often use arguments from morality to justify violating the prohibition on the use of force. The justification follows the standard civil disobedience argument that the moral rightness of using force trumps the legal prohibition. This line of argument fails to recognize that the prohibition on force is not a mere positive rule that is less important in the moral universe than the advocate's normative goal. The prohibition on force cannot be transgressed in the attempt to advance another norm, even another peremptory norm.

The advocacy for humanitarian intervention tends to accept that the concept rests on weak legal grounds, so moral arguments are employed to supplement or substitute for legal ones. The great suffering of victims is used to argue for a lower quantity of evidence to support re-interpretation, modification, or addition to the Charter exceptions for resort to force.[185] Without the moral argument, the legal argument would likely be dismissed out of hand.

[184] Informal Inter-Sessional Meeting of the SWGCA, Assembly of State Parties, International Criminal Court, ICC-ASP/5/SWGCA/INF.1, 5 September 2006, at para. 19. Kress, *Time for Decision* 2009 (n. 65), 1140, citing R. Cryer, *et al.*, *An Introduction to International Criminal Law and Procedure* 2nd edn (Cambridge: Cambridge University Press, 2010), 326–7.

[185] For several of these arguments, Chapter 1.

Another approach is less direct. It accepts that the legal basis for humanitarian intervention is weak but finds sufficient support to leave humanitarian intervention in a 'grey area' of legality, which is apparently sufficient in the international community.[186] Yet, the most important moral principles of international law are found among the *jus cogens* norms. The lawful use of force occurs as an exception to the prohibition on the use of force.

The concept of humanitarian intervention poses the greatest challenge to the prohibition. Unlawful force has been used persistently even since the adoption of Article 2(4). Humanitarian intervention poses a distinctive challenge, however, because its proponents argue directly against the prohibition. Other arguments for the legal right to use force have focused on either characterizing the facts to meet an exception or argue to expand the exceptions. The arguments for humanitarian intervention have been qualitatively and dangerously different. The danger stems from opposing a peremptory norm, which can weaken the entire legal system. The discussion above of the nature of *jus cogens* norms links them to the very purpose of law, as well as the reasons why law is accepted as binding and deserving of respect. Moreover, the prohibition is replaced by an open-ended standard that can be filled in with anyone's notion of 'humanitarian'. The Kurdish cause is a case in point. A persuasive argument can no doubt be made for military intervention on their behalf. That argument can equally plausibly be countered by Turkey, Iraq, and Iran. Under the prohibition, military force cannot be used for the Kurds, certainly not without the consent of the sovereign state governments where the Kurds live. In Chapter 6, alternatives to the use of force in cases such as that of the Kurds will be discussed. Given the alternatives, the prohibition could do great good if its reach is expanded. Humanitarian intervention seeks to restrict the prohibition's reach on the basis of subjective assessments.

In 1991, following the Gulf War, we might have expected another advancement toward a broader peace order. The Cold War was over and, along with it, the false claims of justified force used throughout that era. President George H. W. Bush declared a new world order under the rule of law. Instead, however, the idea of using force for

[186] See Cryer *et al.*, *An Introduction to International Criminal Law* 2010 (n. 184), 326–7.

more purposes, not fewer, grew in popularity in some circles, including among influential human rights advocates. An old idea promoted particularly by Richard Lillich since the 1970s called 'humanitarian intervention' seemed to be taking hold. It began to be used in official arguments in connection with the use of force by NATO in 1999 during the Kosovo crisis.[187] Until then states consistently took the position that force could not be used lawfully for humanitarian reasons except through the collective decisionmaking of the Security Council. Following the bombing of Yugoslavia over mistreatment of Kosovo's ethnic Albanian population in 1999, the United Kingdom spoke officially in terms of aiding in the development of a doctrine of humanitarian intervention. Soon after, the Canadian government created the International Commission on Intervention and State Sovereignty (ICISS) to study the idea and Responsibility to Protect was born.

ICISS issued a report in December 2001.[188] For the most part, the report reinforces existing international law, especially the human rights obligations of states. It also, however, includes a significant departure from the Charter in the following passage:

> E. If the Security Council rejects a proposal or fails to deal with it in a reasonable time, alternative options are:
>
> I. consideration of the matter by the General Assembly in Emergency Special Session under the 'Uniting for Peace' procedure; and
> II. action within area of jurisdiction by regional or sub-regional organizations under Chapter VIII of the Charter, subject to their seeking subsequent authorization from the Security Council.[189]

The provision seems drafted for the case of Kosovo, an after-the-fact attempt at justification. The attempt to open authorization for force beyond the Security Council, however, is a form of derogation from the Article 2(4) prohibition. Even if the ICISS report had been

187 Gray, *International Law and the Use of Force* 2018 (n. 5), 26.
188 International Commission on Intervention and State Sovereignty, *The Responsibility to Protect* (2001), http://responsibilitytoprotect.org/ICISS%20Report.pdf.
189 Ibid., XIII (emphasis added).

adopted as a modification of the Charter with the required affirmative vote of the Security Council and two-thirds of the General Assembly, it could not result, as a matter of law, in a dilution of the prohibition.

Nevertheless, a good deal of attention was paid to Responsibility to Protect (R2P), especially in the academy. Following the US-led invasion of Iraq in March 2003, interest in war for humanitarian purposes seemed to wane with the rising toll of deaths, injury, and destruction. The UN Secretary General's High Level Panel on United Nations Reform, reporting in November 2004,[190] and the Secretary General's own report of September 2005,[191] both included references to R2P but reaffirmed the prohibition on the use of force without Security Council authorization prior to any use of force except in the case of an armed attack. That restatement of the Charter is reflected even more emphatically in the 2005 World Summit Outcome:

> 138. Each individual State has the responsibility to protect its populations from genocide, war crimes, ethnic cleansing and crimes against humanity. This responsibility entails the prevention of such crimes, including their incitement, through appropriate and necessary means. We accept that responsibility and will act in accordance with it. The international community should, as appropriate, encourage and help States to exercise this responsibility and support the United Nations in establishing an early warning capability.
>
> 139. The international community, through the United Nations, also has the responsibility to use appropriate diplomatic, humanitarian and other peaceful means, in accordance with Chapters VI and VIII of the Charter, to help to protect populations from genocide, war crimes, ethnic cleansing and crimes against humanity. In this context, we are prepared to take collective action, in a timely and decisive manner, through the Security Council, in accordance with the Charter, including Chapter VII, on a case-by-case basis and in cooperation with relevant regional organizations as appropriate, should peaceful means be inadequate and national authorities are manifestly failing to protect their populations from genocide, war crimes, ethnic cleansing and crimes against humanity. . . .[192]

[190] See the Secretary-General's High-level Panel on Threats, Challenges and Change, *A More Secure World: Our Shared Responsibility*, UN GAOR, 59th Sess, Supp No. 565, UN Doc A/59 (2004), available at www.un.org/secureworld/.

[191] *In Larger Freedom*, Pt III, available at www.un.org/largerfreedom/resources .html.

[192] UNGA 'World Summit Outcome' UN GAOR 60th Session UN Doc A/60/L.1 (2005) 22–3.

Nevertheless, there remains a persistent view that the unauthorized use of force in pursuance of humanitarian goals is legitimate.[193]

In 2011, the Security Council did authorize the use of force in Libya to protect civilians. In the view of many, NATO forces exceeded the authorization by seeking to change the government of Libyan leader Moammar Ghaddafi. Actually, NATO helped end the regime of Ghaddafi but not to change it. No party was in a position to assume Ghaddafi's place. A brutal civil war followed the killing of Ghaddafi by a mob. The civil war was continuing seven years after the Security Council authorized force to protect civilians.

United States President Barack Obama declared the intervention in Libya the worst foreign policy decision of his presidency. Nevertheless, US Ambassador to the UN Samantha Power was asked in an interview on National Public Radio on 9 September 2013 whether a US attack on Syria would be 'legal', following a suspected use of chemical weapons by the government. She answered that it would be a 'legitimate, necessary, and proportionate response'. Power would not say that it would be lawful, and she is correct: attacking Syria with a view to enforcing the law against chemical weapons without Security Council authorization would violate fundamental law.

In February 2014, Russian armed forces and armoured vehicles moved out of their Black Sea naval base near Sevastopol, Crimea, towards the Crimean regional capital of Simferopol.[194] Ukrainian troops withdrew, protesting. Russia has remained in Crimea ever since while arguing a variety of justifications, including humanitarian intervention on behalf of the Russian-speaking population. The great majority of states have rejected Russian claims and have participated in sanctions against it. Russia's action is noteworthy as

[193] In addition to the ICISS report, the report of the Independent Kosovo Commission likely supported the emergence of this view. The Independent Kosovo Commission declared that the use of force by NATO against Yugoslavia in 1999 was unlawful but nevertheless 'legitimate'. See Independent International Commission on Kosovo, *Kosovo Report: Conflict, International Response and Lessons Learned* 164 (2000). See also, N. J. Wheeler, *Saving Strangers: Humanitarian Intervention in International Society* (Oxford: Oxford University Press, 2000). But see F. Paddeu, 'Excusing Humanitarian Intervention: A Reply to Jure Vidmar', *EJIL*: Talk! (27 April 2017), available at www.ejiltalk.org/excusing-humanitarian-intervention-a-reply-to-jure-vidmar/.

[194] Russian personnel in the first wave were not wearing military insignia. *Keesing's Record of World Events*, 60 (2014), 53188, 53242.

the only seizure of territory from the recognized boundaries of a member state of the United Nations. While Russia's occupation of Ukraine is a clear violation of the prohibition, the prohibition remains a widely and deeply held principle of the international community.

Indeed, its moral underpinnings are widely intuited, perhaps explaining the persistence of one type of argument against it, humanitarianism. In April 2017, United States President Donald Trump ordered an attack on a Syrian air force base reportedly killing nine, including four children, and damaging property.[195] Trump announced that the attack was a response to the Syrian government's alleged use of chemical weapons days earlier, in which 72 died. Syria denied carrying out the chemical attack, and the USA offered no legal justification for its actions.[196] Nevertheless, the French and German governments issued a joint press release stating that the US attacks were a 'just and proportionate' response to the use of chemical weapons.[197] Indeed, the US attacks were generally met with approval in the West.[198]

In April 2018, the Syrian government was again charged with using chemical weapons. The USA attacked again, this time joined by France and Britain.[199] Over 100 missiles were launched. Again,

[195] J. Le Miere, 'Trump's Attack on Syria Killed Four Children, State News Agency Claims', *Newsweek* (7 April 2017), www.newsweek.com/syria-attack-children-civilian-killed-580555.

[196] 'There's no legitimate domestic or international law basis for it, and it's telling that the administration hasn't even tried to provide one.' Hina Shamsi, American Civil Liberties Union, quoted in S. Saddiqui and L. Gabbino, 'Are Donald Trump's Missile Strikes in Syria Legal?', *Guardian*, 7 April 2017, www.theguardian.com/us-news/2017/apr/07/donald-trump-us-missile-strikes-syria-legal.

[197] C. Palazzo and P. Foster, '"Assad Bears Full Responsibility": How the World Reacted to Donald Trump's Missile Strike on Syria', *Telegraph* (UK), 7 April 2017, www.telegraph.co.uk/news/2017/04/07/us-air-strike-syria-world-reacted-donald-trumps-decision-intervene/. See also attempts to find the attacks legal at *EJIL*: Talk!, including A. Z. Borda, 'The Precedent Set by the US Reprisal Against the Use of Chemical Weapons in Syria', *EJIL*: Talk!, 1 May 2017, www.ejiltalk.org/the-precedent-set-by-the-us-reprisal-against-the-use-of-chemical-weapons-in-syria/comment-page-1/#comment-251292.

[198] E. A. Crunden and E. Yu Hsi Lee, 'International Leaders Weigh in on US Strike in Syria', *ThinkProgress* (7 April 2017).

[199] H. Cooper *et al.*, 'US, Britain, and France Strike Syria Over Suspected Chemical Weapons Attack', *New York Times*, 14 April 2018, www.nytimes.com/2018/04/13/world/middleeast/trump-strikes-syria-attack.html

the USA provided no official legal justification. France declared it a use of force to support the norm against chemical weapons use, but without explaining how the unlawful use of force effectively sends a message of the importance of the legal ban on chemical weapons. The United Kingdom government claimed the attack was an exercise of humanitarianism.[200] The attack drew some expressions of 'understanding' and five state members of the UN Security Council voted with the three attacking states in opposing a Russian draft resolution of condemnation. These indications, however, are well short of legally relevant support for the UK justification.[201]

As a matter of positive law, the prohibition remains solid. The greater challenge has come from morally based arguments of humanitarianism. These, however, are asserted in disregard of the legal category of *jus cogens*. The ban on the use of force may not be overridden on the basis of ambiguous claims that a higher moral good will result. The only legal basis for using force in the circumstances would be through the process of Security Council deliberation. The aftermath of the Libya authorization has left Russia and China opposed to future authorization even in cases where a close ally is not involved. This development is consistent with the ethos of the prohibition on the use of force toward the suppression of violence in the world.

## Conclusion

International law exists to eliminate the use of force and to promote peaceful resolution of disputes. These aspirations are at the heart of the system and support the conclusion that the Charter prohibition on the use of force is a peremptory norm. Peremptory norms are international law's higher ethical principles as identified by the application of universal conscience. Peremptory norms permit no derogation. To create a new legal right that violates or limits the breadth of the prohibition on the use of force is a derogation from the prohibition. Peremptory norms are explained by natural law,

[200] Syria Action, UK Government Legal Position, 14 April 2018, www.gov.uk/government/publications/syria-action-uk-government-legal-position/syria-action-uk-government-legal-position.

[201] See, e.g., Statement of the Norwegian Government, Careful Response to Attack in Syria, 16 April 2016, www.newsinenglish.no/2018/04/16/norway-understands-attack-in-syria/.

not positivism. The prohibition on the use of force is also part of an ancient tradition limiting the lawful resort to force. This history as well as natural law theory support the conclusion that it is not only unlawful, it is immoral to violate the prohibition on the use of force, regardless of the aim. There is always an alternative to killing and, thus, no moral exception to the prohibition exists.

In any case of uncertainty, the logic of *jus cogens* requires adherence to peacetime law. The whole body of international law is structured to move toward eliminating war. The exceptions to the prohibition of force are designed to apply in narrowly defined emergencies. It is the body of human rights law that applies normally, as a matter of presumption. In any case of doubt, international law requires erring on the side of peace and peacetime law.

It may seem that these points do not coincide with the real world where the prohibition on the use of force is, as stated at the outset of the chapter, 'under assault'. In an op-ed following the 14 April 2018 US, UK, and French attack on Syria after allegations of chemical weapons use, an international lawyer commented, 'We now have a situation where the permanent members of the Security Council can no longer agree on the basic rules of international law within the Council's core field of activity concerning the maintenance of international peace and security.'[202] The evidence suggests, however, agreement on the law is not the problem. Russia and China have set out clearly what international law requires in this and other cases. The United States, United Kingdom, and France have been clear and correct regarding the international law that applies to Russia respecting Ukraine and China respecting the South China Sea. The problem is not with agreement on the law that applies, but rather with acceptance that the law applies to all, on the basis of equality. The same norm applicable to Russian action in Ukraine applies to French action in Mali. It applies to US and UK action in Syria and Iraq. The issue of equal status before the law and other issues are taken up in the next chapter on the UN Security Council.

[202] V. Kattan, 'How Obama's Lawyers Gave John Bolton the Keys to Armageddon', *Haaretz*, 18 April 2018, www.haaretz.com/us-news/.premium-how-obama-s-lawyers-gave-john-bolton-the-keys-to-armageddon-1.6011850?=&ts=_1524054001298.

# 3

# The UN Security Council for Maintaining the Peace

At 4 am on 14 April 2018, France, the United Kingdom, and the United States launched a barrage of over 100 missiles on three sites in Syria.[1] Serious property damage resulted but few, if any, casualties. The attack followed one week after reports that the Syrian government had again used chemical weapons in rebel-held areas in the sixth year of a brutal civil war. Only the United Kingdom provided a public legal justification of its action under international law:

> The UK is permitted under international law, on an exceptional basis, to take measures in order to alleviate overwhelming humanitarian suffering. The legal basis for the use of force is humanitarian intervention ...[2]

The general understanding within the international law community is that after the 2005 United Nations World Summit, the positive law principle is well established that the UN Security Council must authorize a use of force undertaken for any reason other than self-defence. To counter this principle, the UK put forth an old argument asserting a right to use force without Security Council authorization: When there is a 'blockage', the Council may be ignored.[3]

[1] H. Cooper, T. Gibbons-Neff and B. Hubbard, 'US, Britain and France Strike Syria Over Suspected Chemical Weapons Attack', *New York Times* (13 April 2018), available at www.nytimes.com/2018/04/13/world/middleeast/trump-strikes-syria-attack.html.

[2] UK Prime Minister's Office, 'Syria Action – UK Government Legal Position', 14 April 2018, available at www.gov.uk/government/publications/syria-action-uk-government-legal-position/syria-action-uk-government-legal-position.

[3] M. Weller, 'Syria Air Strikes: Were They Legal?', *BBC* (14 April 2018), available at www.bbc.com/news/world-middle-east-43766556.

An early version of this 'blockage' argument appeared within just a few years of the drafting of the United Nations Charter. Its author was, again, the Australian academic Julius Stone. As with his argument against interpreting UN Charter Article 2(4) as a comprehensive prohibition on the use of force,[4] Stone's aim was to weaken the prohibition. He wanted certain states to have greater rights to use military force. He accurately understood that the Charter provided only two, narrow exceptions to Article 2(4), self-defence in response to an armed attack and Security Council authorization in the case of a threat to, or breach of, the peace. He used the legal standard of effectiveness to assert a ground for eliminating the Security Council requirement.[5] The problem, then and now, is that restricting the Security Council's authorizing role does not create the right for a state to self-authorize. Even if it did, the rule would apply to all states on the basis of equality, thus eliminating the prohibition for all practical purposes.

Stone's argument was countered at the time but has resurfaced periodically. Thomas Franck presented a version of it in his famous piece, 'Who Killed Article 2(4)?'[6] Despite the equally famous response by Louis Henkin, 'The Reports of the Death of Article 2(4) are Greatly Exaggerated',[7] the assertion continues to be invoked periodically that states are free to use force because the UN or the Security Council does not work.[8] It fades again once its full implications are aired.[9]

[4] Chapter 2.

[5] J. Stone, *Legal Controls of International Conflict* (London: Stevens and Sons, 1954), 243–6, 302–4.

[6] See T. M. Franck, 'Who Killed Article 2(4)? Or: Changing Norms Governing the Use of Force by States', *American Journal of International Law*, 64 (1970), 809–37.

[7] L. Henkin, 'The Reports of the Death of Article 2 (4) are Greatly Exaggerated', *American Journal of International Law*, 65 (1971), 544–8.

[8] See, e.g., A. J. Carswell, 'Unblocking the UN Security Council: The Uniting for Peace Resolution', *Journal of Conflict and Security Law*, 18 (2013), 453–80, 454. The author makes an elaborate argument that Security Council decisions respecting Syria and other cases of 'abuse' of the veto justify a new interpretation of the Charter finding the power to authorize the use of force in the General Assembly. Ibid., 476.

[9] See the response to Weller, 'Syria Air Strikes' 2018 (n. 3), in M. Milanovic, 'The Syria Strikes: Still Clearly Illegal', *EJIL: Talk!* (15 April 2018), available at www.ejiltalk.org/the-syria-strikes-still-clearly-illegal/.

This and other arguments related to Security Council authorization invite the inquiry of this chapter: What is the mandate of the Security Council? The Council has been criticized for 'not working', but it has also been criticized for doing too much, acting illegitimately outside the relevant terms of the UN Charter.[10] The Soviet Union levelled this criticism as early as 1950 following the Council's vote – during the Soviet Union's absence – to intervene militarily in the crisis on the Korean peninsula.[11] The charge of acting lawlessly was made again at the end of the Cold War as the Council moved into a variety of new ventures, from authorizing peace enforcement missions, to creating a force intervention brigade, to establishing criminal courts, developing detailed sanctions regimes, administering post-conflict areas, and other activities of a kind more closely associated in the Charter with the duties of the UN General Assembly.

Criticism levelled at the Council, ranging from inaction to hyperactivity, reflect the fact that the Council is an institution, not a rule. As an institution, it falls within the procedural category of law as opposed to the substantive. Legal process or procedure cannot and should not be pinned down with the precision of a substantive rule.[12] Flexibility, even creativity, is appropriate so long as the substantive law governing the procedure is respected. Legal systems have well-developed methods for controlling legal process and restraining inappropriate departures from substantive law. Judicial oversight, elections, and transparency are typical. These are in short supply with respect to the Security Council. They are not entirely absent, however. Most importantly, in any case where procedural safeguards are weak and an institution has considerable power, the substantive limits need to be strict. The purpose of this chapter is to re-present the Council from the perspective of these principles.

In so doing the chapter builds on the previous one. Central to the discussion here, as in Chapter 2, is the prohibition on the use of force. The prohibition is the core substantive principle of the legal

[10] See, e.g., E. C. Luck, 'A Council for All Seasons: The Creation of the Security Council and its Relevance Today', in V. Lowe *et al.* (eds.), *The United Nations Security Council and War: The Evolution of Thought and Practice Since 1945* (Oxford: Oxford University Press, 2008), 61–85, 83–4; and S. D. Murphy, 'The Security Council, Legitimacy, and the Concept of Collective Security After the Cold War', *Columbia Journal of Transnational Law*, 32 (1994), 201–88, 204–6.

[11] See notes 73–5 and accompanying text.

[12] See the discussion in Chapter 6 of international legal process.

regime of peace; the UN Security Council is the most powerful institution for preserving peace.[13] Maintaining the viability and legitimacy of institutions of any kind within the constraints of substantive law is a structural challenge for every legal system. Some of the inherent contradictions of the Security Council make holding the Council to the law all the more difficult. The Charter empowers five UN member states with greater authority than all others in a legal system based on equality of states. The task of the Council is to maintain the peace, yet, its main power is to use military force. The very design of the Council implies that exceptionalism and militarism are acceptable, notions in tension with the prohibition on the use of force as *jus cogens*. The tension is reflected in the UK legal position on attacking Syria in April 2018.

The tensions can be addressed constructively, however, when the rule of law in support of peace is given priority over competing principles. The peace regime does, in fact, need the Security Council, even with its flaws. The world needs an institution devoted to addressing emergencies involving the threat or use of military force. The chapter concludes that the flaws can be ameliorated through greater awareness of the priority of peace, the Council's narrow purpose in preserving the peace, and the law that restrains Council action. The Security Council's job is not fundamentally about authorizing the use of force or legislating. The Charter provides the Council with the power and purpose, in the words of Hans Kelsen, 'to maintain international peace and security by enforcement actions'.[14] The privileges of the Permanent Members are related strictly to that task. They have no greater rights to use

[13] The leading ICJ opinion on the status of the United Nations as an entity under international law with authority to act only as expressly or impliedly provided in the Charter is the *Reparations* Advisory Opinion of 1949. ICJ, *Reparations for Injuries Suffered in the Service of the United Nations*, Advisory Opinion of 11 April 1949, ICJ Reports 1949, 174. The Security Council also has procedural rules. Provisional Rules of Procedure of the UN Security Council, UN Doc. S/96/Rev.7 (1983). When the UN acts within member states, some national law will be relevant to UN personnel in addition to the international law under which they operate.

[14] H. Kelsen, *The Law of the United Nations: A Critical Analysis of its Fundamental Problems* (New York: FA Praeger, 1950), 283. Some criticize the Council for its venture into law making since the end of the Cold War, a process function more appropriately left to the General Assembly. See, e.g., I. Johnstone, 'Legislation and Adjudication in the UN Security Council: Bringing Down the Deliberative Deficit', *American Journal of International Law*, 102 (2008), 275–308; and

force than other states. Indeed, the privileges were allocated together with greater responsibilities, responsibilities that include compliance with international law. The Charter expressly includes this point to prevent abuse of power by the Permanent Members.[15]

The argument here for robust legal limits on the Security Council begins in Part I with a brief discussion of the origins of the Charter design for the Council, followed by an overview of the key Charter provisions relative to the Council's authority. Part II discusses the Council's actions from its first decision in 1947 to its decision over the next seven decades. Important events in that long history are viewed in the light of the prohibition on the use of force as *jus cogens*, a fact that creates the most important restriction on the Security Council. This point of law is rarely if ever discussed in the extensive literature on the Council, despite its important implications. Part III – the final part – will consider ways to enhance law compliance by the Council and thereby how it can more effectively promote the peace. Given the critiques over the years of the Council's failures and shortcomings, many reform plans have been proposed. For political reasons, they remain dead letters. No political impediment stands in the way, however, to holding the Council to the rule of law, especially the law of the Charter and the *jus cogens* norms restricting the use of force.

## I The Council under Law

The roots of the UN and the Council lie in 'the various projects for a universal organization for the maintenance of peace that, from the Middle Ages to the beginning of the 19th century, have been suggested by statesmen and philosophers'.[16] These projects evolved to their greatest sophistication with the establishment of the UN Security Council. Despite the heavy criticism just mentioned, the Council is unlikely to go away or even to experience any great transformation.[17] The permanent five members of the Council –

S. Talmon, 'The Security Council as World Legislature', *American Journal of International Law*, 99 (2005), 175–93.

15 R. B. Russell, *A History of the United Nations Charter* (Washington, DC: Brookings Institution, 1958), 655–6.

16 A. Ross, *The United Nations, Peace and Progress* (Totowa, New Jersey: Bedminster Press, 1966), 4.

17 Luck, 'A Council for All Seasons' 2008 (n. 10), 85.

China, France, Russia, the United Kingdom, and the United States – are unlikely to abandon it nor are other states going to stop campaigning to win elected seats in the foreseeable future.[18] Campaigns continue to seek new permanent members with virtually no prospect of success because the Council is one of the few tangible signs of power in the world. It is an old-fashioned kind of power based on the size of a national military and a long-distant victory in World War II. Despite the solecisms, the designers of the Council had insights into what could be accomplished in 1945, and what would last. They understood the importance of process that combined flexibility under a strong substantive principle. These features of the new UN were inspired by, among other things, the weaknesses of the UN's immediate predecessor, the League of Nations.[19]

The UN Charter Preamble begins with the UN's one and only purpose, 'to save succeeding generations from the scourge of war'.[20] Other purposes, such as promoting human rights, economic prosperity, and arms control, are all related to preserving the peace. The Charter approach to peace is threefold. It provides first for substantive rules prohibiting resort to force and requiring compliance with international law and the peaceful settlement of disputes.[21] It establishes bodies to implement the substance. The two most important organs are the Security Council, which remains in continuous session to deal with immediate threats to the peace and breaches of the peace, and the General Assembly, which has responsibility for responding programmatically to the causes of conflict, especially by developing international law, respect for human rights, and economic prosperity. All six UN organs have a mandate to work to prevent and settle disputes peacefully.[22]

[18] See, e.g., 'German Foreign Minister Heiko Maas at the UN to Lobby for a Security Council Seat', *Deutsche Welle* (27 March 2018), available at www.dw.com/en/german-foreign-minister-heiko-maas-at-un-to-lobby-for-security-council-seat/a-43159228. Even France and the United Kingdom would not give up their permanent seats to the European Union at the time both were committed to a common EU foreign and security policy.

[19] Lowe *et al., The United Nations Security Council and War* 2008 (n. 10), 10–12.

[20] Preamble UN Charter. [21] Art. 2(4) UN Charter.

[22] See Chapters IV (General Assembly), V (Security Council), XIII (Trusteeship Council), XIV (International Court of Justice), and XV (Secretariat) of the UN Charter.

### *A Drafting History*

As discussed in Chapter 2, the UN Charter was built on positive law developments regulating the use of force of the late nineteenth and early twentieth centuries. Natural law restrictions were reflected in the new treaties, international institutions, and new methods for the peaceful settlement of disputes developed in the era. By the middle of the twentieth century, these ideas were carried into the plan for the new organization, the United Nations.

The treaties ending the Thirty Years' War in Europe in 1648 also had a commitment to common action.[23] The Peace of Westphalia prohibited resort to war to impose religion on other states and committed the parties to use arbitration to settle other disputes rather than resort to war. Violation of either treaty provision could be enforced by the other parties acting collectively. A similar arrangement was included in the Treaty of Paris ending the Napoleonic Wars.[24]

When World War I ended, these types of arrangements were adapted to include new thinking with respect to peaceful settlement of international disputes, international institutions, governance, and nationalism. These developments are reflected in the Treaty of Versailles, which provided for a new international organization devoted to peace – the League of Nations. The 1919 Covenant of the League expressly committed states to protect other states from 'external aggression'.[25] The Treaty also included provisions for a Council to enforce the terms of the Covenant; a world court; the break-up of the German, Ottoman, and Austro-Hungarian empires; and the trial of the Kaiser for waging war in violation of treaties.

Article 10 of the Covenant constituted the primary provision against war:

> The Members of the League undertake to respect and preserve as against external aggression the territorial integrity and existing political

[23] Reproduced in C. Parry (ed.), *The Consolidated Treaty Series* 1 (Dobbs Ferry, NY: Oceana Publications, 1969).

[24] C. Parry (ed.), *The Consolidated Treaty Series* 63 (Dobbs Ferry, NY: Oceana Publications, 1969), 171–97.

[25] The Treaty of Versailles, 28 June 1919, reproduced in L. Friedman (ed.), *The Law of War: A Documentary History* 1 (New York: Random House, 1972), 417–34. See also F. P. Walters, *A History of the League of Nations,* (New York: Oxford University Press, 1952).

independence of all Members of the League. In case of any such aggression or in case of any threat or danger of such aggression the Council shall advise upon the means by which this obligation shall be fulfilled.

It was an affirmative agreement to forgo wars of aggression. Article 12 placed limits on lesser uses of force, indicating some support for the view that the use of force to enforce rights was lawful:

The Members of the League agree that if there should arise between them any dispute likely to lead to a rupture, they will submit the matter either to arbitration or to inquiry by the Council, and they agree in no case to resort to war until three months after the award by arbitrators or the report by the Council. In any case under this Article the award of the arbitrators shall be made within a reasonable time, and the report of the Council shall be made within six months after the submission of the dispute.

The Covenant, like the Statute of the Permanent Court of International Justice, which was drafted a year later, reflected both schools of international legal thought of the time. Scholars such as Kelsen saw the Just War Doctrine of natural law reflected in the Covenant, a treaty created through positive law method. For these scholars, the Covenant added procedures and means of enforcement to the ancient prohibition.[26] Others, such as Oppenheim, argued that the use of force was first legally prohibited when it was banned in positive law. For positivists, the Covenant provided the furthest limit on a state's right to use force. It was binding only on states party to the Covenant and only for so long as they continued to extend their consent to be bound.[27]

It went too far for many members of the United States Senate, which had to assent to the United States joining the treaty by a vote of two-thirds in favour. Article 10 was a particular obstacle to senators, including Elihu Root, the founder of the American Society of International Law. The United States never joined the League, and the League never intervened as an organization to protect the territorial integrity of its members. Japan invaded Manchuria, China, in

[26] H. Kelsen, *General Theory of Law and State*, A. Wedberg (trans.) (Cambridge, MA: Harvard University Press, 1945), 335–6.

[27] Oppenheim argued no natural law existed. L. Oppenheim, *International Law: A Treatise: Peace* I (London: Longmans, Green, and Co, 1905), 92. It followed that as of 1906 resort to war was lawful. 'Thus war is not inconsistent with, but a condition regulated by, International Law.' L. Oppenheim, *International Law: A Treatise: War & Neutrality* II (London: Longmans, Green, and Co, 1906), 56.

1931. Italy invaded Ethiopia in 1935. By the time Germany invaded Poland in 1939, the League was effectively dead, although high-ranking political and military leaders of Germany and Japan were prosecuted after the war, in part, for crimes against the peace, including violations of the Covenant of the League.[28]

When it became clear that the USA was never going to join the League, the American peace movement campaigned for their country to continue its diplomatic efforts to advance international law in support of peace. In 1928, US Secretary of State Frank Kellogg joined with his French counterpart Aristide Briand to devise a more straightforward treaty-based prohibition on resort to force than was found in the League Covenant.[29] They drafted the General Treaty for Renunciation of War as an Instrument of National Policy. It consisted of just two operative paragraphs:

> Article I The High Contracting Parties solemnly declare in the names of their respective peoples that they condemn recourse to war for the solution of international controversies, and renounce it as an instrument of national policy in their relations with one another.
>
> Article II The High Contracting Parties agree that the settlement or solution of all disputes or conflicts of whatever nature or of whatever origin they may be, which may arise among them, shall never be sought except by pacific means.[30]

What the Pact did not have was the machinery of the League for preventing and ending violations of the prohibition. Another treaty came into effect the same year, the General Act for the Pacific Settlement of International Disputes, which committed states to use mechanisms of peaceful settlement. Together the two treaties could have gone a long way toward remedying the weaknesses of the League. However, while Kellogg-Briand was widely adopted, the General Act was not.

US President Franklin Roosevelt saw the need to develop an improved form of world organization in 1939, as the world

[28] See, e.g., International Military Tribunal, *Nuremburg Trials*, Judgment of 30 September 1946, Trial of the Major War Criminals before the International Military Tribunal: Nuremberg: 14 November 1945–1 October 1946, 22, 424–8.

[29] O. A. Hathaway and S. J. Shapiro, *The Internationalists: How a Radical Plan to Outlaw War Remade the World* (New York: Simon & Schuster, 2017), chap. 10.

[30] General Treaty for Renunciation of War as an Instrument of National Policy, 27 August 1928, 94 LNTS 57. The Kellogg–Briand Pact is also known as the Briand-Kellogg Pact or Pact of Paris.

descended into war.[31] A State Department official, Leo Pasvolsky, received the initial assignment.[32] Roosevelt and Pasvolsky exercised great influence over the final design, but they were not alone. 'Probably no other major governmental policy has ever been the product of so many minds as the American proposals for an international organization.'[33] Roosevelt wanted a redesign of the League Council. The new body would continue to promote the peaceful settlement of disputes as the central idea, but would also have greater discretion and capacity to enforce the peace.[34] '[T]he provision of continuing machinery for enforcement purposes was the most radical innovation to be written into the new charter, in comparison with the Covenant of the League of Nations. The provision of settlement machinery presented a less novel task.'[35]

All the new ideas hinged on attracting and keeping the major powers committed to the organization. Roosevelt believed he could entice Stalin with the promise of a veto in the Security Council. When the League was established in 1920, the League Council had eight members: four Permanent Members – France, Italy, Japan, and the UK – and four members elected for three-year terms. All eight had a veto, meaning unanimity was required for action. In the new UN Council, the veto was restricted to the Permanent Members only. The new Council had a broader scope of authority over all threats to the peace and breaches of the peace, not just acts of aggression. It also had more flexibility in how it could respond. It did not have to attempt economic sanctions first in every case. It was more attractive to the Permanent Members and that has proven its value as the United Nations approaches its eightieth year. In commenting on the new plan for the Security Council, a French delegate compared it favourably with the League: '[I]t had not been the rule of unanimity which had prevented [League] action, but the absence, from the start, of one great power and the later withdrawal of others.'[36]

[31] S. C. Schlesinger, *Act of Creation: The Founding of the United Nations: A Story of Superpowers, Secret Agents, Wartime Allies and Enemies, and Their Quest for a Peaceful World* (Boulder, CO: Westview Press, 2003), 29–31.

[32] Ibid., 33.

[33] Russell, *A History of the United Nations Charter* 1958 (n. 15), 215.

[34] Ibid., 421.

[35] Ibid., 227–8.

[36] *Documents of the United Nations Conference on International Organization* 12 (1945), 457 (cited in Luck, 'A Council for All Seasons' 2008 (n. 10), 77).

The Permanent Member veto was not, however, simply an enticement to keep the major powers committed to the organization, as important as that was. It also reflected Roosevelt's firm belief that Permanent Member unanimity for action was critical to preserving the peace. He had a point in two respects. Effective action in response to threats to, or breaches of, the peace required the five powers to not be at cross-purposes. As Edward Luck phrases it: 'The prospects for an effective international organization, in essence, would depend on the way the Big Four would use their military assets: showing restraint in their interactions, while displaying the will to act collectively in the common good when needed.'[37] In addition, the way the Security Council was organized prevented a more immediate collapse of relations between the USA, UK, China, and the Soviet Union. The plan kept the Soviet Union tied to its wartime allies in a united front at the final Charter negotiations in San Francisco.

Despite the unity, the obvious negative features of Permanent Member privileges were heavily debated and numerous proposals were made for amendments to the draft Charter. One idea seriously considered was to include Brazil as a Permanent Member of the new Council with the same privileges as the others. Roosevelt had in fact given thought early in the planning to this idea in order to keep the Latin American countries supportive of the new organization. His advisers persuaded him to reject it, in part using the argument that Brazil simply was not a major power. When the idea came up again in San Francisco, it was again rejected by the major powers along with the 'onslaught' of other proposals to limit or eliminate the 'veto privilege'.[38] The New Zealand delegate, Fraser, commented that some of the votes were very close on the subject of the veto. Those voting in support finally accepted the privileges in exchange for the understanding that greater responsibility for peace and security fell to the Permanent Members.[39] Roosevelt rightly predicted his plan would 'preserve the institution and ... insure that it could not be turned against one of its principal founders'.[40]

[37] Luck, 'A Council for All Seasons' 2008 (n. 10), 74.

[38] R. Edis, 'A Job Well Done: The Founding of the United Nations Revisited', *Cambridge Review of International Affairs*, 6 (1992), 29–40, 37. See also *Documents of the United Nations Conference on International Organization* (1945).

[39] *Documents of the United Nations Conference on International Organization* 11 (1945), 108–9. Ibid., 169–173.

[40] Luck, 'A Council for All Seasons' 2008 (n. 10), 81.

Another approach to restraining the Council was to limit its discretion respecting the scope of problems for it to deal with and the range of responses. Proposals were made to define aggression, for example, and to require that upon the occurrence of aggression, the Council would be required to impose sanctions automatically as had the Council of the League.[41] The delegates reached no agreement on a definition of aggression, however, and turned their attention to the content of Articles 1(1) and 1(2). They agreed to impose on the UN as a whole the obligation to comply with international law. The term aggression does make an appearance in Article 39, which empowers the Council to find and act on a 'threat to the peace, breach of the peace, or act of aggression'. The drafting history provides no indication that aggression means anything other than a serious breach of the peace.[42]

Given the extensive use of force by the Permanent Members at present, and the Council's involvement in conflicts where no Permanent Member is a major participant, such as the civil war in Congo, it is interesting to find in the records from San Francisco that the delegates expected the Council to devote most of its time to the peaceful settlement of disputes. Authorization of military force would be rare. 'There would be a small and selective Security Council, which would have primary responsibility on behalf of the whole membership for the pacific settlement of disputes and, when necessary, for the enforcement of peace and security.'[43] At the opening meeting of the commission devoted to Security Council

[41] Russell, *A History of the United Nations Charter* 1958 (n. 15), 669–70.

[42] The UN General Assembly returned to the topic of defining aggression, eventually agreeing that it means any serious violation of Art. 2(4). Arts. 1–3 GA Resolution 3314 (XXIX) of 14 December 1974. Parties to the Statute of the International Criminal Court added the crime of aggression as a crime of individual accountability to the ICC's jurisdiction in 2017. The comparable crime at Nuremberg and Tokyo had been designated 'crimes against the peace'. The ICC formulation makes clear that the crime of aggression subject to prosecution before the ICC is intended to be narrower than aggression that is a serious breach of Art. 2(4). The negotiating history reveals an interest by several NATO member states in excluding violations of Art. 2(4) when a use of force was for humanitarian purposes as in NATO's bombing during the Kosovo crisis. NATO members also wanted to assert expansive claims of self-defence, especially for counter-terrorism. See Chapter 2 and M. E. O'Connell and M. Niyazmatov, 'What is Aggression? Comparing the *Jus Ad Bellum* and the ICC Statute', *Journal of International Criminal Law*, 10 (2012), 189–207, 202–3.

[43] Russell, *A History of the United Nations Charter* 1958 (n. 15), 646.

design at San Francisco, the Norwegian chair stated in his opening remarks that while some differences as to emphasis and approach might exist, there was general agreement on the purpose of the Council. It had to prevent 'the outbreak of another devastating world struggle'.[44] The commission considered amendments to the draft plan to improve the prospects for dispute resolution by, for example, enlarging the Council's membership during particular discussions and requiring the Council to take preliminary steps before authorizing force.[45] A member of the US delegation, Harold Stassen, expressed the hope that the Charter 'Section dealing with the Peaceful Settlement of Disputes, may be the Section that will be used more than any other . . .'.[46]

Nevertheless, the draft plan included the possibility of the Security Council using military force. Three related proposals were considered at San Francisco. One envisioned UN members relinquishing their national militaries to create a UN force.[47] That proposal was not adopted, but two others were combined to make available both UN forces and national forces to the Security Council through agreements with members. The drafters left the details to be worked out later, which never happened.

### *B Charter Rules*

The UN's purpose – to end the use of force – is stated in poetic terms in the Charter preamble and in more prosaic words in Chapter I. Article 1(1) mandates a commitment by all members:

> To maintain international peace and security, and to that end: to take effective collective measures for the prevention and removal of threats to the peace, and for the suppression of acts of aggression or other breaches of the peace, and to bring about by peaceful means, and in conformity with the principles of justice and international law, adjustment or settlement of international disputes or situations which might lead to a breach of the peace.[48]

[44] *Documents of the United Nations Conference on International Organization* 11 (1945), 13.
[45] *Documents of the United Nations Conference on International Organization* 12 (1945).
[46] *Documents of the United Nations Conference on International Organization* 11 (1945), 89.
[47] *Documents of the United Nations Conference on International Organization* 3 (1945), 386.
[48] Art. 1(1) UN Charter.

Article 2(3) provides for the commitment to peaceful settlement of disputes. Article 2(4) is the prohibition on the use of force. These are the objects and purposes of the Charter and are indispensible to interpretation of the Charter as a whole.

Chapter V of the Charter is devoted to the Security Council and begins in Article 24(1) by stating that the Council has 'primary responsibility for the maintenance of international peace and security'.[49] Article 24(2) reiterates that the Council must carry out its responsibilities in conformity with the UN's purposes and principles. The Council must comply with the Charter and with international law in carrying out its mandate. Article 25 is the real source of the Council's power. It pledges member states to accept and carry out the Council's decisions. Those decisions may relate to Chapter VI and the peaceful settlement of disputes, Chapter VII and threats to and breaches of the peace, or Chapter XII and decisions of the International Court of Justice. As Article 24 makes clear, the Council has duties respecting all three areas. All relate to the prohibition on the use of force.

Article 26 of Chapter V, however, is somewhat different. It tasks the Security Council with the 'establishment of a system for the regulation of armaments' that will lead to 'the least diversion for armaments of the world's human and economic resources ...'. The Council was to work with its Military Staff Committee toward this end. The Military Staff Committee had the principal job of developing agreements for national stand-by forces for the use of the Security Council, per Chapter VII, Article 43. Article 26 envisioned the Council and the Military Staff Committee coming up with plans to present to UN members, presumably in the General Assembly. The Military Staff Committee stopped meeting in 1948,

[49] Art. 24 UN Charter

1. In order to ensure prompt and effective action by the United Nations, its Members confer on the Security Council primary responsibility for the maintenance of international peace and security, and agree that in carrying out its duties under this responsibility the Security Council acts on their behalf.
2. In discharging these duties the Security Council shall act in accordance with the Purposes and Principles of the United Nations. The specific powers granted to the Security Council for the discharge of these duties are laid down in Chapters VI, VII, VIII, and XII.
3. The Security Council shall submit annual and, when necessary, special reports to the General Assembly for its consideration.

and the Council has never developed disarmament plans of a general nature. As will be discussed in the next section, the Council has, at the request of the International Atomic Energy Agency, become involved with control of nuclear weapons.[50] It has also considered chemical weapons use.[51] The General Assembly, the more appropriate body for programmatic work, took up the topic in 1978 after 33 years of virtual Council inaction.

The Council has also done little with respect to enforcing judgments of the International Court of Justice.[52] The Council has set up courts, undertaken fact-finding missions, and other actions listed in Chapter VI.[53] Establishing the International Criminal Tribunals for Yugoslavia and Rwanda have been among the Council's most impactful actions for international law. These were established under Chapter VII,[54] despite the references to courts in Chapter VI and the Council's duties with respect to Chapter VI specified in Article 24. The International Court of Justice indicated Article 24's importance in its *Namibia* advisory opinion.[55] Arguably, the Council may take binding action with respect to Chapter VI and the enforcement of ICJ judgments, but by now the Council's practice signals its intent to bind UN members by citing Chapter VII. This need not be the case, however, as will be discussed in Part III of this chapter. The Council may take a broader view of its authority to promote peaceful settlement and compliance with international law.

[50] See notes 90–4 and accompanying text.

[51] See, e.g., 'Security Council Fails to Adopt Three Resolutions on Chemical Weapons Use in Syria', *UN News* (10 April 2018), available at https://news.un.org/en/story/2018/04/1006991.

[52] The Council debated its authority to assist the UK in getting enforcement of an ICJ order of provisional measures in the UK case against Iran for the 1951 seizure of the assets of the Anglo-Iranian Oil Company. The UK withdrew its request prior to a vote. See UN Repertory 5, 'Article 94', available at http://legal.un.org/repertory/art94/english/rep_orig_vol5_art94.pdf.

[53] 'Myanmar: Security Council Meets Leaders Face-to-Face', *UN News* (30 April 2018), available at https://news.un.org/en/story/2018/04/1008582.

[54] SC Res. 827 of 25 May 1993.

[55] ICJ, *Legal Consequences for States of the Continued Presence of South Africa in Namibia (South West Africa) Notwithstanding Security Council Resolution 276 (1970)*, Advisory Opinion of 21 June 1971, ICJ Reports 1971, 52, para. 110. See also D. Schweigman, *The Authority of the Security Council under Chapter VII of the UN Charter: Legal Limits and the Role of the International Court of Justice* (The Hague: Kluwer Law International, 2001), 29–31.

The Council's overwhelming focus has been on Chapter VII where the power to authorize the use of force is located. That is not all that Chapter VII provides, however. Article 39 refers to the Council performing a deliberative or adjudicative function. If the Council finds a threat to, or breach of, the peace, it may make recommendations. Additionally, it may decide on measures per Articles 41 and 42 to 'restore international peace and security.' Under Article 40, the Council may decide on provisional measures to prevent aggravation of a situation pending decisions under Articles 39, 40, and 41. Article 41 then lists examples of measures short of armed force, including economic sanctions. Article 42 provides that the Council may take action by 'air, sea, or land forces as may be necessary to maintain or restore international peace' but only after a determination that coercive measures short of force indicated in Article 41 'would be inadequate or have proved to be inadequate'.[56] Articles 39–42 are a series of steps, reserving the use of force as a last resort in exigent circumstances. Preventing armed force is the goal of Chapter VII. It does not aim at accomplishing other desirable ends, whether the advancement of human rights, protection of the environment, economic development, or even arms control.[57]

The action by air, sea, or land forces was to be by UN forces as provided for under Article 43. Article 43 requires all UN members to make armed forces and facilities available to the Security Council under special agreements. Those agreements were never formed.

[56] Article 39 provides:

> The Security Council shall determine the existence of any threat to the peace, breach of the peace, or act of aggression and shall make recommendations, or decide what measures shall be taken in accordance with Articles 41 and 42, to maintain or restore international peace and security.

Article 42 provides:

> Should the Security Council consider that measures provided for in Article 41 would be inadequate or have proved to be inadequate, it may take such action by air, sea, or land forces as may be necessary to maintain or restore international peace and security. Such action may include demonstrations, blockade, and other operations by air, sea, or land forces of Members of the United Nations.

[57] At the 2005 World Summit in New York, UN members clarified their view that the Security Council was authorized to act under Chap. VII, which includes Arts. 39 and 42, in situations of severe humanitarian crisis, despite the reference in Art. 39 to 'international peace'. See 2005 World Summit Outcome, GA Res. A/60/1 of 16 September 2005, para. 139. See also notes 111–40 and accompanying text.

In their place the Security Council has undertaken a variety of approaches, some more and some less consistent with the law governing Council action. The 2018 Report of the International Law Association's Committee on the Use of Force accepts that the Council may authorize force regardless of Article 43 agreements and without being organized under the UN blue flag. The International Law Association (ILA) Report finds a basis for this position by reading Articles 42 and 48 of Chapter VII together. Article 48 provides that 'action required to carry out the decisions of the Security Council . . . shall be taken by all the Members of the United Nations or by some of them, as the Security Council may determine'.[58] The plain meaning of Article 48 is that the Council need not call upon all UN members for every action. It is a stretch to find it somehow allows for the Council to authorize national military action regardless of Article 43 agreements. Still, the Council has interpreted Articles 43 this way for so long that its legal right to do so is unquestioned. UN members had an opportunity to clarify this point during the World Summit in 2005 but did not.[59] Regardless of these ad hoc developments, the main point here is that authorization of force by the Council remains as a legal matter an action appropriate in limited, emergency situations.

The exceptional nature of Council-authorized force is further underscored by other provisions of Chapter VII. Article 42, in particular, indicates that the Council needs to restrict resort to or authorization of force to a last resort. Once the Council has found a threat to or breach of the peace as provided in Article 39, it may authorize force only after determining, per Article 42, that measures other than armed force would be 'inadequate'.[60] In addition, because the Council is bound by general international law as indicated by Article 24, any use of force undertaken on the basis of Council authorization must comply with the principles of necessity

[58] International Law Association Committee on the Use of Force, 'Draft Report on Aggression', (March 2018), 9. See also, N. Blokker, 'Outsourcing the Use of Force: Towards More Security Council Control of Authorized Operations?', in M. Weller (ed.), *The Oxford Handbook of the Use of Force in International Law* (Oxford: Oxford University Press, 2015), 202–26, 213.

[59] 2005 World Summit Outcome, GA Res. A/60/1 of 16 September 2005, paras. 77–80.

[60] The Security Council has no pattern of violating principles of attribution. On the requirement to comply with necessity and proportionality, see ILA, 'Draft Report on Aggression and the Use of Force' 2018 (n. 58), 10–11.

and proportionality that condition all lawful coercive action.[61] The Council has no special privilege in this regard. States authorized to use force by the Security Council undoubtedly are obligated to respect necessity and proportionality. These restrictions cannot be ignored on the basis of a Security Council authorization, given that the Security Council itself is not permitted to ignore them. Force must be necessary to achieve the Council's mandate. The type of force envisioned must be calibrated to the threat or breach of the peace that triggers the mandate.

States have from time to time claimed a right to use force based on an implication of a Council resolution, rather than an express authorization. The United States and the United Kingdom argued that Council resolutions authorizing force against Iraq in 1990 continued to permit the use of force against that country over many years in maintaining 'no-fly zones' and, finally, a full-scale invasion in 2003.[62] The United States attempted to defend its use of force in 1999 against Serbia during the Kosovo crisis as implied by Security Council resolutions.[63] NATO members asserted that the limited terms of an authorizing resolution to protect civilians in 2011 in Libya could be stretched to include removing the government by military force.[64]

Given the peremptory status of the prohibition on the use of force, however, such claims are unpersuasive. Any right to resort to force, as a legal matter, must be based on express authorization and conform to the terms of the authorization. Not only is this conclusion compelled by the concept of *jus cogens*, it is consistent with the fact that any Security Council authorization of the use of force in the absence of Article 43 agreements rests on a weak or implied basis. The rule in standard legal interpretation is that a right or power may only be implied from an express right or power.[65]

[61] On necessity and proportionality in relation to Security Council authorization, see J. Gardam, *Necessity, Proportionality and the Use of Force by States* (Cambridge: Cambridge University Press, 2004), 188–212; and ILA, 'Report on Aggression and the Use of Force' 2018 (n. 58), 10–11. See also Chapter 2.

[62] S. D. Murphy, 'Assessing the Legality of Invading Iraq', *Georgetown Law Journal*, 92 (2004), 173–257, 175–6.

[63] M. E. O'Connell, 'The UN, NATO, and International Law after Kosovo', *Human Rights Quarterly*, 22 (2000), 57–89, 78.

[64] See SC Res. 1973 of 17 March 2011.

[65] ICJ, *Reparations*, Advisory Opinion (n. 13), 182–4.

Many of the points above respecting the principles governing Security Council action are rarely discussed. By contrast, a single provision, Article 51, receives extensive attention. Article 51 permits the use of force without Security Council authorization. Nevertheless, Article 51 imposes real constraints on unilateral action, including a temporal limit. The right lasts only until the Security Council takes 'measures necessary to maintain international peace and security'.[66] This and other limits have attracted objections, which will be discussed in the next chapter.[67] It is clear from the drafting history, however, that the Council's authority was to remain paramount, even in cases of self-defence. Article 51 was designed to allow organizations such as the Rio Treaty Organization to use force in collective self-defence in emergencies. Again, the experience of World War II was uppermost in the drafters' minds. Collective self-defence arrangements might deter aggression by a state with a larger military against a state with a smaller one.

While permitting collective self-defence arrangements, the Charter also makes clear that military alliances may only use force for any purpose other than self-defence with Security Council authorization. Chapter VIII is devoted to regional organizations and specifies in Article 53 that 'no enforcement action shall be taken under regional arrangements or by regional agencies without the authorization of the Security Council . . .'. The ICJ clarified in the *Certain Expenses* case that 'enforcement action' means the use of military force.[68]

[66] Art. 51 UN Charter provides:

> Nothing in the present Charter shall impair the inherent right of individual or collective self-defence if an armed attack occurs against a Member of the United Nations, until the Security Council has taken measures necessary to maintain international peace and security. Measures taken by Members in the exercise of this right of self-defence shall be immediately reported to the Security Council and shall not in any way affect the authority and responsibility of the Security Council under the present Charter to take at any time such action as it deems necessary in order to maintain or restore international peace and security.

[67] See, e.g., Y. Dinstein, *War, Aggression, and Self-Defence*, 3rd edn (Cambridge: Cambridge University Press, 2001).

[68] ICJ, *Certain Expenses of the United Nations (Article 17, paragraph 2, of the Charter)*, Advisory Opinion of 20 July 1962, ICJ Reports 1962, 164.

## II The Council in Action

The plan for the Council had been one thing. The reality, inevitably, something else. Relations among the Permanent Members were already difficult prior to San Francisco. Still, the Council began well from the perspective of prohibiting the use of force. Even as the Cold War deepened, positive developments did occur. In some respects, action by the Council after the end of the Cold War has proven more challenging to restricting resort to force and honouring the legal prohibition. The consistently poor results of ambitious post-Cold War military interventions provide grounds for advocating renewed respect for the reason the UN was established in the first place.

### *A Cold War*

As just mentioned, the Security Council started auspiciously. In 1948, it organized the United Nations Truce Supervision Organization (UNTSO) to oversee an armistice following fierce fighting to establish the State of Israel in the British Mandate of Palestine.[69] In 1949, the Security Council authorized a similar mission to the border of Pakistan and India, the UN Military Observer Group in India and Pakistan (UNMOGIP).[70] Both missions remain deployed seventy years later.

In 1950, however, the crisis on the Korean Peninsula led to the first significant departures from the prescribed procedures for the Council developed during the long years of World War II and in San Francisco. As the World War ended, the United States and the Soviet Union competed to replace Japan as it withdrew rapidly from wide swaths of occupied Asia. The US military took control of Korea south of the 38th parallel. The Soviet Union extended its influence north of the parallel. Talks ensued to re-unify the country but to no avail. The USA organized elections in the south in 1948 and withdrew. In June 1950, the Soviet Union, with the help of the new Chinese communist leadership, induced North Korea to attack the South.[71]

69 United Nations Peacekeeping, 'Our History', available at https://peacekeeping.un.org/en/our-history.

70 Ibid.

71 See J. P. Glennon (ed.), 'Korea', in *Foreign Relations of the United States* 7 (Washington DC: United States Government Printing Office, 1950), 291–329; and C.-I. Ohn, 'The Causes of the Korean War (1950–1953)', *International Journal of Korean Studies*, XIV (Fall/Winter 2010), 19–44.

On news of the attack, the United States representative to the Security Council requested authorization to lead a United Nations counter-attack. The Soviet Union was boycotting the Security Council at the time to protest the refusal to give China's seat to the new communist government. The Korea resolutions passed.[72] It was a controversial move given the language of the Charter in Article 27(3) that decisions of the Security Council on all but procedural matters 'shall be made by an affirmative vote of nine members including the concurring votes of the permanent member ...'. The Korean War continued until 1953 when, after about 2.5 million deaths, the two sides agreed to an armistice re-establishing the de facto border at the 38th parallel. The Soviet Union, and subsequently Russia, never boycotted Security Council meetings again.

Indeed, when the Soviet Union returned to the Council, it took up the presidency and, through control of the agenda, restricted discussion of the Korea crisis. The United States then sought 'alternative ways to enable the UN to take decisions legitimizing US-led military action ...'.[73] The USA and its allies sponsored a resolution in the General Assembly, titled the Uniting for Peace Resolution. It provided, most relevantly, that 'if the Security Council, because of lack of unanimity of the permanent members, fails to exercise its primary responsibility for the maintenance of international peace and security ... the General Assembly shall consider the matter immediately with a view to making appropriate recommendations ... including ... the use of armed force where necessary ...'.[74] The General Assembly has no authority to authorize force and has never sought to do so under Uniting for Peace. Nevertheless, the Uniting for Peace Resolution introduced the idea of the General Assembly or some other body authorizing force in place of the Security Council. UN Secretary-General Ban Ki-moon pointed to Uniting for Peace again in 2009, as an alternative to the Security Council for authorizing force for humanitarian purposes.[75]

[72] SC Res. 83 of 27 June 1950, 84 of 7 July 1950, and 85 of 31 July 1950.

[73] D. Zaum, 'The Security Council, the General Assembly, and War: The Uniting for Peace Resolution', in Lowe et al., *The United Nations Security Council and War* 2008 (n. 10), 154–74, 157.

[74] GA Res. 377A (V) of 3 November 1950.

[75] Report of the Secretary-General, 'Implementing the Responsibility to Protect', UN Doc. A/63/677 (2009).

The Uniting for Peace Resolution had one less negative impact. It provides for the General Assembly to come into emergency session to discuss crises and make recommendations. The General Assembly came into emergency session during the Suez Crisis of 1956. Tensions in the Middle East erupted into armed conflict following Egypt's takeover of the Suez Canal from a British-French consortium on 26 July 1956. France, Israel, and the United Kingdom developed an outlandish plan for retaking the canal in which Israel would attack Egypt, then France and the UK would intervene between the two warring states to restore peace and, at the same time, retake the canal. Israel duly attacked on the night of 29 October. On 30 October, the United States called an emergency session of the Security Council. France and the UK issued an ultimatum to Egypt and Israel to cease fire and withdraw ten miles from the Canal area. The two then vetoed other proposals for a ceasefire. On 31 October after announcing that Egypt had rejected their ultimatum, France and the UK also intervened. A meeting of the General Assembly under the Uniting for Peace Resolution was convened. With the agreement of all parties, the United Nations Emergency Force (UNEF I) was organized to enforce a ceasefire and supervise the withdrawal of foreign forces.[76] France and the UK withdrew their troops by the end of December 1956. Israel withdrew by the end of March 1957.

UNEF I is considered the first of a series of highly successful UN Peacekeeping Missions.[77] Secretary-General Dag Hammarskjöld drew on its success to develop what became known as 'classic' or 'traditional' peacekeeping.[78] Traditional peacekeeping involves four criteria: consent from all the parties, neutrality in the conflict, an effective ceasefire, and resort to force only for personal defence.[79] Hammarskjöld argued the concept was not *ultra vires* for the UN because it combined elements of Chapter VI and

[76] GA Res. 1000 (ES-I) of 5 November 1956; and GA Res. 1001 (ES-I) of 7 November 1956.

[77] S. D. Bailey and S. Daws, *The Procedure of the UN Security Council* 3rd edn (Oxford: Oxford University Press, 1998), 356 (update to the 4th edn, available online).

[78] Report of the UN Secretary-General, 'Summary Study of the Experience Derived from the Establishment and Operation of the Force', UN Doc. A/3943 (1958).

[79] N. White, 'Peacekeeping or War-fighting?', in N. White and C. Henderson (eds.), *Research Handbook on Conflict and Security Law:* Jus Ad Bellum, Jus in Bello, Jus Post Bellum (Cheltenham:Edward Elgar, 2013), 572–97, 574.

Chapter VII of the Charter. Further, it did not require Security Council authorization because of the limited force contemplated, and the element of consent meaning traditional peacekeeping does not trigger Article 2(4). Supporting a ceasefire gave the missions a concrete and realizable objective, in contrast to later peace enforcement missions.[80] The four criteria came to characterize 'traditional peacekeeping', which drew its legality from general international law, as opposed to the UN Charter. All seventeen traditional or classic peacekeeping missions genuinely supported the maintenance of peace.[81] With the end of the Cold War, the successful formula was abandoned for missions with Security Council authorization to use offensive force. The results of these missions are far from the uniform success of traditional peacekeeping, as will be discussed presently.

Uniting for Peace and traditional peacekeeping were avenues of UN action that avoided being shut down by a Permanent Member veto. On one extraordinary occasion, a Permanent Member of the Security Council did not veto a resolution against it. In 1964, the Council condemned the United Kingdom's bombing of Fort Harib in Yemen.[82] The Council found that the UK's bombing of targets in Yemen were undertaken as reprisals for raids into an area the UK was trying to form into the Federation of South Arabia and the Crown Colony of Aden. The Council resolved in Resolution 188 that reprisals are 'incompatible with the purposes and principles of the United Nations'.[83]

The Council condemnation likely provided assistance to the UK in extricating itself from yet another difficult end-of-empire challenge. In the same year, the UK turned to the Council again for assistance in transforming the British colony of Southern Rhodesia. The UK was preparing to turn over local administration to majority rule. White colonists resisted, in part because they were already facing organized, violent pressure in respect of their privileged position in the country. On 11 November 1965, whites, under the leadership of Ian Smith, made a unilateral declaration of

[80] Ibid., 572–83. [81] United Nations Peacekeeping (n. 69).

[82] See B. M. Leiser, 'The Morality of Reprisals', *Ethics*, 85 (1975), 159–163, 159 n. 1.

[83] SC Res. 188 of 9 April 1964, para. 1. It is noteworthy and to the UK's credit that it did not veto the resolution.

independence (UDI) from the UK and prepared to fight organized armed liberation groups. The UK did not use military force to take back control of the colony but did turn to the Security Council, which adopted a resolution the next day condemning the UDI. On 20 November, the Security Council made a finding of threats to peace and security and called on UN members to 'desist' from supplying arms, equipment, and military material.

A year later, the UN passed a more comprehensive, clearly mandatory set of sanctions aimed at ending white rule. Portugal, concerned about maintaining its own colonial control in southern Africa, offered Smith assistance from the start. Liberation fighters throughout the region supported each other with weapons and safe havens. A controversy emerged, however, as to whether the Security Council was acting to counter a threat to and breach of the peace or in the interest of promoting human rights.[84] Myres McDougal and Michael Reisman, defending the Council's action on the facts of violence in the area, included the interesting argument that racism could trigger humanitarian intervention by states. McDougal and Reisman plainly supported a broader understanding of the Council's authority to act with respect to human rights than the plain terms of the Charter indicate. It was a position that would develop after the end of the Cold War.[85]

Despite the actions in the Rhodesia crisis and those against apartheid policies in South Africa,[86] the Council 'proved reluctant to engage in an expansive definition of threats for most of the Cold War period'.[87] The UN has the duty to promote human rights, as

[84] For an account of the legal controversy, see, M. S. McDougal and W. M. Reisman, 'Rhodesia and the United Nations: The Lawfulness of International Concern', *American Journal of International Law*, 62 (1968), 1–19.

[85] Ibid., 10–13. Vera Gowlland-Debbas went much farther, arguing that the Security Council was enforcing human rights in the Rhodesia crisis, regardless of any link to peace and security. She used this analysis in an effective argument after the Cold War to gain support for the proposition that the Security Council has the power and the duty to engage militarily in human rights crises. See V. Gowlland-Debbas, *Collective Responses to Illegal Acts in International Law: United Nations Action in the Question of Southern Rhodesia* (Dordrecht: Martinus-Nijhoff, 1990). See also notes 104–40 and accompanying text.

[86] Already in 1960, the Council had called upon the Union of South Africa to base law and policy on racial equality. SC Res. 134 of 1 April 1960.

[87] J. M. Welsh, 'The Security Council and Humanitarian Intervention', in Lowe *et al., The United Nations Security Council and War* 2008 (n. 10), 535–62, 537. But see V. Gowlland-Debbas, 'The Security Council as Enforcer of Human Rights',

indicated in the Preamble, Article 1(1), Article 1(2), and Article 55, but the drafters conceived that such promotion would be through the development of treaties and other measures to which all states would contribute voluntarily. Promoting human rights was not considered interference in internal affairs. With respect to other issues, however, throughout the Cold War UN members took seriously at least the principle of non-intervention provided in Charter Article 2(7).[88] Article 2(7) makes an exception for cases arising under Chapter VII, but those were expected to be the immediate threats to, and breaches of, international peace and security as understood in 1945. Building respect for human rights and economic development could not be accomplished with UN military forces.

Arms control presents a similar challenge, but arms control, unlike human rights or economic development, has long been considered a direct cause of war. Tsar Nicholas II called the First Hague Peace Conference in 1899, for example, to promote peace through arms control. In recognition of the linkage, arms control is among the Security Council's duties, but the task migrated to the General Assembly where it likely should have been from the start. In one important area, however, the Security Council does remain active: nuclear non-proliferation. A United Nations specialized agency, the International Atomic Energy Agency (IAEA), was established in 1957 to ensure that peaceful uses of atomic energy were not diverted to military uses.[89] The IAEA Statute requires the agency to draft safeguard agreements with states other than the Security Council Permanent Five. Those agreements provide for a reference to the Security Council and General Assembly if a party is found to be in non-compliance. In 1968, the Nuclear Non-Proliferation Treaty was adopted, providing again for IAEA safeguard agreements and measures against non-compliance, including referral to the Security Council and the General Assembly. The first referral to the Security

in B. Fassbender (ed.), *Securing Human Rights? Achievements and Challenges of the UN Security Council* (Oxford: Oxford University Press, 2011), 36–73.

88 'Nothing contained in the present Charter shall authorize the United Nations to intervene in matters which are essentially within the domestic jurisdiction of any state or shall require the Members to submit such matters to settlement under the present Charter; but this principle shall not prejudice the application of enforcement measures under Chapter VII.' Art. 2(7) UN Charter.

89 See the website of the IAEA for treaties related to the organization, www.iaea.org. See also, D. H. Joyner, *Interpreting the Nuclear Non-Proliferation Treaty* (New York: Oxford University Press, 2011).

Council did not occur until after the end of the Cold War when the IAEA referred North Korea in 1993.

In 1981, however, the Council did become involved in a crisis that squarely raised the peace-nuclear proliferation issue. On 7 June, Israeli jets bombed a nuclear reactor in Iraq being constructed by a French company. Iraq requested an emergency meeting of the Security Council. The IAEA, Iraq, and Israel all spoke at the multi-day meeting. Israel's representative was a respected professor of international law, Yehuda Blum, who made a case that the attack was lawful as an exercise of anticipatory self-defence under Article 51. The Council found 'the military attack by Israel in clear violation of the Charter of the United Nations and the norms of international conduct'.[90] The US representative to the UN Security Council, Ambassador Jeane Kirkpatrick, stated that the United States, too, understood Israel had violated the Charter, in particular because it had not exhausted peaceful alternatives before striking.[91] Many representatives were impressed by the testimony of the Director General of the International Atomic Energy Agency who testified that the IAEA had found no evidence of unlawful weapons development by the Iraqi government.[92] Not only did the IAEA find no diversion of nuclear material, but Israel put forward no evidence that an attack was highly imminent, let alone underway.[93] Blum had quoted Sir Humphrey Waldock's lectures in The Hague for the right to use force prior to absorbing the impact of the 'armed attack' referred to in Article 51. Blum cut the quotation just short of the part supplied by the Iraqi representative. Waldock went on to say the attack, nevertheless, had to be underway.

By the end of the Cold War, the law of the Charter was largely intact. In the first decades after 1945, knowledge of the purpose and meaning of the post-war agreements remained in living memory. The Cold War played a role as well. The existence of the Soviet Union reminded US government officials and academics to take care in arguing for new rules on the use of force. The same

90 See SC Res. 487 of 19 June 1981, and accompanying debate.

91 SCOR, 36th Sess. UN Doc. S/PV.2288 and Corr.1 (1981), paras. 27–30.

92 Ibid., para. 19.

93 Some writers have suggested that governments now approve of the Israeli attack but provide no official statements to that effect. See W. M. Reisman, 'International Legal Responses to Terrorism', *Houston Journal of International Law*, 22 (1999), 3–61, 17–18.

consideration seems to have influenced the Soviets. Both superpowers tended to manipulate the facts to fit the law rather than the law to fit the facts, in attempting to publicly justify uses of force. The 1956 Soviet invasion of Hungary was justified by an invitation, which the Soviets obtained by plotting with a high-ranking member of the Hungarian government, János Kádár, to claim he was the legitimate head of government, moving aside the choice of the reformers, Imre Nagy.[94] The Soviets followed a similar approach in obtaining invitations to intervene in Czechoslovakia in 1968[95] and Afghanistan in 1979.[96] The United States characterized Vietnam as two separate countries. The USA claimed to be joining South Vietnam in collective self-defence against the North. In 1983, the United States obtained an invitation to intervene in Grenada where it replaced the government. The invitation was obtained from the British Governor-General. He likely did not have the authority to issue it and had to backdate it.[97]

The superpowers used some care to prevent a direct military conflict between them. The law of the Charter established a substantive framework to limit how far they would go. The Security Council offered a place and a process for communication between two states existentially opposed to the other. They did not, however, reject armed conflict in the form of proxy wars, intervention in spheres of influence, and other uses of military force. The many armed conflicts of the Cold War inflicted extraordinary suffering, and yet, when the era ended with the collapse of the Soviet Union, rather than a new commitment to peace, the use of military force as a tool to implement policy held new attraction. The reasons for implementing the prohibition on the use of force in positive law seemed forgotten for the next quarter century.

[94] C. Gati, *Failed Illusions: Moscow, Washington, Budapest, and the 1956 Hungarian Revolt* (Washington, DC: Woodrow Wilson Center Press, 2006), 17, 232–3.

[95] P. Windsor and A. Roberts, *Czechoslovakia 1968: Reform, Repression and Resistance* (New York: Columbia University Press, 1969), 102–111.

[96] M. E. O'Connell, 'Soviet Prisoners in the Afghan Conflict', *Columbia Journal of Transnational Law*, 23 (1985), 497–504.

[97] C. C. Joyner, 'The United States Action in Grenada: Reflections on the Lawfulness of Invasion', *American Journal of International Law*, 78 (1984), 131–75, 137–9.

### *B Post-Cold War*

Again, things began relatively well as the Cold War was ending with respect to the Council and action for the maintenance of peace. In August 1990, the Council voted unanimously to condemn Iraq for violating Article 2(4) of the United Nations Charter by invading Kuwait and claiming to re-absorb it as Iraq's long-lost '19th province'. Kuwait's own small armed forces made some attempt to defend the nation as was their right under Article 51, but those forces were quickly overwhelmed. The UN Security Council became involved and after a period of attempting to use economic sanctions to persuade Iraq to withdraw, the Council authorized a coalition of states to use force to liberate Kuwait. The coalition forces quickly drove Iraq's armed forces out of Kuwait and beyond a swath of territory that became a demilitarized zone for Kuwait's future security. Famously, the coalition did not proceed to Baghdad to remove Saddam Hussein from power because doing so, in the view of coalition leaders, was not necessary to the liberation of Kuwait.[98] Indeed, fighting unrelated to the liberation of Kuwait could not be justified under the principle of necessity since it was clearly beyond the force required to remove the occupier. Failing to respect the principle of necessity would make any killing and destruction both unnecessary and disproportionate.

US President George H. W. Bush declared that the liberation of Kuwait by the near-unanimous effort of the international community would be the beginning of a new world order 'where the rule of law ... governs the conduct of nations', and 'in which a credible United Nations can use its peacekeeping role to fulfill the promise and vision of the UN's founders'.[99] Some interpreted his meaning to be not a new order of peace, but one in which military force would and should be used to promote human rights and self-determination. In fact, what the coalition forces had accomplished in 1991 was the pushing of one army across a recognized international border. The victory was not about military force as a useful

[98] The US Secretary of Defense of the time, Richard Cheney, had advocated regime change and continued to do so until it was accomplished in the 2003 invasion of Iraq. See P. Rowe (ed.), *The Gulf War 1990–1991 in International and English Law* (London: Sweet & Maxwell, 1993).

[99] President George H. W. Bush, 'Address to the Nation Announcing Allied Military Action in the Persian Gulf', 16 January 1991.

tool for the painstaking building of legal institutions and good governance within states. Failing to realize this, the post-Cold War world has been plagued by armed conflict. The most deadly has been the war in the Democratic Republic of the Congo, which is roughly estimated to have cost over 6 million lives as of 2016.

Indeed, the misuse of military force began just as Kuwait was being liberated. The Kurds of northern Iraq and the Shia population of southern Iraq attempted to free themselves from Saddam Hussein. The Security Council debated how to respond to the uprisings. The USA did not believe there was legal authority to intervene to assist the rebels. France argued for a humanitarian intervention regardless of the law.[100] That argument was rejected, but the British offered a view that the Security Council resolutions authorizing the use of force to liberate Kuwait had vague references to peace in the area that could suffice to provide air cover and other limited assistance to the two populations.[101] From the modest start, American and British air patrols remained over Iraq until the two countries, together with Australia, invaded in 2003. Periodically, Russia and France protested the 'no-fly' zones but were ignored.[102]

Later in 1991, human rights campaigners called for military action on behalf of populations attempting to secede from Yugoslavia. The Security Council's first action was to impose an arms embargo on all parties. Belgrade supported the move. In November 1991, Zagreb, Croatia, and Belgrade agreed to the formation of a peacekeeping force, the United Nations Protection Force (UNPROFOR). It was the first of a new style of 'peacekeeping' mission. The Council approved the deployment without a ceasefire in place. On the contrary, peacekeepers were sent to stop the fighting.

On 3 December 1992, the Security Council authorized a mission to Somalia in response to widespread famine triggered in part by government collapse and the violent competition among warlords to take control. In Resolution 794, the Security Council authorized 'all necessary means to establish as soon as possible a secure environment for humanitarian relief operations . . .'. In Resolution 814,

[100] M. E. O'Connell, 'Continuing Limits on UN Intervention in Civil War', *Indiana Law Journal*, 67 (1992), 903–14, 905.
[101] Ibid., 906–7. [102] Ibid., 909.

the Council ordered troops wearing blue helmets – some under UN command and others under US command – to disarm warring parties and armed bands. UN Secretary-General Boutros Boutros-Ghali said this was the first time the UN had 'decided . . . to intervene militarily for strictly humanitarian purposes'.[103] Twenty-five years later, the situation in Somalia has not improved.

The same could be said for other areas of Security Council activism where UN and non-UN forces with mandates to use all necessary means have intervened. These places have included Congo, Central African Republic, Mali, Burkina Faso, Ivory Coast, South Sudan, and others. In Haiti, UN peacekeepers may have caused more problems than they solved by spreading cholera. Traditional peacekeeping has been criticized for helping to keep conflict frozen, as has been the case with respect to Cyprus. Post-Cold War interventions, however, have failed to even freeze brutal conflicts, let alone end them.

Rwanda may be the worst case from every possible perspective. The UN Security Council authorized a peace enforcement mission to Rwanda in late 1993, despite a report to the UN in the spring of that year discussing mass killings and other indications of the violent and unstable situation in the country. An advance mission estimated in September that a peacekeeping force of 4,260 would be needed to support the tentative political deal between the contending Hutus and Tutsis. Unaccountably, Kofi Annan, then Under Secretary-General for Peacekeeping, only requested 2,548 troops.[104] Belgium and Bangladesh made the only troop contributions at first: 400 each. It took over five months to reach the total number requested by Annan. Within weeks of that date, the genocide began. Within 100 days an estimated 800,000 people were dead in Rwanda, mostly Tutsis. Following years of civil war, Tutsi rebels had taken refuge in Uganda and Kenya. They were on the verge of making a push back into Rwanda when the Hutu-controlled government decided to slaughter anyone who might assist them when they arrived.

103 Annual Report of the UN Secretary-General on the Work of the Organization, UN Doc. A/48/1 (1993).

104 UN, 'Rwanda-UNAMIR: Background', available at https://peacekeeping.un.org/mission/past/unamirS.htm.

The UN presence may have lulled people into a false sense of security. The force was inadequate and UN Headquarters knew it. This author asked Sir Brian Urqhart, known as the father of UN Peacekeeping and someone close to Annan, why Annan did not inform the Security Council that he could not find sufficient troops to carry out the Council's mandate in Rwanda. Urquhart answered simply that Annan could not say no to the Security Council. Instead, an inadequate force was faced with an impossible situation, which may account for why Annan did not authorize the peacekeepers under the Canadian General Romeo Dallaire to do more, such as taking control of a weapons cache in January 1994.[105] Tutsi rebels made it to Rwanda and took control despite – or perhaps because of – the frenzy of killing within the country. Hutus then fled to neighbouring Zaire, soon to be renamed the Democratic Republic of Congo. Hutu forces joined the entrenched armed conflict that continues in the Congo at time of writing.[106]

In the aftermath of Rwanda, scholars and politicians concluded that the genocide there and mass killing in Bosnia were the result of too little fighting by the UN, not the fact that outside military intervention is not suited to resolving such conflicts. Secretary-General Boutros-Ghali seemed to have learned the lesson of trying to change complex situations with military force and sought a return to traditional peacekeeping.[107] Internal conflict is far more complicated, in almost all cases, than transboundary aggression.[108]

Boutros-Ghali was out, however, and Kofi Annan succeeded him as Secretary-General. Books by journalists such as Samantha Power's *A Problem from Hell* did more to shape the debate than sober

[105] UN, 'Report of the Independent Inquiry into the Actions of the United Nations During the 1994 Genocide in Rwanda', 15 December 1999, available at https://reliefweb.int/report/rwanda/report-independent-inquiry-actions-united-nations-during-1994-genocide-rwanda.

[106] For a detailed description of the first years of the conflict in Congo, see ICJ, *Armed Activities in the Territory of the Congo* (*Democratic Republic of Congo* v. *Uganda*), Judgment of 19 December 2005, ICJ Reports 2005, 168.

[107] See Report of the Secretary-General, Supplement to An Agenda for Peace, UN Doc. A/50/60-S/1995/1 (1995).

[108] I. Davidson, 'Not the Way to Do It: Military Intervention in Civil Wars is Unlikely to Procure Peace', *Financial Times* (3 August 1994), 14; A. Roberts, 'The Road to Hell... A Critique of Humanitarian Intervention', *Harvard International Review*, 16 (Fall 1993), 10–13, 63, 11–12. See also Chapter 5.

scholarship by people such as Adam Roberts. In 1999, US President Bill Clinton and his Secretary of State, Madeleine Albright, wanted no more Rwandas or Srebrenicas on their watch. Thus, with the willing support of the UK's Prime Minister Tony Blair, they were able to rally all NATO members to support a 78-day bombing campaign of Serbia to attempt to end persecution of Kosovo's majority ethnic Albanian population. The campaign had no Security Council authorization. Only Belgium argued it was lawful as an humanitarian intervention. The USA gave no official legal justification for a major use of military force for perhaps the first time since the adoption of the UN Charter. An estimated 20,000 people died once NATO bombing started in contrast to dozens killed in the crisis in the previous year. No plan for mass killing of Kosovars was found. Serbia's leader, Slobodan Milosevic, had been under political pressure to leave power. That pressure was suspended while the bombs fell. The aftermath has been a kind of unstable limbo for Kosovo, its full sovereign statehood opposed by Serbia, Russia, China, and others. Kosovo is not a member of the UN. Government corruption is a serious problem, the economic base is virtually non-existent, and young people seek to leave.[109]

In some quarters, the lesson from the Kosovo experience has been paradoxically to support weakening the restrictions on force. Within the UN, ten Peacekeeping Missions with mandates that were adopted or renewed after 2000 all provide for or even encourage the use of force to deter threats to civilian populations.[110] Various governments and academics undertook debates, investigations, and reports into the difficult legal question of whether the UN Charter had been effectively modified to permit unilateral 'humanitarian intervention' in the years after the Cold War. The events of 9/11, however, shifted world attention dramatically to the problem of terrorism, which erupted out of challenges in the Middle East

[109] D. Franchini and A. Tzanakopoulos, 'The Kosovo Crisis-1999', in O. Corten, T. Ruys and A. Hofer, *The Use of Force in International Law: A Case-Based Approach* (Oxford: Oxford University Press, 2018), 594–622; and M. E. O'Connell, 'The UN, NATO, and International Law After Kosovo', *Human Rights Quarterly*, 22 (2000), 57–89.

[110] United Nations Peacekeeping Operations, available at www.un.org/en/peacekeeping/operations/. See also J. Karlsrud, 'The UN at War: Examining the Consequences of Peace-Enforcement Mandates for the UN Peacekeeping Operations in the CAR, the DRC and Mali', *Third World Quarterly*, 36 (2015), 40–54.

with origins in colonialism, armed interventions, and civil war. In 2003, after intense sessions at the Security Council, the USA, UK, and Australia invaded Iraq, ostensibly to end a programme of weapons of mass destruction. The Security Council had not authorized the intervention. US Secretary of State Colin Powell remarked, when asked about the legality of the invasion, that it was as lawful as Kosovo. In 2005, the UN membership as a whole made clear that humanitarian intervention must be authorized by the Security Council to be lawful. The UK challenged this decision in April 2018 in its attempted legal justification for the use of force against Syria discussed at the outset of the chapter.

War for humanitarian and purposes other than countering an unlawful first resort to military force have proven highly problematic. The military objectives are vague and doubts about legality affect morale, planning, and alliances. Humanitarian intervention is a particularly challenging concept for military strategists.[111] After decades of debate, it remains elusive. Legal process is designed to deal with such concepts. The Security Council was designed to deal with 'threats to the peace', also a vague concept. To keep legal process legal, however, and distinctive from policymaking, substantive rules must apply to limit procedure – the vaguer the issue, the more substantive procedural law is needed. Article 51 provides a concrete legal standard for the use of force in self-defence – an armed attack. With this standard, less process is needed. Unilateral decisions are tolerable. Almost every other problem for which armed force has been proposed as a remedy is qualitatively different, including, or especially, humanitarian crises. For these, process solutions are needed. Security Council process consists of the relevant provisions of the Charter and international law. This law requires a finding of threat to or breach of the peace and a determination that any response meets the principles of necessity and proportionality.

Acceptance of this perspective is reflected in the UN World Summit Outcome document. After the Secretary-General's review of the UN following the 2003 Iraq invasion, the membership did

[111] For a catalogue of problems with the concept of 'humanitarian intervention' including vagueness, see M. E. O'Connell, 'Review of Mark Gibney, "International Human Rights Law: Returning to Universal Principles" (2008)'; and of T. Weiss, '"Humanitarian Intervention: Ideas in Action" (2007)', *Perspectives on Politics*, 7 (2009), 712–13.

indicate its readiness for the Security Council to be involved in responding to humanitarian crises, but the reference also indicates that the lawful use of military force requires Council authorization. No alternative body is empowered to authorize, let alone states acting alone or in ad hoc coalitions:

> 138. Each individual State has the responsibility to protect its populations from genocide, war crimes, ethnic cleansing and crimes against humanity. This responsibility entails the prevention of such crimes, including their incitement, through appropriate and necessary means. We accept that responsibility and will act in accordance with it. The international community should, as appropriate, encourage and help States to exercise this responsibility and support the United Nations in establishing an early warning capability.
>
> 139. The international community, through the United Nations, also has the responsibility to use appropriate diplomatic, humanitarian and other peaceful means, in accordance with Chapters VI and VIII of the Charter, to help to protect populations from genocide, war crimes, ethnic cleansing and crimes against humanity. In this context, we are prepared to take collective action, in a timely and decisive manner, through the Security Council, in accordance with the Charter, including Chapter VII, on a case-by-case basis and in cooperation with relevant regional organizations as appropriate, should peaceful means be inadequate and national authorities are manifestly failing to protect their populations from genocide, war crimes, ethnic cleansing and crimes against humanity ...[112]

No finding was made in March 2011 that peaceful means would be inadequate when the United Nations Security Council authorized the imposition of a no-fly zone to protect civilians from the Libyan government of Colonel Ghaddafi. About 172 peaceful demonstrators had been killed in the capital, Tripoli, in February 2011. As soon as the Council resolution passed, NATO began a campaign far in excess of a no-fly zone. NATO forces came to the aid of government opposition forces, assisting them in driving Colonel Ghaddafi from Tripoli and to his death at the hands of a mob. When challenged that the Security Council resolution did not authorize regime change, the answer has been that the only effective way to protect civilians was to remove Ghaddafi from power.[113] The critical terms for some

[112] 2005 World Summit Outcome, GA Res. A/60/1 of 16 September 2005, paras. 138–9.

[113] H. Roberts, 'Who Said Gaddafi Had to Go?', *London Review of Books* (17 November 2011), available at www.lrb.co.uk/v33/n22/hugh-roberts/who-said-gaddafi-had-to-go .

intervening states were, 'protect civilians'. Beyond the issue of whether NATO exceeded its authority under Resolution 1973, is the question, should the Security Council have authorized even a no-fly zone?

The evidence from the Libya crisis reveals no indication of the necessity of using force.[114] Hugh Roberts, at the time of the Libya intervention with the International Crisis Group, wrote:

> The claim that 'the international community' had no choice but to intervene military and that the alternative was to do nothing is false. An active, practical, non-violent alternative was proposed, and deliberately rejected. The argument for a no-fly zone and then for a military intervention employing 'all necessary measures' was that only this could stop the regime's repression and protect civilians. Yet many argued that the way to protect civilians was not to intensify the conflict by intervening on one side or the other, but to end it by securing a ceasefire followed by political negotiations.[115]

The International Crisis Group advocated the formation of a contact group to negotiate among the Libyan groups. The African Union offered high-level mediation, which Colonel Ghaddafi accepted but the rebels and their Western sponsors rejected.

These and other facts demonstrate the intervention was anything but a last resort. Nor was real success probable. President Obama spoke of Ghaddafi going but did not say how removing him would assist civilians. Richard Falk has concluded that military intervention has for decades led only to general failure. He predicted a similar failure as a result of the Libya intervention. The first six months of fighting cost an estimated 30,000 lives. Libya became the scene of lawlessness, militant activity, and vicious human rights violations, especially against minorities and immigrants. On the other hand, foreign oil interests are prospering.[116]

[114] M. E. O'Connell, Remarks, 'Revolution and Intervention in the Middle East', *Proceedings of the Annual Meeting (American Society of International Law)*, 105 (2011), 555–75, 563–4.

[115] Roberts, 'Who Said Gaddafi Had to Go?' 2011 (n. 113).

[116] For a critical comment on humanitarian intervention, see R. Falk, 'Can Humanitarian Intervention ever be Humanitarian?' (4 August 2011), available at http://mwcnews.net/focus/editorial/12577-humanitarian-intervention.html?tmpl=component. L. Müller, 'The Force Intervention Brigade – United Nations Peacekeeping and Peace Enforcement', *Journal of Conflict and Security Law*, 3 (2015), 359–80.

In November 2013, several hundred M23 militants were able to seize the city of Goma in Eastern Congo without meeting resistance from the '1,500 peacekeepers of the United Nations Organization Stabilization Mission in the Democratic Republic of Congo (MONUSCO) who were deployed in the city'.[117] Just eighteen months earlier, M23 had been part of Congo's Army under a peace agreement brokered in 2009. M23 members mutinied when trials began of fighters who should have enjoyed, in their view, amnesty under the terms of the agreement.[118] The fall of Goma was seen as a major blow to the UN's reputation.[119] States in the region began to call for UN capacity to engage a force like M23. Rather than conclude more should have been done to support the peace agreement, the UN turned to using more force by setting up the Force Intervention Brigade (FIB).[120]

The FIB is a laboratory of sorts 'for testing new peacekeeping techniques'.[121] It was 'authorized to carry out "targeted offensive operations" to "neutralize" and "disarm" more than ten rebel armed groups in the east of DR Congo'.[122] The brigade was made up of 3,069 troops from Tanzania, South Africa, and Malawi, with specialized units for infantry, artillery, special forces, and reconnaissance. UN staff emphasized that the FIB was created on an exceptional basis and would not create a precedent. This was an answer in part to members opposed to the creation of the FIB. Among their concerns was the development of expectations that the FIB would be 'hailed as "best practice"'[123] and initiate a 'shift toward counterinsurgency-style

[117] O. Ilyshev, 'The UN Force Intervention Brigade in DR Congo: "Offensive" Peacekeeping', *International Affairs*, 62 (2016), 139–52, 139.

[118] Müller, (n. 116), 362; and BBC News, 'Q&A: DR Congo's M23 Rebels' (5 November 2013), available at www.bbc.com/news/world-africa-20438531; see also Peace Agreement Between the Government and *le Congres National pour la Defense du Peuple* (CNDP), DRC-CNDP, 23 March 2009.

[119] Karlsrud, 'The UN at War' 2015 (n. 110), 44–5.

[120] Ilyshev, 'The UN Force Intervention Brigade in DR Congo' 2016 (n. 117), 140.

[121] T. Piiparinen, 'Beyond the Technological Turn: Reconsidering the Significance of the Intervention Brigade and Peacekeeping Drones for UN Conflict Management', *Global Governance*, 21 (2015), 141–60, 141.

[122] Ilyshev, 'The UN Force Intervention Brigade in DR Congo' 2016 (n. 117), 140 (quoting SC Res. 2098 of 28 March 2013, para. 2(b)).

[123] L. Gberie, 'Intervention Brigade: End Game in the Congo?', *African Renewal Online*, (August 2013), available at www.un.org/africarenewal/magazine/august-2013/intervention-brigade-end-game-congo.

operations by the United Nations'.[124] There were grounds for these concerns when, following the FIB's initial success against the M23, the Security Council began to pass resolutions incorporating reference to some of the strategies used in the FIB's operations into other peacekeeping mandates and operations, including MONUSCO's.[125]

The Democratic Republic of Congo (DRC)'s leaders balked, accusing the UN of using MONUSCO and the FIB to 'force its will on sovereign Kinshasa'.[126] The DRC ended cooperation with the UN to prevent the FIB from becoming an 'occupation force'.[127] The DRC not only unilaterally ended its military cooperation with the UN, but also cooperation with 'UN programs on a security sector reform on human rights, and on disarmament, demobilization and reintegration'.[128] This was proof for many scholars that '[w]hile this new initiative [the creation of the FIB] could improve the UN's efforts to protect civilians, particularly by deterring rebel attacks through a show of force, it also raise[d] a number of risks and challenges for MONUSCO, the DRC, and the region as a whole'.[129]

Five years later, a record number of UN peacekeepers have died, and none of the conflicts in which the FIB intervened is resolved.[130] In Congo, not only have militant groups continued to inflict heavy casualties, some of the FIB's engagements have also resulted in many civilian deaths,[131] negating the original

[124] P. Cammaert and F. Blyth, 'The UN Intervention Brigade in the Democratic Republic of the Congo', International Peace Institute (July 2013), 6, available at www.ipinst.org/wp-content/uploads/publications/ipi_e_pub_un_intervention_brigade_rev.pdf.

[125] See, e.g., UN News Center, 'Kosovo: UN to Create Trust Fund, Following Panel Report on Alleged Rights Violations by Mission' (26 May 2017), available at www.un.org/apps/news/story.asp?NewsID=56852#.WTAHityZSM8 (discussing how '[t]he [UN Security] Council created a UN peace enforcement mission in Mali, MINUSMA, which has a robust use of force mandate. . . just a few weeks after [it created] the DRC Intervention Brigade, ... [which] seems to indicate an ongoing evolution (revolution?) in UN peacekeeping').

[126] Ilyshev, 'The UN Force Intervention Brigade in DR Congo' 2016 (n. 117), 147.

[127] Ibid., 148. [128] Ibid., 146–7.

[129] Cammaert and Blyth, 'The UN Force Intervention Brigade in the Democratic Republic of the Congo' 2013 (n. 124), 1.

[130] R. Gladstone, 'UN Peacekeepers Must "Not Fear to Use Force", Report Recommends', *New York Times* (23 January 2018), A8. See also, Ilyshev, 'The UN Force Intervention Brigade in DR Congo' 2016 (n. 117), 149.

[131] 'Democratic Republic of Congo: Stabilisation Agenda at Risk', *Africa Research Bulletin: Political, Social, & Cultural Series*, 51 (2015), 20393–5, 20393–4; see also

purpose of authorizing the creation of the FIB.[132] In a grim incident with overtones of the UN's failure in Rwanda in 1994, 'the Congolese army halted its operation against ADF [militants] in the vicinity of Beni in the unjustified expectation that the sheer presence of the [B]rigade in that area would make militants stop attacking civilians'.[133] The ADF carried out retaliatory killings of several hundred civilians.[134] Increasing the amount of military force employed has been generally counter-productive.[135] Peacekeeping Missions are increasingly characterized by failure, and, yet, Secretary-General Guterres's adviser demands that the UN respond to failure by acting still more 'aggressively'.[136]

The arguments for using greater force and for relaxing UN Charter rules to permit it seem to be made on the basis of the false assumption that force is effective for achieving protection of human rights, democracy, and other desiderata.[137] Rather than relax the law against violence, strengthening and extending it will support the use of alternative solutions. Rather than 'paralysing' states or the Security Council, the limits on force channel action into non-violent and more potentially successful avenues.

Cammaert and Blyth, 'The UN Force Intervention Brigade in the Democratic Republic of the Congo' 2013 (n. 124), 9.

132 SC Res. 2098 of 28 March 2013, para. 12(a); 'Stabilisation Agenda at Risk' 2015 (n. 131), 20394 (quoting Jason Stearns, director of the Congo Research Group at New York University); Cammaert and Blyth, 'The UN Force Intervention Brigade in the Democratic Republic of the Congo' 2013 (n. 124), 9.

133 Ilyshev, 'The UN Force Intervention Brigade in DR Congo' 2016 (n. 117), 150.

134 Ibid., 149.

135 Cammaert and Blyth, 'The UN Force Intervention Brigade in the Democratic Republic of the Congo' 2013 (n. 124), 8.

136 See Gladstone (n. 130) and Müller (n. 117), 360.

137 See, e.g., D. Bethlehem, 'Self-Defense Against an Imminent or Actual Armed Attack by Nonstate Actors', *American Journal of International Law*, 106 (2012), 770–7 (advocating a significant expansion of the right to resort to major military force in the counter-terrorism context); L. Feinstein and A.-M. Slaughter, 'A Duty to Prevent', *Foreign Affairs*, 83 (January/February 2004), 136–50 (advocating that organizations in addition to the Security Council have the power to authorize military intervention for such purposes as arms control); M. J. Glennon, 'The New Interventionism: The Search for a Just International Law', *Foreign Affairs*, 78 (May/June 1999), 2–7 (advocating a greater right to use military intervention for 'humanitarian' purposes by, for example, allowing NATO and other organizations to have the right to authorize military intervention in addition to the Security Council).

The problem of cyber security may finally demonstrate the limits of military force in a way that humanitarian intervention and intervention for democracy and arms control have failed to do so far. While diligent attempts are being made to cast cyber space as battlespace and to find the law governing the use of military force, both *jus ad bellum* and *jus in bello*, as somehow applicable, the reality is that the use of the internet is as a device for communication and commerce.[138] When governments deploy so-called 'cyber weapons,' they destroy or steal property. If computer code is linked to a means of doing kinetic damage, the line has been crossed to military force and the realm of the Security Council. The Council is only likely to respond when malicious physical damage appears. Cyberattacks on Estonia and Iran are examples of the limits to the Security Council's role. Cyber problems, like terrorism, are better left to law enforcement. What the world needs now is not attenuated arguments to fit cyber or terrorist attacks into the category of war but, rather, an international body to complement the Council for international cooperation on law enforcement. Interpol needs to become a true global law enforcement agency.

The lessons of the post-Cold War period respecting the Security Council include two: return to first principles for the Council and create new processes for the global problems that do not fit the Council's remit. The Russian use of force in Ukraine and ongoing occupation of Crimea underscore these lessons. The Cold War ended with the Security Council acting unanimously and effectively to counter a clear and egregious act of aggression by Iraq against Kuwait. Twenty-three years to the month after that success for law and process against war, Russia moved into Crimea and supported secessionist movements in Eastern Ukraine. In the long history

[138] See the two sides represented during thirteen years of debate over cyber governance at the United Nations. One side was led by the USA and UK; the other by Russia, China, and Cuba. O. Bowcott, 'Dispute along Cold War Lines Led to Collapse of UN Cyberwarfare Talks', *Guardian* (23 August 2017), available at www.theguardian.com/world/2017/aug/23/un-cyberwarfare-negotiations-collapsed-in-june-it-emerges. The debate broke down over the fundamental dispute regarding whether Article 51 of the UN Charter applies to cyberattacks. The US-UK side was adamant that it does. Russia and its partners objected that the US-UK position was based on interest in using conventional military attacks to respond to cyberattacks. The Russian side pointed out that this misconceived the nature of cyberspace. For more on self-defence, see Chapter 4.

since the drafting of the Charter, this is a rare attempt to take territory from a UN member state.

The explanation has multiple, complex aspects. One critical factor is the weakening of respect for the prohibition on the use of force through the many experiments in using force of the post-Cold War era. To have a successful act of aggression perpetrated in 2014 is a critical indication of the need for reform. While the USA has been involved in more unlawful uses of force than any other state since the end of the Cold War, with the post-Cold War period ending and new political trends emerging, it is surely in the interest of the USA and all states to rekindle respect for the prohibition on force. The very arguments NATO states used to attempt to justify the intervention in Kosovo have been used by Russia with respect to Ukraine.

## III A New Emphasis on Legal Process

With this understanding of the substantive legal framework and actual experience of the Council in mind, a picture of the Council for the future comes into focus. The way forward for the Security Council as an institution for maintaining the peace is through re-emphasizing the legal framework around Council action.

### *A The Value of Council Law Compliance*

Proposals for Security Council reform abound. They typically incorporate plans to expand membership or alter the veto right.[139] Greater representation and participation are well-known answers to governance issues. In the case of the Security Council, however, such proposals conflict with the legal and political reality that without Permanent Member agreement, the membership of the Council cannot change. The Permanent Members control the process of legal change through the veto.[140] They can be expected to continue to block proposals for enlargement or other changes that might dilute their special status.[141] Law offers another way to control

[139] See notes 32–48 and accompanying text. [140] Arts. 108, 109(2) UN Charter.

[141] France did issue a statement in favour of Security Council expansion to include its EU partner Germany. Permanent Mission of France to the United Nations, 'France and the UN Reform', 26 March 2018, available at https://onu.delegfrance.org/France-and-the-UN-Reform-8615. The other four Permanent Members do not support expansion, however, as France knows, and France

institutions besides membership and elections to membership. It is the procedural law that governs institutional action. Promoting respect for the law not only offers a viable way to reform the Council, it is a realizable approach given that the very status of Council members is based on a legal arrangement.

Respect for the law of the Charter is the basis of Security Council power. When members carry out Security Council mandates to impose economic measures or other actions, it is owing to the sense of legal obligation. Renewing the understanding of the international law governing Security Council action supports what Council members want: prestige, and what the international community wants: an institution that works on their behalf using lawful methods to achieve peace. As Anne Peters explained eloquently:

> Interrelated considerations of legitimacy and effectiveness suggest acknowledging legal limits for the Security Council. The Council's behaviour is morally consistent and thus credible only if the Council itself satisfies the standards it imposes on its members. … Members are likely to comply with what they perceive as lawful decisions. If one does not concede to the members the authority to contest a flagrantly illegal act of the Council with legal arguments, they will try to sneak out secretly, and simply obstruct Security Council resolutions.[142]

In a perceptive analysis of why states continue to defer to the Council's authority respecting the use of force, Nico Krisch writes that 'we can observe a convergence of interests of most states around upholding, as a minimum, a strong anti-interventionist norm with the Security Council at its centre. Given this convergence, there are few coordination problems in defending this norm against revisionist powers, and its relative strength is thus not surprising.'[143] He makes a possible exception for humanitarian intervention but that was in 2006. Today, consensus appears strong that use of force for such reasons require Security Council authorization for the very fact that it is a subjective standard that needs to be adjudicated in the appropriate legal process. The fact that of the

does not support the types of reforms that the others would support, such as stepping aside in favour of an EU seat. See also note 18.

142 A. Peters, 'Article 25', in B. Simma *et al.* (eds.), *The Charter of the United Nations: A Commentary* 3rd edn (Oxford: Oxford University Press, 2012), 787–854, 810.

143 N. Krisch, 'The Security Council and the Great Powers', in Lowe *et al.*, *The United Nations Security Council and War* 2008 (n. 10), 133–53, 149.

three states that engaged in air strikes in April 2018, only the UK cited humanitarian intervention is an exceptional case that tends to prove the point. Despite this relatively positive conclusion, Krisch also notes that the foundations of Council authority are 'shaky'.[144] Given the consensus in the world around Security Council authority, it is in the interest of all to shore up those foundations through demanding compliance with the relevant international law by all Council members all of the time.

How to achieve this renewal of commitment to the law is a task of legal education. A component of legal education includes understanding the social problem the law is addressing. Two concrete problems include the declining respect for the Council at a time when the international community needs a powerful institution for peace. Another problem is related to the first. As seen throughout Part II of this chapter, Security Council departures from the law are linked to failure to keep the peace.

The Security Council's moves from peacekeeping to peace enforcement to intervention, for example, have failed. By contrast, traditional peacekeeping, has worked and can work again. Traditional peacekeeping worked because it involved all the parties to a conflict. The parties, the UN, and other partners worked for ceasefires and obtained consent before sending neutral and impartial troops in blue helmets. Consent is needed in cases where the Security Council needs to reach unanimous agreement. Rather than see the veto as an obstacle, it can motivate a more appropriate solution.[145] The key is to follow the law.

The Security Council has extraordinary power – Article 25 requires UN members to carry out Council orders. The Council has authority to override otherwise applicable treaty obligations of member states.[146] The Council's power is, as just set out, a special type of power – legal power. Wartime realities led to acceptance that five states would have privileges, even beyond the privileges bestowed on four states in the League Council, but military strength remains today only a dim background reason that the vast majority of UN members accept the binding nature of UN Security Council mandates. Most members have no fear they will be subject to

144 Ibid., 147. 145 Chapter 6.

146 Lowe *et al.*, *The United Nations Security Council and War* 2008 (n. 10), 37 (citing Art. 103 and Lockerbie).

Council coercion. The Council's power rests, therefore, principally on the respect members pay to it. The UK wants Iran to comply with Security Council mandates respecting its nuclear programme. Yet, the UK arrogates to itself the decision that attacking Syria is permissible on an exceptional basis.[147] Such reasoning can only undermine the role of the Council in the critical duty of maintaining the peace. The value of complying with this law should be self-evident. Beyond the more intangible benefits of law compliance, failing to adhere to the law governing resort to armed force has been linked to failure in accomplishing the very purpose of using force.

### *B The Full Sweep of the Law*

The law relevant to the Council in the maintenance of peace begins with the peremptory prohibition on the use of force. This fact is rarely mentioned in discussions of the law on the use of force, the role of *jus cogens* vis-à-vis unilateral resort to force, or the law governing the Security Council and the use of force. Plainly, it needs to be discussed for a full understanding of norms relevant to the Council. The Security Council is also bound, of course, by the Charter. The lively debate that went on for some decades about how far the Council is in fact bound appears to be mostly settled, owing to one point about *jus cogens* that has appeared in the literature: the Security Council may not authorize the violation of a peremptory norm. Finally, the Council is also required to comply with general principles, especially necessity and proportionality. Some authors once expressed doubt about this, but the doubt rested on a narrow view of general principles.

'The prohibition of the use of force by States undoubtedly forms part of *ius cogens*.'[148] This proposition, the main subject of Chapter 2, enjoys wide consensus. A certain amount of skepticism remains that a principle with exceptions should be treated as absolute and non-derogable.[149] The view here, as explained in Chapter 2, is that self-defence is part of what constitutes the prohibition on the use of force. So is Security Council authorization.

[147] See notes 2–9 and accompanying text.

[148] A. Orakhelashvili, *Peremptory Norms in International Law* (Oxford: Oxford University Press, 2008), 50.

[149] Chapter 2.

The narrow allowance for the Council to permit the use of force to respond to breaches of the peace is part of the prohibition on the use of force. It is the enforcement provision. Law against murder includes an exception for police use of force to save a life from being taken unlawfully.

Sir Elihu Lauterpacht, sitting as judge ad hoc in the *Bosnia* v. *Serbia* case, helped create the widespread understanding that the Council is not only bound by relevant general international law but by *jus cogens*: '[O]ne only has to state the proposition thus – that a Security Council Resolution may even require participation in genocide – for its unacceptability to be apparent.'[150] Judge Weeramantry made a more general point in the same case. He looked to the history of the UN Charter for evidence that Security Council powers 'must be exercised in accordance with well-established principles of international law'.[151] The International Criminal Tribunal for Yugoslavia also found it 'clear ... that the Security Council plays a pivotal role and exercises a very wide discretion ... But this does not mean that its powers are unlimited ... In any case, neither the text nor the spirit of the Charter conceives of the Security Council as *legibus solutus* (unbound by law).'[152] The weight of authority is today on the side of seeing the Security Council as clearly bound by law beyond the Charter,[153] which includes *jus cogens*.

The argument for interpreting the Charter as leaving the Security Council unfettered in peace and security matters is based principally on the lack of any express provision listing restrictions. The argument gained support from the International Court of Justice's advisory opinion on Namibia. The ICJ cited a statement

[150] ICJ, *Application of the Convention on the Prevention and Punishments of the Crime of Genocide* (*Bosnia and Herzegovina* v. *Yugoslavia* (Serbia and Montenegro)), Provisional Measures, Order of 13 September 1993, Separate Opinion of Judge Lauterpacht, ICJ Reports 1993, 444, para. 100.

[151] ICJ, *Questions of Interpretation and Application of the 1971 Montreal Convention Arising from the Aerial Incident at Lockerbie* (*Libyan Arab Jamahiriya* v. *United Kingdom*), Provisional Measures, Order of 14 April 1992, Dissenting Opinion of Judge Weeramantry, ICJ Reports 1992, 65.

[152] ICTY, *Prosecutor* v. *Tadić (Jurisdiction) (Appeals Chamber)*, Decision of 2 October 1995, *International Law Reports* 105, 465, para. 28.

[153] This has been the position of all three editions of the Simma Commentary on the United Nations Charter. See B. Simma *et al.* (eds.), *The Charter of the United Nations: A Commentary* 2012 (n. 144), 818.

of the Secretary-General that '[T]he Members of the United Nations have conferred upon the Security Council powers commensurate with its responsibility for the maintenance of peace and security. The only limitations are the fundamental principles and purposes found in Chapter I of the Charter.'[154] Chapter I, Article 1(1) includes as a purpose of the UN bringing 'about by peaceful means, and in conformity with the principles of justice and international law, adjustment or settlement of international disputes'. Article 1(1) could be seen as linking 'conformity' with international law as a requirement of settlements reached to end international disputes rather than general action by the Security Council. The argument seems to ignore the terms of Article 24, however. Article 24(2) of the Charter states that 'in discharging [its] duties the Security Council shall act in accordance with the Purposes and Principles of the United Nations'. Chapter I sets out the purposes and principles, including in Article 1(1) conformity with international law.[155]

The fact that international law includes the prohibition on the use of force leads to clear implications for Council action. Derogation is not permissible and that includes attempts to legalize uses of force beyond the Charter's terms respecting self-defence and Security Council authorization. The Charter represents a move to create a more robust prohibition on the use of force. Including the prohibition in positive law has had that effect. Narrowing the right of self-defence to response to an armed attack also supports the prohibition. The changes fit the doctrine of *jus cogens* because they are not derogations. They are expansions of the reach of the prohibition. To reverse the direction and to create broader rights to use force would be to derogate. Thus, the proper interpretation of Security Council authority is not toward expansion but rather limitation.

The Security Council may authorize resort to force if there is a threat to the peace, breach of the peace, or act of aggression. States acting without Security Council authorization may only use force in individual and collective self-defence. Clearly, the Council may respond to a wider variety of concerns, so long as it does not

[154] ICJ, *Legal Consequences for States of the Continued Presence of South Africa in Namibia (South West Africa) Notwithstanding Security Council Resolution 276 (1970)*, Advisory Opinion of 21 June 1971, ICJ Reports 1971, 52, para. 110.

[155] B. Simma *et al.* (eds.), *The Charter of the United Nations, A Commentary* 2nd edn (Oxford: Oxford University Press, 2002), 52.

authorize force. In fact, in contrast to the unilateral use of force, UN members have not sought to expressly expand the Security Council's authority. One possible example concerns the references to the use of force to respond to humanitarian crises in the World Summit Outcome document. These vague references, however, can and should be interpreted consistently with the Security Council's existing powers. The Council may respond to restore international peace in ways that will be effective. As the discussion of Libya makes clear, military force is rarely, if ever, the right solution to humanitarian crises, certainly not those crises posing no threat to international peace.

Nor is it the case that the Security Council may not act in such situations. It may authorize action short of a use of force that would violate the prohibition. Economic measures and other steps coordinated with the General Assembly are always open to the Council, so long as they respect human rights law. Indeed, many of the problems created in the area of counter-terrorism could have been avoided if the Council had taken human rights more seriously into account, not to mention coordination with the General Assembly. Countering terrorism has long been the job of the General Assembly, given that it is the sort of problem that responds best to programmes that support, for example, the rule of law. Military force in response to terrorist organizations and individual suspects has proven counter-productive in suppressing terrorism by being destructive of the rule of law, among other factors.

In addition to the Charter, general principles govern the Security Council. One author, however, has concluded that 'as a matter of hierarchy there are no general principles of law by which the Council must abide'.[156] The author relies on Akehurst for the view that general principles exist to fill gaps combined with Jennings's view that gaps in international law have become rare. The view of general principles taken here is not inconsistent with Akehurst and Jennings but reaches the opposite conclusion. The Security Council is bound. A principle such as necessity is part of the law regardless of its appearance in a treaty. It is not demonstrable through the process of customary international law. It is an inherent principle that must exist. The methods of treaty and custom do not produce such principles, leaving the need for

[156] Schweigman, *The Authority of the Security Council* 2001 (n. 55), 201.

a third source to explain the full set of legal principles. Positivists since Elihu Root have been uncomfortable explaining how general principles can exist in international law if not explainable as treaties and custom, but they accept the category. The difficulty lies with positivism, however, not general principles. The nature of general principles and other such issues can always be put to the International Court of Justice for an advisory opinion. The old concern that the Council should not be subject to judicial review is, at the least, no longer a matter of debate. The ICJ touches on Security Council authority often. Making use of the Court's advisory jurisdiction can signal the Council's understanding of the supremacy of law and the importance of institutions for peaceful settlement.[157]

The fact that the Council is governed by general principles needs to be raised more prominently. The Libya case demonstrates why.

[157] Security Council Report, 'In Hindsight: The Security Council and the International Court of Justice', 28 December 2016, available at www.securitycouncilreport.org/monthly-forecast/2017-01/in_hindsight_the_security_council_and_the_international_court_of_justice.php:

> The UN Charter envisioned a symbiotic relationship between the Security Council and the International Court of Justice (ICJ), the principal judicial organ of the UN. However, the Council has scarcely made use of the ICJ as an instrument, or 'tool', in the exercise of its responsibility for the maintenance of international peace and security. In its latest research report on the rule of law of 20 December 2016, Security Council Report examines the relationship between the Security Council and the ICJ, including options for enhancing that relationship to assist the Council in its work . . .
>
> To date, the Council has only recommended that states refer their dispute to the ICJ under Article 36(3) on one occasion, in the *Corfu Channel Case* – the first proceeding of the ICJ – when on 9 April 1947 in resolution 22 it recommended that Albania and the UK immediately refer their dispute to the Court. The resolution was adopted with eight votes in favour and two abstentions, from Poland and the USSR, while the UK, as a party to the dispute, abstained from voting in accordance with Article 27(3) of the Charter. Similarly, the Council has requested only one advisory opinion from the Court, on 29 July 1970 in resolution 284, when it asked for an advisory opinion on the legal consequences for states of South Africa's continued presence in Namibia. As for non-compliance, the Council has yet to use its powers under Article 94(2) to enforce a judgment. However, one attempt to have the Council exercise that authority was when Nicaragua requested, in a letter to the president of the Council on 17 October 1986, an emergency meeting to consider the failure of the US to execute the ICJ's judgment of 27 June 1986 against it in the *Military and Paramilitary Activities in and against Nicaragua Case.* The US vetoed a draft resolution calling for full and immediate compliance with the ICJ judgment on 28 October 1986.

See also Chapter 6 of this Volume.

So do Council resolutions sending under-resourced, poorly trained peace enforcement missions into war fighting situations. They will predictably fail to accomplish the Security Council's purpose. In some cases, the situation will be worse off. Authorizing such missions violates the principle of necessity.

This does not mean the Council stops acting. It does mean that in some cases the Council is legally bound to find alternatives to authorizing armed force. Traditional peacekeeping, economic sanctions, and initiatives undertaken with the General Assembly on the basis of recommendations rather than mandates are all available. In many cases these approaches will achieve better results than the use of force.

## Conclusion

The Security Council as a whole and individual members of the Council, especially the five Permanent Members, have much to gain or at the least to retain in taking a more robust stand in support of international law. When members defy the law or argue for self-serving, thin interpretations, it not only weakens the prohibition on the use of force, it retards attempts to build respect for law in other contexts. It weakens the very basis for the attractiveness of Permanent Member status. Preserving the sense of the importance of the Council is a political argument to encourage a new era of respect for law by the Permanent Members. The normative reason centres on the benefits for humanity from law compliance. Unlawful military intervention even to stop a tyrant's use of excessive force against peaceful demonstrators has counter-productive results. Diplomacy, targeted sanctions, positive incentives supporting good governance, and respect for the rule of law have all produced superior results at far lower costs, certainly over time.[158]

The use of military force by Permanent Members of the Security Council in defiance of the law sends a message that disrespect of the law is acceptable. The United States, Britain, and Australia claimed to be enforcing Security Council resolutions when they invaded Iraq in 2003, yet the other Permanent Members and a majority of rotating members all agreed the Council had not authorized the invasion.[159] The rhetoric around a possible attack on Syria in 2013

[158] See notes 104–41 and accompanying text.
[159] See notes 101–3 and accompanying text.

and actual attacks in 2017 and 2018, have been even more counter-intuitive. In order to enforce the Chemical Weapons Convention, military force has been used without Security Council authorization. Not only does such argumentation defy common sense, it flies in the face of evidence reviewed above of so many uses of military force in violation of law that have failed.

The results of such interventions demonstrate how inappropriate the use of military force is to advance complex social goals such as promoting the rule of law, enforcing treaty obligations, protecting human rights, achieving arms control, or establishing effective government institutions. Social science research indicates that the unlawful use of force fuels a cycle of violence by encouraging resort to further violence rather than using non-lethal mechanisms for change. The fact that doctors, teachers, farmers and others in Syria in 2012 believed they could remove the government of Assad by taking up arms only makes sense if they believed they would attract the assistance of NATO as their counterparts in Libya and Kosovo did. The hope of outside military intervention helps account for the turn away from non-violence.[160]

Rebuilding commitment to non-violence can begin with reform of the Security Council. This chapter has proposed three avenues of reform. The Council can lead by example, scrupulously following the international law governing the use of force. The Council can adhere faithfully to the Charter, which privileges peaceful settlement over authorizing offensive force. Most importantly, the Security Council can reject Realist ideology with its focus on militarism over legalism.

The 2017 report to the Secretary-General on the crisis in peacekeeping demonstrates tangibly and dramatically Realism's irrational and destructive impact.[161] The report insists that the way to cure peacekeeping is to use more offensive force, not less. The author concedes increasing the use of offensive force will

[160] E.g., A. J. Kuperman, 'The Moral Hazard of Humanitarian Intervention: Lessons from the Balkans', *International Studies Quarterly*, 52 (2008), 49–80, 50–1; T. W. Crawford and A. J. Kuperman (eds.), *Gambling on Humanitarian Intervention: Moral Hazard, Rebellion and Civil War* (Abingdon: Routledge, 2006).

[161] C. A. dos Santos Cruz, *Improving Security of United Nations Peacekeepers: We Need to Change the Way We Are Doing Business* (19 December 2017), https://peacekeeping.un.org/sites/default/files/improving_security_of_united_nations_peacekeepers_report.pdf.

require more money and more troops at the very moment UN members appear highly unlikely to contribute more of either. The author seems unable to see the world through a different lens. The aesthetic philosophy of peace through law points back to traditional peacekeeping. Traditional peacekeeping is lawful, less expensive, and more successful than post-Cold War peace enforcement. Getting there will require weakening the hold of Realism. Weakening the hold of Realism on the Security Council could have the added benefit of loosening Realism's deep influence in the other use of force topics of concern in this book, including self-defence, the topic of the next chapter.

# 4

# The Limited Exception for Self-Defence

On 3 March 2014, at United Nations Headquarters in New York, Ukraine's interim government representatives presented evidence of 16,000 Russian troops entering Crimea in the previous days. US Secretary of State John Kerry declared the Russian action an act of aggression. Ukraine activated reserve units and requested military assistance from the United States and European states.[1] Ukraine was told, however, not to risk an armed confrontation with Russia.[2] On 15 March, pro-Russian Crimeans declared the province independent, then held a hastily organized referendum to say yes or no to joining the Russian Federation.[3] The outcome heavily favoured joining. On 18 March, Russian President Vladimir Putin announced that Russia had annexed Crimea.[4] One week later, Ukrainian troops withdrew from the peninsula.[5]

1 A. Smale and S. Erlanger, 'Ukraine Mobilizes Reserve Troops, Threatening War', *New York Times* (1 March 2014), available at www.nytimes.com/2014/03/02/world/europe/ukraine.html. See also, M. E. O'Connell, 'The Crisis in Ukraine–2014', in T. Ruys, O. Corten and A. Hofer (eds.), *The Use of Force in International Law: A Case-Based Approach* (Oxford: Oxford University Press, 2018), 855–72.

2 J. Rogin and E. Lake, 'US Told Ukraine To Stand Down as Putin Invaded', *Bloomberg View* (21 August 2015), available at www.bloomberg.com/view/articles/2015–08-21/u-s-told-ukraine-to-stand-down-as-putin-invaded.

3 'Crimea Referendum: Voters "Back Russia Union"', *BBC* (16 March 2014), available at www.bbc.com/news/world-europe-26606097.

4 'Ukraine Profile – Timeline', *BBC* (5 June 2018), available at www.bbc.com/news/world-europe-18010123.

5 C. Phipps and B. Quinn, 'Ukraine Pulls Forces Out of Crimea as Russia Takes Over Military Bases', *Guardian* (24 March 2014), available at www.theguardian.com/world/2014/mar/24/ukraine-crimea-russia-military-bases-live.

As these events were unfolding, reports emerged of an armed Russian presence in the Donbass region of eastern Ukraine apparently supporting pro-Russia separatist militias there.[6] By July, Ukrainian armed forces were on the verge of defeating these militias when significant additional Russian military assistance arrived.[7] Ukrainian forces began to suffer losses and Russian forces threatened to move beyond the Donbass to central Ukraine. Officials in Kiev reached a ceasefire with the militias and with Russia in September. The agreement, known as Minsk I, lasted about a week before fighting resumed. By January 2015, the fighting was again heavy. In February, German Chancellor Angela Merkel and French President François Hollande worked to broker a new agreement, Minsk II, between Ukraine and Russia with the Organisation for Security and Co-operation in Europe (OSCE) in a monitoring role. Minsk II envisaged extensive decentralization for Luhansk and Donetsk, as well as regional elections. By January 2018, fighting had resumed, and Minsk II was all but dead.

Explanations of why the Russia–Ukraine conflict erupted in 2014 are complex. Among them are:

> the decline of the normative and legal order that was established during the Cold War and reinforced in the years immediately following its end. The core of this order is found in the UN Charter, especially Chapter VI on the peaceful resolution of disputes, which provides clear, legally binding principles about the non-use of force to settle international disputes and respect for the territorial integrity of all UN member states. In Russia's view, the West has violated these principles especially in the 1999 attack on Serbia over Kosovo, which Moscow interprets as the West invalidating its own commitment to these legal principles.[8]

A thesis of this book is that the prohibition on the use of force endures even in the face of contrary state practice. The *jus cogens*

6 'Donbass' refers to the Donetsk River Basin, which is found in the eastern Ukrainian provinces of Donetsk, Luhansk, and Kharkiv. Two groups have proclaimed independence, the Donetsk People's Republic (DPR) and Luhansk People's Republic (LPR).

7 'Downing of Passenger Airliner by Separatists', *Keesing's Contemporary Archives* 60 (2014), 53477–8. 'Ukraine Crisis: "Column from Russia" Crosses Border', *BBC* (25 August 2014), available at www.bbc.com/news/world-europe-28924945.

8 P. T. Hopmann, 'Negotiating the Ukraine-Crimea Crisis', in F. O. Hampson and M. Troitskiy (eds.), *Tug of War: Negotiating Security in Eurasia* (Waterloo, Canada: Centre for International Governance Innovation, 2017), 101–116, 102.

nature of the prohibition means that regardless of persistent violations the principle remains valid and binding.[9] These features of *jus cogens* have important implications for the self-defence exception. Writers interested in expanding the legal right to resort to force have long looked to self-defence as the most promising avenue for broadening the legal right to use force.[10] The choice is understandable given that self-defence has been accepted as a right as long as resort to force has been restricted. The Charter contains a specific exception in Article 51, which not only allows for the use of force but permits self-judging by states acting unilaterally or in coalition with allies. Writers have used the permissiveness of Article 51 to argue for ever greater concessions. Their arguments have been countered by citing positive law.[11] This chapter adds to the positive law counter by considering self-defence as an integral part of the peremptory prohibition.[12]

As part of the peremptory prohibition and as an exception to a general rule prohibiting force, the situations in which self-defence

[9] Gray contrasts the 'hundreds of communications to the Security Council in which states claim to be the victims of armed attacks' on the basis of the standard legal criteria for the right of self-defence with the 'focus of writers on controversial cases' giving the impression that far-reaching claims of a right of self-defence are 'normal rather than exceptional'. C. Gray, *International Law and the Use of Force* 4th edn (Oxford: Oxford University Press, 2018), 123.

[10] See, e.g., D. W. Bowett, *Self-Defence in International Law* (New York: Frederick A. Praeger, 1958); J. Stone, *Aggression and World Order: A Critique of United Nations Theories of Aggression* (Sydney: Maitland Publications, 1958); C. Greenwood, 'International Law and the United States' Air Operation Against Libya', *West Virginia Law Review*, 89 (1987), 933–60; A. D. Sofaer, 'On the Necessity of Preemption', *European Journal of International Law*, 14 (2003), 209–26; D. Bethlehem, 'Self-Defense Against an Imminent or Actual Armed Attack by Nonstate Actors', *American Journal of International Law*, 106 (2012) 770–7; and A. S. Deeks, '"Unwilling or Unable": Toward a Normative Framework for Extraterritorial Self-Defense', *Virginia Journal of International Law*, 52 (2012), 483–550. See also notes 78–81 and accompanying text.

[11] Gray finds that at least until 9/11, 'few states claimed wide rights of self-defence'. Gray, *International Law and the Use of Force* 2018 (n. 9), 175. Henderson finds even well after 9/11 'little appetite for either formal *reform* of the rules or an extreme interpretation of them.' C. Henderson, *The Use of Force and International Law* (Cambridge: Cambridge University Press, 2018), 271–2. See also, generally, O. Corten, *Le Droit contre la Guerre* 2nd edn (Paris: Editions Pedone, 2014); and Y. Dinstein, *War, Aggression and Self-Defence* 5th edn (Cambridge: Cambridge University Press, 2012). For critical analysis of particular proposals for expanding the right to use force in self-defence, see notes 82, 96, and 106 and accompanying text.

[12] See Chapter 2 and notes 85–96 and accompanying text.

is permissible may shrink over time but not expand. As with the UN Security Council and its power to authorize force, the peremptory nature of the prohibition on the use of force sets the parameters for understanding self-defence. The very sizeable literature on self-defence tends to categorize self-defence as a positive law rule, giving rise to the view that it is open to expansion.[13] No one expects the Charter to be amended to allow more force. Instead, government officials and writers have attempted to re-interpret the Charter's terms. They have even solicited government statements to manufacture state practice and *opinio juris* – the elements of new customary rules – in their attempts to supersede the Charter's plain terms.[14]

A few writers have had considerable impact, such as Derek Bowett, who argued that the correspondence over the 1837 *Caroline* incident between Great Britain and the United States referenced a right to attack in self-defence if a prior attack is 'imminent'. Article 51, however, clearly requires that the right is triggered 'if an armed attack occurs'.[15] Understandably, states that have invested extraordinary resources in building massive militaries want the flexibility to use them. Governments are certainly under heavy pressure by the public to guarantee security and by industry to buy and use ever more products and services. Attacking other states sends a dramatic message of action and apparent power.[16] To date, government officials have also shown an interest in claiming the legal right to attack. Inevitably, however, when legal advisers always give yes for an answer to the question of legality, officials will see no point in asking the question.[17]

[13] Henderson, *The Use of Force* 2018 (n. 11), 271 (describing self-defence as a combination of treaty and customary international law).

[14] Kattan found evidence in WikiLeaks documents that US and UK officials set out to expand the right to use force through developing a new rule of customary international law. V. Kattan, 'Furthering the "War on Terrorism" through International Law: How the United States and the United Kingdom Resurrected the Bush Doctrine on Using Preventive Military Force to Combat Terrorism', *Journal on the Use of Force and International Law*, 5 (2018), 97–144, 114–17 note 110. This approach, at the least, conflicts with the treatymaking and amending process. See also Chapter 2.

[15] Bowett, *Self-Defence in International Law* 1958 (n. 10), 58–60, 142–4.

[16] See M. Zenko, 'America's First Reality TV War', *Foreign Policy*, (16 April 2018) (on Trump's decision to attack Syria in April 2018 being about a dramatic political gesture), available at http://foreignpolicy.com/2018/04/16/americas-first-reality-tv-war/.

[17] The decades of ever thinner arguments justifying the use force may have reached the vanishing point. Almost no attempt was made to justify the use of

This chapter tells a different story. It is one in which despite frequent violations of the limits on self-defence, those limits persist. Since the drafting of the UN Charter, scholars have regularly offered new interpretations that permit governments to use force in response to ever-changing factual situations.[18] This accommodationist legal reasoning has led to contempt for the law or at least confusion between law and policy. Lawyers have methodology that sets their discipline apart from policymaking and politics. The analysis here restates the exception for self-defence following, as appropriate, either positive or natural law methodology.

This restatement of the law of self-defence begins with a conceptual discussion of what self-defence means, and how it relates to the general prohibition on the use of force.[19] Self-defence, like the general prohibition, entered into international law as part of the Just War tradition. It was then codified in positive law, specifically as UN Charter Article 51.[20] Article 51 requires an armed attack, meaning it provides a more concrete limitation on force than was found in pre-Charter law. This development is consistent with the logic of *jus cogens*, which supports greater restriction of forbidden conduct over time, not less. The chapter's final part considers three topics long on the international security agenda that regularly feature in the arguments for expanding the right to resort to force in self-defence: the use of force against weapons programmes and weapons shipments, to rescue hostages, and to counter terrorism.[21]

force against Syria by the USA in 2017 or 2018 or by France in 2018. See, e.g., US President Donald Trump's and French President Emmanuel Macron's statements, 'President Trump on Syria Strikes', *New York Times* (13 April 2018), available at www.nytimes.com/2018/04/13/world/middleeast/trump-syria-air strikes-full-transcript.html; 'Statements by Theresa May and Emmanuel Macron on the Syria Strike', *New York Times* (13 April 2018), available at www.nytimes .com/2018/04/13/world/europe/theresa-mays-statement-on-the-syria-strike .html.

[18] See, e.g., Bowett, *Self-Defence in International Law* 1958 (n. 10); Stone, *Aggression and World Order* 1958 (n. 10); Greenwood, 'International Law and the United States' Air Operation Against Libya' 1987 (n. 10); Sofaer, 'On the Necessity of Pre-emption' 2003 (n. 10); and Bethlehem, 'Self-Defense Against an Imminent or Actual Armed Attack by Nonstate Actors' 2012 (n. 10).

[19] See notes 21–54 and accompanying text.

[20] See notes 70–4 and accompanying text.

[21] See notes 148–224 and accompanying text. In respect of this choice of topics, Gray concurs that these challenges to the law of self-defence have been particularly problematic to the integrity of the law: 'Thus the natural focus of writers on controversial cases where states invoke self-defence in protection of

## I The Nature of Self-Defence

'The right of self-defence' is a familiar phrase in international law. The actual legal meaning of self-defence is not as familiar. Invoking 'the magical reference' to Article 51 seems to suffice.[22] Self-defence 'is one of those vague and irreproachable abstractions like Justice, Truth, and Honour, which few attempt to define, let alone challenge'.[23] Since the end of the Cold War, those who wish to see the right to resort to force expanded have used these positive associations with self-defence to bolster their case.[24] The reality of using military force is often overlooked. Resort to armed force involves killing and destruction. It is permitted in narrow circumstances when the terms of Article 51 and other applicable international law restrictions are met.[25] Only a narrow right of self-defence is consistent with the international community's consensus moral principles on intentional killing.

'Self-defence' is a term of art in international law. The right of self-defence means the right to use major military force on the territory of a foreign sovereign state. It is more than the defensive action a state may take on its own territory. Because of what the right allows, it is narrow. The appropriate domestic analogy is to the rare time an individual may kill without punishment. Self-defence in both domestic and international law is permitted when halting an attack underway or responding just after an attack to stop the next one. In the case of international law, a state may retake territory occupied as a result of the initial unlawful use of force. If, however, the party attempting to retake territory has broken off the attempt for an extended period, measures other than force in self-defence

nationals, anticipatory or pre-emptive self-defence, and response to terrorism inevitably gives an unbalanced picture and distorts our perception of state practice; it helps to give the impression that the far-reaching claims of states like the USA and Israel are normal rather than exceptional.' Gray, *International Law and the Use of Force* 2018 (n. 9), 123.

[22] Gray, *International Law and the Use of Force* 2018 (n. 9), 175.

[23] M. A. Weightman, 'Self-Defense in International Law', *Virginia Law Review*, 37 (1951), 1095–115, 1095.

[24] The type of argument is, of course, not new, just the actual references to moral causes. In the Cold War, the Reagan Doctrine was associated with uses of force to promote democracy and capitalism. The Brezhnev Doctrine promoted Soviet-style communism.

[25] M. E. O'Connell, 'Lawful Self-Defense to Terrorism', *University of Pittsburgh Law Review*, 63 (2002), 889–908, 889–90.

even in the occupied territory may be required.[26] The key feature of the right of self-defence by states is using significant armed force against another state, beyond the defender's own territory. Defensive action not involving significant force is better referred to by other terms, such as intervention, retorsion, and countermeasures.[27]

Comparing the concept of self-defence in various legal systems yields three core features:

1 Self-defence is a permissible violent response to the use of unlawful violence. The purpose of self-defence is to prevent or end injury to a person or property.
2 The use of force in self-defence must be necessary, meaning the danger must be real and present. There must be no alternative to using force. The defence must be proportionate to the danger and 'cease when the danger ceases'.[28]
3 Self-defence is an exception to the prohibition on the use of force. The burden of proving the right of self-defence is on the party claiming it.[29]

The allowance for self-defence is for protection in the moment of attack, not to exact revenge, to send a message, to punish, or to secure longer-term protection through deterrence and the like. 'In essence, then, the right of self-defence ... is severely circumscribed.'[30]

[26] This is the import of the arbitral decision in the *Jus Ad Bellum* case between Ethiopia and Eritrea. Eritrea Ethiopia Claims Commission, *Ethiopia's Claims 1–8: Jus Ad Bellum,* Partial Award of 19 December 2005, Reports of International Arbitral Awards 26, 464–5, paras. 9–10. Ethiopia occupied territory belonging to Eritrea after the long years of civil war that finally ended with a separation of the two countries. Eritrea won an arbitral award respecting the boundary but has no right to retake by force the area awarded to it. The rule restricting force even in the event of retaking occupied territory would apply to North and South Korea, where the two sides have long respected a de facto border, as well as Ukraine and Russia respecting Crimea but not Eastern Ukraine.

[27] See Responsibility of States for Internationally Wrongful Acts, GA Res. 56/83 of 12 December 2001.

[28] These three points are a consolidation of the six points Weightman attributes to Giraud. Weightman, 'Self-Defense in International Law' 1951 (n. 23), 1097, citing Giraud, 'Le Théorie de la Légitime Défense', *Academie de Droit International: Recueil des Cours,* 3 (1934), 691–860.

[29] I. Brownlie, *International Law and the Use of Force by States* (Oxford: Clarendon Press, 1963), 214–15; and B. V. A. Röling, 'The Ban on the Use of Force and the UN Charter' in A. Cassese (ed.), *The Current Legal Regulation of the Use of Force* (Dordrecht: Martinus Nijhoff Publishers, 1986), 3–8, 4–5.

[30] Weightman, 'Self-Defense in International Law' 1951 (n. 23), 1097.

In Waldock's 1952 lectures on international law and the use of force at the Hague Academy, he expressed the view that '[t]here are few more important questions in international law than the proper limits of the right of self-defence'. He went on to explain the limited nature of the right and linked it to the domestic law concept:

> In the 19th century it was not infrequently said that States possessed an inherent right not simply of self-defence but of self-preservation. ... But a right of self-preservation is a much wider concept than a right of self-defence. It leads only too easily to the doctrine of necessity ... and the doctrine of necessity is a rejection of law. Self-preservation might allow one State to do a grave wrong to another on the plea of saving its own military, economic or political interests. It is a concept which cannot be kept within proper bounds ... In municipal law, ... it is only self-defence and not self-preservation which may justify an otherwise criminal use of violence against another person.[31]

Self-defence is a concept that can be kept within legal bounds, in contrast to self-preservation, because it is a response in the moment of objective danger – a real emergency. Self-preservation relates to challenges of a more diffuse or less immediate kind.

The limit on self-defence to responding in the moment is significant. Reacting after the danger has passed moves the action out of the category of self-defence. Once the immediate danger has passed a violent response becomes punitive rather than defensive and is properly designated a 'reprisal'.[32] For the Spanish Scholastic Vitoria, 'defence can only be resorted to at the very moment of the danger ... and so when the necessity of defence has passed there

[31] C. H. M. Waldock, 'The Regulation of the Use of Force by Individual States in International Law' in *Collected Courses of the Hague Academy of International Law* (Leiden: Martinus Nijhoff Publishers, 1951), 451–517, 461–2. But see Brownlie who considers that until 1920 the right of self-defence was identical to a right of self-preservation. Brownlie, *International Law and the Use of Force by States* 1963 (n. 29), 46.

[32] 'Reprisals ... can be considered as acts of forcible self-help, involving an unlawful use of force falling short of war, by one state in response to a prior violation of international law by another. "Armed reprisals" is the most suitable label for such actions ... [Reprisals aim] "at either impelling the delinquent state to discontinue the wrongdoing, or at punishing it, or both."' S. Darcy, 'Retaliation and Reprisal', in M. Weller (ed.), *The Oxford Handbook of the Use of Force in International Law* (Oxford: Oxford University Press, 2015), 879–96, 881–2. See also notes 91–6 and accompanying text.

is an end to the lawfulness of war'.[33] Self-defence is an emergency and temporary measure.

Augustine, known as the father of the Just War Doctrine, introduced the concept to persuade Christian communities to defend themselves from attack. Strict pacifist Christians were allowing members of a heretical sect known as the Donatists to use violence against them. The Donatists also claimed to be Christians but interpreted the scriptures differently. They heeded Christ's admonition to his followers to put away their swords.[34] The Donatists never used swords but did use clubs, bare fists, and other means to rob and beat those who would not defend themselves. Augustine found in the philosophy of Aristotle and the legal reasoning of Cicero that sometimes the only way to attain peace is to use force.[35] He retained the Christian emphasis on peace but taught that force in self-defence, to recover property, and to punish a wrong could be consistent with scripture.[36]

Augustine's inclusion of self-defence as the most important exception to Christian opposition to violence has evolved to the point that today force in self-defence is the only exception in the Catechism of the Catholic Church.[37] After Augustine, Just War teaching merged into international law with Grotius, who followed Aquinas and the Scholastics in including self-defence as a just cause of war.[38] He distinguished self-defence from other just causes as the one basis that would endure even if international law was no longer

[33] F. de Vitoria, 'On the Law of War', in J. B. Scott, E. Nys (eds.) and J. P. Bate (trans.), *The Classics of International Law: De Indis et De Ivre Belli Relectiones* (Buffalo: William S. Hein & Co, 1995), 163–87, 168.

[34] W. G. Grewe and M. Byers (trans./rev.), *The Epochs of International Law* (Berlin: Walter de Gruyter, 2000), 108.

[35] The Roman society of which Cicero was a part developed religious law known as the *jus fetiale* that restricted the lawful resort to force to a short list, including: in response to attacks on Roman territory, to violations of treaties, or to attacks on ambassadors. C. Phillipson, *International Law and Custom of Ancient Greece and Rome* 2 (London: MacMillan & Co, 1911), 315–48.

[36] 'Letter of Augustine to Boniface', in L. Friedman (ed.), *The Law of War: A Documentary History* I (New York: Random House, 1972), 7.

[37] Catechism of the Catholic Church, Part 3, sec. 2, ch. 2, art. 5(III), para. 2309, available at www.vatican.va/archive/ENG0015/__P81.HTM.

[38] H. Grotius, 'The Law of War and Peace (1646)', chap. 3, in J. B. Scott (ed.) and F. W. Kelsey (trans.), *The Classics of International Law* (New York: Oceana Publications, 1964); see also, Weightman, 'Self-Defense in International Law' 1951 (n. 23), 1099–100; Brownlie, *International Law and the Use of Force by States* 1963 (n. 29), 13; and G. I. A. D. Draper, 'Grotius' Place in the Development of Legal Ideas about War', in H. Bull, B. Kingsbury and A. Roberts (eds.), *Hugo*

needed in the event a supranational authority replaced the system of states.[39] Grotius took a more restrictive view of self-defence than some of his fellow Protestants. Gentili, for example, argued that self-defence could be stretched to permit a state to pre-emptively attack another to prevent the other from becoming too powerful: 'Do not all men with complete justice oppose on one side the Turks and on the other the Spaniards, who are planning and plotting universal dominion? ... [I]t is better to provide that men should not acquire too great power, than to be obliged to seek a remedy later ... '[40]

Grotius also extended his restrictive view to oppose rebellion by citizens against their own governments.[41] In this, at least, Grotius shared a view in common with the English political philosopher, and his contemporary, Thomas Hobbes.[42] An English political philosopher of a later period, John Locke, however, disagreed with Grotius and Hobbes, finding a compelling right to take up arms against a tyrannical government. For Locke, 'the right of self-defence in response to unlawful use of power by the political magistrate(s) is clear and absolute: citizens can defend themselves by means of force, if necessary'.[43] Locke plainly influenced the early American revolutionaries, later national liberation movements, and today's arguments for humanitarian intervention on behalf of armed opposition fighters.[44] Locke's focus, however, was the relationship between individuals and government. He was not focused on the problem that concerned Grotius, namely ending and avoiding the disastrous armed conflicts between European states as the Holy Roman Empire broke apart.[45]

*Grotius and International Relations* (Oxford: Clarendon Press, 1990), 177–207, 194.

39 Weightman, 'Self-Defense in International Law' 1951 (n. 23), 1099–100.

40 A. Gentili, 'De Jure Belli Libri Tres', in J. B. Scott (ed.) and J. C. Rolfe (trans.), *The Classics of International Law* (Buffalo: William S. Hein & Co, 1995), 64–5. Weightman, 'Self-Defense in International Law' 1951 (n. 23), 1101.

41 Grotius, *The Law of War and Peace* 1646 (n. 38), 103–111.

42 T. Hobbes, *Leviathan, or The Matter, Forme, & Power of a Common-wealth: Ecclesiasticall and Civill* (London: Andrew Crooke, 1651), 88–9.

43 K. Lidén and H. Syse, 'The Politics of Peace and Law: Realism, Internationalism, and the Cosmopolitan Challenge', in C. M. Bailliet and K. M. Larsen (eds.), *Promoting Peace Through International Law* (Oxford: Oxford University Press, 2015), 21–42, 29–30.

44 Chapter 5.

45 See generally J. Locke, *Two Treatises of Government and a Letter Concerning Toleration*, C. L. Sherman (ed.) (original 1689/1690) (New York: Appleton-Century-Crofts, 1937).

Not only was Locke concerned with a different level of social organization, he was mistaken to think that rebellion against government is a form of self-defence. What Locke urged is the offensive, not defensive, use of force. Arguments in favour of a right of oppressed people to take up arms and overthrow their governments or secede reflect the same erroneous understanding. A common example used to support this argument is the Warsaw Ghetto Uprising as both precedent for such a right and the need for it.[46] Those who organized against the Nazis in Poland were fighting a war of self-defence. They were local resisters against an invading foreign force. The comparison is inapposite to the case of people in Chechnya, Kosovo, Libya, or Syria who have created armed opposition forces against their own governments. Fighters in these more recent conflicts engaged in rebellion or insurrection, not self-defence except in an attenuated sense.[47]

The understanding that self-defence is a narrow right of interstate use of force analogous to personal self-defence against an attacker remained ascendant until the impact of the rise of science and the suppression of natural law. In the mid-eighteenth century, Vattel, in line with Gentili, began to question the possibility of law above sovereigns.[48] By the nineteenth century, European international law scholars were adopting the position that sovereignty is absolute, meaning the state was absolutely free 'from control by any higher power over its actions'.[49] Governments could enter into agreements that bound them through consent, at least for such time as they continued to extend that consent. Non-consensual restrictions, such as those found in the Just War Doctrine, simply cannot bind as law and were increasingly viewed as moral or religious concepts only. Without a general restriction on resort to war, no state needed the exception of self-defence to justify armed action against another state.

As a discussed already in previous chapters, the Just War Doctrine as part of international law never disappeared entirely.[50] Just War

[46] See, e.g., J. A. Hessbruegge, *Human Rights and Personal Self-Defense in International Law* (Oxford: Oxford University Press, 2017), 312–13, 333.

[47] Chapter 5.

[48] E. de Vattel, *The Law of Nations* (London: G. G. and J. Robinson, 1797), lxiii.

[49] Weightman, 'Self-Defense in International Law' 1951 (n. 23), 1102.

[50] See M. E. O'Connell, 'The Just War Tradition and International Law against War: The Myth of Discordant Doctrines', *Journal of the Society of Christian Ethics*, 35 (2015), 33–51, 38. A. Tischer, *Offizielle Kriegsbegründungen in der Frühen*

restrictions were challenged certainly by writers on the ground that these restrictions could only be explained by natural law. States agreed to the first general positive law restriction on resort to force at the 1899 Hague Peace Conference.[51] Prior to the adoption of positive law, interestingly, anti-natural law writers did not simply abandon the Just War Doctrine in favour of a completely unrestricted right to resort to war. Instead, they introduced ever more liberal rights to use force. It was a gradual move away from international law limits. Scholars such as Hall, Wheaton, and Lawrence offered new concepts in place of restrictive self-defence, concepts like 'self-preservation' and 'self-help'.[52] These 'profligate' doctrines were nearly the same as saying states faced no restrictions since almost any concern could be put forward as a ground for the exercise of self-preservation.[53] Inevitably, the scholars offering these ideas thought in terms of a single state – usually their own – and its prerogatives. They failed to consider, in a foreshadowing of current times, how such open-ended rights could work in a multistate system. 'If State A may justify an attack upon State B on the grounds of self-preservation, then what has happened to State B's right of self-defence?'[54] An unrestricted or even just a broad right of self-defence results in no viable legal prohibition on the use of force and that situation conflicts with the very possibility of law at the interstate level.

In distinction to the anti-natural law scholars of the nineteenth century, government officials, who had to deal with other governments, retained a restrictive understanding of self-defence. British and American officials exchanged correspondence between 1838 and 1842 over the destruction in 1837 by British forces of an American vessel named the *Caroline*.[55] Americans who supported a

*Neuzeit: Herrscherkommunikation in Europa zwischen Souveränität und korporativem Selbstverständnis* (Münster: LIT Verlag, 2012),22, 220; and H. Simon, 'The Myth of *Liberum Ius Ad Bellum*: Justifying War in 19th-Century Legal Theory and Political Practice', *European Journal of International Law*, 29 (2018), 113–36.

51 See J. L. Tryon, 'Hague Conferences', *Yale Law Journal*, 20 (1910–11), 470–85.

52 Weightman, 'Self-Defense in International Law' 1951 (n. 23), 1103.

53 Ibid., 1107. 54 Ibid., 1104.

55 See citations in n. 15 and documents related to the *Caroline* incident of 1837 produced by the American and British governments, which reflect detailed rules regulating the right of self-defence in a way that makes no sense unless self-defence is an exception to a prohibition on the use of force. See J. B. Moore, *Digest of International Law* 1 (Washington, DC: Government Printing Office, 1906), 680 *et seq*. See also, 'The Caroline', *The Avalon Project*, Lillian Goldman Law Library, Yale Law School, available at http://avalon.law.yale.edu/19th_cen

rebellion in Canada against the British government used the *Caroline* to smuggle weapons and materiel to rebels. British forces set the ship on fire while it was docked in the USA, then sent it over Niagara Falls. An unknown number of lives were lost. Official correspondence related to the incident demonstrates that both the USA and Britain recognized the existence of detailed rules of international law governing resort to force in self-defence. US Secretary of State Daniel Webster explained that the British had no right to destroy the *Caroline* because the ship did not present a danger that was 'instant, overwhelming, leaving no choice of means, and no moment of deliberation'. Webster added that even when resort to force is lawful it may not be 'unreasonable or excessive'. It is 'limited by ... necessity'.[56] Special Minister Lord Ashburton replied to Webster 'that we are perfectly agreed as to the general principles of international law applicable to this unfortunate case'.[57]

Positive law instruments related to the resort to and conduct of war began to appear by the middle of the nineteenth century. The 1856 Paris Declaration on Maritime Law contained regulations on the conduct of maritime warfare. It also outlawed privateering, the practice by governments of giving commissions to private persons to attack and rob ships of enemy states. The first of the Geneva Conventions devoted to protecting the victims of war was agreed in 1864. Peace campaigners were also active in this period promoting alternatives to resort to force to settle international disputes according to international law. The peace movement helped

tury/br-1842d.asp. For a detailed account of the incident itself, see J. E. Noyes, 'The Caroline: International Law Limits on Resort to Force' in J. E. Noyes, L. A. Dickinson and M. W. Janis (eds.), *International Law Stories* (New York: Foundation Press, 2007), chap. 9. See also R. Y. Jennings, 'The Caroline and McLeod Cases', *American Journal of International Law*, 32 (1938), 82–99; M. Wood, 'The Caroline Incident – 1837', in Ruys *et al.*, *The Use of Force in International Law* 2018 (n. 1), 5–14; and Brownlie, *International Law and the Use of Force by States* 1963 (n. 29), 42–4.

56 'The Caroline', *The Avalon Project* (n. 55), Webster Note to Ashburton, 24 April 1841.

57 'The Caroline', *The Avalon Project* (n. 55), Ashburton Note to Webster, 28 July 1842. On the importance of the correspondence to the contemporary understanding of necessity and proportionality in the law of self-defence, see O. Schachter, 'The Right of States to Use Armed Force', *Michigan Law Review*, 82 (1984), 1620–46, 1634–5.

persuade the American and British governments to settle a dispute over Britain's neutral duties during the US Civil War through the use of arbitration in 1872.[58] The United States won the case, and Britain paid $15 million in damages.

The most important early step toward codifying the prohibition on force came during the Hague Conferences of 1899 and 1907. The participants agreed to a good deal of new positive law on peaceful settlement of disputes, restrictions on resort to war, and on the conduct of armed conflict.[59] The next major development was the adoption of the Covenant of the League in 1919.[60] It required that states party to a dispute go to arbitration rather than resort to war. It further barred members of the League from going to war at all with another member of the League that had accepted the arbitral award. While not as extensive as the Just War Doctrine's prohibitions, it was an important development in the positive law.[61] The drafters of the Covenant saw no need to include an exception for self-defence.

A decade later, the United States wished to promote the prohibition of war as a matter of positive law despite the USA's failure to join the League. Secretary of State Frank Kellogg worked with his counterpart, French Foreign Minister Aristide Briand, to create the General Treaty for the Renunciation of War as an Instrument of National Policy, known as the Kellogg-Briand Pact.[62] The Pact was a dramatically simple statement rejecting war. After some discussion respecting its compatibility with the Covenant for members of the League, and whether the Pact was redundant for League members, most states concluded that the two anti-war documents were compatible.[63] Like the Covenant, the Pact was also silent as to self-defence.[64] Unlike the Covenant, the Pact's comprehensive

58 Grewe, *The Epochs of International Law* 2000 (n. 34), 518.

59 Tryon, 'Hague Conferences' 1910–11, 473–4 (n. 51), 479–81.

60 Covenant of the League of Nations, 28 June 1919, available at http://avalon.law.yale.edu/20th_century/leagcov.asp.

61 Weightman, 'Self-Defense in International Law' 1951 (n. 23), 1108.

62 The treaty is also known as the 'Pact of Paris' or, in France, the 'Briand-Kellogg Pact'. The complete text and list of signatories may be found at Yale's Avalon Project website, http://avalon.law.yale.edu/20th_century/kbpact.asp.

63 Brownlie, *International Law and the Use of Force by States* 1963 (n. 29), 246.

64 The US State Department's Office of the Historian offers this interpretation of the Pact with respect to self-defence: 'After the severe losses of the First World War, the idea of declaring war to be illegal was immensely popular in

prohibition on force raised the question whether it outlawed war in self-defence. To clarify this and 'following the lead of the United States, the signatory nations appended a series of notes which declared in more or less similar language that the "inherent" right of self-defence was unimpaired by the treaty. Why "inherent"? This can only suggest that self-defence is a natural right, i.e., one above and apart from rules, treaties, and conventions of positive international law.'[65]

The law was such that as Germany, Italy, and Japan prepared for wars of conquest, they invoked various versions of self-defence to justify their actions.[66] When the three formed an alliance, Hitler described it as 'an act of self-defence'.[67] During the war, Germany sought to justify attacks on Norway and the Low Countries as pre-emptive self-defence.[68] Imperial Japan argued it needed to secure vital natural resources, especially oil, through invasion and occupation. The claims of both states were rejected by the Tokyo and Nuremberg Tribunals. The high-ranking accused were found guilty of crimes against the peace for violating positive and natural law norms. No defendant successfully argued his state had lawfully exercised the right of self-defence.[69]

As the Nuremberg Charter was being drafted, the negotiations for the final version of the UN Charter were also underway. The Charter expressly re-establishes the link between self-defence and natural law. The English version of Article 51 includes the reference to 'inherent right'. In the French version the term is 'droit natural' – 'natural law'. Article 51 became the first positive law version of the right of self-defence in international law. At first, Article 51 could be understood as narrower than the positive law right. As discussed

international public opinion. Because the language of the pact established the important point that only wars of aggression – not military acts of self-defense – would be covered under the pact, many nations had no objections to signing it.' See https://history.state.gov/milestones/1921-1936/kellogg.

65 Ibid.

66 Joachim von Ribbentrop was indicted at Nuremberg for, among other crimes, his legal justification for the pre-emptive attacks on Norway, Denmark, and the Low Countries. International Military Tribunal (IMT), *Trial of the Major War Criminals Before the International Military Tribunal, Nuremberg*, 10 (14 November 1945–1 October 1946, 68–70); and R. W. Coakley, 'The War Against Japan in American Military History', in *United States Military History*, http://www.history.army.mil/books/amh/amh-23.htm, chap. 23.

67 Adolf Hitler, Speech to the German People (22 June 1941).

68 IMT, *Trial of the Major War Criminals* (n. 66). 69 Ibid.

throughout this book, however, once a wider scope of a *jus cogens* norm is discerned there is no going back. Article 51 is now the natural and positive law provision for self-defence. The purpose of including an express provision on self-defence was the 'necessity of preserving regional systems like the Inter-American one'.[70]

Recall that Article 51 was a late addition to the Charter. It was drafted and re-drafted in San Francisco to reach a version that would not weaken the new UN with competing bodies also possessing authority to authorize the use of force. Latin American countries in particular worried that the Treaty of Chapultepec – which promised mutual security aid – and the plan for the future Rio Treaty Organisation would violate the new Charter. Australia, too, raised concerns at Dumbarton Oaks, near Washington, DC, where the final preparatory talks were held prior to San Francisco. Would the Security Council react or react in time for the security of a place like Australia, considered to be remote by other UN members?[71] During the final conference, the US delegation worked diligently drafting and re-drafting a new provision that would allow regional organizations for mutual security while retaining the UN and the UN Security Council's supremacy. The British and Soviets were slow to accept the new article, but the US Secretary of State, Stettinius, explained that the US Senate would expect to see a provision for the inter-American system.[72] The final version of Article 51 was approved on 21 May 1945, after the Soviet delegation received approval from Moscow.[73] It remains unchanged:

> Nothing in the present Charter shall impair the inherent right of individual or collective self-defence if an armed attack occurs against a member of the United Nations, until the Security Council has taken measures necessary to maintain international peace and security. Measures taken by members in the exercise of this right of self-defence shall be immediately reported to the Security Council and shall not in any way affect the authority and responsibility of the Security Council under the present Charter to take at any time such action as it deems necessary in order to maintain or restore international peace and security.[74]

[70] *Documents of the United Nations Conference on International Organisation* 12 (1945), 680; and Weightman, 'Self-Defense in International Law' 1951 (n. 23), 1111.

[71] R. B. Russell, *A History of the United Nations Charter* (Washington, DC: Brookings Institution, 1958), 695–6.

[72] Ibid., 699. [73] Ibid., 702–3.

[74] English and French were the two original authentic languages of the Charter. It is helpful to compare the French version to the English version to understand

The most powerful military alliance in the world, the North Atlantic Treaty Organization (NATO) was founded in 1949. It is organized around the terms of Article 51, as Article 5 of the North Atlantic Treaty makes clear:

> The Parties agree that an armed attack against one or more of them in Europe or North America shall be considered an attack against them all and consequently they agree that, if such an armed attack occurs, each of them, in exercise of the right of individual or collective self-defence recognised by Article 51 of the Charter of the United Nations, will assist the Party or Parties so attacked by taking forthwith, individually and in concert with the other Parties, such action as it deems necessary, including the use of armed force, to restore and maintain the security of the North Atlantic area.
>
> Any such armed attack and all measures taken as a result thereof shall immediately be reported to the Security Council. Such measures shall be terminated when the Security Council has taken the measures necessary to restore and maintain international peace and security.[75]

The concept of self-defence extends to the right to use otherwise prohibited violence in the moment of danger to halt an attack underway or to prevent the next blow. It is a right at odds with the monopoly over violence legally restricted to governmental authorities within states, or the international community as a whole among states. Owing to this tension, the law permitting self-defence draws the right narrowly.

## II The Law of Self-Defence

As the case of NATO amply demonstrates, Article 51 succeeded in its intended role of permitting the establishment of regional security organizations while at the same time preventing those organizations from supplanting the Security Council or subverting the prohibition on the use of force in Article 2(4). That success may be fading as the UN and the Security Council appear to be in decline, and NATO, an organization designed to defend against

the meaning of both. See generally, J. L. Kunz, 'Privileges and Immunities of International Organizations', *American Journal of International Law*, 41 (1947), 828–62. It is worth noting, however, that Stassen likely drafted the original version in English.

75 Art. 5 North Atlantic Treaty, 4 April 1949, available at www.nato.int/cps/ic/natohq/official_texts_17120.htm.

the long-defunct Soviet Union, expands and moves away from its purpose as a collective self-defence organization. The USA tried to substitute NATO, as an organization of democratic states, for the UN Security Council in authorizing the use of force in the Kosovo crisis.[76] It tried something similar during the 1962 Cuban Missile Crisis, to be discussed below under the heading of self-defence and arms control.[77]

These examples are exceptions. For the most part, the USA and other Security Council members see the value of a Security Council with unique authority, as discussed in Chapter 3. The one remaining option for using force within the law is, therefore, Article 51. Governments and writers interested in expansive rights to use force began, soon after San Francisco, to treat Article 51 not as an exception to a general rule but as a licence, something equivalent to the Security Council's right to use force should the other tools at its disposal, such as terminating diplomatic relations and economic sanctions, prove inadequate. This trend seems to have begun, again, with Julius Stone, who took as his starting place not Article 2(4), but Article 51. Stone cast Article 51 as a permissive right allowing force in persuing justice, not a measure of last resort in response to armed attack.[78]

Stone's premise is that the world is a place of conflict and those who see the possibility of harmonious relations at the international level are deceiving themselves.[79] He championed liberalism within states and argued that liberal states are superior and deserving of preferential rights. Stone sought to support this position citing principles of sociology. He also used sociology as a justification for ignoring standard methodology. He dismissed, for example, the reference

[76] NATO engaged in fighting for the first time during the Kosovo crisis, which had nothing to do with collective self-defence of its members. The war not only violated the UN Charter, it was *ultra vires* the North Atlantic Treaty. M. E. O'Connell, 'The UN, NATO, and International Law after Kosovo', *Human Rights Quarterly*, 22 (2000), 57–89, 57. NATO also engaged in the 2011 Libya intervention, plainly exceeding the terms of the authorizing Security Council resolution, Resolution 1973, but also the limits of necessity and proportionality. See Chapter 3.

[77] See notes 155–61 and accompanying text.

[78] Stone, *Aggression and World Order* 1958 (n. 10), 43, 94–5, 181–3. See also Röling, 'The Ban on the Use of Force and the UN Charter' 1986 (n. 29), 4–5.

[79] J. Stone, 'A Sociological Perspective on International Law', in R. St. J. MacDonald and D. M. Johnston (eds.), *The Structure and Process of International Law: Essays in Legal Philosophy, Doctrine, and Policy* (Dordrecht: Martinus Nijhof, 1983), 264–303, 290–2.

to 'armed attack' in Article 51 and other restrictive language in the Charter as not in the interest of individuals who are at the centre of the reason states exist.[80] Stone argued further that because the Security Council was unable to take 'effective' collective measures, states were free to use force in self-defence as each judged appropriate.[81] Brownlie found Stone indulged in policy, not legal analysis,[82] and Stone's policy favoured the use of force for some but not all. Nevertheless, as discussed in Chapter 2, Stone's approach of re-interpreting the words of the Charter has been influential with those supporting classical legal interpretation: the 'realist–traditionalists' and those favouring expanding resort to force: the 'expansionists'.[83] This move to equivalence pervades scholarship on self-defence. The expanders see their approach as just as legitimate as the restrictionists, or more so. They see themselves as creatively interpreting the law to achieve security for human beings in light of changing realities. The approach is presented as fundamentally a moral one, which was Stone's own starting place.

The majority of restrictionists see the value of their position as grounded in the consensus around positivist methodology of international law. Positivism does impart greater objectivity in establishing rules, but also leaves the law governing self-defence vulnerable to the aims of expansionists. Expansionists promise greater personal security or protection of human rights if restrictive rules on use of force are relaxed to allow greater resort to force. These can be persuasive arguments that occlude the fact that *jus cogens* cannot be weakened with contrary state practice.[84]

[80] Stone gives 1951 as the date for his first public criticism of the standard interpretation of Article 2(4) as a general prohibition on resort to force. See J. Stone, 'Force and the Charter in the Seventies', *Syracuse Journal of International Law and Commerce*, 2 (1974), 1–17, 6, 13.

[81] Stone, *Aggression and World Order* 1958 (n. 10), 93–8.

[82] I. Brownlie, 'Recent Appraisals of Legal Regulation of the Use of Force', *International and Comparative Law Quarterly*, 8 (1959), 707–1, 708.

[83] C. Kress, 'Time for Decision: Some Thoughts on the Immediate Future of the Crime of Aggression: A Reply to Andreas Paulus', *European Journal of International Law*, 20 (2009), 1129–46, 1140 n. 42. See also Gray on 'wide' versus 'narrow' interpreters of the law on self-defence, Gray, *International Law and the Use of Force* 2018 (n. 9), 124–5.

[84] See, e.g., Gray, *International Law and the Use of Force* 2018 (n. 9), chaps. 4 and 5. Gray carefully catalogues developments toward ever looser treatment of self-defence restrictions. Her tone is consistently critical of these developments, but she is constrained by her positivist methodology in ultimately rejecting them

Article 51 is particularly vulnerable to these creative arguments because it permits self-judging. The references to 'armed attack occurs' and 'until the Security Council acts' were intended to cabin the discretion of victim states. Creative lawyers, however, have worked to weaken both limits. A number of those arguments are analysed here in the light of *jus cogens*. This shift in perspective reveals the flaws in the expansionist approach. It is an approach with a certain appeal, but fails to incorporate the moral and historic foundations of the legal regime of peace and humanity's broader consensus regarding the regime's object and purpose.

### A *General Aspects of Self-Defence Law*

By its plain terms, Article 51 provides only a narrow right of self-defence. It restricts the use of force in self-defence to situations where 'an armed attack occurs', and requires self-defence to be reported to the Security Council.[85] These terms are to be understood in the context of *jus cogens*. *Jus cogens* norms never shrink but may expand.[86] This means that the restrictive terms of Article 51 may not be superseded by state practice, let alone narrowed through interpretation.[87] Expansionists may attempt to assert interpretations that yield greater flexibility regarding force but good faith interpretation will not result in limiting the reach of a *jus cogens* norm.[88]

The approach to interpretation here would apply even if Article 2 (4) were not a peremptory norm. Article 51, as the negotiating history shows, was included in the Charter not as an exception to Article 2(4) but as an exception to the Security Council's sole authority to authorize uses of force. The Council's authority was initially conceived of as the only permissible exception to the prohibition on force because the Security Council would use a multilateral deliberative process, avoiding self-serving judgments by a

and concludes frequently 'it remains to be seen' whether this or that 'doctrine' of expansion will succeed. See, e.g., ibid., 261.

85 See, generally, M. E. O'Connell, C. Tams and D. Tladi, 'Self-Defense against Non-State Actors', in A. Peters and C. Marxsen (eds.), *The Max Planck Trialogues on Peace and War Series*, (Cambridge University Press, 2019).

86 Chapters 1, 2, and 3.

87 Art. 53 VCLT.

88 Brownlie, *International Law and the Use of Force* Cambridge: 1963 (n. 29), 214; and Röling, 'The Ban on the Use of Force and the U.N. Charter' 1986 (n. 29), 4–5.

state with a vested interest in using force. Article 51 was included to allow for an exception to the exception of Security Council authority. If exceptions to general rules are to be narrowly construed,[89] exceptions to exceptions must be yet more narrowly interpreted.[90] Exceptions are interpreted in light of the object and purpose of the primary rule, which is the prohibition on the use of force.

Another general aspect of self-defence – one also related to interpretation that is rarely discussed – is the requirement that the purpose of the force be defence. Article 51's armed attack requirement and the requirement of necessity both channel the right to strictly defensive purpose.[91] The requirement of defensive purpose helps explain why certain categories of armed force, such as reprisals, are per se unlawful. As discussed, 'self-defence' is a term of art in the law.[92] It refers to the use of force to respond in the moment of danger to force that is about to result or is resulting in death or physical injury.

Retaliatory attacks after the danger has passed and pre-emptive attacks before the danger is occurring are clearly prohibited by international law. Retaliation or reprisals are after-the-fact responses that do not fit the exception for self-defence.[93] Such

[89] Röling, 'The Ban on the Use of Force and the U.N. Charter' 1986 (n. 29), 4–5; and Introduction to this Volume.

[90] Several prominent American cases interpreting international law provide additional examples. In *Parsons & Whittemore Overseas Co Inc v. Societe Generale De L'Industrie Du Papier (RATKA)*, 508 F.2d 969, 973–974 (US 2d Cir. Ct. of Appeal 1974), the court narrowly applied the public policy exception in the United Nations Convention on the Recognition and Enforcement of Foreign Arbital Awards. In *Siderman de Blake v. Republic of Argentina*, 965 F.2d 699, 720 (US 9th Cir. Ct. of Appeal 1992), the court interpreted the waiver of sovereign immunity narrowly, which 'conforms to the general rule of a narrow construction of the exception'.

[91] S. A. Alexandrov, *Self-Defence against the Use of Force in International Law* (The Hague: Kluwer International Law, 1996), 17–18.

[92] See notes 22–75 and accompanying text.

[93] 'Few propositions about international law have enjoyed more support than the proposition that, under the Charter of the United Nations, the use of force by way of reprisals is illegal.' D. Bowett, 'Reprisals Involving Recourse to Armed Force', *American Journal of International Law*, 66 (1972), 1–36, 1. Bowett supports this conclusion by spending most of the article attempting to create a new justification for resort to reprisals. See, e.g., ibid., at 26–8. For an author who shares Bowett's interest in seeing a new exception for reprisals, see W. O'Brien, 'Reprisals, Deterrence and Self-Defense in Counterterror Operations', *Virginia Journal of International Law*, 30 (1990), 421–78. For a thorough rejection of the arguments in favour of lawful reprisals, see R. Barsotti, 'Armed Reprisals', in A. Cassese (ed.), *Current Legal Regulation of the Use of Force* (1986), 79–110. By 2018,

attacks were launched against Syria and the Islamic State in Syria in 2017 and 2018 by France, Iran, the United Kingdom, and the United States.[94] The attack on ISIS by Iran in 2017 was retaliation for terrorist killings in Tehran.[95] The General Assembly confirmed the illegality of armed reprisals in its 1970 *Declaration on Principles of International Law Concerning Friendly Relations and Cooperation among States*.[96] The General Assembly agreed that states have a 'duty to refrain from acts of reprisal involving the use of force' against other states.[97] The attacks by France, the UK, and the USA were to punish alleged chemical weapons use by the Syrian government. The attack by Iran was to avenge terrorist violence against its parliament.

States have also claimed a right to use force in self-defence in anticipation of an attack or to pre-empt an attack in both the arms control and terrorism contexts. These situations are the flipside of the reprisal case. They are equally unlawful for not responding to danger in the moment as well as for failing to comply with the restriction on using force only if an armed attack occurs.[98] Claims to be acting in anticipation of an armed attack have gained a good deal of support since the 9/11 attacks in the USA and will be discussed in more detail in the next section and later with respect to countering arms proliferation. All of these claims consistently fail to meet the conditions of lawful self-defence because they are rarely a defensive response to violence in the moment.

Gray found the law against reprisals unchanged. Gray, *International Law and the Use of Force* 2018 (n. 9), 160, 162, and 205.

94 H. Cooper, T. Gibbons-Neff, and B. Hubbard, 'US, Britain and France Strike Over Suspected Chemical Weapons Attack', *New York Times* (13 April 2018), available at www.nytimes.com/2018/04/13/world/middleeast/trump-strikes-syria-attack.html. J. Le Miere, 'Trump's Attack on Syria Killed Four Children, State News Agency Claims', *Newsweek* (7 April 2017, 11:10 am), available at www.newsweek.com/syria-attack-children-civilian-killed-580555.

95 S. K. Dehghan, 'Iran Targets "Terrorists" in Missile Strike on Isis-held Syrian Town', *Guardian* (18 June 2017, 6:25 pm), available at www.theguardian.com/world/2017/jun/18/iran-targets-terrorists-in-missile-strike-on-isis-held-syrian-town.

96 GA Res. 2625 (XXV) of 24 October 1970. 97 Ibid.

98 M. E. O'Connell, 'The Myth of Preemptive Self-Defense', ASIL Terrorism Task Force, 6 August 2002, available at www.nyccriminallawyer.com/wp-content/uploads/2014/07/oconnell.pdf.

### *B Specific Provisions of Article 51*

Article 51 has two objective conditions that must be met for the lawful use of force in self-defence. The requirements are armed attack and report to the Security Council. Both provisions serve the purpose of maintaining the supremacy of Article 2(4) and of the Council. The US delegation in San Francisco saw the phrase 'if an armed attack occurs' as permitting the narrowest right of self-defence possible while still permitting regional groups to organize for mutual security.

In 1984, Nicaragua brought a case in the International Court of Justice against the United States for the unlawful use of force on its territory. The ICJ judgment in the case remains the most important decision in international law on the use of force in self-defence. The court held for jurisdictional reasons it could not apply the Charter directly. It nevertheless found that the requirement of an armed attack is the *sine qua non* of the post-Charter right of self-defence.[99] The USA had attempted to defend its actions as collective self-defence with El Salvador in response to weapons shipments and other aid by Nicaragua to rebels fighting to overthrow El Salvador's government. The court clarified that the armed attack must be significant to trigger the right of a defending state to use military force on the attacking state's territory. Minor uses of force, including minor armed attacks, will not give rise to the right of self-defence.[100]

The ICJ found that conduct triggering self-defence must be more serious than a 'mere frontier incident':

> The Court sees no reason to deny that, in customary law, the prohibition of armed attacks may apply to the sending by a State of armed bands to the territory of another State, if such an operation, because of its scale and effects, would have been classified as an armed attack rather than as a mere frontier incident had it been carried out by regular armed forces. But the Court does not believe that the concept of 'armed attack' includes not only acts by armed bands where such acts occur on a significant scale but also assistance to rebels in the form of the provision of weapons or logistical or

[99] ICJ, *Military and Paramilitary Activities in and against Nicaragua* (*Nicaragua* v. *United States*), Merits, Judgment of 27 June 1986, ICJ Reports 1986, 103, para. 195. See also ICJ, *Oil Platforms* (*Iran* v. *United States*), Merits, Judgment of 6 November 2003, ICJ Reports 2003, 195–6, para. 72.

[100] ICJ, *Military and Paramilitary Activities* (n. 99), para. 195.

other support. Such assistance may be regarded as a threat or use of force, or amount to intervention in the internal or external affairs of other States.[101]

In a later passage, the court states more directly that it excludes weapons shipments and the provision of supplies from the armed attack category: '[T]he Court has indicated that while the concept of an armed attack includes the dispatch by one State of armed bands into the territory of another State, the supply of arms and other support to such bands cannot be equated with armed attack.'[102]

The ICJ's reference to the sending of armed bands is from the General Assembly's Definition of Aggression.[103] The Definition lists other acts that trigger the right of self-defence, when, as the ICJ emphasized, the act reaches a serious level. Such acts include invasion of territory, bombardment of territory, blockade of ports, attack on air, sea, or land forces, and the 'sending ... of armed bands, groups, irregulars or mercenaries, which carry out acts of armed force against another State of such gravity as to amount to the acts listed above, or its substantial involvement therein'.[104]

The court characterized US interference with Nicaragua's airspace by overflight of military planes to have been a violation of Nicaraguan sovereignty, but not a violation of the prohibition on the use of force.[105] Nicaragua's supply of weapons to armed groups fighting to overthrow El Salvador's government were similarly examples of unlawful intervention, not armed attack. They were either not significant enough or lacked the character of an armed attack of the kind that can trigger the right to use major military force on a foreign sovereign state's territory. Such an attack must be more than a 'mere frontier incident'.[106] In the 2003 *Oil Platforms* case, the court held again, citing *Nicaragua*, that 'it is necessary to distinguish "the most grave forms of the use of force (those constituting an armed attack) from other less grave forms." ... "In the case of individual self-defence, the exercise of this right is subject to the State concerned having been the victim of an armed attack" ... .'[107]

[101] Ibid. [102] Ibid., para. 247.
[103] See GA Res. 3314 (XXIX) of 14 December 1974. [104] Ibid.
[105] ICJ, *Military and Paramilitary Activities* (n. 99), para. 292.
[106] Ibid., para. 195. [107] ICJ, *Oil Platforms* (n. 99), para. 51.

These findings support the conclusion that economic, cyber, and other types of coercive measures that do not have direct kinetic effects are unlikely to constitute the use of armed force as prohibited in Article 2(4). This conclusion is consistent with the view that Article 2(4) does not speak to this conduct. It prohibits armed force. States may respond to attacks in the non-kinetic category with countermeasures and other defensive action, but not military force in self-defence.[108]

The ICJ in the *Oil Platforms* and *Congo* cases confirmed the key interpretations of the law on use of force enunciated in the *Nicaragua* case. The Ethiopia–Eritrea Claims Commission also underscored the importance of restricting self-defence to cases of significant armed attack.[109] As the ICJ said in *Oil Platforms*:

> … [I]n order to establish that it was legally justified in attacking the Iranian platforms in exercise of the right of individual self-defence, the United States has to show that attacks had been made upon it for which Iran was responsible; and that those attacks were of such a nature as to be qualified as 'armed attacks' within the meaning of that expression in Article 51 of the United Nations Charter, and as understood in customary law on the use of force. As the Court observed in the case concerning *Military and Paramilitary Activities in and against Nicaragua*, it is necessary to distinguish 'the most grave forms of the use of force (those constituting an armed attack) from other less grave forms' (*ICJ Reports 1986*, p. 101, para. 191), since 'In the case of individual self-defence, the exercise of this right is subject to the State concerned having been the victim of an armed attack' (*ibid.*, p. 103, para. 195).[110]

Since the end of the Korean War, North Korea has committed a series of wrongs against its neighbours. It has kidnapped people, launched missiles, and attacked ships. At times, the neighbours have responded forcefully. In 2001, Japanese Coast Guard vessels exchanged fire with a North Korean vessel in Japan's exclusive

108 For more on why cyberattacks do not amount to armed attacks applying the ICJ's analysis in the *Nicaragua* case, see M. E. O'Connell, 'Cyber Security Without Cyber War', *Journal of International Conflict & Security Law*, 17 (2012), 187–209. For a different view see International Group of Experts, *Tallinn Manual on the International Law Applicable to Cyber Warfare* (Cambridge: Cambridge University Press, 2013).

109 Eritrea–Ethiopia Claims, *Jus Ad Bellum* (n. 26), 465–6, paras. 10–11. See also, Gray, *International Law and the Use of Force* 2018 (n. 9), 153–7.

110 ICJ, *Oil Platforms* (n. 99), para. 51.

economic zone. The North Korean vessel exploded and sank.[111] In 2002, an exchange of fire lasting twenty-one minutes between North and South Korea resulted in a patrol boat being sunk and four South Korean sailors being killed. It was referred to as an 'incident', 'armed provocation', 'border incursion', 'clash', and the like. It was not reported to the Security Council.[112] On 26 March 2010, a South Korean warship sank in waters disputed between North and South Korea. Forty-six South Korean sailors perished in the incident. North Korea denied responsibility. South Korea did not counter-attack or bring the incident to the Security Council.[113] These provocations clearly violate international law but have not been treated as the type of attacks that could lawfully trigger self-defence. Some may be below the Article 2(4) threshold, such as kidnapping; others are not significant enough to trigger the right of self-defence on North Korean territory.

One view holds that the hesitation to counter-attack in self-defence is owing to North Korea's possession of nuclear weapons and the fear that attacking it would lead to a use of those weapons and a response in kind from the USA. North Korea, however, did not develop a useable nuclear warhead until 2006.[114] Yet, South Korea and Japan have exercised restraint for many years prior to that date. No doubt fear of even a conventionally armed escalation in fighting has played a role in restraining counter-attacks. The prohibition on the use of force must also be credited. A rationale for restraints on self-defence is to deter escalation. The self-defence rule and the concern that gave rise to it are well integrated. The existence of the rule is a reminder of the rationale. Restraint in the case of North Korea is linked to the paired rule and rationale.

[111] K. Morikawa, Comments on the Draft Initial Report on the Meaning of Armed Conflict in International Law, 20 August 2008 (on file with the author).

[112] D. Kirk, 'North and South Korea Trade Charges Over Naval Clash', *New York Times* (30 June 2002), available at www.nytimes.com/2002/06/30/world/north-and-south-korea-trade-charges-over-naval-clash.html.

[113] C. Sang-Hun, 'North Korea Denies Sinking Navy Ship', *New York Times* (17 April 2010), available at www.nytimes.com/2010/04/18/world/asia/18korea.html. South Korea has reported to the Security Council when it believed the North breached Security Council mandates respecting its nuclear programme. See, Letter dated 6 April 2009 from the Permanent Representative of the Republic of Korea to the United Nations addressed to the President of the Security Council, UN Doc. S/2009/186 (2009), referring to UN SC Res. 1718.

[114] 'North Korea Claims First Nuclear Test', *Guardian* (9 October 2006), https://www.theguardian.com/world/2006/oct/09/northkorea.

The need for an actual armed attack was first emphasized in 1956 when the UK, France, and Israel planned to use force against Egypt. In an apologia after the Suez Crisis, a British academic, Derek Bowett, published a book arguing against the armed attack requirement.[115] He pointed out that the law of self-defence prior to the Charter had no such requirement and that the 'inherent right' mentioned in Article 51 was a reference to law pre-Charter. In other words, Bowett interpreted Article 51 as allowing self-defence even without an armed attack as well as requiring an armed attack.[116] The argument defies logic not to mention standard rules of interpretation. Bowett's attempt to read out the armed attack requirement is unpersuasive. His argument was constructed for a particular purpose. What remains puzzling is why the argument persists. Twenty-five years after Bowett's book appeared, the ICJ confirmed in the *Nicaragua* case that the law outside the Charter – the court said customary international law, better seen as *jus cogens* – has expanded to restrict self-defence to responses to an armed attack. The court found that the reference in Article 51 to 'inherent right' did bring forward pre-Charter law but only principles that further restrict self-defence, such as necessity and proportionality.[117] These principles are consistent with the requirement of armed attack.

Article 51 has one additional objective provision, the requirement to report uses of force in self-defence to the Security Council: 'Measures taken by members in the exercise of this right of self-defence shall be immediately reported to the Security Council.' The ICJ drew inferences in the *Nicaragua* case from the fact that El Salvador had not reported to the Security Council that it was exercising collective self-defence with the United States against Nicaragua. In fact, the court mentioned it found no evidence of an invitation by El Salvador to the USA.[118] In the decades since the *Nicaragua* judgment, the USA and other states have dutifully informed the Security Council of uses of force. Gray finds this so much 'lip service', but it serves the purpose of underscoring the complete lack of a legal basis for using force in the many cases in which no report is made.

In 2014, Iraq sent a letter to the Security Council on the subject of military action against ISIS, and its need for assistance. Iraq did not

[115] See Bowett, *Self-Defence in International Law* 1958 (n. 10). [116] Ibid., 184–5.
[117] ICJ, *Military and Paramilitary Activities* (n. 99), 94. [118] Ibid., 194.

cite Article 51.[119] That was appropriate in that Iraq was facing an internal military challenge by a non-state actor armed group, not an armed attack by another sovereign state. Chapter 5 discusses the obligations of non-state actors to comply with the prohibition on the use of force. Such groups are not party to the UN Charter. Iraq's letter had another purpose as well. It stressed the need for its sovereignty to be respected by those states coming to its aid. Iraq has developed detailed agreements to ensure that states assisting it conform to Iraqi government requirements. A use of force on Iraqi territory not in conformity with Iraq's terms is a violation of Article 2 (4).[120] Iraq's approach is consistent with the view that its campaign against ISIS was a civil war, not a war of self-defence. This characterization makes sense from the perspective of both the law and facts involved. At the same time, the anti-ISIS campaign coincided with extreme interpretations of self-defence in the interest of unfettered right of military action. These are discussed below under self-defence and terrorism.

### C *Restrictions in General International Law*

General law beyond the Charter imposes further limits on the lawful exercise of self-defence. The principles of necessity, proportionality, and state responsibility all condition resort to force and are equally subject to interpretation consistent with the peremptory status of the prohibition on resort to force.

The principles of necessity and proportionality apply to all coercive action.[121] Necessity is assessed based on the lawful object of the coercive action. Armed force is permitted if and to the extent it is necessary to achieve defence. If a state can make that showing, it must then show that the method of force used will not result in a disproportionate loss of life and destruction compared to the value of the objective. 'As part of the basic core of self-defence all states

119 Letter dated 20 September 2014 from the Permanent Representative of Iraq to the United Nations addressed to the President of the Security Council, UN Doc. S/2014/691(2014).

120 See GA Res. 3314 (XXIX) of 14 December 1974.

121 See M. E. O'Connell, 'The Limited Necessity of Resort to Force Force', in D. Stephens and P. Babie (eds.), *Imagining Law: Essays in Conversation with Judith Gardam* (Adelaide: University of Adelaide Press, 2016), 37–60.

agree that self-defence must be necessary and proportionate.'[122] These principles also form an integral part of the prohibition.

Necessity and proportionality are not expressly mentioned in the Charter, but the ICJ has referred to the obligation to comply with them in most of its cases involving the *jus ad bellum.* As mentioned above in connection with Bowett's analysis, the ICJ explained in the *Nicaragua* case that the principles of necessity and proportionality were part of the law of self-defence prior to the adoption of the Charter in 1945.[123] The Charter's reference to the 'inherent right of self-defense' in Article 51 is a reference to principles part of general law that the Charter did not clearly amend. In *Legality of the Threat or Use of Nuclear Weapons (Nuclear Weapons),* the ICJ found 'a "specific rule whereby self-defense would warrant only measures which are proportional to the armed attack and necessary to respond to it, a rule well established in customary international law." This dual condition applies equally to Article 51 of the Charter, whatever the means of force employed.'[124]

The ICJ's application of necessity and proportionality to a claim of self-defence by the USA in the *Oil Platforms* case, brought against it by Iran, is particularly instructive. The court confirmed prior decisions that meeting the requirements of necessity and proportionality are integral to lawful self-defence. It then applied the principles to specific US actions following attacks on two ships in the Persian Gulf during the Iran-Iraq War:

On 16 October 1987, the Kuwaiti tanker *Sea Isle City,* reflagged to the United States, was hit by a missile near Kuwait harbour. The United States attributed this attack to Iran, and three days later, on 19 October 1987, it attacked Iranian offshore oil production installations, claiming to be acting in self-defence … On 14 April 1988, the warship USS *Samuel B. Roberts* struck a mine in international waters near Bahrain while returning from an escort mission; four days later the United States, again asserting the right of self-defence, employed its naval forces to attack and destroy simultaneously the Nasr ['Sirri'] and Salman ['Sassan'] complexes.[125]

122 Gray, *International Law and the Use of Force* (n. 9), 157.
123 See notes 110–15 and accompanying text.
124 ICJ, *Legality of the Threat or Use of Nuclear Weapons (Nuclear Weapons),* Advisory Opinion of 8 July 1996, ICJ Reports 1996, 245, para. 41 (quoting ICJ Reports 1986 at 94, para. 176). See also ICJ *Military and Paramilitary Activities* (n. 99), para. 176; *Oil Platforms* (n. 99), para. 76.
125 ICJ, *Oil Platforms* (n. 99), para. 25.

The court ruled that the USA had submitted insufficient evidence to prove Iran had placed the mine that the *Samuel B. Roberts* struck or fired the missile that struck the *Sea Isle City*. Even if attribution had been proven, however, the court doubted the necessity of the US counter-attacks:

[T]he Court is not satisfied that the attacks on the platforms were necessary to respond to these incidents. ... [T]here is no evidence that the United States complained to Iran of the military activities of the platforms, in the same way as it complained repeatedly of minelaying and attacks on neutral shipping, which does not suggest that the targeting of the platforms was seen as a necessary act. ... [I]n the case of the attack of 19 October 1987, the United States forces attacked the R-4 platform as a 'target of opportunity', not one previously identified as an appropriate military target ...

The judgment was split respecting proportionality:

[T]he attack of 19 October 1987 might, had the Court found that it was necessary in response to the *Sea Isle City* incident as an armed attack committed by Iran, have been considered proportionate. In the case of the attacks of 18 April 1988, ... the Court cannot assess in isolation the proportionality of that action to the attack to which it was said to be a response; it cannot close its eyes to the scale of the whole operation, which involved, *inter alia*, the destruction of two Iranian frigates and a number of other naval vessels and aircraft. As a response to the mining, by an unidentified agency, of a single United States warship, which was severely damaged but not sunk, and without loss of life, neither 'Operation Praying Mantis' as a whole, nor even that part of it that destroyed the Salman and Nasr platforms, can be regarded, in the circumstances of this case, as a proportionate use of force in self-defence.[126]

The *Oil Platforms* judgment underscores the need for an actual armed attack for providing the guideposts of lawful defensive action. Acting in anticipation or to pre-empt an attack renders the necessity and proportionality assessments mere guesswork, which is too uncertain a basis to justify killing and destruction. In *Oil Platforms*, the USA had only limited success in shaping a proportionate response and that was in a case where it was responding to actual attacks. Designing a response requires caution. It also requires respect for the presumption against the use of force. The

[126] ICJ, *Oil Platforms* (n. 99), paras 76–7.

armed attack requirement places real limits on, for example, interfering with websites or other assets unless part of an initial significant and kinetic armed attack.[127] Meeting the requirements of necessity and proportionality seems impossible where the attack at issue is hypothetical, rather than actual.[128]

Beyond necessity and proportionality, the ICJ has emphasized the need for the triggering attack to be attributable to the state against which force in self-defence will be exercised. The court has discussed the attribution requirement in the self-defence context in *Nicaragua, Oil Platforms, Congo,* and in *The Wall* advisory opinion.[129] The *Oil Platforms* case set out the need for clear and convincing evidence of a state's actual responsibility for an armed attack before that State may be counter-attacked in self-defence.[130]

*The Wall* advisory opinion arose from a General Assembly request respecting the legality and consequences of illegality of the security barrier or wall that Israel built at some points within the Occupied Palestinian Territories (OPT). Israel argued it had the legal right to build within the OPT as an exercise of self-defence under Article 51.[131] It reasoned that if it had the right to use armed force, then less potentially lethal measures are logically permitted. The court, however, said Article 51 was not relevant to the case. Israel exercised control over the OPT and was, therefore, an occupying power.[132] Invoking Article 51 in such a case would be analogous to a government invoking Article 51 in responding to a high level of violence by a non-state actor on its own territory. Even if violence reached a

[127] In 2008, Georgia attacked Russian troops in a peacekeeping role in South Ossetia. In turn, Russia invaded Georgia, advancing to within thirty miles of the capital Tbilisi. Both sides interfered with internet sites unrelated to command and control of weapons and troops involved in actual fighting. For facts, see, Report of the Independent International Fact-Finding Mission on the Conflict in Georgia (2009), available at www.mpil.de/en/pub/publications/archive/independent_international_fact.cfm.

[128] But see N. Tsagourias, 'Necessity and the Use of Force: A Special Regime', *Netherlands Yearbook of International Law,* 41 (2010), 11–44, 12–13. Tsagourias argues necessity is related to a 'right of self-preservation' and permits self-defence regardless of an armed attack. See also, R. D. Sloane, 'On the Use and Abuse of Necessity in the Law of State Responsibility', *American Journal of International Law,* 106 (2012), 447–508, 455.

[129] ICJ, *Legal Consequences of the Construction of a Wall in the Occupied Palestinian Territory,* Advisory Opinion of 9 July 2004, ICJ Reports 2004, para. 139 (the court uses the term 'imputable', a synonym for 'attributable' to a state).

[130] See note 108 and accompanying text.

[131] ICJ, *Construction of a Wall* (n. 129), para. 138.

[132] Ibid., para. 139.

level that seriously challenged Israeli control, the situation of the OPT is complicated. The Security Council long ago required Israel to withdraw from the OPT.[133] Under the Council's resolutions, if fighting led to an Israeli withdrawal, Israel could only fight back in self-defence if Palestinians attacked into Israel.

Judge Rosalyn Higgins added a separate opinion objecting to the majority's decision that Article 51 did not apply. She pointed out that Article 51 does not specify that a triggering armed attack must be by a sovereign state.[134] Her observation in support of the Israeli case fails to acknowledge, however, that Charter provisions such as Article 51 are aimed at the member states of the UN. More importantly, she appears to agree with the majority that Israel is in occupation of the OPT.[135] She does not then address the majority's main point that Article 51 plays no role in a zone of occupation.[136]

As the majority implies, states do not invoke Article 51 when in occupation or against internal armed rebellion. In the *Congo* case, the court hints at a different possible conclusion if the armed group is able to launch 'large-scale attacks'.[137] The court's comment is brief but implies that where a non-state actor controls enough territory to be capable of launching major attacks, a situation that perhaps reaches de facto statehood could trigger Article 51. The affirmative point from the case is that Congo did not control the militias that Uganda charged with cross-border attacks. In the circumstances, Uganda's duty was to defend from its own side of the border.[138] Other cases that seem to present the de facto state scenario, however – Kurds in Iraq and Syria fighting Turkey; ISIS in Syria and Iraq fighting the respective governments – indicate that the de jure government's consent to such attacks can and should be obtained.

Otherwise, the attacking state is using violence against a place and a population in violation of not only attribution principles but

[133] See SC Res. 242 of 22 November 1967.
[134] ICJ, *Construction of a Wall*, (n. 129), Separate Opinion of Judge Higgins, 215, para. 33.
[135] Ibid., para. 34.
[136] Compare the situation with Israeli invasions of Lebanon in 1982 and 2006. For facts and analysis of Israel–Lebanon, see, Gray, *International Law and the Use of Force* (n. 9), 23, 101–2, 104, 145, 163, 202, 210, 213–16, 227–30, 342.
[137] ICJ, *Armed Activities on the Territory of the Congo* (*Democratic Republic of the Congo* v. *Uganda*), Judgment of 19 December 2005, ICJ Reports 2005, 223, para. 147.
[138] Ibid.

the basic concepts of fairness that underlie them. To punish a person or community for something they did not do is the definition of unfairness. It is a form of collective punishment, which is expressly forbidden in international humanitarian law.[139] The law of state responsibility specifies that consequences follow from wrongdoing.[140] To determine the party that must bear the consequences, the law of state responsibility includes principles of attribution. The need to establish attribution follows from the principle of legality. Former UK legal adviser Daniel Bethlehem has, however, proposed a right to attack states that are 'unable or unwilling' to control terrorist actors within their jurisdiction. The proposal may be intended to displace all the elements required for self-defence – significant armed attack, necessity, proportionality, and attribution – to allow a state to justify attacking another state by declaring it 'unable or unwilling'. The utter vagueness of such a declaration would undermine any restraint in the regime of self-defence.[141] Nevertheless, a few states began to cite 'unable or unwilling' as official justification for killing in 2015.[142] In doing so, they are citing a principle in derogation of *jus cogens.*[143]

In addition, principles of attribution are general principles. They do not follow the process associated with customary international law. Bethlehem together with US State Department lawyers

[139] Geneva Convention (IV) relative to the Protection of Civilian Persons in Time of War (12 August 1949), https://ihl-databases.icrc.org/ihl/385ec082b509e76c41256739003e636d/6756482d86146898c125641e004aa3c5, Art 33.

[140] 'Every internationally wrongful act of a State entails the international responsibility of that State.' International Law Commission, *Responsibility of States for Internationally Wrongful Acts,* UNGA, 55th Sess, Supp. No. 10, UN Doc A/56/10 (12 December 2001), Art. 1.

[141] Gray writes, 'As part of its doctrine of self-defence against non-state actors, the USA includes the "unwilling or unable" test and a wide interpretation of imminence. Again these elements are more controversial than the USA indicates. The "unwilling or unable" doctrine was claimed be the USA to be merely an application of the requirement that self-defence be necessary. But this doctrine is something more radical, and significantly extends the scope of self-defence.' Gray, *International Law and the Use of Force* (n. 9), 243 (footnotes omitted.)

[142] See UN Doc. S/2015/693, 9 September 2015 (Australia); UN Doc. S/2015/221, 31 March 2015 (Canada); UN Doc. S/2015/563, 24 July 2015 (Turkey); UN Doc. S/2014/695, 23 September 2014 (USA).

[143] The first use of the expression appears to have been in 1976 by the US representative to the UN when he spoke in support of Israel's rescue operation at Entebbe, Uganda. See notes 183–8 and accompanying text.

attempted to construct state practice and *opinio juris* to support 'unwilling/unable'. It is not clear that such an intentional effort can change rules of customary international law. Regardless, such efforts certainly cannot change general principles.[144] Even if attribution principles were customary law and not general principles, evidence of state practice and *opinio juris* is woefully inadequate, despite Bethlehem's efforts to support a use of force. Few states have attempted to justify a use of force by invoking 'unable/unwilling' as part of customary international law and those states have invoked other justifications in addition to 'unable/unwilling'.[145] The case for *opinio juris* is almost non-existent.[146] To the extent any state has acted on the basis of 'unwilling/unable' alone, it has violated Article 2(4).

This section has applied the art of interpreting *jus cogens* to the right of self-defence. Since the time of Augustine, self-defence has been conceived as part of the prohibition on the use of force. The defender counters force with limited force to re-establish peace. This is the basic concept that was included in the UN Charter's specific provision on self-defence, Article 51. Article 51 restricts self-judging self-defence to response to armed attack. It requires a report to the Security Council. The design is of a narrow, temporary right made narrower by the general principles that condition it: necessity, proportionality, and the law of responsibility. This understanding of self-defence has been challenged since 1945, persistently in the three categories discussed in Part III.

## III A Case for Strict Limits

As mentioned in previous chapters, Cold War challenges to the law of self-defence tended to revolve around characterization of facts. While some states also challenged the law, the greater number of direct challenges to the law have occurred since the end of the Cold

[144] J. Brunée and S. J. Toope, 'Self-Defence Against Non-State Actors: Are Powerful States Willing but Unable to Change International Law?', *International and Comparative Law Quarterly*, 67 (2018), 263–86.

[145] See note 143.

[146] Some have claimed that the opinion and practice of specially affected states has greater weight in the formation of customary international law rules than others. Whether this is true for any rule of customary international law, it is not true of rules related to the use of force as all states are affected.

War. This part looks at legal arguments around ending weapons programmes and shipments,[147] rescuing nationals,[148] and countering terrorism.[149] Successful arms control has always involved treaties, not the use of force. Low-level force can be justified in the rescue of nationals but is regulated under the law of countermeasures, not self-defence. Successful terrorism suppression has involved both law enforcement and treaties. The examples in this part demonstrate that political leaders in several states with major militaries persist in using force and claiming a right to self-defence to do so in all three categories, despite poor results.

### *A Arms Control versus Self-Defence*

The drafters of the UN Charter saw weapons as directly linked to the causes of armed conflict. Unlike the other, less direct links – human rights violations, economic privation, and disrespect for international law – the problem of arms proliferation was assigned to the Security Council in Article 26. The Charter allocates the other causes to the General Assembly. States continue today to view weapons as an acute security concern. Some states have even attempted to argue they have the right to use force in anticipation of or to pre-empt weapons shipments or development programmes. These arguments have typically stressed that waiting for the actual unlawful use of a weapon, in particular weapons of mass destruction, will be too late for effective self-defence. As technology and techniques have developed to evade detection, arguments for a right to attack earlier and earlier on ever thinner evidence of a future attack are being made.[150]

The logic of *jus cogens* with its presumption of peace requires the opposite response. Nuclear weapons, chemical and biological weapons, cyberattacks, suicide bombings, and fully autonomous artificial

[147] Notes 151–81 and accompanying texts.

[148] Notes 182–92 and accompanying texts.

[149] Notes 193–224 and accompanying texts.

[150] One of the most memorable and consequential of such arguments was by US National Security Adviser Condoleeza Rice. In an interview on CNN, Rice argued for war against Iraq, saying: 'The problem here is that there will always be some uncertainty about how quickly [Saddam Hussein] can acquire nuclear weapons. But we don't want the smoking gun to be a mushroom cloud.' *CNN* (8 September 2002), available at transcripts.cnn.com/TRANSCRIPTS/0209/08/le.00.html. The acquisition of nuclear weapons does not trigger Article 51.

intelligence (AI) weapons, as well as nanotechnology clearly pose challenges to national security, but more specifically to the right to life.[151] Effective responses to the dangers weapons pose will involve efforts across the international community to raise taboos against such weapons and to create and research effective defences.[152] Undermining restrictions on self-defence will not aid these efforts. It will incentivize research on ever more lethal means of killing instead of antidotes. Incentives should be in the opposite direction, a direction that can be encouraged by law.[153]

Interestingly, this understanding that the law of self-defence does not permit attacking arms shipments or weapons programmes was widely respected until the end of the Cold War. This is all the more interesting as states provided weapons to non-state actor armed groups fighting governments regularly after 1945. Such shipments have not been considered an attack on the state. States only rarely threatened or used unlawful military force to stop the spread of weapons or advances in weapons programmes. That adherence changed with the end of the Cold War and more dramatically after 9/11. A few cases prior to the end of the Cold War helped solidify the understanding that a weapons shipment does not amount to an armed attack under Article 51. In 1962, the USA used an unlawful threat of force in the form of a naval blockade to prevent Soviet shipments of missiles from reaching Cuba.[154] In

[151] See M. E. O'Connell, '21st Century Arms Control Challenges: Drones, Cyber Weapons, Killer Robots, and WMDs', *Washington University Global Studies Law Review*, 13 (2014), 515–33.

[152] On creating taboos against weapons, see, articles cited in C. Gray, 'The Charter Limitations on the Use of Force: Theory and Practice', in V. Lowe, A. Roberts, J. Welsh and D. Zaum (eds.), *The United Nations Security Council and War: The Evolution of Thought and Practice Since 1945* (Oxford: Oxford University Press, 2008). On the importance of defences to so-called cyber weapons, etc., see M. E. O'Connell, 'Cyber Security Without Cyber War' 2012 (n. 108), 187–209.

[153] The use of AI to create fully autonomous weapons is under review by the conference on certain conventional weapons in Geneva. Researchers at Google understand the concerns and have demanded that their company withdraw from research on artificial intelligence for the US DOD. S. Shane and D. Wakbayashi, '"The Business of War": Google Employees Protest Work for the Pentagon', *New York Times* (4 April 2018), www.nytimes.com/2018/04/04/technology/google-letter-ceo-pentagon-project.html.

[154] A. Orakhelashvili, 'The Cuban Missile Crisis – 1962', in O. Corten, T. Ruys and A. Hofer, *The Use of Force in International Law: A Case-Based Approach* (Oxford: Oxford University Press, 2018), 97–107.

1981, Israel attacked Iraq, destroying a nuclear reactor under construction and killing eleven while claiming a right of self-defence. In 1986, the ICJ ruled that weapons shipments by the government of Nicaragua to rebels in El Salvador were not an armed attack on El Salvador.

The paradox of using force for arms control while claiming self-defence was thoroughly vetted in the White House during the Cuban Missile Crisis of October 1962. The incident has fascinated the world of political science, international relations, and international law for decades. The United States detected that the Soviet Union was installing missiles in Cuba within easy striking distance of the United States. President John F. Kennedy, his brother Robert Kennedy, as well as military, policy, and legal advisers debated options ranging from air strikes to no action. The legal advisers cautioned against unilateral air strikes, saying that the only legal basis for doing so was Article 51. The US would have to characterize the missile sites as the equivalent of an armed attack to meet the requirement of Article 51.[155] The US itself had missiles in Turkey that the Soviets could equally characterize as an armed attack. The idea of a naval blockade to prevent the missiles from reaching the launch site was agreed. Under the pre-Charter law, instituting a naval blockade was an act of war. To obscure its unlawful character, the USA called the blockade a 'quarantine' and sought authorization for it, not from the Security Council, but the Organization of American States.[156]

State Department lawyers developed an argument to justify going to the Rio Treaty Organization:[157]

**1. Authorization Under the Rio Treaty**

The Rio Treaty ... provides for collective action, not only in the case of armed attack, ... but also:

155 T. Ruys, 'Israel's Airstrike Against Iraq's Osiriq Nuclear Reactor – 1981', in O. Corten, T. Ruys and A. Hofer, *The Use of Force in International Law: A Case-Based Approach* (Oxford: Oxford University Press, 2018), 329–41.

156 Blockades and embargoes are perhaps better seen as threats of force that become a use of force only upon armed action to defend them. Threats of force are unlawful but plainly tolerated far more widely than actual killing and destruction.

157 The memo, 'Legal Basis for the Quarantine of Cuba', was written by Thomas Ehrlich and is reproduced in T. Ehrlich and M. E. O'Connell, *International Law and the Use of Force* (Little, Brown, & Co, 1993), 148–54.

> 'if the inviolability or the integrity of the territory or the sovereignty or political independence of any American State should be affected by an aggression which is not an armed attack . . . or by any other fact or situation that might endanger the peace of America ... '
>
> In such cases, the Organ of Consultation ... is to, 'meet immediately in order to agree on the measures which must be taken in case of aggression to assist the victim of the aggression or, in any case, the measures which should be taken for the common defense and for the maintenance of the peace and security of the Continent.'
>
> ...
>
> These measures ... include 'use of armed force'.

The Organ of Consultation duly met on 23 October and adopted 'recommendations' that included 'the use of armed force' as 'necessary to ensure that the Government of Cuba cannot continue to receive from the Sino–Soviet powers military material and related supplies'.[158] The memo continued by reviewing Chapter VIII of the UN Charter, the provisions on regional organizations, implying that so long as the use of force is a recommendation only, the regional organization does not usurp the Security Council's authority. The major omission, of course, is that a recommendation is not authorization and only the Security Council has the power to permit a use of force by states outside Article 51.

Soviet ships did not test the US resolve to interdict them. The ships turned back short of the line. Yet, the real end of the crisis occurred when the US agreed to remove its own missile sites from Turkey.[159] Treaty arrangements like the one reached by the US and the Soviet Union on this occasion, bargains reached through exchange of consideration and monitoring mechanisms, have a consistent record of success in arms control. The use of force may delay a programme; it has rarely ended one. Indeed, in some cases the use of force has only motivated a state to continue with a weapons programme, redoubling efforts to keep it secret and secure.

That was the clear lesson learned by Iraq's Saddam Hussein after an Israeli use of force in 1981 destroyed a nuclear reactor being built by French and Italian companies at Osirik, Iraq. The Security Council unanimously condemned Israel's bombing as a violation of the United Nations Charter. A noted Israeli professor of

[158] Ibid. [159] Orakhelashvili, 'The Cuban Missile Crisis' 2018 (n. 154).

international law, Yehuda Blum, presented a detailed legal analysis to the Council on why Israel's attack was a lawful act of self-defence under Article 51 of the Charter. He stressed the future danger to Israel of Iraq having nuclear weapons, insisting that Israel had to act before it was too late.[160] Security Council members rejected the argument, emphasizing that Israel had not been attacked by Iraq. Concerns over future risk were to be brought to the Council. States have no right to attack under Article 51 in advance of an armed attack occurring.

For a number of years, writers pointed to another Israeli attack, on Egypt in 1967, as evidence that the Security Council would permit anticipatory self-defence – attacking before an armed attack has occurred when the attack is soon to occur. In fact, the Security Council did not deliberate on such facts in 1967. Israel represented to the Council and General Assembly that Egypt had attacked first.[161] The facts are now established that not only did Egypt not attack, Israel had intelligence that it would not attack.[162] Dinstein has written that Israel may have made a good-faith mistake in 1967.[163] This appears unlikely given the evidence Israel had; regardless, the presumption against the use of force obviates mistake as a defence to a violation of Article 2(4).

During the 1981 Osirik debate, the US representative to the Security Council, Jeanne Kirkpatrick, stated that the United States, too, understood that Israel had violated the Charter, in particular because Israeli leaders had not exhausted peaceful alternatives. The USA emphasized that there was no 'necessity' to attack. Many representatives were impressed by the testimony of the Director General of the International Atomic Energy Agency who

[160] See SC Res. 487 of 19 June 1981 and accompanying debate.

[161] *1967 Yearbook of the United Nations,* 175–7. In reporting on its initial use of force Israel's representative to the Security Council stated that Egyptian forces had actually crossed into Israeli-held territory. By 17 June, when the General Assembly began its debate on the crisis, Israel's foreign minister no longer spoke of actual Egyptian attacks, but only of Egyptian forces approaching Israel's borders. Ibid., 196.

[162] 'Le général Rabin ne pense pas que Nasser voulait la guerre', *Le Monde,* 19 February 1968; see also J. Quigley, 'The United Nations Action Against Iraq: A Precedent for Israel's Arab Territories?', *Duke Journal of Comparative & International Law,* 2 (1992), 195–228, 203–13.

[163] Y. Dinstein, *War, Aggression and Self-Defence* 4th edn (Cambridge: Cambridge University Press, 2005), 192.

testified that the IAEA had found no evidence of unlawful weapons development by the Iraqi government. The IAEA had found no diversion of nuclear material. Following Israel's attack, Iraq did pursue the acquisition of nuclear weapons, but did so secretly in protected sites.[164] Following the 1991 Gulf War, the United Nations undertook concerted steps to ensure the elimination of all traces of weapons of mass destruction (WMD) in Iraq. Those efforts fully succeeded before the USA, UK, and Australia invaded in 2003. The Iraq case indicates what works in arms control.

The states invading in 2003 attempted to argue the Security Council had authorized their use of force when the Council authorized force for the liberation and protection of Kuwait after Iraq's invasion in 1990–1. In 2003, Iraq had no WMD programme and the global consensus was that the invading states had no legal right to invade even if it had. The aftermath has been a costly debacle that left Iraq a fertile field for the rise of a virulent militant organization, ISIS.

Despite the precedent of Iraq, Israel persists in the view that attacking suspected weapons development sites and weapons shipments is imperative for Israeli national security. It attacked Syria in 2007 to destroy a suspected nuclear weapons production facility. Israel apparently requested US assistance in the operation, but President Bush declined. Not, presumably, because it would be unlawful, rather, the President felt the need to be cautious following the failed invasion of Iraq in 2003, which had no weapons of mass destruction or any hint of an effort to acquire them. President Bush wrote in his memoir that he needed stronger intelligence in the case of Syria. 'I cannot justify an attack on a sovereign nation unless my intelligence agencies stand up and say it's a weapons program.'[165]

Since the outbreak of civil war in Syria in 2012, Israel's attacks on Syria have been persistent.[166] In 2013, President Obama appeared set to join Israel in attacking Syria. He threatened to use force

164 NTI (Nuclear Threat Initiative), *Country Assessment: Iraq*, available at www.nti.org/country-profiles/iraq last accessed 23 January, 2014).

165 D. Makovsky, 'The Silent Strike', *New Yorker* (17 September 2012), available at www.newyorker.com/magazine/2012/09/17/the-silent-strike.

166 See B. Piven, 'Timeline: Israeli Attacks on Syria Targets', *Al Jazeera* (5 May 2013), available at www.aljazeera.com/indepth/features/2013/05/20135512739431489.html.

following a use of chemical weapons during the civil war. The USA did not cite any basis in international law to justify such a use of force. Rather, references were made to the use of force in the Kosovo crisis in 1999. US Ambassador to the UN Samantha Power was asked in an interview whether a US attack on Syria would be 'legal'. She answered that it would be a 'legitimate, necessary and proportionate response'.[167] She lobbied in the USA in August and September of 2013, for using military force to punish Syria's President Assad and those allied with him, following the use of chemical weapons.[168]

Perhaps President Obama's lawyers understood that Power's reasoning could have a seriously detrimental impact on the law restraining the use of force. At any rate, Obama invoked the one ground available under the Charter for attacking Syria, self-defence:

The President is authorized to use the Armed Forces of the United States as he determines to be necessary and appropriate in connection with the use of chemical weapons or other weapons of mass destruction in the conflict in Syria in order to:

(1) prevent or deter the use or proliferation (including the transfer to terrorist groups or other state or non-state actors), within, to or from Syria, of any weapons of mass destruction, including chemical or biological weapons or components of or materials used in such weapons; or
(2) protect the United States and its allies and partners against the threat posed by such weapons.[169]

The president likely had Congress in mind when making this argument. Congress, however, refused to give Obama authorization. Instead, the USA, together with Russia, convinced the Syrian

[167] M. Memmott, 'Strike on Syria: Meaningless Gesture or Necessary Response?', *National Public Radio* (9 September 2013), available at www.npr.org/blogs/thetwo-way/2013/09/09/220611202/strike-on-syria-meaningless-gesture-or-necessary-response.

[168] Morning Edition, 'US Ambassador Samantha Power Presses For Strike On Syria', *National Public Radio* (9 September 2013), available at www.npr.org/2013/09/09/220586231/u-s-ambassador-susan-rice-makes-case-for-strikes-on-syria.

[169] White House Draft Resolution Authorizing the Use of United States Armed Forces, 31 August 2013, available at https://obamawhitehouse.archives.gov/sites/default/files/docs/aumfresolutiontext.pdf.

government to join the Chemical Weapons Convention.[170] The USA, Russia, and others succeeded in removing and destroying tonnes of chemical munitions. Reports of chemical weapons use continued after the destruction. If Syria has been the perpetrator, it is still a positive thing that significant stockpiles have been destroyed. In 2015, the USA joined with Russia, China, France, Germany, the UK, and the EU to reach an agreement with Iran to end its nuclear programme in exchange for sanctions relief.

At the same time that these agreements were being reached, attacks on Syria by Israel and other states without legal justification continued. Israel attacked to 'advance broader strategic goals, such as deterring Iranian and Syrian forces from crossing "red lines" that Israel seeks to communicate concerning the conveyance of arms and presence of foreign troops in Syria. ... Israel is basing its actions on a ... preventive self-defense doctrine.'[171] Israel has also attacked trucks travelling to Lebanon reportedly to deliver weapons. According to one Israeli Air Force official, the attacks have been relentless.[172] Israeli international lawyers advocate seeing Israel's attacks on Syria as a legitimate extension of the right of self-defence given Security Council inactivity. In other words, they are relying on the old argument put forward by Stone and others.[173]

President Trump has attacked Syria twice following reports of chemical weapons use in 2017 and again in 2018.[174] The USA issued no legal justification on either occasion. In 2018, the UK and France joined the attack. The UK said it had the right to attack Syria as

[170] 'Last of Syria's Chemical Weapons Shipped Out', *BBC* (23 June 2014), www.bbc.com/news/world-middle-east-27974379.

[171] A. Cohen and E. Chachko, 'The Israel-Iran-Syria Clash and the Law on the Use of Force', *Lawfare* (14 February 2018), available at https://lawfareblog.com/israel-iran-syria-clash-and-law-use-force.

[172] Ibid.

[173] Stone, *Aggression and World Order* (n. 10). See also, Röling, 'The Ban on the Use of Force and the UN Charter' 1986 (n. 29), 5. ('The fact is that, for Stone's purposes, no reading of Art. 51 is sufficiently broad to cover the range of circumstances in which, under contemporary international conditions, a State might have compelling reasons to protect its interests by a morally justified use of force.' Ibid.)

[174] T. Mak, 'Critics Want the Legal Rationale for Strikes on Syria. The White House Says its Secret', *NPR* (12 April 2008), https://www.npr.org/2018/04/12/601674175/critics-want-legal-rationale-for-strikes-on-syria-the-white-house-says-its-secre.

'humanitarian intervention'.[175] France provided no legal justification. President Trump has also made it clear he is willing to use force against both North Korea and Iran to end their respective nuclear programmes.[176]

### *B Rescue of Nationals versus Self-Defence*

Oscar Schachter wrote with respect to rescue operations that 'when lives are in imminent danger, a good case exists for an exercise of self-defense through a rescue attempt. Such attempts must be limited to the rescue and must not serve as a basis for political pressure or reprisal.'[177] Schacter quotes the US Ambassador to the United Nations on the subject of Israel's Entebbe operation in 1976, for authority. Scranton's formula is, however, narrower than Schachter's. '[T]here is a well-established right to use limited force for the protection of one's own nationals from an imminent threat of injury or death in a situation where the state in whose territory they are located either is *unwilling or unable* to protect them.' He also added that the force must be limited to that 'necessary and appropriate to protect threatened nationals from injury'.[178]

In a footnote, Schachter says Scranton is relying on Waldock and cites Waldock's Hague Lectures.[179] Waldock does conclude that rescue of the state's own nationals is a justifiable act, not of self-defence, however, but of 'self-help' if the restrictions mentioned in the *Caroline* correspondence are strictly followed. 'There must be (1) an imminent threat of injury to nationals, (2) a *failure or inability* on the part of the territorial sovereign to protect them and

[175] Prime Minister's Office, 'Syria Action – UK Government Legal Position' (14 April 2018), www.gov.uk/government/publications/syria-action-uk-government-legal-position/syria-action-uk-government-legal-position.

[176] Respecting North Korea, see, Remarks by Donald Trump to the 72nd Session of the United Nations General Assembly, 19 September 2017, www.whitehouse.gov/the-press-office/2017/09/19/remarks-president-trump-72nd-session-united-nations-general-assembly; and Chapter 2. With respect to Iran, see M. Landler, 'Trump's Twitter Threat vs. Iran: Loud but Hardly Clear', *New York Times* (23 July 2018), www.nytimes.com/2018/07/23/us/politics/iran-donald-trump-policy.html.

[177] O. Schachter, 'In Defense of Rules on the Use of Force', *University of Chicago Law Review*, 53 (1986), 113–46, 139.

[178] Ibid., 139, n. 107 (emphasis added). [179] Ibid.

(3) measures of protection strictly confined to the object of protecting them against injury.'[180] Waldock's reference to 'self-help' rather than 'self-defence' was plainly intentional. He is describing a countermeasure, not self-defence.

Still, it seems a number of scholars put rescue in the self-defence category. When they do, they often describe the level of permissible force to be the same as that allowed in response to a significant armed attack per Article 51. Yet, to be a lawful countermeasure the level of force must be far below that permitted for self-defence. A well-known example exposes the issue of excessive force. In 1976, Israel rescued over 100 passengers on board a hijacked Air France flight.[181] The plane landed at Entebbe Airport in Uganda where Idi Amin had Ugandan troops assist the hijackers in holding the plane and the passengers while negotiations ensued. After a week, 100 Israeli commandoes managed to rescue almost all of the hostages in a daring night raid.[182] In doing so, three hostages were killed, as well as one Israeli soldier, all of the hijackers, and forty-five Ugandan soldiers. Thirty Ugandan Air Force planes were destroyed on the ground. The mission was praised by the United States and several West European states but was condemned by many East European, African, and Middle Eastern states. The UN Secretary-General Kurt Waldheim decried the violation of Uganda's territory. The Security Council,

[180] C. H. M. Waldock, 'The Regulation of the Use of Force by Individual States in International Law', 1952 (n. 31), 451, 467 (emphasis added).

[181] For the facts of the Entebbe, Uganda, operation, see C. Kress and B. K. Nussberger, 'The Entebbe Raid – 1976', in T. Ruys, O. Corten and A. Hofer (eds.), *The Use of Force in International Law: A Case-Based Approach* (Oxford: Oxford University Press, 2018), 220–33. The raid was condemned by most in the non-aligned movement. See R. Berg, 'Entebbe Raid Sparked Joy and Anger', *BBC News*, 3 July 2006, available at http://news.bbc.co.uk/2/hi/middle_east/5110266.stm.

The USA tried to use this justification regarding the invasions of Grenada and the Dominican Republic. It is by now known that US citizens were not in danger in either case. See J. Quigley, 'The United States Invasion of Grenada: Stranger than Fiction', *University of Miami Inter-American Law Review*, 18 (1986-7), 271–352; and C. Walter, 'The US Intervention in the Dominican Republic – 1965', in T. Ruys, O. Corten, and A. Hofer (eds.), *The Use of Force in International Law: A Case-Based Approach* (Oxford: Oxford University Press, 2018), 118–130.

[182] A. M. Weisburd, *Use of Force: The Practice of States Since World War II* (University Park, PA: Pennsylvania University Press, 1997), 276–7.

however, took no action beyond hearing Uganda's charges and Israel's defence.[183]

The United States attempted a rescue mission in 1980 of the fifty-three persons being held hostage in the US embassy in Tehran, Iran. In principle, the USA had the right to try to rescue its nationals, even using limited military force. Yet, the operation to rescue the hostages had a number of practical obstacles associated with it. In the end, the commandoes sent to carry out the rescue never made it to Tehran, owing to two transport helicopters crashing and a third helicopter returning to the aircraft carrier after encountering a sandstorm.[184]

On 11 September 2000, over 150 British troops rescued five British soldiers and their interpreter taken captive by rebel forces, called the West Side Boys, in Sierra Leone. Again, as in the Entebbe rescue, excessive force seems to have been used. The six hostages were successfully freed from their captors within about ninety minutes, but the British rescuers continued battling the West Side Boys for hours to retrieve equipment and to, apparently, weaken the militants as a fighting force. The West Side Boys putative leader was captured. One British soldier was killed but over seventy militants died.[185]

A good example of a lawful rescue is the 2012 case of the American Jessica Buchanan and the Dane Poul Thisted in Somalia by US Navy SEALs.[186] The two Westerners were taken hostage for ransom. Somalia, being virtually without government, could not secure their release. The SEALs did, killing some of the hostage-takers in the effort, but, according to media accounts, they moved in and out of Somalia rapidly without unnecessary killing or destruction.

183 Berg, 'Entebbe Raid Sparked Joy and Anger' 2006 (n. 181).

184 'Hostage Rescue Mission Ends in Disaster', *History.com*, www.history.com/this-day-in-history/hostage-rescue-mission-ends-in-disaster.

185 K. Sengupta, 'British Soldier Killed in Sierra Leone', *Independent* (11 September 2000), available at www.independent.co.uk/news/world/africa/british-soldier-killed-in-sierra-leone-699335.html; see also W. Fowler, *Operation Barras: The SAS Rescue Mission: Sierra Leone 2000* (London: Cassell Military, 2005).

186 K. DeYoung and G. Jaffe, 'Navy SEALs Rescue Kidnapped Aid Workers Jessica Buchanan and Poul Hagen Thisted in Somalia', *Washington Post* (25 January 2012), available at www.washingtonpost.com/world/national-security/us-forces-rescue-kidnapped-aid-workers-jessica-buchanan-and-poul-hagen-thisted-in-somalia/2012/01/25/gIQA7WopPQ_story.html.

The detention of Abu Khattala in Libya in 2014 also demonstrates the elements of lawful countermeasures using minimal force. US military personnel involved in the operation followed police-type law enforcement rules. They deployed only the force necessary to detain Khattala, so there was no apparent violation of Article 2(4). Further, the breakdown of authority in Libya was such that under the international law of countermeasures, the USA could claim the right to carry out a law enforcement action there even in violation of Libyan sovereignty. In the circumstances, the countermeasure was necessary as the only way to bring Khattala to justice for his role in the killing of US diplomatic personnel. The carefully executed mission resulted in no casualties, indicating it was proportionate to the injury suffered by the US – lack of Libyan due diligence respecting criminal law enforcement.[187]

### C *Terrorism versus Self-Defence*

As so many of the incidents just described indicate, terrorism is a persistent challenge to the international community. The decision of the USA and Western European states to use military force outside their borders in response to terrorism is, however, largely a post-Cold War phenomenon. Until then, most states classified terrorism as a problem of national criminal law, not the international right of self-defence.

In 1985, Israel attacked the Palestine Liberation Organization (PLO) headquarters in Tunis in response to attacks by PLO members in Israel. Israel argued in justification that it had exercised its right of self-defence given Tunisia's failure to control terrorists on its territory. The Security Council was not persuaded that Tunisia was legally responsible for the PLO's violence against Israel or that Israel's response was proportionate. The Council condemned 'vigorously the act of armed aggression perpetrated by Israel against Tunisian territory' by a vote of 14–0 with the USA abstaining.[188] The Council also condemned the PLO for violence

[187] On states' obligations of due diligence respecting non-state actor armed groups, see ICJ, *Armed Activities* (n. 137), 268, para. 301. See also J. Gathii, 'Irregular Forces and Self-Defense Under the UN Charter', in M. E. O'Connell (ed.), *What is War? An Investigation in the Wake of 9/11* (Brill: Martinus Nijhof, 2012), 97–108.

[188] SC Res. 573 of 4 October 1985.

in its struggle with Israel, finding no justification for the PLO's methods under the right of self-determination. In 1988, Israel sent a commando team to Tunis to kill the PLO's number two, Khalil Wazir, also known as Abu Jihad. The Security Council condemned Israel in Resolution 611 for carrying out an 'assassination'. The US refused to veto the resolution. US Ambassador Herbert Okun 'referred to Tunisia as a friend of the United States and said "the perpetration of political assassination on Tunisian soil stands in stark contrast to Tunisia's longstanding tradition of non-violence"'.[189]

One of the first incidents indicating the coming change in attitudes towards terrorism suppression occurred just a year later in 1986. US President Ronald Reagan ordered an air attack on Libyan military sites following terrorist incidents linked to the Libyan government under Moammar Ghaddafi. The incidents included the bombing of a Berlin disco frequented by American service members.[190] For Reagan, these incidents were beyond criminal acts. They triggered the right to use force in self-defence under Article 51 because they were perpetrated by a sovereign state, and the USA revealed to allies intelligence that more such attacks were planned. Even strict interpreters of the UN Charter like Louis Henkin began to support the 'accumulation of events' theory. It substituted many smaller attacks for the one significant event needed under Article 51 to trigger the right of self-defence.[191]

When the Cold War ended, Reagan's preliminary steps developed into a major road cutting through the law of self-defence. President Bill Clinton bombed Sudan and Afghanistan to punish al-Qaeda for terrorist attacks on the United States embassies in Kenya and Tanzania in 1998.[192] Clinton made no attempt to link al-Qaeda to the government of either state. Indeed, the factory destroyed in

[189] C. Hughes, 'Security Council Condemns Wazir Slaying, US Abstains', *Associated Press* (25 April 1988), available at 1988 WL 3779956.

[190] See C. Greenwood, 'International Law and the United States' Air Operation Against Libya', *West Virginia Law Review*, 89 (1987), 933–60.

[191] L. Henkin, *Collected Courses of the Hague Academy of International Law* 114 (Leiden: Martinus Nijhoff, 1989); see L. Henkin, *Right v. Might: International Law and the Use of Force* (New York: Council on Foreign Relations Press, 1989).

[192] See J. Lobel, 'The Use of Force to Respond to Terrorist Attacks: The Bombing of Sudan and Afghanistan', *Yale Journal of International Law*, 24 (1999), 537–57.

Sudan was selected on the basis of intelligence errors.[193] When the USA turned to the Security Council it found support, since so many states face terrorism challenges: from Chechens in Russia to Uighurs in China. Still, the Council's resolutions continued to characterize the problem as one of crime and the proper responses in the realm of criminal justice. In 1999, the Security Council imposed sanctions on Afghanistan to pressure it to hand over al-Qaeda's leader, Osama bin Laden, and later condemned 'all acts, methods and practices of terrorism as criminal and unjustifiable, regardless of their motivation'.[194]

Clinton, however, was apparently feeling unconstrained by the international law on the use of force and was emboldened by new weapons technology. He led the sole superpower of the time, a country promoting human rights, new international institutions, and courts. The sense of American exceptionalism among Clinton's advisers, however, translated into policies in violation of international law, as though the US president were above the law. Clinton ordered the war against Serbia over Kosovo.[195] It was the first use of major military force by the USA since 1945 in which the USA offered no legal justification under the Charter. A few months later, Clinton modified a presidential executive order banning assassination that had been in place since the 1970s. He did so to provide the CIA with domestic authorization to use the newly weaponized Predator drone to hunt for and assassinate Osama bin Laden, leader of al-Qaeda, thought to be in Afghanistan at the time.[196]

By 2001, Clinton was out and the new president, George W. Bush, was promising a more modest American foreign policy. Apparently, Bush was unaware of the long-term plans of his vice president, Dick Cheney, and Secretary of Defense, Donald Rumsfeld, to effect

[193] E. Cannizzaro and A. Rasi, 'The US Strikes in Sudan and Afghanistan – 1998', in T. Ruys, O. Corten, and A. Hofer (eds.), *The Use of Force in International Law: A Case-Based Approach* (Oxford: Oxford University Press, 2018), 541–74.

[194] SC Res. 1269 of 19 October 1999.

[195] D. Franchini and A. Tzanakopoulos, 'The Kosovo Crisis – 1999', in T. Ruys, O. Corten and A. Hofer (eds.), *The Use of Force in International Law: A Case-Based Approach* (Oxford: Oxford University Press, 2018), 594–62.

[196] Bin Laden was killed in 2011 in Pakistan, shot in his home by a US Special Forces commando. M. Bowden, 'The Death of Osama Bin Laden: How the US Finally Got its Man', *The Guardian* (12 October 2012), www.theguardian.com/world/2012/oct/12/death-osama-bin-laden-us.

regime change in Iraq. His Secretary of State, Colin Powell, had perhaps the greatest commitment to international law in the new foreign policy team. The State Department legal adviser was William Howard Taft IV, someone linked by family and temperament to the long tradition of Republican commitment to international law.[197] In July 2001, the US Ambassador to Israel, Martin Indyk, stated on Israeli television in connection with Israeli targeted killing of suspected terrorists: 'The United States government is very clearly on the record as against targeted assassinations. They are extrajudicial killings, and we do not support that.'[198]

Then, on 11 September 2001 (9/11), US President George W. Bush declared a 'global war on terror' against al-Qaeda. It began with war in Afghanistan under a claim of self-defence. Secretary Powell stated publicly that the US war aims in Afghanistan were limited; they did not include entering Kabul and ending the Taliban regime. The focus was on al-Qaeda in keeping with the principles of necessity and proportionality.[199] Rumsfeld, however, overruled Powell. Almost two decades later, the USA was still fighting in Afghanistan.

The Security Council helped to advance the move from responding to terrorism as crime to responding in self-defence. In Resolution 1368, adopted on 12 September 2001, the Council cited the 'inherent right of self-defence' in the Resolution's preamble.[200] The Council did not authorize the use of force or make findings with respect to any of the other conditions of lawful self-defence. Critically, the Council said nothing about attribution, necessity, or proportionality. Nevertheless, the resolution helped launch America's 'global war on terrorism' – purportedly a war of self-defence.[201]

[197] His great-grandfather was William Howard Taft, a former president of the United States, an advocate for international courts, and an able international arbitrator. He decided the famous Tinoco Claims cases. See his biography at http://www.friedfrank.com/index.cfm?pageID=42&itemID=620.

[198] J. Greenberg, 'Israel Affirms Policy of Assassinating Militants', *New York Times* (5 July 2001), available at www.nytimes.com/2001/07/05/world/israel-affirms-policy-of-assassinating-militants.html.

[199] See W. La Feber, 'The Rise and Fall of Colin Powell and the Powell Doctrine', *Political Science Quarterly*, (Spring 2009), 71–93.

[200] SC Res. 1368 of 12 September 2001; SC Res. 1373 of 28 September 2001. The most concrete obligation of Resolution 1373 concerned controls on financing of terrorist organizations.

[201] SC Res. 2249 of 20 November 2015 is sometimes invoked as well.

President Bush declared that the 'war' would 'not end until every terrorist group of global reach has been found, stopped, and defeated'.[202] In the months that followed, the administration invoked the core privileges available to lawful belligerents during an armed conflict, including an expanded right to kill, a right to detain without trial, and a right to search and seize cargo of foreign-flagged vessels.[203] Bush authorized the CIA to detain or kill al-Qaeda suspects wherever found, using remotely piloted drones and other means. As new terrorist groups emerged either by splitting from al-Qaeda or inspired by it, such as ISIS, Al Shabab, and Boko Haram, the United States expanded the scope of its targeted killing operations accordingly.[204]

In November 2002, the CIA, based in Djibouti, East Africa, launched a Hellfire missile from a Predator drone at a passenger vehicle in Yemen, killing the six men inside.[205] Yemen recognized no armed conflict on its territory at the time of the strike, nor was the United States at war with Yemen. The CIA carried out the operation because the US Air Force questioned the legality of the operation.[206] Also in 2002, a Department of Defense official said al-Qaeda suspects could be killed without warning wherever they were

202 See George W. Bush, 'President's Address to the Nation on the Terrorist Attacks', *Weekly Compilation of Presidential Documents,* 37 (11 September 2001) 1301; 'President's Address to a Joint Session of Congress on the United States Response to the Terrorist Attacks of September 11', *Weekly Compilation of Presidential Documents* 1347, 1348 37 (20 September 2001), 1347, 1348; 'Training Camps and Taliban Military Installations in Afghanistan', *Weekly Compilation of Presidential Documents* 37 (7 October 2001), 1432; 'President's Address Before a Joint Session of the Congress on the State of the Union', *Weekly Compilation of Presidential Documents* 39 (28 January 2003) 109, www.gpo.gov/fdsys/browse/collection.action?collectionCode=CPD.

203 See M. E. O'Connell, 'Ad Hoc War', in H. Fischer *et al.* (eds.), *Krisensicherung und Humanitärer Schutz – Crisis Management and Humanitarian Protection* (Berlin: BMV Berliner-Wissenschaft, 2004), 405.

204 See generally, L. Wright, *The Terror Years: From Al Qaeda to the Islamic State* (New York: Alfred A. Knopf, 2016). On targeted killing of suspected terrorists see C. Woods, *Sudden Justice: America's Secret Drone Wars* (Oxford: Oxford University Press, 2015).

205 D. McManus, 'A US License to Kill, a New Policy Permits the CIA to Assassinate Terrorists, and Officials Say a Yemen Hit Went Perfectly. Others Worry About Next Time', *LA Times,* (11 January 2003) A1, http://articles.latimes.com/2003/jan/11/world/fg-predator11.

206 Ibid.

found.[207] In 2006, a Department of Justice official said in Congressional testimony that the President could order targeted killings inside the United States on the basis of the new kind of war – the global war on terror.[208]

In 2010, the Obama administration tried to put overseas killings of terrorism suspects on somewhat more rational, if no less unlawful, grounds.[209] Bowett's old 'inherent right' argument was used again. It provided the flexibility needed to justify anything the USA's administrations had done.[210] By 2013, Obama was backtracking. He attempted to institute a policy of 'zero civilian casualties', which brought nearly to an end the practice of targeted killing by drones outside Iraq and Afghanistan.[211] Even in those countries, air attacks declined.

Obama could plainly see by his second term that lawless targeted killing does not suppress terrorism. On the contrary, indications are that targeted killing is counter-productive.[212] By 2014, ISIS, one of the most brutal and successful of all terrorist organizations inspired by al-Qaeda, was rolling through Iraq, defeating Western-trained units of Iraq's regular armed forces. ISIS at its peak controlled a swath of territory that straddled the Iraqi and Syrian border. It was

[207] A. Dworkin, 'Law and the Campaign against Terrorism', *Global Policy Forum* (16 December 2002), available at https://www.globalpolicy.org/component/content/article/163/28224.html.

[208] K. Ossenova, 'DOJ Official: President May Have Power to Order Terror Suspects Killed in US', *Jurist* (5 February 2006), available at www.jurist.org/paperchase/2006/02/doj-official-president-may-have-power.php.

[209] H. Koh made clear that new terminology was being used in an answer to a question from the author at the American Society of International Law Annual Meeting on 26 March 2010. It is not clear, however, that the new terms refer to a substantive change. The exchange was recorded and broadcast on NPR. See A. Shapiro, 'US Drone Strikes Are Justified, Legal Adviser Says', *NPR* (26 March 2010), available at www.npr.org/templates/story/story.php?storyId=125206000.

[210] H. Koh, 'The Obama Administration and International Law', *American Society of International Law* (25 March 2010), available at www.state.gov/documents/organization/179305.pdf.

[211] White House, 'Fact Sheet: US Policy Standards and Procedures in Counterterrorism Operations Outside the United States and Areas of Active Hostilities', (23 May 2012), https://obamawhitehouse.archives.gov/the-press-office/2013/05/23/fact-sheet-us-policy-standards-and-procedures-use-force-counterterrorism.

[212] N. Hopkins, 'US Drone Attacks "Counter-Productive", Former Obama Security Adviser Claims', *Guardian* (7 January 2013), available www.theguardian.com/world/2013/jan/07/obama-adviser-criticises-drone-policy.

able to accomplish this feat owing to the chaotic civil war in Syria and the chaotic, harsh government in Iraq. ISIS emerged in Iraq as a backlash to the treatment meted out to Sunnis by the Shia-controlled government.[213] It spilled over the border, becoming another of the dozens of armed groups fighting to remove the Assad government from power or take control of parts of the country. Syria, too, has treated ISIS as an internal insurgent force. Both Syria and Iraq invited outside assistance to support them against ISIS and other armed rebels.

The Iraqi and Syrian governments are friendly toward each other and have coordinated against their common enemy ISIS. The USA, UK, and several other states that came to Iraq's assistance did not, however, want to assist the Syrian government. Indeed, several were aiding non-state actor groups at war with the Syrian government.[214] The USA, UK, Canada, France, and Turkey explained in letters to the Security Council that they were fighting ISIS in collective self-defence with Iraq and in their own self-defence.[215]

Meanwhile, at the Security Council the negative implications of invoking Article 51 in responding to terrorism became clearer. In a comprehensive resolution in the aftermath of terrorist incidents in five cities during 2015, the Council indicated 'all necessary means be used against ISIS control of Iraqi and Syrian territory'. The Council also emphasized member states' obligations to act in compliance with international law. Most of Resolution 2249 speaks to the need for solidarity against terrorism.[216] No reference is made to Article 51.[217] Also in 2015, the United Kingdom used a drone strike to kill twenty-one-year-old British national Reyad Khan and three

213 See generally, A. Soufan, *Anatomy of Terror: From the Death of Bin Laden to the Rise of the Islamic State* (New York: W.W. Norton & Co, 2017).

214 Gray, *International Law and the Use of Force* 2018 (n. 9), 191, n. 365.

215 Ibid., 191, notes 364 and 365.

216 SC Res. 2249 of 20 November 2015 mentions terrorist attacks in Sousse, Ankara, Sinaï, Beirut, and Paris without citing Article 51. Since 2015, additional attacks have been carried out in Nice (2016), Brussels (2016), Istanbul (2016), Berlin (2016), Manchester (2017), London (2017), and Tehran (2017).

217 For an expansionist perspective, see M. Weller, 'Permanent Imminence of Armed Attacks: Resolution 2249 (2015); and the Right to Self-Defence Against Designated Terrorist Groups', *EJIL: Talk!* (25 November 2015), available at www.ejiltalk.org/permanent-imminence-of-armed-attacks-resolution-2249-2015-and-the-right-to-self-defence-against-designated-terrorist-groups/.

men near him.[218] While the killing cannot be justified, certainly not as an exercise of self-defence under Article 51 of the UN Charter, the UK seems to realize this. A subsequent parliamentary committee report linked the killing to the conflict against ISIS, not British self-defence. The report is factually false on this point but did insert a more legally plausible basis than that cited by Prime Minister David Cameron.

Prior to the end of the Cold War, the USA, UK, and others promoted law enforcement measures against terrorism. After the Cold War, decades of assassination and the use of excessive military force followed, providing evidence that as a practical matter, law enforcement is more effective. Regardless of effectiveness, the use of military force against intermittent attacks by criminal gangs violates the prohibition on the use of force. Such unlawful killing is, therefore, also violative of the fundamental right to life.[219]

## Conclusion

For decades writers and government officials have used their talents to argue for new interpretations to expand the exception for self-defence. These efforts have been carried out to advance the interests of particular states from the perspective of Realist understandings of the world. The arguments pay a certain respect to the law. They do not represent the wholesale disregard of those who make no argument at all or dismiss international law as a 'sham'. Still, expanding the exception is little better than completely dismissing Article 2(4).

Embedded in the arguments, from Stone's gibes at the UN to Trump's silence on reprisal attacks, is the idea that the state or states

[218] Such arguments have been referred to as 'abusive' and 'openly instrumental', e.g., O. Corten, 'A Plea Against the Abusive Invocation of Self-Defence as a Response to Terrorism', *EJIL*: Talk! (14 July 2016), available at www.ejiltalk.org/a-plea-against-the-abusive-invocation-of-self-defence-as-a-response-to-terrorism/; and J. von Bernstorff, 'Drone Strikes, Terrorism and the Zombie: On the Construction of an Administrative Law of Transnational Executions', *ESIL Reflection* 5:7 (11 July 2016), available at www.esil-sedi.eu/node/1368.

[219] Special Rapporteur on Extrajudicial, Summary, or Arbitrary Executions, 'Report of the Special Rapporteur, Asma Jahangir: Civil and Political Rights, Including the Questions of Disappearances and Summary Executions', UN Doc. E/CN.4/2003/3 (13 January 2003), paras. 37–9.

asserting the right to act regardless of Security Council authorization or the terms of the Charter are morally entitled to do so. It is the only perspective that makes sense of permitting unilateral action in violation of the law while not destroying the law in its entirety. None of the arguments for special privilege calls for generally dismantling the system. Even the states that so frequently violate the prohibition on the use of force apparently understand the chaos that would ensue without some sense of legal order. What these arguments implicitly envision, therefore, is a two-class system.

This belief in privilege and exceptionalism has dogged respect for the prohibition on the use of force since the end of the Cold War. When the Western world and the socialist world faced off, the principle of legal equality was not so easily dismissed. With the end of the Soviet Union, the USA and some of its closest allies lost this circumspection. The USA's failure to lead on the basis of respect for equality before the law may be the single greatest reason for the problems of the world order system a generation later. With the USA now challenged for sole superpower status by China, and with researchers creating ever more automated technologies to kill, the time is right for the international legal community to renew understanding of and commitment to the *jus cogens* norm against the use of force except in authentic self-defence. It is time to move beyond mere renewal to consideration of expansion to restrict invitation to internal armed conflict and rebellion.

# 5

# Restricting Exceptions for Invitation and Rebellion

Mali held the record in 2018 as the most dangerous place in the world for UN peacekeepers.[1] This was the case five years into a complex military intervention spearheaded by France to respond to an uprising involving multiple, competing armed groups that included the nation's military, which staged a successful coup at the start of the crisis.[2] A French journalist blamed the high number of peacekeeper deaths on the fact that UN Blue Helmets, as distinct from their French colleagues, had not been permitted to use offensive force. Blue Helmets in Mali 'are shot like hares'.[3] The journalist's comment reflects the confused state of UN Peacekeeping today, as well as the continuing high confidence in military force typical of the post-Cold War era.[4] He overlooks that even though

[1] 'Several French Soldiers Injured in Latest Mali Attack', *France 24* (16 April 2018), available at www.france24.com/en/20180415-french-soldiers-injured-mali-jihadi-attack-timbuktu-terrorism-touareg-mnla-gsim-aqip.

[2] G. Chauzal and T. van Damme, 'The Roots of Mali's Conflict: Moving Beyond the 2012 Crisis', *CRU Report* (Clingendael, Netherlands: Institute of International Relations, 2015), 30–6; 'The Situation in Mali', Report of the UN Secretary General, UN Docs. S/2012/894, S/2013/189; S. Brüne, H.-G. Ehrhart and H.-G. Justenhoven (eds.), *Frankreich, Deutschland, and die EU in Mali, Chancen, Risiken, Herausforderungen* (Baden Baden, Germany: Nomos/Münster: Aschendorff Verlag, 2015); and C. Gray, *International Law and the Use of Force* 4th edn (Oxford: Oxford University Press, 2018), 335.

[3] 'Several French Soldiers Injured in Latest Mali Attack' 2018 (n. 1).

[4] These two factors can be seen in Mali, where Permanent Security Council members France and the United States have lobbied for UN peacekeepers to use ever greater levels of lethal force while other states have opposed peacekeepers being involved in offensive military operations in general and in counter-terrorism operations in particular. See SC Res. 2295 of 29 of June 2016; Gray, *International Law and the Use of Force* 2018 (n. 2), 335–9; and a report to the Secretary General, Carlos Alberto dos

France uses offensive force liberally, it, too, has lost dozens of soldiers, has killed hundreds of opposition fighters, and, yet, the conflict continues.[5] Civilians are killed by both sides. The situation there and in other long-running, seemingly intractable conflicts call for a fresh look at the international law regulating intervention and insurgency in light of the peremptory prohibition on the use of force.[6]

Most contemporary conflicts are the predictable outcome of persistent external military intervention and internal resort to violent rebellion.[7] France has long been part of this pattern, colonizing Mali in 1891 for the purpose of wealth extraction and maintaining control 'by whatever means necessary'.[8] Mali achieved independence in 1960 but its post-colonial governments have been 'riven by corruption and narrow loyalties, with leaders who were most often unwilling to pursue or incapable of pursuing a truly national, democratic vision of development'.[9] Mali's problems have been made worse by the violence and instability in neighbouring states, to which France has contributed. The implosion of Libya has had serious regional repercussions. In 2011, France took the lead in advocating for intervention and regime change there. The resulting chaos put large numbers of 'men and arms into play in northern Mali at a particularly dangerous moment . . . '.[10]

Despite the debacle in Libya, in early 2013, France again sent troops into an African country, its former colony Mali. Mark LeVine foresaw that 'just as previous African interventions generated the

Santos Cruz, *Improving Security of United Nations Peacekeepers: We Need to Change the Way We Are Doing Business* (19 December 2017). Additional examples are provided in Chapters 3 and 4.

5 Ministère des Armeés, République Française, 'Opération *Barkhane*', *Dossier de Presse* (April 2018), available at www.defense.gouv.fr/operations/operations/sahel/dossier-de-presentation-de-l-operation-barkhane/operation-barkhane.

6 'Intervention by invitation' will also be referred to here as 'consent to intervene' or simply, 'consent' or 'invitation'. 'Insurgency' will also be referred to as 'rebellion'. Both insurgency and rebellion mean an organized armed challenge to a state's government with the aim of either replacing the government of the state as a whole or taking control of a part of a state.

7 See, e.g., Uppsala Conflict Data Programme, available at http://ucdp.uu.se/#/encyclopedia.

8 M. LeVine, 'France in Mali: The Longue Durée of Imperial Blowback', *Al Jazeera* (19 January 2013), available at www.aljazeera.com/indepth/opinion/2013/01/2013119153558185275.html.

9 Ibid. 10 Ibid.

blowback that helped create the present Malian crisis, the present intervention ... will no doubt produce its own blowback, which will claim the lives of many more Africans, French, American and other Western citizens'.[11] It will also claim the lives of more UN peace-keepers from across the globe.

Armed responses to complex social conflict have consistently proven counter-productive. Such responses often violate the international legal principle of non-intervention. Yet, international lawyers defend the French intervention in Mali as justified on the basis of 'intervention by invitation'.[12] Paradoxically, the right of people to take up arms in rebellion is also defended – either indirectly on the basis that international law is silent respecting rebellion,[13] or directly on the policy ground that international law should permit oppressed people to fight their oppressors.[14] As with the other exceptions to the prohibition on the use of force, however, international law places strict limits on the right to intervene as well as any possible right to take up arms in rebellion.[15]

Some of these restrictions are evident in the French Foreign Minister's statement on France's legal basis for military action in Mali. First, he asserts that France had an invitation from a party with the legal right to issue it. He then puts forward a collection of other arguments, each insufficient to justify using force in Mali but perhaps giving the impression of an adequate basis through 'an accumulation of arguments' approach:

> Firstly, the appeal and the request made by Mali's legitimate government ... ; and secondly, all the United Nations resolutions, which not only allow but require those countries capable of doing so to support the fight against terrorists in this matter [;] ... Article 51 [;] ... the request by ECOWAS, the

[11] Ibid.

[12] G. H. Fox, 'Intervention by Invitation', in M. Weller (ed.), *The Oxford Handbook of the Use of Force in International Law* (Oxford: Oxford University Press, 2015), 816–40, 827.

[13] For a discussion of international law's traditional neutrality respecting the question of the legality of rebellion, see O. Corten, 'La rébellion et le droit international: le principe de neutralité en tension', *Collected Courses of The Hague Academy of International Law, Receuil des Cours* 374 (Leiden: Brill, 2015), 53–312.

[14] For a normative argument in favour of rebellion, see J. A. Hessbruegge, *Human Rights and Personal Self-Defense in International Law* (New York: Oxford University Press, 2017), chap. 7.

[15] See notes 129–200 and accompanying text.

Economic Community of West African States, and the position taken by the African Union . . .[16]

None of these references on the facts of the case in Mali provides a legal basis for French intervention. The UN Security Council resolutions referred to an African-led force, called the International Support Mission in Mali (AFISMA), which did not include France.[17] Regional organizations like ECOWAS and the African Union have no authority to authorize military intervention.[18] The mention of Article 51 is puzzling, as France was not attacked by Mali.[19] While the Security Council had not criticized intervenors after five years of fighting, a lack of criticism or acquiescence is not the same as authorization. In sum, France had no adequate legal basis for its military intervention in Mali. International law does not permit combining several weak arguments to create one sufficient one.[20]

Bannelier and Christakis also see the basis of France's presence in Mali as questionable and caution that '[t]he consensus surrounding the legality of foreign intervention by invitation in Mali should not lead to the conclusion that third states have an unlimited right to military intervention on the basis of the consent of the authorities of the state where the intervention takes place'.[21] They consider Mali 'a precedent

[16] 'Mali: Press Conference by M Laurent Fabius', French Minister of Foreign Affairs (14 January 2013), available at http://basedoc.diplomatie.gouv.fr/vues/Kiosque/FranceDiplomatie/kiosque.php?fichier=baen2013-01-14.html, cited in K. Bannelier and T. Christakis, 'The Intervention of France and Others in Mali', in O. Corten, T. Ruys and A. Hofer (eds.), *The Use of Force in International Law: A Case-Based Approach* (Oxford: Oxford University Press, 2018), 812–27, 815–16.

[17] SC Res. 2085 of 20 December 2012.

[18] Chapter 3; and see the discussion of the African Union Charter provision providing for prior consent for pro-democratic invasion below at notes 125–7 and accompanying text.

[19] Chapter 4.

[20] The USA has tried to combine several inadequate arguments into a single sufficient one on several occasions, see, e.g., the arguments put forward to justify the invasion of Panama. M. N. Leich, 'Contemporary Practice of the United States Relating to International Law', *American Journal of International Law*, 84 (1990), 536–49, 547–8; and 'Letter Dated 20 December 1989 from the Permanent Representative of the United States of America to the United Nations Addressed to the President of the Security Council', UN Doc. S/21035 (1989). Compare the approach to the 'pin prick' argument where a number of low-level attacks are combined to substitute for an attack significant enough to trigger the right to respond in self-defence. See Chapter 4.

[21] Bannelier and Christakis, 'The Intervention of France and Others in Mali' 2018 (n. 16), 819.

*against* an unlimited right to military intervention by invitation . . .'[22] and propose a new criterion for lawful use of force on the basis of an invitation.[23] They suggest that if a state's purpose in intervening is to counter terrorism, the intervention should be considered lawful. Their proposal has the virtue of being narrower than other claims to a right to intervention by invitation. It is not narrow enough to avoid conflict with the peremptory norm prohibiting the use of force.

Rather than proposing new versions of a right to intervene, this chapter looks in the opposite direction for new restrictions not only on intervention but also respecting the right to rebel.[24] France intervened in Mali in 2013 following a rebellion that began in 2012 by the Tuareg people of northern Mali against the central government based in the southern capital of Bamako.[25] It was the fourth major Tuareg rebellion since Mali gained independence. During the 2013 uprising, other armed groups quickly overwhelmed the Tuareg campaign, including groups committed to ideologies and tactics linked to al-Qaeda and ISIS. The Tuaregs, and many other communities in Mali, have had legitimate grievances against the central government, but an argument asserting that those grievances support a right to kill fails to fully appreciate the moral underpinnings of the *jus ad bellum* and the implications of the *jus cogens* prohibition. It is time to consider restricting – not expanding – the right of rebellion under the *jus ad bellum.*

Even if the principle of law regulating the use of force were not *jus cogens,* plenty of practical reasons exist to support restrictive rules on intervention and insurgency. As pointed out throughout this book, military force in connection with suppressing terrorism, advancing human rights, or establishing good governance has a poor history of success – certainly over time. Social science research is quite explicit that the imposition of government by outside parties is unlikely to lead to democracy or better governance outcomes.[26] The history of Mali

[22] Ibid. (emphasis in the original).

[23] See notes 111–28 and accompanying text.

[24] E.g., Hessbruegge, *Human Rights and Personal Self-Defense* 2017 (n. 14).

[25] Chauzal and van Damme, 'The Roots of Mali's Conflict' 2015 (n. 2), 30–6.

[26] See, e.g., E. Chenoweth and M. J. Stephan, *Why Civil Resistance Works: The Strategic Logic of Nonviolent Conflict* (New York: Columbia University Press, 2011); G. Peic and D. Reiter, 'Foreign-Imposed Regime Change, State Power and Civil War Onset, 1920–2004', *British Journal of Political Science,* 41 (2011), 453–75; and F. Ledwidge, *Losing Small Wars: British Military Failure in the 9/11 Wars* 2nd edn (New Haven: Yale University Press, 2017).

and so many of its neighbours provides ample evidence of this conclusion. During Security Council discussions, both China and Russia raised concerns about another UN 'militarized' intervention.[27] As this chapter will also show, the law has developed over time to reflect the limited effectiveness of using force in complex social, political, and cultural settings. When force is both unlawful and ineffective, it is also immoral. All three standards for judging conduct call for strict limitations on intervention and rebellion.

Instead of outside military intervention, the people of Mali deserve a bold new approach, one exemplifying courage, creativity, and patience. Discussions toward a new approach to peace and stability in Mali are overdue. The cycle of rebellion, corruption, war, intervention, and rebellion needs to end. The president of Niger said of the French deployment that it was 'the most popular of all French interventions in Africa'.[28] The perspective of this statement reflects an important part of the problem. After so many interventions, people are conditioned to think intervention is the only option. They seem to have lost the moral imagination to see beyond ongoing violence toward avoiding violence. Advocates of intervention and rebellion seem to overlook the clear evidence of military failure in these situations. They seem to grasp at anything to do something. They even seem to forget the basic principle of humanitarian assistance: first, do no harm.[29] As Richard Falk writes: 'The record of military intervention during the last several decades is one of almost unbroken failure if either the human costs or political outcomes are taken into proper account.'[30]

[27] Russia, for example, stated in the debate over authorizing the UN Peacekeeping Mission that 'we are disturbed by the growing shift towards the military aspects of United Nations peacekeeping'. SC Verbatim Record (25 April 2013), UN Doc. S/PV.6952, 2. China did not see France's intervention as coming within the Security Council authorization and wanted it to withdraw. Chinese analysts saw France's intervention as tied to President Hollande's interest in boosting his popularity and other reasons of self-interest, nor did China foresee a positive outcome. China worried most of all about French 'neo-interventionism' under the excuse of fighting terrorism. Yun Sun, 'How China Views France's Intervention in Mali: An Analysis', *Brookings* (23 January 2013), available at www.brookings.edu/opinions/how-china-views-frances-intervention-in-mali-an-analysis/.

[28] Bannelier and Christakis, 'The Intervention of France and Others in Mali' 2018 (n. 16), 815.

[29] See Hippocratic Oath: 'First, do no harm . . . '.

[30] R. Falk, 'Libya: Will We Ever Learn? Kicking the Intervention Habit', 11 March 2011, available at www.voltairenet.org/article168826.html.

A better future for Mali involves 'innovative solutions and creative ways to re-invent the presence of the state across the territory. Ancient or contemporary endogenous models, examples from neighbouring countries or reform of some existing institutions could lead to peace in the long run and to trust between communities.'[31] Such a future requires more from international law. It requires reversing the long slide toward perceiving ever-wider rights to intervene and rebel.

## I Restricting Intervention by Invitation

As with self-defence and Security Council authorization, writers interested in expanding exceptions to the prohibition on force have also looked to what is often referred to as the third exception to Article 2(4), intervention by invitation or with the consent of a party to a conflict.[32] The expansionists have argued steadily for ever looser qualifications as to who may invite, in what circumstances, and in what counts as an invitation or consent. France invoked an invitation of questionable validity to justify intervening in Mali in 2013.[33] France's basis for intervening in the Syrian Civil War against the government was more questionable still. By 2018, states were intervening on all sides of both the Syrian and Yemeni civil wars, each intervenor claiming the right to do so under international law, mostly on the basis of an invitation.[34] Prior to the Charter, international lawyers tended to be unified in seeing strict limits on

[31] Chauzal and van Damme, 'The Roots of Mali's Conflict' 2015 (n. 2), 58.

[32] See, e.g., C. Henderson, *The Use of Force and International Law* (Cambridge: Cambridge University Press, 2018), citing in accord, O. Corten, *The Law Against War: The Prohibition on the Use of Force in Contemporary International Law* (Oxford: Hart Publishing, 2010), 253; and Fox, 'Intervention by Invitation' 2015 (n. 12), 816. See also, Gray, *International Law and the Use of Force* (n. 2), chap. 3. This author once took the same position but in light of the research for this chapter no longer does. See, e.g., M. E. O'Connell, 'The Prohibition on the Use of Force', in N. D. White and C. Henderson (eds.), *Research Handbook on International Conflict and Security Law:* Jus Ad Bellum, Jus in Bello, Jus Post Bellum (Cheltenham: Edward Elgar, 2013), 89–119.

[33] Note 20 and accompanying text.

[34] France was intervening on the side of the opposition in the Syrian Civil War within months of the International Committee of the Red Cross declaring that the fighting had reached the level of civil war in mid-2012. M. Chulov, 'France Funding Syrian Rebels in New Push to Oust Assad', *Guardian* (7 December 2012), available at www.theguardian.com/world/2012/dec/07/france-funding-syrian-rebels. 'Syria in a Civil War, Red Cross Says', *BBC* (15 July 2012), available at www.bbc.com/news/world-middle-east-18849362.

intervention by invitation.[35] The imperative of *jus cogens* leads back to those restrictions and forward to new ones.

### *A The Charter and Invitation*

Article 2(4) could well be interpreted as forbidding a state from using force on the territory of another state even with the consent of that other state's government. It was for that very reason that Article 51 was added to the draft during the negotiating conference in San Francisco in 1945.[36] Article 51 provides a right of individual and collective self-defence if an armed attack occurs. The International Court of Justice clarified in the *Nicaragua* case that lawful collective self-defence includes the requirement of an actual invitation from the state claiming to be the victim of an armed attack by another state. The court found no evidence El Salvador had extended an invitation to the United States. Indeed, it found no evidence that El Salvador felt it needed US assistance against Nicaragua in the first place.[37] El Salvador had not, for example, reported to the Security Council that it was under an armed attack by Nicaragua.[38] The USA also failed to provide a report informing the Security Council of the facts and legal basis justifying its use of military force against Nicaragua.[39]

[35] On the restrictions respecting intervention in civil war, see, Gray, *International Law and the Use of Force* 2018 (n. 2), chap. 3; C. Gray, 'The Charter Limitations on the Use of Force: Theory and Practice', in V. Lowe, A. Roberts, J. Welsh, D. Zaum (eds.), *The United Nations Security Council and War, The Evolution of Thought and Practice Since 1945* (Oxford: Oxford University Press, 2008), 86–98, 93. On restrictions respecting intervention for other purposes, see I. Brownlie, *International Law and the Use of Force by States* (Oxford: Clarendon Press 1963), 317–27. Positivists tend deny this position but as discussed in earlier chapters, the basis for the denial is the fact the theory of positivism does not encompass a prohibition on force prior to 1899 and, even then, the prohibition is limited until the Kellogg-Briand Pact. The reality of international law as a hybrid of natural law, positive law, and procedure leads to a different understanding. See Chapter 2.

[36] Chapter 4.

[37] ICJ, *Military and Paramilitary Activities in and against Nicaragua* (*Nicaragua* v. *United States*), Merits, Judgment of 27 June 1986, ICJ Reports 1986, paras. 200, 235–6.

[38] Ibid.

[39] Ibid. Cf. 'September 11, 2001: Attack on America: Letter of United States Representative John Negroponte to the President of the Security Council' (7 October 2001), available at http://avalon.law.yale.edu/sept11/un_006.asp.

The ICJ decision in the *Wall* advisory opinion also clarifies that Article 51 provides for a narrow right of a state to respond to an armed attack for which another sovereign state is responsible.[40] The UK tried to justify its 1944–5 intervention in the Greek civil war as lawful 'collective defence against indirect aggression' by communists.[41] The UK would later argue that such intervention 'is in the spirit of the Charter'. The UK used the terminology of self-defence, but, as a legal matter, Article 51 was intended to apply in cases of armed attacks by foreign states or perhaps, quasi-state entities.[42] As the addition of Article 51 demonstrates, the San Francisco delegates agreed that the natural right of self-defence, included a narrow right of collective self-defence, but they otherwise understood Article 2(4) to be a comprehensive prohibition on force. Wolfgang Friedmann shared this view and rejected any right to intervene in a civil war on the basis of Article 51.

Bannelier and Christakis's proposal to allow intervention for the purpose of countering terrorism even without a government's invitation seems to be an attempt to combine two insufficient bases to create one adequate one. A state may well invite assistance in an effort to counter terrorism on its territory. A state may also use force on another state's territory without permission when it has been the victim of an armed attack. In Mali, Syria, Somalia, and other places, some intervenors have no invitation and most have not been the victims of an armed attack. Bannelier and Christakis presumably believe their proposal is warranted on the basis of state practice and *opinio juris*, but, the evidence of these elements is thin. Even were it stronger, state practice and *opinio juris* cannot lead to a derogation from *jus cogens* through expanding situations permitting force.

At the time the Charter was drafted, state delegates would have been aware of the existing position in international law and intervention.[43] The common understanding was that international law restricts 'intervention in a conflict serious enough to be characterized as a civil war ... even at the invitation of the

[40] ICJ, *Legal Consequences of the Construction of a Wall in the Occupied Palestinian Territory*, Advisory Opinion of 9 July 2004, ICJ Reports 2004, 194, para. 139.
[41] Brownlie, *International Law and the Use of Force by States* 1963 (n. 35), 325.
[42] ICJ, *Construction of a Wall* (n. 40), Separate Opinion of Judge Higgins, 215, para. 33.
[43] See notes 136–60 and accompanying text.

government, unless there had been prior outside intervention'.[44] Quincy Wright, one of the leading scholars on international law and civil war in the mid-twentieth century, explained that the rule, 'as it developed in the nineteenth century, considered revolutionary change an internal affair of the state, and ... held that other states must not intervene on behalf of either the government or the insurgents, if the results of the revolt are uncertain. They must not even recognize the insurgents until they have in fact established themselves as the government of the state or of a revolting community.'[45] Oppenheim, the great opponent of natural law limits on a state's prerogative to use force, also considered that international law restricted intervention in internal conflict.[46] '[A] foreign state commits an international delinquency by assisting insurgents in spite of being at peace with the legitimate Government.'[47]

In addition to the Charter, the UN General Assembly's Declaration on Friendly Relations provides that '[A]ll states have a duty to refrain from organizing, instigating, assisting or participating in acts of civil strife or terrorist acts in another State'.[48] This is a direct ban on assistance to opposition groups at least in the earliest stages of an insurrection. Intervention on the side of a government only until an insurgency reaches the level of belligerency is also implied by the ICJ's decision in *Congo*. Congo invited assistance from neighbouring states to suppress internal conflict. The ICJ specified that withdrawing consent requires no formal, express evidence. The Court made no comment on the right to issue invitations in the first place, but the right is implied in the discussion of terminating them.[49]

44 Gray, 'The Charter Limitations on the Use of Force: Theory and Practice' 2008 (n. 35), 93. See also notes 125–8 and accompanying text.

45 Q. Wright, 'International Law and Civil Strife', *Proceedings American Society of International Law*, 53 (1959), 145–52, 149. See also, Q. Wright, 'Changes in the Conception of War', *American Journal of International Law*, 18 (1924), 755–67, 759; and Q. Wright, 'Legal Aspects of the Viet-Nam Situation', *American Journal of International Law*, 60 (1966), 750–69.

46 Chapter 2.

47 H. Lauterpacht, *Oppenheim's International Law* vol. II 6th edn (London: Longmans, Green, and Co, 1940), 522.

48 Declaration on Principles of International Law Concerning Friendly Relations and Co-operation among States in Accordance with the Charter of the United Nations, GA Res. 2625 (XXV) of 24 October 1970.

49 ICJ, *Armed Activities on the Territory of the Congo* (*Democratic Republic of the Congo* v. *Uganda*), Judgment of 19 December 2005, ICJ Reports 2005, paras. 92–105.

Brownlie, however, found versions of the pre-Charter rule that made it unlawful 'to assist a Government in suppressing an insurrection . . . ',[50] apparently even if the insurrection has no chance of reaching belligerency. The rule makes logical sense. If a government needs outside assistance in suppressing a military challenge to its control, the need is evidence that the opposition has a chance of success. During the Spanish Civil War of the late 1930s, states agreed in the Non-Intervention Pact to refrain from intervening on either side even prior to General Franco's forces reaching the strength to credibly challenge the government.[51] A rule against any intervention makes practical sense, and it makes moral sense given the peremptory status of the prohibition on the use of force. Establishing this understanding as the appropriate one will be discussed further in the third section below on *jus cogens* and invitation. The conclusion here is that, at the least, pre-Charter law restricted intervention to a government until the point when organized armed opposition reached belligerency, meaning it acquired the potential to challenge the government for control.[52] The belligerency rule provided a relatively objective point for triggering the bar on assistance.

Still, the pre-Charter literature recognizes that determining whether an armed group had reached belligerency was often difficult. Insurgents had to demonstrate sufficient organization, resources, and success in early hostilities to indicate a good chance of defeating the government. A state intervening or continuing an intervention once the opposition reached belligerency became a party to the armed conflict.[53] The belligerency rule also implies that the government retains its status as the government to the extent practicable until its chance of defeating the opposition is clearly lost. In the case of fighting in which no party emerges as able to

[50] Brownlie, *International Law and the Use of Force by States* 1963 (n. 35), 323, quoting A. D. McNair, 'The Law Relating to the Civil War in Spain', *Law Quarterly Review*, 53 (1937), 471–99, 474.

[51] W. Friedmann, 'Intervention, Civil War and the Rôle of International Law', *Proceedings of the American Society of International Law*, 59 (1965), 67–81, 72.

[52] For an even broader view that resort to war was not limited by law prior to 1945, see E. Lieblich, 'The Soviet Intervention in Hungary – 1956', in Corten *et al.*, *The Use of Force in International Law* 2018 (n. 16), 48–66, 58–60. ('Before the UN Charter . . . war was generally a sovereign prerogative.') See also Chapter 2.

[53] B. R. Roth, 'The Virtues of Bright Lines: Self-Determination, Secession, and External Intervention', *German Law Journal*, 16 (2015), 384–415, 412, n. 101.

maintain durable control, as has been the case in Somalia and Yemen, no outside intervention is permitted. This aspect of the rule has been regularly dishonoured since the drafting of the Charter. Rather than use the standard criteria for determining the existence of a government, intervenors use other criteria or claim the lack of a government in a 'failed state' means there is no barrier to intervention.[54]

To the extent invitation to intervene is valid, it must still be made by an express and public invitation. The international community must be able to conclude that a state's actions on the territory of another state have the valid consent of that state and are not unlawful interference. Public evidence of treaties and legal licenses, such as consent, are needed for the international legal system to work.[55] According to the Commentary on the Articles on State Responsibility, consent as a general matter must 'be freely given and clearly established. It must be actually expressed by the State rather than merely presumed on the basis that the State would have consented if it had been asked.'[56] When the request is for military assistance at a stage before opposition forces have reached belligerency, the invitation or consent must be given by the 'legitimate' government – one in effective control.[57]

When Iraq invaded Kuwait in 1990, the government of Kuwait fled. In that case, the government in exile remained the government owing to the fact that the United Nations Security Council and most of the rest of the world treated the Kuwaiti government in exile as the legitimate government. That was a case of interstate use of force and violation of Article 2(4). If the Kuwaiti government had been ousted by opposition forces within Kuwait the situation would have been different. Since the Tinoco Claims decision, effective control has been the legal test to determine the result of internal

[54] See notes 58–110 and accompanying text.

[55] Since World War I 'secret treaties' have been denounced. This is not so much due to an express rule against them but owing to their incongruity in a rule of law system enforced by the community itself. On this point see S. A. Shah, *International Law and Drone Strikes in Pakistan: The Legal and Socio-Political Aspects* (Abingdon: Routledge, 2015), 102.

[56] GA 56th Sess, Supp. No. 10, UN Doc. A/56/10, International Law Commission, 'Responsibility of States for Internationally Wrongful Acts', Art. 20 'Consent' and Commentary, para. 6.

[57] L. Doswald-Beck, 'The Legal Validity of Military Intervention by Invitation of the Government', *British Yearbook of International Law*, 56 (1985), 189–252, 191.

governmental change – whether by election, military coup, or civil war. International law does not yet, apparently, prohibit civil war, so accepting the results of such wars does not undermine an international law rule against rebellion. As a practical matter, so many governments take power by express or implied violations of constitutions or principles of democracy it would be difficult under international law to penalize such governments through mandating non-recognition. Nevertheless, recognizing a government installed through outside military intervention does tend to undermine the rule against the interstate use of force.

### *B The Cold War and Post-Cold War Eras of Ever-Expanding Invitations*

Writers in the early years of the Cold War continued to support the pre-Charter rule that only governments could request outside assistance against internal opponents until opponents reached a state of belligerency.[58] In the course of the 1960s and 1970s, however, debates at the UN began to feature arguments calling for the right to assist national liberation struggles.[59] These arguments tended to leave the nature of the lawful intervention vague – it could entail non-lethal aid, for example. With the end of the Cold War, a broad array of opposition groups asserted claims to receive military support against oppressive governments.[60] This section looks at a number of interventions on the side of opposition forces, which evidence declining respect for legal limits on invitation.

As mentioned, the UK intervened in the Greek Civil War claiming to be in 'collective defence against indirect aggression' by communists.[61] The USA gave the same reason for its intervention in Lebanon in 1958.[62] In 1956, the Soviet Union sent 60,000 troops into Hungary to crush a popular movement aimed at moving Hungary away from Soviet dominance. The Soviets justified the intervention on the basis of an invitation, but to get the invitation,

[58] Brownlie, *International Law and the Use of Force by States* 1963 (n. 35), 317.
[59] See, e.g., R. E. Gorelick, 'Wars of National Liberation: *Jus Ad Bellum*', *Case Western Reserve Journal of International Law*, 11 (1979), 71–93.
[60] See note 131.
[61] Brownlie, *International Law and the Use of Force by States* 1963 (n. 35), 325.
[62] Friedmann, 'Intervention, Civil War and the Rôle of International Law' 1965 (n. 51), 72.

they plotted with a high-ranking member of the Hungarian government, János Kádár, to represent himself as the true government, moving aside the choice of the reformers, Imre Nagy.[63] The Soviets followed a similar approach in obtaining invitations to intervene in Czechoslovakia in 1968,[64] and Afghanistan in 1979.[65]

In the case of Afghanistan, the Soviets moved troops into the country to support a takeover by Babrak Karmal. During the confusion, Afghanistan's leader Hafizullah Amin was killed. The weight of evidence indicates Soviet troops assassinated him.[66] Karmal then invited the Soviet Union to assist Afghanistan in fighting militants determined to install a version of Islamic government. These fighters, known as Mujahideen, were influenced by a wave of religious revival that also swept the conservative Muslim cleric Ayatollah Khomeini into power in Iran in 1979. As part of this wave, a Saudi engineer from a wealthy family, Osama bin Laden, travelled to Afghanistan to join the fight against the Soviets. He and other Mujahideen received US government backing. The USA justified this assistance as countering the unlawful Soviet intervention.[67]

Almost three decades before the 1979 Soviet intervention in Afghanistan, the USA was backing anti-communist fighters and political leaders in Vietnam. During World War II, Japan had occupied the French colony of Vietnam. Communist guerrilla fighters resisted them with US backing. After the war, the USA supported the French return to Vietnam as part of a worldwide anti-communist strategy, but the nationalists who fought the

[63] C. Gati, *Failed Illusions: Moscow, Washington, Budapest, and the 1956 Hungarian Revolt* (Washington, DC: Woodrow Wilson Center Press, 2006), 17, 231–3. See also, Lieblich, 'The Soviet Intervention in Hungary' 2018 (n. 52).

[64] P. Windsor and A. Roberts, *Czechoslovakia 1968: Reform, Repression and Resistance* (London: Institute for Strategic Studies, 1969), 97–111.

[65] See M. E. O'Connell, 'Soviet Prisoners in the Afghan Conflict', *Columbia Journal of Transnational Law*, 23 (1985), 497–504.

[66] Ibid. See also, G. Nolte and J. Barkholdt, 'The Soviet Intervention in Afghanistan – 1979–80', in Corten *et al.*, *The Use of Force in International Law* 2018 (n. 16), 297–305, 297–8, notes 9–10. Nolte and Barkholdt say the circumstances of Amin's death are 'not entirely clear' but cite only the Soviet Union for the position that Afghans and not Soviet troops might have killed Amin.

[67] See generally, L. Wright, *The Looming Tower: Al-Qaeda and the Road to 9/11* (New York: Alfred A. Knopf, 2006).

Japanese now turned to fighting the French.[68] The French suffered a major military defeat at Dien Bein Phu in 1954 and began the process of withdrawal. Under an agreement reached later that year, Vietnam was temporarily divided into north and south pending elections in 1956 to establish a unified country under one government. Those elections were never held. With the support of the USA, Ngo Dinh Diem declared the south independent in 1955.[69] The USA supported Diem as an opponent of communism until the CIA assassinated him in 1963. For the next decade, the USA fought on behalf of South Vietnam against the North, claiming to be acting in collective self-defence under Article 51.[70]

In 1960–1963 and again in 1964, Belgium intervened in its former colony, Congo, claiming the need to rescue Belgian citizens and others.[71] The USA assisted Belgium in both periods, including by assassinating the Congolese nationalist leader, Patrice Lumumba, in 1961.[72] Lumumba was attempting to limit Western influence by building ties to the Soviet Union. The USA intervened in the Dominican Republic in April 1965 where violence broke out among rival political factions. Again, US officials cited the need to rescue nationals but also mentioned a request from Dominican authorities.[73] The intervening force grew rapidly to 10,000 troops, then combined with a newly created peacekeeping force of the Organization of American States to reach 12,000. At the point the

[68] For a general history of the origins of the US intervention in Vietnam, see, F. Logevall, *Embers of War: The Fall of an Empire and the Making of America's Vietnam* (New York: Random House, 2012).

[69] For a history of the US role in the fighting between North and South Vietnam, see G. Herring, *America's Longest War: The United States and Vietnam, 1950–1975* (New York: McGraw-Hill, 1996).

[70] On the USA, Vietnam, and international law, see, Wright, 'Legal Aspects of the Viet-Nam Situation' 1966 (n. 45).

[71] See R. Kolb, 'The Belgian Intervention in the Congo – 1960 and 1964', in Corten *et al., The Use of Force in International Law* 2018 (n. 16), 76–84.

[72] G. Nzongola-Ntalaja, 'Patrice Lumumba: The Most Important Assassination of the 20th Century', *Guardian* (17 January 2011), available at www.theguardian.com/global-development/poverty-matters/2011/jan/17/patrice-lumumba-50th-anniversary-assassination.

[73] C. Walter, 'The US Intervention in the Dominican Republic – 1965', in Corten *et al., The Use of Force in International Law* 2018 (n. 16), 118–130, 123. See also, G. Nolte, 'Intervention by Invitation', Max Planck Encyclopedia of Public International Law available at http://opil.ouplaw.com/view/10.1093/law:epil/9780199231690/law-9780199231690-e1702?rskey=gdQPrA&result=1&prd=EPIL (last updated 2010).

OAS force was created, the USA shifted its justification from rescue to authorization by an organization. US troops remained a year and a half, withdrawing finally in September 1966. During the turmoil of 1965, identifying any party with authority to issue an invitation in the Dominican Republic would have been difficult.

The UN General Assembly adopted its Declaration on the Inadmissibility of Intervention at this turbulent moment. The Declaration provides for situations like that of the Dominican Republic: '[N]o State shall organise, assist, foment, finance, incite or tolerate subversive, terrorist or armed activities directed towards the violent overthrow of the regime of another State, or interfere in civil strife in another State.'[74] The obligation on states is to stay out of the civil strife. The USA failed in this duty once again in 1983, when it intervened in Grenada.[75] It obtained an invitation from the British Governor-General, who lacked authority to issue it and, at any rate, had to backdate it to prior to the invasion.[76] The USA then replaced Grenada's government.

Even the UK joined in a UN General Assembly resolution condemning America's use of force against Grenada. The vote was all the more striking given the otherwise close relations between US President Ronald Reagan and British Prime Minister Margaret Thatcher. Yet, the vote was understandable given the continuing UK ties to Grenada, including on security matters. In addition, the UK stood firm respecting the illegality of military intervention against a government. In 1984, the UK government published a 'Foreign Policy Document' which stated that governments may invite assistance, so long as it was the result of true consent. International law prohibits assistance, however, in a situation of civil war in which contending parties are in control of territory.[77]

The post-Cold War period was hailed as a new moment in which democracy and market economies would flourish worldwide.

[74] Declaration on the Inadmissibility of Intervention in the Domestic Affairs of States and the Protection of their Independence and Sovereignty, GA Res. 2131 (XX) of 21 December 1965, para. 2.

[75] See J. Quigley, 'The United States Invasion of Grenada: Stranger than Fiction', *University of Miami Inter-American Law Review*, 18 (1986–7), 271–352; and C. C. Joyner, 'The United States Action in Grenada: Reflections on the Lawfulness of Invasion', *American Journal of International Law*, 78 (1984), 131–75. See also Chapter 4.

[76] Joyner, 'The United States Action in Grenada' 1984 (n. 75), 137–9.

[77] G. Marston (ed.), 'United Kingdom Materials on International Law 1986', *British Yearbook of International Law*, 57 (1986), 487–654, 614.

A noticeable change occurred in the practice of intervention by invitation as well. The USA ended for a time its practice of assassinating leaders to obtain invitations. Instead, it turned to military intervention with or without an invitation. It did so despite the link between the Soviet Union's collapse and intervention.

The Soviet invasion of Afghanistan played a clear role in the demise of the Soviet Union in 1989. Another factor was the Helsinki Watch movement that formed after the agreement to the Helsinki Accords.[78] The movement helped spread interest in democracy and human rights throughout the Eastern bloc. The new interest led people to organize for peaceful, yet revolutionary, political, economic, and ideological changes.[79] After the successful military action to liberate Kuwait following Iraq's invasion in 1990, however, calls started from an NGO that began with Helsinki, Human Rights Watch. It was joined by neo-conservatives in the call to spread democracy in Iraq and beyond through the use of force. As the fighting to liberate Kuwait ended on 28 February 1991, Kurds in northern Iraq and Shia in the south began rebellions.[80] The Kurds had long aimed to create their own ethnically-defined state, encompassing Kurdish communities in Iraq, Iran, Syria, Turkey, and Armenia.[81] The Shia rising was more spontaneous, a reaction to the perception that Iraq's leader Saddam Hussein and his Sunni Muslim allies were weakened after two failed wars against Iran in the 1980s and against Kuwait. The Shia, with help from groups in Iran, succeeded during the month of March in taking

[78] See Office of the Historian, US Department of State, 'Helsinki Final Act, 1975', *Milestones*, available at https://history.state.gov/milestones/1969–1976/helsinki.

[79] S. Crawshaw, 'Fall of the Berlin Wall: A People's Uprising That Grew Until It Remade Europe', *Independent* (28 October 2014), available at www.independent.co.uk/news/world/world-history/fall-of-the-berlin-wall-a-people-s-uprising-that-grew-until-it-remade-europe-9824273.html.

[80] M. Zenko, 'Who is to Blame for the Doomed Iraqi Uprisings of 1991?', *National Interest* (7 March 2016), available at https://nationalinterest.org/blog/the-buzz/behind-the-doomed-iraqi-uprisings-1991–15425.

[81] 'Who Are the Kurds?', *BBC* (31 October 2017), available at www.bbc.com/news/world-middle-east-29702440; and 'Iraqi Kurdistan Profile – Timeline', *BBC* (31 October 2017), available at www.bbc.com/news/world-middle-east-15467672. See also, T. Gazzini, 'Intervention in Iraq's Kurdish Region and the Creation of the No-Fly Zone in Northern and Southern Iraq – 1991–2003', in Corten *et al., The Use of Force in International Law* 2018 (n. 16), 469–81.

control of a dozen cities but not the capital, Baghdad. Within weeks, Saddam had regrouped and brutally repressed the Shia uprising.

Despite the fact that US President George H. W. Bush had made radio broadcasts that encouraged Iraqis to act against Saddam, the USA held to the legal position it had no basis to intervene.[82] France agreed with the US legal analysis. Nevertheless, French Foreign Minister Roland Dumas pronounced that '[l]aw is one thing, but the safeguard of a population is something at least as precious'.[83] He said France would try to get the law changed. The most France obtained at the UN was Security Council Resolution 688 in which the Council found that Iraqi attacks on the Kurds constituted a threat to peace in the region. On the basis of that resolution, the USA, UK, and, for a while, France patrolled the skies above Iraq, preventing Iraqi airstrikes on the Kurdish and Shiite regions. The human rights organization Middle East Watch claimed the Council's resolutions authorized humanitarian intervention to aid the Kurds.[84]

Within a month of the Security Council's resolution on behalf of the Kurds, armed groups in Yugoslavia began insurgencies aimed at creating new, independent states. The Netherlands supported the groups and raised the possibility of intervening on their behalf.[85] The Dutch acknowledged, however, the need for Security Council authorization. The Council subsequently authorized the first of the 'peace enforcement' operations. The consequences of this well-

[82] B. Gellman, 'Kurds Contend US Encouraged Rebellion Via "Voice of Free Iraq"', *Washington Post* (9 April 1991), available at www.washingtonpost.com/archive/politics/1991/04/09/kurds-contend-us-encouraged-rebellion-via-voice-of-free-iraq/a28c33b4–0bcf-4005–849b-8202ba1f36de/?noredirect=on&utm_term=.51e39e9303b1.

[83] P. Webster, 'French Minister Rushes to Scene: Guardian Correspondents Report on World Outrage at the Iraqi Regime's Systematic Slaughter of Kurdish and Shi'ite Rebels', *Guardian* (4 April 1991), 24.

[84] Middle East Watch Report, November 1991. See also, Gazzini, 'Intervention in Iraq's Kurdish Region and the Creation of the No-Fly Zones in Northern and Southern Iraq – 1991–2003' 2018 (n. 81).

[85] 'The Netherlands ... proposed today that Western European countries consider deploying a "lightly armed" force in Yugoslavia because an international team of 200 civilian observers had so far been unable to end the fighting. Dutch officials said the idea of the force was not to impose a cease-fire but rather to use a European show of arms to discourage a resumption of warfare after a new cease-fire goes into effect.' A. Riding, 'European Force is Proposed for Croatia', *New York Times* (17 September 1991), A3, available at www.nytimes.com/1991/09/17/world/european-force-is-proposed-for-croatia.html.

meaning but poorly conceived initiative is discussed in Chapter 3. For the justification of invitation, the Council's action was a milestone on the road to weakening the legal limits against outside military force aimed at changing internal political and social situations.[86] The USA supported these resolutions but did not provide troops. It also supported an arms embargo to prevent fighting from escalating, but then smuggled weapons in defiance of the embargo to Bosnian Muslim fighters.[87]

Independence movements were emerging in the former Soviet Union, too. In August 1991, during an attempted military coup against Mikhail Gorbachev, Russia, Ukraine, and other Soviet republics declared sovereign, independent statehood. In September 1991, a former Soviet Air Force Major General, Dzhokhar Dudayev, seized power in the Republic of Chechnya and declared it, too, independent – the independent Republic of Ichkeria. Russia responded first by supporting Dudayev's opponents, then by arming them. By 1994, regular Russian forces were leading the armed effort to end the secession. Foreign fighters joined the anti-Russia forces. Some of the foreign fighters were, however, Wahabi Muslims practising a stricter form of the faith than Chechnya's Sufis. Internal tensions among Moscow's opponents together with the new leadership of Vladimir Putin combined in 2000 for a decisive Russian defeat of the separatist government.[88] Outside states generally abstained from interference in the Caucasus conflicts except to protest excessive use of force and human rights violations.[89]

Certainly the USA was busy elsewhere. It was carrying out air strikes in Iraq to maintain control of air space until 2004.[90]

[86] SC Res. 713 of 25 September 1991.

[87] See Cees Wiebes, *Intelligence and the War in Bosnia: 1992–1995* (Münster: LIT Verlag, 2003).

[88] See generally, C. King, *The Ghost of Freedom: A History of the Caucasus* (Oxford: Oxford University Press, 2008).

[89] The European Court of Human Rights has decided a number of cases against Russia based on conduct in the Caucasus conflicts. ECtHR, *Isayeva* v. *Russia*, Judgment of 24 February 2005, Application No. 57950/00; ECtHR, *Khashiyev & Akayeva* v. *Russia*, Judgment of 24 February 2005, Application Nos. 57942/00 and 57945/00; and ECtHR, *Abuyeva & Others* v. *Russia*, Judgment of 2 December 2010, Application No. 27065/05.

[90] For details of US and UK air operations over Iraq from the liberation of Kuwait in Operation Desert Storm in early 1991 through the heavy attacks of Operation Desert Fox in late 1998, see, United States Department of Defense Archive available at http://archive.defense.gov/specials/desert_fox/.

Between 1992 and 1995, it was active in Somalia's internal conflicts, sometimes involved in fighting. In October 1993, 18 US soldiers were killed in Mogadishu and their bodies desecrated, discouraging the use of US ground forces until 9/11.[91] In 1998, the USA bombed Sudan and Afghanistan in revenge for al-Qaeda terrorist attacks on the US embassies in Kenya and Tanzania.[92] Also in 1998, the US made its first request to NATO members to authorize attacking Serbia over the treatment of the ethnic Albanian population living in the Serbian province of Kosovo.[93]

Serbia agreed to permit human rights monitors in December and NATO called off the plan to bomb. Then, on the basis of false evidence that forty-five people had been murdered in Račak, Kosovo, in January 1999, the US Secretary of State ended the monitoring arrangement and again threatened Serbia with bombing unless it withdrew its troops. NATO's threat was carried out beginning in March and continued for seventy-eight days until Russia prevailed on the Serb leader, Slobodan Milosevic, to agree to move troops out of Kosovo. Russia assured Milosevic that its force would enter Kosovo quickly to counter NATO's presence.[94]

Following the attacks of 11 September 2001 in the USA by al-Qaeda, under the control of the United States's old ally Osama bin Laden, the USA began to intervene in internal conflicts with seemingly little sense of restraint. The first post-9/11 intervention was in the civil war in Afghanistan where the USA joined with the Northern Alliance against the Taliban.[95] A government acceptable to the USA and European allies took over in mid-2002. The USA has been fighting to keep first that government then its successors in power for years, far exceeding the duration of all past wars in which the USA has participated.

[91] See M. Bowden, *Black Hawk Down: A Story of Modern War* (New York: Grove Press, 1999).

[92] See J. Lobel, 'The Use of Force to Respond to Terrorist Attacks: The Bombing of Sudan and Afghanistan', *Yale Journal of International Law*, 24 (1999), 537–58.

[93] See D. Franchini and A. Tzanakopoulos, 'The Kosovo Crisis – 1999', in Corten *et al.*, *The Use of Force in International Law* 2018 (n. 16), 594–622; and M. E. O'Connell, 'The UN, NATO, and International Law After Kosovo', *Human Rights Quarterly*, 22 (2000), 57–89.

[94] Franchini and Tzanakopoulos, 'The Kosovo Crisis – 1999' 2018 (n. 93), 596–7.

[95] M. Byers, 'The Intervention in Afghanistan – 2001', in Corten *et al.*, *The Use of Force in International Law* 2018 (n. 16), 625–38.

Post-9/11 interventions did not stop with Afghanistan. The Bush administration soon argued it could use military force in self-defence anywhere in the world where al-Qaeda was present.[96] In 2002, President Bush authorized attacks in Yemen, a country finally at peace after many years of civil war. By 2012, following repeated uses of force by the USA, as well as governmental corruption, the influence of the Arab Spring, the Saudi-Iranian competition, and other factors, Yemen disintegrated into all-out civil war once again, sparking an overwhelming humanitarian catastrophe.[97] US President Donald Trump's first action as Commander-in-Chief was to authorize a Navy SEAL operation in Yemen on 5 February 2017. The USA and allied forces likely received false intelligence about the presence of al-Qaeda in a small village near the front line of the civil war. They attacked and ten children under the age of thirteen were killed, as well as about two dozen women and men. The people of the village had been fighting on the same side as Saudi Arabia and the USA. Saudi Arabia said it was intervening in the civil war on the side of the 'government', but their ally Hadi had fled Yemen in 2015, and the Houthi opposition, backed by Iran, controlled 'significant' territory.[98] Hadi had little if any authority to issue an invitation.

In addition to the post-9/11 interventions in Afghanistan and Yemen, the USA intervened in Iraq, Pakistan, Somalia, the

[96] The United States Congress has supported the President's use of military force:

> That the President is authorized to use all necessary and appropriate force against those nations, organizations, or persons he determines planned, authorized, committed, or aided the terrorist attacks that occurred on September 11, 2001, or harbored such organizations or persons, in order to prevent any future acts of international terrorism against the United States by such nations, organizations or persons.

Authorization for Use of Military Force, Public Law 107–40, 115 Statutes 224 (18 September 2001).

[97] 'Yemen Crisis: Who is Fighting Whom?', *BBC* (30 January 2018), available at www.bbc.com/news/world-middle-east-29319423. See also, L. Fero and T. Ruys, 'The Saudi-Led Military Intervention in Yemen's Civil War – 2015' in Corten *et al., The Use of Force in International Law* 2018 (n. 16), 899–911.

[98] L. Fero and T. Ruys, 'The Saudi-Led Military Intervention in Yemen's Civil War – 2015' (n. 97), 907–911. The authors question the continuing value of the territorial control test, given that Hadi was widely recognized as having the authority to invite intervention. In light of the *jus cogens* prohibition on force, however, a subjective test cannot replace the more objective and restrictive test of control.

Philippines, Nigeria, Libya, Niger, and Syria.[99] A variety of legal grounds have been offered. The US representative to the Security Council sent a letter in 2014 on the legality of intervening in Syria:

> ISIL and other terrorist groups in Syria are a threat not only to Iraq, but also to many other countries, including the United States and our partners in the region and beyond. States must be able to defend themselves, in accordance with the inherent right of individual and collective self-defence, as reflected in Article 51 of the Charter of the United Nations, when, as is the case here, the government of the State where the threat is located is unwilling or unable to prevent the use of its territory for such attacks. The Syrian regime has shown that it cannot and will not confront these safe havens effectively itself. Accordingly, the United States has initiated necessary and proportionate military actions in Syria in order to eliminate the ongoing ISIL threat to Iraq . . .[100]

Of the many concerns this letter raises, the most significant for a discussion of the right to intervene in internal conflict is the reference to Syria being 'unwilling or unable' to control terrorist groups. The representative is using 'unable/unwilling' where states have been using invitation. The letter indicates the USA has an actual invitation from Iraq. Syria likely would have issued one as well. The USA, however, did not want an invitation from Syria given the nature of the Syrian regime. A proponent of the 'unable/unwilling' argument has paired it with invitation or consent, saying: 'Consent may be strategic or operational, generic or ad hoc, express or implied.'[101] A state that is 'unable' or 'unwilling' to handle a problem is, for Bethlehem, giving implied consent. Syria's military efforts against opposition groups, including ISIS, indicate it was able and willing. It invited assistance to bolster its effort – just not from the USA, UK, or France.[102]

[99] See the website of the United States Department of Defense, available at www.defense.gov.

[100] UN Doc. S/2014/695, 'Letter dated 23 September 2014 from the Permanent Representative of the United States of America to the United Nations addressed to the Secretary-General'. See also, B. Egan/State Department, 'International Law, Legal Diplomacy, and the Counter-ISIL Campaign', Address at the American Society of International Law, *Lawfare* (1 April 2016), available at www.lawfareblog.com/state-department-legal-adviser-brian-egans-speech-asil.

[101] D. Bethlehem, 'Self-Defense Against an Imminent or Actual Armed Attack by Nonstate Actors', *American Journal of International Law*, 106 (2012), 770–7, 777.

[102] See, e.g., I. Black and D. Roberts, 'ISIS Air Strikes: Obama's Plan Condemned by Syria, Russia and Iran', *Guardian* (12 September 2014), available at www

In February 2014, Russia took advantage of unrest in Ukraine to move troops into the country, taking control of the Crimean peninsula. Russia's representative in the Security Council mentioned a raft of justifications, including invitation by Crimeans and their wish to be part of Russia. 'It is clear that the achievement of the right to self-determination in the form of separation from an existing state is an extraordinary measure. However, in the case of Crimea, it obviously arose as a result of the legal vacuum created by the violent coup against the legitimate Government carried out by nationalist radicals in Kyiv, as well as by their direct threats to impose their order throughout the territory of Ukraine.'[103] The president of Ukraine, Viktor Yanukovych, had in fact requested Russian assistance in re-establishing order in Ukraine. At the same time, however, he was fleeing the country to Russia.

Russia's President Putin referred to an invitation by 'Crimean authorities' to intervene as well as 'the well-known Kosovo precedent – a precedent our western colleagues created with their own hands in a very similar situation … '.[104] Pro-Russian leaders in Crimea compared their situation with that of Kosovar Albanians in the 1990s, asserting they had as much a right to request outside military intervention to aid their secession as the Kosovars. A few weeks later Yanukovych 'retracted' his invitation, which he admitted he was never in a position to give.[105] Russia did not withdraw, rather it granted the request for assistance from insurgents in Eastern Ukraine to help them fight to separate from Kiev. The USA condemned Russian action in Ukraine as 'aggression' and organized economic sanctions aimed at inducing Russia to remove its troops.[106] Then, less than six months later, the USA and Russia found

.theguardian.com/world/2014/sep/11/assad-moscow-tehran-condemn-obama-isis-air-strike-plan.

[103] UN Doc. S/PV.7134 of 13 March 2014, 15, cited in O. Corten, 'The Russian Intervention in the Ukrainian Crisis: Was *Jus Contra Belllum* "Confirmed Rather than Weakened"?', *Journal on the Use of Force and International Law*, 2 (2015), 17–41, 24, note 57.

[104] 'Address by the President of the Russian Federation', available at eng.kremlin.ru/news/6889, cited in M. Nikouei and M. Zamani, 'The Secession of Crimea: Where Does International Law Stand?', *Nordic Journal of International Law*, 85 (2016), 37–64, 54.

[105] T. D. Grant, 'Current Developments: Annexation of Crimea', *American Journal of International Law*, 109 (2015), 68–95, 82.

[106] W. Dunham, 'Kerry Condemns Russia's "Incredible Act of Aggression" in Ukraine', *Reuters* (2 March 2014), available at www.reuters.com/article/us-

themselves fighting in a common cause to defeat ISIS.[107] The USA and Russia reached agreement to 'deconflict' so that the focus of fighting would be on ISIS, not each other.[108] At the end of 2014, the USA reached a formal agreement with Afghanistan to continue assisting the government against the Taliban and later ISIS.[109]

These complicated interventions defy the traditional rule restricting intervention in civil war to the side of the government until the opposition reaches a stage without outside assistance of being able to challenge the government. The cases certainly do not support a rule of non-intervention on any side. They nonetheless underscore the wisdom of the more stringent rule. Despite considerable outside assistance to Syrian opposition fighters, these groups had little chance from the outset of winning an armed conflict with regular Syrian forces. The same has been true in Eastern Ukraine. In Afghanistan, the government has tried for seventeen years to defeat the Taliban and now ISIS. In Mali in 2013, France invoked the invitation of a government that would not exist but for French military support. Similarly, Yemen has had no government with a credible right to invite outside assistance since 2011.[110]

### *C* Jus Cogens *and Invitation*

The discussion above is a litany of intervention in disrespect for the traditional rule. Nevertheless, standard scholarly analysis on intervention from the perspective of positive law tends to conclude that the traditional rule remains in place. State practice and *opinio*

ukraine-crisis-usa-kerry-idUSBREA210DG20140302; and United States Department of State, 'Ukraine and Russia Sanctions' (visited 27 February 2017), available at www.state.gov/e/eb/tfs/spi/ukrainerussia.

107 See A. Soufan, *Anatomy of Terror: From the Death of Bin Laden to the Rise of the Islamic State* (New York: W.W. Norton & Co, 2017).

108 G. Rayner, B. Riley-Smith, and A. Luhn, 'US-Russia "Hotline" for Syrian Air Strikes Could Help Avoid Conflict Escalating', *Telegraph* (13 April 2018), available at www.telegraph.co.uk/news/2018/04/12/us-russia-hotline-syrian-air-strikes-could-help-avoid-conflict/.

109 Security and Defense Cooperation Agreement Between the United States of America and the Islamic Republic of Afghanistan, 30 September 2014, available at www.state.gov/documents/organization/244487.pdf.

110 See A. Aneja, 'Political Vacuum as Wounded Saleh Leaves for Saudi Arabia', *The Hindu* (5 June 2011), available at www.thehindu.com/news/international/political-vacuum-as-wounded-saleh-leaves-for-saudi-arabia/article2079250.ece.

*juris*[111] do not support a new more permissive rule.[112] The cases, while significant, are relatively few and the *opinio juris* is equivocal at best.[113] Even if the evidence were stronger for a more permissive customary law rule, the peremptory norm prohibiting the use of force invalidates any expansion of lawful resort to armed intervention. The traditional rule restricting intervention remains in place unless the international community discerns that a more restrictive rule applies. This section considers the case for a rule restricting any outside intervention in internal conflict.

In most of the cases reviewed above, opposition forces would never have reached a stage of challenging the government without outside military assistance. If such assistance amounts to the equivalent of a significant armed attack, the government has the right to invite assistance in collective self-defence. In the rare case, however, where an opposition reaches the status of belligerency through its own efforts, the traditional rule prohibits any party from receiving outside assistance. As related to the peremptory norm, the traditional rule of no outside assistance at the stage of belligerency endures.

The traditional rule also means no assistance to counter assistance. There is certainly no express rule in the positive law permitting counter-intervention on behalf of the opposition. It may seem that counter-intervention is the only way to effectively sanction a government for receiving assistance, but this is incorrect. The Security Council and General Assembly may organize collective measures. Non-military sanctions by states acting individually may also be lawful. In addition, until the opposition is established as a government in effective control, it lacks capacity to request outside military assistance in any case. The exercise of military force on the territory of another state against the government, even a government facing a serious challenge, violates Article 2(4). The better view is that no right of counter-intervention exists. In states with no

[111] Corten and Gray conclude that the traditional rule has not been altered by state practice and *opinio juris*. Interestingly, both authors add policy arguments to their analysis of the positive law. Corten, 'La rébellion et le droit international' 2015 (n. 13), 290–5; and Gray, *International Law and the Use of Force* 2018 (n. 2), 118–19.

[112] Ibid.

[113] See, e.g., D. McManus, 'A US License To Kill', *LA Times* (11 January 2003), A1, available at http://articles.latimes.com/2003/jan/11/world/fg-predator11.

government in control, as has been the case in Libya, Somalia, and Yemen, the duty of the international community is to act against all intervention lacking express Security Council authorization, not pick a side to assist into power.

This restrictive view of outside assistance is consistent not only with the peremptory norm against the use of force but also the concerns Louise Doswald-Beck has pointed to respecting escalation of conflict and interference with self-determination. The more restrictive rule is also more protective of the principle of equality. Equality is the 'most basic principle of international law'.[114] Without the principle of equality, 'it is impossible to maintain even a minimum of universal international order'.[115] Groups that require outside intervention to control a state do not have the sufficient acceptance of their population. In such circumstances, an outside state determines the national government. Such interference is the antithesis of equality, independence, and self-determination. While all states should be concerned with human rights and good governance in every other state, these goods must be promoted through mechanisms other than military force. Killing and destruction are unlawful, immoral, and ineffective ways of responding to oppressive regimes.[116]

In the mid-1960s, Wolfgang Friedman observed that states were unwilling to honour the distinction between governments and opposition groups:

> So deep are the political conflicts leading to intervention and counter-intervention ... the distinction between the rights of incumbent governments and of substantial movements of rebellion has lost all meaning. In none of the important recent internal-international conflicts have the contending outside states even bothered to accord the status of 'insurgents' or 'belligerents' to the other side. In these circumstances, there is much justification for the view ... that no meaningful legal distinction can be made with regard to claims for outside assistance, as between the incumbent government and insurgents.[117]

[114] Friedmann, 'Intervention, Civil War and the Rôle of International Law' 1965 (n. 51), 67.

[115] Ibid.

[116] Ibid., 73–4. See also, See, e.g., Gray, *International Law and the Use of Force* 2018 (n. 2), 119.

[117] Friedmann, 'Intervention, Civil War and the Rôle of International Law' 1965 (n. 51), 72–3.

Even states attempting to avoid ideological bias in assessing the status of a party to a conflict might nevertheless be confronted with genuine issues of fact as to 'which side would ultimately establish itself as the legal representative of the state . . .'.[118] Without clarity on the point, the case becomes stronger for a non-intervention rule.

Friedmann concluded that not only states but also the UN Security Council should stay out of civil war. The Charter can be interpreted as permitting Security Council action in civil war. Articles 24 and 39 refer to 'any threat to the peace, breach of the peace or act of aggression', but this view is 'more than countered by the increased turbulence of a multitude of unsettled international conditions in an increasing number of countries'.[119] The 2011 case of Libya and other UN interventions in civil wars prove the correctness of Friedmann's position.[120] His views provide further support for the argument in Chapter 3 to end UN Peacekeeping that does not conform to traditional criteria: existence of a ceasefire, consent of all parties, impartiality, and minimal force for personal self-defence only.[121] Since classical peacekeeping requires an actual ceasefire, peacekeepers are not called upon to intervene in an armed conflict.

In 2005, despite intervention's dismal record, UN members agreed in the World Summit Outcome Document that the Security Council does have legal authority to authorize intervention in some civil wars. While Articles 24 and 39 indicate the Council has the power to authorize intervention, the last clause of Article 39 seems to negate this by stating the Council is restricted to restoring 'international peace and security'. The Outcome Document provides that serious governmental violations of human rights within one state are a matter of international peace and security. As such, internal conflict may fall within the Security Council's jurisdiction.[122] What the membership may not do, however, in light of *jus cogens*, is expand the Security Council's

118 Ibid., 73. 119 Ibid., 74.
120 See also, M E. O'Connell, 'Continuing Limits on UN Intervention in Civil War', *Indiana Law Journal*, 67 (1992), 903–13.
121 Chapter 3.
122 2005 World Summit Outcome, UN Doc. A/RES/60/1, 24 October 2005, para. 138.

power to authorize military force. The Council may address internal conflict using non-lethal alternatives. Additionally, the principles of necessity and proportionality raise barriers to military intervention in addition to those of the Charter.

If the Security Council's role in internal armed conflict is limited, other international organizations have no military role. Treaties have been adopted that purport to provide prior consent to intervention in certain situations.[123] Brownlie points to the 'particularly difficult question' where governments have agreed in advance to intervene to preserve a government in power. 'Can a party to such an agreement intervene to overthrow a *de facto* government which has effectively replaced the former government? A number of jurists have denied that such a treaty is valid.'[124] Yet, after Brownlie published this position, states have continued to agree in advance to intervention and have intervened in West Africa, for example, at the request of a government that has lost control.[125] Yet, such prior consent cannot as a legal matter override the termination of consent by a government at the time when intervention is under consideration. In the case of a government requesting that an organization assist, if that government cannot maintain power without outside intervention, its claim to be the government is undermined. Where no group exercises governmental control, a situation seen in Somalia, Libya, and Yemen in the 2000s, the prohibition on the use of force directs all intervenors to stay out – state or organization.

[123] Treaty of Guarantee, signed at Nicosia, 16 August 1960, UNTS 5475, available at https://peacemaker.un.org/sites/peacemaker.un.org/files/CY%20GR%20TR_600816_Treaty%20of%20Guarantee.pdf; Art. 4, Protocol on Amendments to the Constitutive Act of the African Union, adopted by the First Extra-Ordinary Session of the Assembly of the African Union, Addis Ababa (Ethiopia), 3 February 2003; and, respecting the more complicated basis of ECOWAS intervention, see J. I. Levitt, 'Pro-Democratic Intervention in Africa', *Wisconsin International Law Journal*, 24 (2006), 785–834; J. D. Gagnon, 'ECOWAS's Right to Intervene in Côte d'Ivoire to Install Alassane Ouattara as President-Elect', *Notre Dame Journal of International & Comparative Law*, 3 (2013), 51–72; and see M. S. Helal, 'The ECOWAS Intervention in The Gambia – 2016', in Corten *et al.*, *The Use of Force in International Law* 2018 (n. 16), 912–32.

[124] Brownlie, *International Law and the Use of Force by States* 1963 (n. 35), 321.

[125] See, e.g., Helal, 'The ECOWAS Intervention in The Gambia – 2016' 2018 (n. 123); and Gagnon, 'ECOWAS's Right to Intervene in Côte D'Ivoire to Install Alassane Ouattara as President-Elect' 2013 (n. 123).

In brief, governments may invite outside military assistance in situations that are well short of armed conflict occurring on their territory, a threshold to be discussed in the next section. Non-state actors have no legal right to request outside military assistance to act against governments. Aiding non-state actors may amount to an armed attack and trigger the right of self-defence under Article 51. If, however, a non-state actor is able to challenge a government, outside military assistance to that governments must also end. Failure of an outside state to withdraw at that point not only violates the peremptory norm against the use of force but also the closely-related principles of non-intervention, equality, independence, and self-determination. In situations of doubt as to whether a group is the government under international law, whether a government has issued an invitation, or whether an opposition group has reached belligerency, each issue will be decided in favour of the presumption of peace. In other words, close questions are resolved on the side of non-intervention.

## II Restricting Resort to Rebellion

The crisis in Mali described at the outset of this chapter began when the Tuareg people attempted their fourth armed rebellion against the government. The rebellion triggered a chain of events that included France's military intervention. In the case of Mali and many others, there is a close connection between rebellion and intervention. Groups organize to overthrow governments or to secede, then they or the government request outside assistance. The rule against such assistance was just discussed. The analysis now turns to the right of people to rebel in the first place. A range of views can be found from writers who find nothing in the *jus ad bellum* on this question to those now advocating for recognition of a right of oppressed people to fight in self-defence under the *jus ad bellum*.[126] Applying the lens of *jus cogens* leads to a different

[126] See, e.g., Corten, 'La rébellion et le droit international' 2015 (n. 13), 91, 107, finding nothing in international law speaking to the legality or illegality of rebellion prior to or after the adoption of the UN Charter in 1945. For an argument in favour of expanding the exceptions to the prohibition to include rebellion, see Hessbruegge, *Human Rights and Personal Self-Defense in International Law* 2017 (n. 14), chap. 7.

conclusion. The prohibition on the use of force and other aspects of the *jus ad bellum* apply to resort to force against the government. These principles restrict the right to violent rebellion and support in its place the use of alternatives to organized killing and destruction.

The question of whether there is a right of rebellion is discussed far less often than the other use of force issues analysed in the book so far. This is true even though internal armed conflict has been a worse problem since 1945 than interstate war.[127] Most armed conflict today combines aspects of both. Since the end of the Cold War, major armed conflicts, including Iraq's invasion of Kuwait, the Eritrea–Ethiopia War, the Afghanistan War, the Iraq War, the intervention in Libya, and Russia's intervention in Ukraine, have involved direct conflict between sovereign states but also internal conflict against the governments involved. Even conflicts that began as more purely civil wars – Congo, Mali, Somalia, Syria, the Philippines, and Yugoslavia, for example – invariably became internationalized with the intervention of foreign sovereign states.[128] The civil wars in Russia (Chechnya), Sri Lanka, and Colombia involved more minimal outside intervention. Every persistent civil war, however, inevitably includes external intervention in support of one side or another, at the very least in the form of providing weapons to rebels.[129]

In general, the situations that can be described as civil war or internal armed conflict involve an organized group of people who decide to take up arms against the government. The focus here is on the point when the decision to resort to force results in significant

[127] Uppsala Conflict Data Programme (n. 7). See also, D. Armitage, *Civil Wars, A History in Ideas* (New York: Alfred A. Knopf, 2017), 3–27.

[128] For a discussion of the importance and difficulty of classifying conflicts as international, non-international, and others, see, Gray, *International Law and the Use of Force* 2018 (n. 2), 85–6. This part uses the terms 'civil war' and 'internal armed conflict' synonymously and in distinction to 'international armed conflict'. The terms 'non-international armed conflict' will not be used given the distortion of its original meaning as another term for civil war after 9/11.

[129] See, e.g., C. J. Chivers, E. Schmitt, and M. Mazzetti, 'In Turnabout, Syria Rebels Get Libyan Weapons', *New York Times* (21 June 2013), available at www.nytimes.com/2013/06/22/world/africa/in-a-turnabout-syria-rebels-get-libyan-weapons.html. Even where rebels procure weapons from private sellers in violation of national law, if weapons nevertheless reach fighters it indicates a failure of due diligence by the outside state, which implicates state responsibility.

armed fighting. At that point, under international law, the armed group has triggered armed conflict.[130] International law imposes a duty on governments not to respond with excessive force to protestors, criminal gangs, or low-level armed opposition. Excessive force will violate the right to life, due process, and other human rights. Less is known about the opposition's duties in such situations. When the government uses excessive force, some writers say the victims have a right to engage in armed force in response. Advocates of humanitarian intervention also argue for a right of states to intervene on behalf of armed action against government oppression. When they do so they inevitably accept, at least implicitly, the legality of non-state actors taking up arms against the government. Claims for humanitarian intervention consistently involve aiding a non-state actor armed group, such as the Kosovo Liberation Army or the Free Syrian Army.

Thus, advocacy for a right of humanitarian intervention is indirect advocacy for a right of rebellion. Intervenors, however, rarely consider that fighting to defeat government forces needs advanced planning, weapons, training, and resources. The insurgencies that endure tend to involve units of the armed forces that defect, so that opposition groups have trained fighters.[131] Under most national law this sort of activity is unlawful. Even in the Latin American states where constitutions indicate a legal right to overthrow the government, advanced planning for military action is not permitted.[132]

[130] ILA Committee on the Use of Force, 'Final Report on the Meaning of Armed Conflict under International Law' (2010), available at https://ila.vettoreweb.com/Storage/Download.aspx?DbStorageId=1266&StorageFileGuid=84ac02f3-e51a-4308-adf0-e94256758f38. For an application of the definition of armed conflict as set out in the ILA Report, see *BBC*, 'Syria in a Civil War, Red Cross Says', (15 July 2012), available at www.bbc.com/news/world-middle-east-18849362.

[131] See, e.g., the case of Libya, D. Babington, 'Over 100 Libyan Army Members Defect from Gaddafi', *Reuters* (30 May 2011), www.reuters.com/article/us-libya-officers/over-100-libyan-army-members-defect-from-gaddafi-idUSTRE74T41820110530; and regarding ISIS, H. Hendawi and Q. Abdul-Zahra, 'ISIS Top Brass Is Iraqi Army's Former Best and Brightest', *Haaretz* (8 August 2015), www.haaretz.com/isis-top-brass-is-iraqi-army-s-former-1.5384550.

[132] T. Ginsburg, D. Lansberg-Rodriguez and M. Versteeg, 'When to Overthrow your Government: The Right to Resist in the World's Constitutions', *UCLA Law Review*, 60 (2013), 1184–260, 1240–1. See, e.g., Art. 3 Political Constitution of the Republic of Honduras of 1982.

Early advocates of humanitarian intervention and responsibility to protect (R2P) tended to look at the nature of the crisis, not the conditions of effective military action on behalf of victims. Advocates for a right of groups within states to fight their governments under the *jus ad bellum* typically fail to address the practical problem of organizing to fight. When they fail to do so, they fail to apply the analysis required by the principle of necessity. They fail to consider whether there is a chance of success.[133]

Such advocacy for rebellion tends not only to be impractical as a matter of positive law, it even more clearly conflicts with the peremptory norm prohibiting force. Rather than wasting efforts in a vain attempt at expanding the *jus ad bellum* to embrace a right of rebellion, human rights advocates would use their time and talent more effectively in seeking alternatives to war in confronting government violations of human rights and other wrongs. Chapter 6 turns to these alternatives not only to identify them, but to explain how they can be represented in a more attractive light.

### *A The Charter and Insurgency*

Olivier Corten is correct that the UN Charter does not expressly address the use of force within states.[134] The Charter was written for member states and their interstate rights and duties. Article 2(4) and 51 are addressed to interstate uses of force. The UN Security Council is mandated to act against threats and breaches of 'international peace and security'. The Charter promotes human rights and economic prosperity, which are to be enjoyed by individuals

[133] Hessbruegge, *Human Rights and Personal Self-Defense in International Law* 2017 (n. 14), chap. 7; and see A. Marsavelski, 'The Crime of Terrorism and the Right of Revolution in International Law', *Connecticut Journal of International Law*, 28 (2013), 243–96, 267–73. Hessbruegge advocates for the right of armed opposition to oppressive governments but does not follow his point through to the question of prior organization for a chance of success. Advocates of the use of torture in so-called 'ticking time bomb' situations similarly omit the need to train torturers to perform in the way proponents advocate. See, e.g., the argument of a prominent Harvard law professor, Alan M. Dershowitz, 'Stop Winking at Torture and Codify It: US Must Decide Which Interrogation Tactics Are Allowable and Which Aren't', *LA Times* (13 June 2004), available at http://articles.latimes.com/2004/jun/13/opinion/oe-dersh13.

[134] Corten, 'La Rebéllion et le Droit International: Le Principe de Neutralité en Tension' 2015 (n. 13). See also, G. Nolte, *Eingreifen auf Einladung* (Heidelberg: Springer, 1999).

and communities. It has no express mention of a similar kind respecting insurgency or rebellion. This silence suggests that the Charter does not prohibit the organized, anti-government use of force by non-state actors. Other indications, however, narrow any positive law right of rebellion considerably. The *jus cogens* prohibition goes farther, restricting resort to internal as well as international armed conflict.[135]

The Charter drafters did debate aspects of the problem of internal armed conflict. The Spanish Civil War had been a harbinger of the wider world war to follow.[136] The wartime German, Italian, and Japanese governments fell at home and were pushed out of occupation zones by forces that included irregular fighters, aided by the Allies. Yet, during and after the war, Britain's Prime Minister Winston Churchill made it clear the UK intended to maintain the empire. Churchill diverted efforts against the Axis powers to quash independence movements in Britain's colonies.[137] As discussed above, the British helped the French retake control of Vietnam in preference to the nationalist Vietnamese forces who had battled Japanese occupation.[138] This complicated situation was mirrored in the relevant international law prior to and after the adoption of the Charter. The four new Geneva Conventions of 1949 for the protection of victims of armed conflict, for example, attempted to mitigate some of the more extreme impacts of fighting in non-international armed conflicts by imposing new duties but without significantly weakening the privileged status of sovereign states.[139]

The question of the legal right to rebel also reflected the complications of civil war. Just War thinkers had generally stood in opposition to rebellion but not uniformly. The English political philosopher John Locke, writing in 1689, took a stand clearly in favour of rebellion. Locke argued firmly for the priority of individual liberty in contrast to the priority of social order. The weakness of his argument lies in his failure to justify why killing

135 Section C, notes 110–127.

136 On the Spanish Civil War, see A. Beevor, *The Battle for Spain, The Spanish Civil War, 1936–1939* (New York: Penguin Books, 2006).

137 On Churchill and the British Empire, see R. Toye, *Churchill's Empire* (New York: St Martin's Press, 2010).

138 See notes 67–9 and accompanying text.

139 See, e.g., L. Moir, *The Law of Internal Armed Conflict* (Cambridge: Cambridge University Press, 2002), 23–9.

versus other methods of securing liberty is defensible.[140] Locke's contemporary, the German scholar of natural law and international law Samuel Pufendorf, agreed.[141] Their views added weight to the pro-rebellion side of a long-running debate.

The great figures of the Just War Doctrine, Saints Augustine and Aquinas, had reasons to be opposed to rebellion. Augustine argued, it will be recalled from Chapter 2, for limited exceptions to the pure pacifism of early Christians. He taught that force was justifiable for self-defence by individuals and communities. Communities could also recover property and punish wrongdoing, but only as decreed by a right authority, a prince or other legitimate leader of government.[142] This principle of right authority also served as a bar to war against the prince by his own people who lacked the authority to initiate war. Augustine called on the Roman authorities of his time to use armed force against the violent Donatist sect for 'acts constituting rebellion'.[143]

Augustine accepted that a rule against rebellion might entail tolerating injustice in the case of a tyrannical ruler but considered that the terrible costs of war were not worth the potential benefit in such cases.[144] Augustine's most important follower in the matter of justifiable war, St Thomas Aquinas, was more equivocal respecting rebellion against a tyrant.[145] Aquinas's first requirement is that a legitimate authority make the decision. He had two arguments for 'why special authority is needed for war-making, one based on the juridical principle "no higher redress" (just war becomes operative

140 K. Lidén and H. Syse, 'The Politics of Peace and Law: Realism, Internationalism, and the Cosmopolitan Challenge', in C. Marcela Bailliet and K. M. Larsen (eds.), *Promoting Peace Through International Law* (Oxford: Oxford University Press, 2015), 21–42, 29–30.

141 S. Pufendorf, *Two Books of the Elements of Universal Jurisprudence* (Buffalo: William S. Hein & Co, J. B. Scott (ed.), W. A. Oldfather (trans.) 1660 (1995)), 292–3 (Observation V, sec. 22).

142 Augustine, 'Against Faustus the Manichean', bk. XXII, chaps. 74–5, 78, cited in G. M. Reichberg, H. Syse and E. Begby (eds.), *The Ethics of War: Classic and Contemporary Readings* (Malden, MA: Blackwell Publishing, 2006), 81–2.

143 J. T. Johnson, '*Ad Fontes*: The Question of Rebellion and Moral Tradition on the Use of Force', *Journal of Ethics and International Affairs* (6 January 2014), available at www.ethicsandinternationalaffairs.org/2014/ad-fontes-the-question-of-rebellion-and-moral-tradition-on-the-use-of-force/.

144 Ibid.

145 Aquinas is not as consistent respecting these points as his predecessor, Augustine, or his successor, Grotius. See generally, G. M. Reichberg, 'Legitimate Authority: Aquinas's First Requirement of a Just War', *The Thomist*, 76 (2012), 337–69.

only in the absence of established judicial procedures)'. The other argument concerned the more practical point that the 'defense of the common good requires a chain of command with the prince at its head'.[146]

Violent opposition to authority, 'strife', on the other hand, 'is always sinful ... For if an officer of a prince or judge, in virtue of their public authority, should attack certain men and these defend themselves, it is not the former who is said to be guilty of strife, but those who resist ...'[147] Aquinas considered 'sedition', which is the incitement to rebellion, a mortal sin.[148] Yet, he provides a significant exception to these strictures by saying that the duty of obedience is owed to a legitimate authority only. 'Those who achieve ruling power by violence are not truly rulers: hence nor are their subjects bound to obey them, except in the circumstances already mentioned.'[149] Tyrants 'hold authority in appearance only'.[150] Aquinas, like Augustine, understood the great suffering caused by war, and was circumspect in finding resort to it justifiable. At various points in his writing, however, he also accepts the need of the people to 'slay' a tyrant.[151]

Aquinas's follower, the Scholastic Francisco Suárez, added yet more complicating observations. Suárez opposed using force against the prince merely to protect property even in a case of injustice, but he supported a person's right to defend her life against the sovereign, including by killing him. He did advise caution in the case of killing rulers to avoid the disorder that might follow.[152] Martin Luther, by contrast, took an uncompromising stand against rebellion, calling on the nobility to show no mercy in repressing the Peasants' Revolt of 1524 and 1525. 'No matter how

146 Ibid., 338.

147 T. Aquinas, 'Question 41: On Strife', *Summa Theologica*, in Reichberg *et al.* (eds.), *The Ethics of War* 2006 (n. 145), 182–3.

148 T. Aquinas, 'Question 42: On Sedition', *Summa Theologica*, in Reichberg *et al.* (eds.), *The Ethics of War* 2006 (n. 145), 183–6.

149 T. Aquinas, *Scriptum Super Libros Sententiarum* 2, R. P. Mandonnet (ed.) (Paris: Sumptibus P. Lethielleux. 1929), 1127–33 (distinction 44, q. 2, arts. 2–3).

150 Reichberg, 'Legitimate Authority: Aquinas's First Requirement of a Just War' (n. 145), 349. See also *De regno ad regim Cypri* vol. I, chap. 6, cited in ibid., 350, n. 45.

151 See, e.g., Aquinas, *Scriptum Super Libros Sententiarum* 2 1929 (n. 149), 1127–33 (distinction 44, q. 2, arts. 2–3).

152 F. Suárez, *Defence of the Catholic and Apostolic Faith Against the Errors of Anglicanism* 2, P. L. P. Simpson (trans.) (New York: Lucairos Occasio Press, 2013), bk. 6, chap. 4.

just their complaints, a peasants' victory would mean lawlessness, disorder, bloodshed and suffering. The armed forces should "stab, kill, and strangle" them.'[153]

Grotius, like the Scholastics he emulated, also understood the great cost of war. In *The Law of War and Peace*, he emphasized restrictions on the right to resort to war and advocated alternatives, including non-violent civil disobedience to unjust laws,[154] the use of courts, and the use of interstate arbitration.[155] He warned that if a 'promiscuous right of resistance be allowed, there would no longer [be] a state, but a multitude without a union'. He advised that when compliance with law conflicts with higher law or morality, the answer is non-violence:

By nature all men have the right of resisting in order to ward off injury, as we have said above. But as civil society was instituted in order to maintain public tranquility, the state forthwith acquires over us and our possessions a greater right, to the extent necessary to accomplish this end. The state, therefore, in the interest of public peace and order, can limit that common right of resistance. That such was the purpose of the state we cannot doubt, since it could not in any other way achieve its end. If, in fact, the right of resistance should remain without restraint, there will no longer be a state, but only a non-social horde, such as that of the Cyclopes, among whom—

Each bears rule
O'er wife and offspring.
A mob confused, where none the other heeds.[156]

Grotius's contemporary Thomas Hobbes, for all of the differences between the two men,[157] took the same view of rebellion. The two agreed that states are organized for the very purpose of establishing order through law and legal institutions.[158] For Immanuel Kant, too, no legal system can permit rebellion because that is to recognize rebellion as superior to the legal order.[159]

[153] M. Luther, 'Against the Robbing and Murdering Hordes of Peasants' (1525), reproduced in K. C. Sessions (comp.), *Reformation and Authority; The Meaning of the Peasants' Revolt* (Lexington, MA: Heath, 1968).
[154] H. Grotius, *De Jure Belli ac Pacis* (1625) J. B. Scott (ed.), F. W. Kelsey (trans.) (Oxford: The Clarendon Press, 1925) vol. II 138 (book I, chap. IV, sec. I, para. 3).
[155] Ibid., 558–63 (book II, chap. XXIII, sec. III-VII).
[156] Ibid., 139 (book I, chap. IV, sec. II, para. 1), citing Homer, *Odyssey*, IX. 114 f.).
[157] See Introduction.
[158] T. Hobbes, *Leviathan* (1651), C. B. Macpherson (ed.) (Middlesex: Penguin Books, 1968), 228–39 (chap. 18).
[159] I. Kant, *The Science of Right* (1790) W. Hastie (trans.) (Online: Infomotions, 2000), 63.

Locke and Pufendorf saw things differently a generation after Hobbes and Grotius. Locke's promotion of individual rights against government even to the point of taking up arms and Pufendorf's finding in natural law a right to rebel helped launch the age of revolution that followed.[160] In 1776, the prominent citizens of Britain's original thirteen colonies in North America drafted a Declaration of Independence, setting out a legal and moral case for finding the English king an unjust and even tyrannical ruler over the colonies. The declaration says little about why war is lawful in such circumstances other than the indirect references to lack of response from petitions and court cases.[161]

The French Revolution followed the American War of Independence with the variation that the French fought and killed the ruling family at home, not in overseas colonies. The French legal and moral claims for the right to rebel were the same, however: injustice. In the decades that followed, throughout Central and South America, revolutionaries fought the Spanish and Portuguese. To this day, the constitutions of several Latin America states and beyond endorse the right of revolution.[162] Not so in the United States, where taking up arms against the government as southern states did in 1861 was treasonous. The USA also changed its attitude toward colonization when, in 1898, it acquired overseas colonies from Spain, even fighting a brutal war with Filipino independence fighters.[163] After the French Revolution, France, too, fought for empire first in Europe through Napoleon's efforts at conquest, then beyond in Africa and Asia. Other European states

[160] J. Locke, 'Two Treatises of Government', in *The Works of John Locke* 5 (London: Thoms Tegg, W. Sharpe and Son, 1823), chap. 18; and Pufendorf, *Two Books of the Elements of Universal Jurisprudence* 1660 (n. 141), 292–3 (Observation V, sec. 22).

[161] 'We, therefore, the Representatives of the united States of America, in General Congress, Assembled, appealing to the Supreme Judge of the world for the rectitude of our intentions, do, in the Name, and by Authority of the good People of these Colonies, solemnly publish and declare, That these united Colonies are, and of Right ought to be Free and Independent States, that they are Absolved from all Allegiance to the British Crown, and that all political connection between them and the State of Great Britain, is and ought to be totally dissolved; and that as Free and Independent States, they have full Power to levy War, conclude Peace, contract Alliances, establish Commerce, and to do all other Acts and Things which Independent States may of a right do.' American Declaration of Independence (4 July 1776).

[162] Ginsburg *et al.*, 'When to Overthrow your Government' 2013 (n. 132), 1240–1.

[163] See the Treaty of Paris of 1898, 10 December 1898, USTS 343.

joined France, violently competing for control on their own continent and abroad.[164]

By the twentieth century, the rule in international law to deal with this turmoil included the pragmatic principle that the government in effective control regardless of how it came to power is the government. The implication of such a rule is that international law neither permitted nor forbade rebellion against the government.[165] Hans Kelsen, prior to the adoption of the UN Charter, took the position that international law was neutral on the question of rebellion.[166] World War I began, however, when a secret Serbian nationalist group assassinated Archduke Franz Ferdinand, the Austro-Hungarian Empire's heir to the throne. After the War, a great effort was made to align borders to nationality as a way of defusing the causes of internal instability, violence, and civil war that so often triggered wider conflicts.[167] This was also the period of great strides to outlaw war in positive law and promote peaceful alternatives, including mediation, arbitration, and adjudication.[168]

## *B Expansion and Insurrection*

Two decades later, three conflicting ideas on rebellion formed the backdrop to UN Charter negotiations: the principle that international law is neutral on the right of rebellion, support for rebellion in cases of serious oppression, and opposition to rebellion and armed conflict of any kind. Opponents of armed conflict have

164 On international law and imperialism, see A. Anghie, *Imperialism, Sovereignty, and the Making of International Law* (Cambridge: Cambridge University Press, 2005).

165 See, e.g., Tinoco Claims Arbitration (*Great Britain* v. *Costa Rica*), *Report of International Arbitral Awards* 1 (1923), 369–99; 'Judicial Decisions involving Questions of International Law: Arbitration between Great Britain and Costa Rica', *American Journal of International Law*, 18 (1924), 147–74.

166 H. Kelsen, *General Theory of Law and State*, A. Wedberg (trans.) (Cambridge, MA: Harvard University Press, 1945), 368.

167 See K. Knop, *Diversity and Self-Determination in International Law* (Cambridge: Cambridge University Press, 2002), 12–14.

168 Waldock refers to the 'increased odium attaching to war' even as the vitality of the Just War Doctrine declined. C. H. M. Waldock, 'The Regulation of the Use of Force by Individual States in International Law', *Recueil des Cours* 81 (1951), 451–517, 457. See also, M. E. O'Connell, 'Peace and War' in A. Peters and B. Fassbender, (eds.) *Oxford Handbook of the History of International Law* (Oxford: Oxford University Press, 2012), 272–93.

consistently paired that opposition with support for non-violent means of change. The final text of the Charter does not favour any one of these three. It has no express prohibition or permission for people to use military force against their governments. The drafters understood that people living under colonial domination and authoritarianism wanted a voice in government. The drafters were well aware, too, of the atrocities committed before and during World War II by governments against their populations at home. The drafters agreed that human rights protections are needed for any chance at global peace.

> In this broad field, the precedents of the League of Nations were of little help; the minorities treaties that had been made under the League auspices, as part of the settlements after the First World War, were generally considered inadequate as a protective device. From the technicians' point of view, these interrelated problems presented an extremely difficult task of international organization. They concerned some of the most jealously guarded aspects of national sovereignty, and the general conception on which [US] Department of State studies were based was that of an international organization that would not derogate from the essential sovereignty of its members – that would, in other words, affect that sovereignty only by the general agreement of all its member states. The means to achieve *international* protection of human rights were hard to develop within the limits set. Nevertheless, the issues were too important to be ignored in planning for an international organization that set its objectives in terms of world peace.[169]

The drafter's solution is a comprise in which the Charter demands protection for human rights, self-determination,[170] and the peaceful settlement of disputes. The prohibition on the use of force states that 'all Members shall refrain in their *international relations* from the threat or use of force . . .'.[171] Internal sovereignty is protected in Article 2(7): 'Nothing contained in the present Charter shall authorize the United Nations to intervene in matters which are essentially within the domestic jurisdiction of any state or shall require the Members to submit such matters to settlement under

169 R. Russell, *A History of the United Nations Charter* (Washington, DC: The Brookings Institution, 1958), 211–12.

170 Arts 1(2), 55, UN Charter.

171 Art. 2(4) UN Charter (emphasis added). See also, Gray, *International Law and the Use of Force* 2018 (n. 2), 75.

the present Charter; but this principle shall not prejudice the application of enforcement measures under Chapter VII.'

In 1947, the UN General Assembly requested that the International Law Commission prepare a declaration on the rights and duties of states. In 1949, the Assembly acknowledged the ILC's work, which included the statement that '[e]very State has the duty to refrain from fomenting civil strife in the territory of another State, and to prevent the organization within its territory of activities calculated to foment such civil strife'.[172] The provision expresses clear concern with violent opposition against governments, regardless of the reason. Yet, the restriction addresses aid to rebels, not the per se question of the rebels' own activities. In 1948, the General Assembly adopted the Universal Declaration of Human Rights, which says in the Preamble that 'it is essential, if man is not to be compelled to have recourse, as a last resort, to rebellion against tyranny and oppression, that human rights should be protected by the rule of law'.[173] The principal drafter, René Cassin, wanted to add an affirmative right of armed resistance in the operative part of the Declaration, but he was opposed by those who found no such right to exist in international law.[174]

By 1970, UN members, especially the newly independent states that formed the Non-aligned Movement (NAM) and the Group of 77 (G-77), began to push for recognition by the UN and within international law of the right of people living under alien domination and racist regimes to use military force. The NAM and G-77 also demanded that international law permit assistance to armed national liberation groups. Some authors today conclude that customary international law evolved at this time to permit rebellion for self-determination and to permit military assistance to national liberation fighters.[175] The better view, however, is that the situation remained ambiguous.

[172] Art. 4, Draft Declaration on the Rights and Duties of States, GA Res. 375 (IV) of 6 December 1949.

[173] GA Res. 217A (III) of 10 December 1948.

[174] J. Morsink, *The Universal Declaration of Human Rights: Origins, Drafting, and Intent* (Philadelphia: University of Pennsylvania Press, 1999), 302–12.

[175] Hessbruegge apparently takes this position. Hessbruegge, *Human Rights and Personal Self-Defense in International Law* 2017 (n. 14), 316, n. 104, citing, among others, A. Eide, L. Barlaug, and C. Chinana, 'The Right to Oppose Violations of Human Rights: Basis, Conditions, and Limitations', in UNESCO, *Violations of*

On the twenty-fifth anniversary of the UN Charter, the General Assembly adopted the Declaration on the Principles of International Law Concerning Friendly Relations and Co-operation among States in Accordance with the Charter of the United Nations.[176] The declaration repeated the duty not to intervene,[177] and to 'refrain from organizing, instigating, assisting or participating in acts of civil strife or terrorist acts in another State'.[178] It also, however, affirmed the right of self-determination and provided:

> Every State has the duty to refrain from any forcible action which deprives peoples ... of their right to self-determination and freedom and independence. In their actions against, and resistance to, such forcible action in pursuit of the exercise of their right to self-determination, such peoples are entitled to seek and to receive support in accordance with the purposes and principles of the Charter.[179]

The language arguably supports the right to throw off oppressive regimes through the use of military force and possibly of a right to receive outside military assistance.[180] The more persuasive understanding is that 'support' cannot mean military assistance, but rather non-military, diplomatic, and other forms of non-military aid.[181] Tolerance of violence against government, however, is clear. Just four years later, the General Assembly adopted the 1974 Definition of Aggression, which, on one hand, renders it an act of aggression to send 'armed bands, groups, irregulars or mercenaries' to carry out 'acts of armed force against another State' but also requires respect for the right of people living under various

*Human Rights: Possible Rights of Recourse and Forms of Resistance* (Paris: UNESCO, 1984), 34–66, 60.

176 Declaration on Principles of International Law Concerning Friendly Relations and Co-operation among States in Accordance with the Charter of the United Nations, GA Res. 2625 (XXV) of 24 October 1970.

177 Ibid. 178 Ibid. 179 Ibid.

180 A. Tanca, 'The Prohibition of Force in the U.N. Declaration on Friendly Relations of 1970', in A. Cassese (ed.), *The Current Legal Regulation of the Use of Force* (Dordrecht: Martinus Nijhoff, 1986), 397–412, 407.

181 Abi-Saab considers that some military assistance could be provided such as the provision of sanctuary or the supply of arms. It is not clear, however, on what basis any military assistance could be provided without violating Article 2(4). G. Abi-Saab, 'The Third World and the Future of the International Legal Order', *Revue Egyptienne de Droit International*, 29 (1973), 27–66, 47–8. See N. D. White, 'Defending Humanity: When Force is Justified and Why, Book Review', *Melbourne Journal of International Law*, 10 (2009), 379–93, 391.

forms of oppression to 'struggle' and to 'seek and receive support'.[182] These seemingly contradictory provisions are reconcilable under the Charter if the support provided to people struggling against oppression is non-lethal aid.[183] The Definition provides no further clarity on the right of armed rebellion. In the actual world of armed struggle, charismatic, violent revolutionaries such as Che Guevara, Fidel Castro, and Robert Mugabe were more than matched by Mahatma Gandhi, Martin Luther King, and Nelson Mandela. The tragedy of conflicts like the Algerian Civil War and the need for reconciliation led Mandela eventually to reject armed action and successfully end apartheid in South Africa.[184] He became a champion of non-violence.

Nevertheless, pro-force proponents grew steadily, including within the international law and human rights community. Those who supported rebellion and aid to rebels in the 1960s and 1970s tended to restrict their views to colonialism and white minority rule. The line between those categories of human rights violations and other types was, however, not obvious. References began to be made in the debates about military intervention and armed struggle to human rights more generally.[185] In 1973, for example, Jean-Pierre L. Fonteyne concluded that it was lawful to resort to force against colonial regimes and should equally be lawful to resort to force to advance other forms of human rights protection. He was

[182] Arts. 3, 7, Definition of Aggression, GA Res. 3314 (XXIX) of 14 December 1974.

[183] The Definition of Aggression has remained an important topic as the UN moved forward over the years toward a permanent international criminal court to succeed the Nuremberg and Tokyo Tribunals. Several scholars and government officials have sought to restrict future prosecutions of the crime of aggression consistently with their advocacy for expanding the right to use force. For example, H. H. Koh and T. F. Buchwald, 'The Crime of Aggression: The United States Perspective', *American Journal of International Law*, 109 (2015), 257–95; J. Bellinger, 'USG Concerns with the ICC Aggression Amendments', *Lawfare* (5 January 2016), available at www.lawfareblog.com/usg-concerns-icc-aggression-amendments; C. Kreß and L. von Holtzendorff, 'The Kampala Compromise on the Crime of Aggression', *Journal of International Criminal Justice*, 8 (2010), 1179–217.

[184] Nelson Mandela was the co-recipient of the 1993 Nobel Peace Prize. The Norwegian Nobel Institute website contains more on why he won. www.nobelprize.org/nobel_prizes/peace/laureates/1993/.

[185] J.-P. L. Fonteyne, 'Appendix B: Forcible Self-Help by States to Protect Human Rights: Recent Views from the United Nations', in R. B. Lillich (ed.), *Humanitarian Intervention and the United Nations* (Charlottesville: University Press of Virginia, 1973), 197–221, 206–9, 213–14.

encouraged by the willingness to assist people 'struggling for self-determination or freedom from apartheid and other discriminatory practices',[186] but also wanted to convince 'States that other situations where fundamental human rights are seriously violated should be subjected to the same reasoning – accepting exceptional measures to meet emergency situations'.[187]

A law professor at the University of Virginia, Richard Lillich, associated himself with Fonteyne's argument, writing that he 'supervised' the appendix featuring Fonteyne's comment. Lillich was a principal advocate of humanitarian intervention – outside military force on behalf of people within states. He believed people had the right to rebel against oppressive governments whether on behalf of armed non-state actors or not. Lillich cited the East Pakistani separatists, aided by India, and Ugandan opposition fighters, aided by Tanzania, as precedents for a developing right of military intervention.[188]

Lillich used these examples presumably to show an emerging principle of customary international law permitting humanitarian intervention. Decades later, the state practice for such a principle remains anaemic and the *opinio juris* virtually non-existent.[189] Not only is a right of humanitarian intervention too vague to serve as a viable legal norm, it conflicts with the *jus cogens* prohibition on force. At best, humanitarian intervention could supply only indirect support for a right of rebellion. Given that such intervention is itself unlawful it provides no support.

Another development further undermines any claim that rebellion is or should be lawful under the *jus ad bellum* as a matter of positive law. In 1977, states party to the 1949 Geneva Conventions adopted two additional protocols to update the Conventions given the phenomenon of post-World War II internal armed conflicts. The International Committee of the Red Cross (ICRC) reacted to the Vietnam War and the Biafran War by expanding the reach of international humanitarian treaty law. Parties to the Geneva Conventions engaged in contentious debates over the ICRC's proposals, finally agreeing to create two protocols instead of one.[190]

186 Ibid., 220–1. 187 Ibid., 221. 188 Ibid. 189 See Chapters 2 and 3.

190 J. Pictet, C. Pilloud *et al.*, *International Committee of the Red Cross, Commentary on the Additional Protocols of 8 June 1977 to the Geneva Conventions of 12 August 1949*, Y. Sandoz *et al.* (eds.) (Dordrecht, NL: Nijhoff, 1987).

Additional Protocol I elevated fighters in national liberation struggles to the status of privileged combatants, persons immune from prosecution for the deaths they cause in fighting that complies with IHL.[191] Opposition fighters in internal conflicts for any other cause remained classified for international law purposes as criminals.[192] The United States opposed the new classification. President Ronald Reagan explained that the USA would not join Additional Protocol I because of the change to the status of irregular fighters.[193]

Nevertheless, the USA has encouraged opposition fighters to take up arms against the governments of other states. Already in 1980, the USA was sending weapons and other resources to the Mujahedeen fighting Afghanistan's government controlled at the time by the Soviet Union. The USA, France, the UK, and Russia have also encouraged non-state actor fighters in Libya, Syria, Ukraine, and many other places. They apparently continue to oppose granting the combatant's privilege on a wider basis to irregular fighters.

The soft notion of 'liberation struggle', fighting for self-determination as a good, has not remained within the confines of anti-colonial and anti-apartheid conflicts. With the end of the Cold War, human rights groups based in the West argued for the legality of intervention in many situations, including on behalf of insurgents seeking to secede from Iraq and Yugoslavia beginning in 1991. In part owing to lobbying by these groups, NATO bombed what remained of Yugoslavia, Serbia, and Montenegro for seventy-eight days in 1999 on behalf of the Albanian ethnic population of Kosovo. The USA had made common cause with the Kosovo Liberation Army, a militant group that used terror tactics to pressure Serbia and Montenegro into withdrawing from Kosovo. Despite the poor results of the NATO intervention,[194] in 2003, the USA, UK, and Australia invaded Iraq ostensibly to rid the country of

[191] Protocol Additional to the Geneva Conventions of 12 August 1949, and relating to the Protections of Victims of International Armed Conflicts (Protocol I), 8 June 1977, 1125 UNTS 3, Arts. 1(4) and 43.

[192] Protocol Additional to the Geneva Conventions of 12 August 1949, and relating to the Protections of Victims of Non-International Armed Conflicts (Protocol II), 8 June 1977, 1125 UNTS 609, Art. 6.

[193] Ronald Reagan, Letter of Transmittal, The White House (29 January 1987), available at www.loc.gov/rr/frd/Military_Law/pdf/protocol-II-100–2.pdf.

[194] See Chapters 2 and 3.

weapons of mass destruction, but also to fulfil the ideological goals of a group of American politicians and scholars known as 'neo-conservatives'. Neo-conservatives believe if the USA imposes democratic governments on states, it can better control them to advance its own national interests.[195]

Later in 2003, following the invasion, as discussed in previous chapters, UN Secretary-General Kofi Annan undertook a review of UN principles and institutional processes related to the use of force. The final document in that process offers one point in support of groups fighting their governments:

139. The international community, through the United Nations, also has the responsibility to use appropriate diplomatic, humanitarian and other peaceful means, in accordance with Chapters VI and VIII of the Charter, to help to protect populations from genocide, war crimes, ethnic cleansing and crimes against humanity. In this context, we are prepared to take collective action, in a timely and decisive manner, through the Security Council, in accordance with the Charter, including Chapter VII, on a case-by-case basis and in cooperation with relevant regional organizations as appropriate, should peaceful means be inadequate and national authorities are manifestly failing to protect their populations ...

In 2009, Secretary-General Ban Ki-Moon added a gloss to Paragraph 139:

When a State refuses to accept international prevention and protection assistance, commits egregious crimes and violations relating to the responsibility to protect and fails to respond to less coercive measures, it is, in effect, challenging the international community to live up to its own responsibilities under paragraph 139 of the Summit Outcome. Such collective measures could be authorized by the Security Council under Articles 41 or 42 of the Charter, by the General Assembly under the 'Uniting for peace' procedure ... or by regional or subregional arrangements under Article 53, with the prior authorization of the Security Council.[196]

[195] Anne Norton ascribes to neo-conservatives, followers of the University of Chicago philosopher Leo Strauss, a rejection of any restraint on the right to resort to war to achieve their goals. A. Norton, *Leo Strauss and the Politics of American Empire* (New Haven: Yale University Press, 2004), 123, 148.

[196] UN Doc. A/63/677, 12 January 2009, para. 56.

This formulation not only erroneously implies that the General Assembly may authorize the use of force, it also fails to discourage armed rebellion aided by outside military intervention.[197]

The Arab Spring that began sweeping through the Middle East and North Africa in 2010 included Libya. Libya's quixotic, authoritarian leader, Muammar Gadhafi, responded to protests in February 2011 with force that killed several hundred.[198] Soon after, a high-ranking military officer and other troops defected from the regular Libyan forces to form an armed opposition in Benghazi. Gadhafi wildly threatened to kill them and everyone else in Benghazi. The UN Security Council authorized NATO members and other states to use military force to protect civilians at risk in the pending clash.[199] NATO, however, aimed its effort at fighting Gadhafi, not simply protecting civilians.[200] It bombed from March until September, decimating Libya's armed forces. Gadhafi was murdered by a mob in front of French soldiers in September 2011. NATO withdrew soon after and general civil war engulfed the country. The conflict transformed Libya to a place not only of widespread violence and disorder but a conduit of mass migration to Europe. Thousands have died in the desperate search for the chance at a decent life. The crisis has led in turn to instability throughout Europe. Augustine's warning about the chaos and disorder of rebellion continues to apply.

The Libyan case and others provide powerful evidence of the misplaced faith in military force to advance complex social goals of security, prosperity, good governance, respect for human rights, and protection of the environment. As Christine Chinkin and Mary Kaldor express it, true security 'entails a law-based rather

[197] GA Res. 377 (V) of 3 November 1950.

[198] 'Battle for Libya: Key Moments', *Al Jazeera* (30 April 2017) www.aljazeera.com/indepth/spotlight/libya/2011/10/20111020104244706760.html

[199] H. Roberts, 'Who Said Gaddafi Had to Go?', *London Review of Books*, 17 November 2011, available at www.lrb.co.uk/v33/n22/hugh-roberts/who-said-gaddafi-had-to-go.

[200] Once the intervention began, UK and French government officials began to argue that only with regime change could civilians be protected. At the time of the Security Council debate such an attenuated claim was not in the discussion. The UK and French officials at the UN cited time and again that Libyan forces were on the road to the town of Benghazi. The only logical deduction from this line of argument was that the aim of a military intervention in Libya would be to stop that force on the road.

than a war-based approach . . . '.[201] Yet, expansionists continue to make proposals for new exceptions to the prohibition on force. While admitting that '[n]onviolent campaigns are more effective', and that legal authorities do not support him, Hessbruegge, nevertheless, wants 'a right of armed struggle against mass atrocities' as part of the *jus ad bellum*.[202] He envisions this as right beyond the need of a group to defend itself from armed attack to a right to plan, organize, resource, and practise offensive military operations against armed forces of a government that the group determines is oppressing them. The proposal incorporates the other conditions of the lawful use of force, most importantly the principles of necessity and proportionality. Those principles alone, however, would render the use of military force unlawful in most of these situations.[203]

The proposal, like that for humanitarian intervention, rests on the idea of last resort. Hessbruegge asserts that a right of people to rebel should be available when 'nonviolent resistance leads only to more government atrocities'.[204] Again, however, this condition undermines the proposal. Groups cannot know when non-violent resistance will lead 'only' to more atrocities. They cannot know if their military effort will lead to success and a better life for all. What they can know is that to succeed against an army, they need a high level of military organization. In Libya in 2011, military units defected but not in sufficient numbers to have a chance against regular Libyan forces. Then, even with NATO's assistance, the leaderless, war-torn country sank into further lawlessness and violence. The story in Syria, Iraq, and Mali for opposition fighters and their supporters has been more dire still.[205]

[201] C. Chinkin and M. Kaldor, *International Law and New Wars* (Cambridge: Cambridge University Press, 2017), 528.

[202] Hessbruegge, *Human Rights and Personal Self-Defense in International Law* 2017 (n. 14), 325, 332 and *passim*.

[203] See, e.g., how the compliance with the principle of necessity would have prevented the Libyan intervention, M. E. O'Connell, Remarks, 'Revolution and Intervention in the Middle East', *Proceedings of the Annual Meeting (American Society of International Law)* 105 (2011), 555–75, 563–4.

[204] Hessbruegge, *Human Rights and Personal Self-Defense in International Law* 2017 (n. 14), 332.

[205] On Syria, see, F. Nawa, 'Pro-Opposition Syrians in Turkey Grapple with Losing the War', *PRI* (9 April 2018), available at www.pri.org/stories/2018-04-09/pro-opposition-syrians-turkey-grapple-losing-war. On Libya, see, Roberts, 'Who Said Gaddafi Had to Go?' 2011 (n. 199). On Mali, see note 2 and accompanying text.

Oppressed people cannot know if their non-violent or violent resistance will succeed. What they can know is that if they choose violence, they will kill men and women in the armed forces and other government agencies as well as many bystanders to attempt to secure their own human rights. Arguments for humanitarian intervention or the right to rebel often focus on a monster at the head of government, persons who rarely die in the fighting – Gadhafi was an exceptional case. The persons who will die are police, soldiers, letter carriers, fire fighters, and the people near them who draw no government pay check. In the thousands of pages promoting killing in these cases, the question Brownlie put to Lillich in the 1970s remains unanswered. How many innocent people should the law permit to die to secure the rights of others? Add to this moral challenge the fact that military campaigns begun by rebels rarely succeed in creating a government that does not oppress.

One final point on expanding the right to use force to rebellion, expansionists discuss only creating a new legal right to resort to force. They fail to consider that exercising the right means preparing well in advance. Resources are needed to buy weapons and train fighters. Most governments will impose a great cost on such efforts to organize and the more oppressive the government, the more brutal the response. Rather than promote the human rights of the oppressed, the proposal keeps alive the myth that military force is at times the only way forward.

Proposing a right of rebellion in the *jus ad bellum* is another example of misplaced reliance on the use of force. Hessbruegge writes that without the right of rebellion international law 'abandons victims of mass atrocities to their fate by denying them international legal recognition of *the only action they can take to save themselves* in extreme situations'.[206] Killing is never the only available action. On the contrary it is typically counterproductive and, therefore, not an 'available' action. This reality, combined with evidence of the positive law, and most importantly, the norm of *jus cogens* adds up to the conclusion that armed rebellion is unlawful today. The next section discusses the role of *jus cogens* in this conclusion in greater depth.

[206] Hessbruegge, *Human Rights and Personal Self-Defense in International Law* 2017 (n. 14), 332.

### C *Jus Cogens and Insurrection*

In marked contrast to events in its neighbour Libya, in Tunisia in 2010, civil society groups worked actively to prevent civil war. In 2015, four organizations that led the national dialogue for peaceful change, the Tunisian Quartet, won the Nobel Peace Prize. The Norwegian Nobel Committee gave this explanation:

> [T]he Nobel Peace Prize for 2015 is to be awarded to the Tunisian National Dialogue Quartet for its decisive contribution to the building of a pluralistic democracy in Tunisia in the wake of the Jasmine Revolution of 2011. The Quartet was formed in the summer of 2013 when the democratization process was in danger of collapsing as a result of political assassinations and widespread social unrest. It established an alternative, peaceful political process at a time when the country was on the brink of civil war. It was thus instrumental in enabling Tunisia, in the space of a few years, to establish a constitutional system of government guaranteeing fundamental rights for the entire population, irrespective of gender, political conviction or religious belief.[207]

The Quartet, Mandela, King, Gandhi, and so many others explain how revolutionary change is possible without revolutionary wars. The right of rebellion has never had the status of self-defence with respect to the prohibition on the use of force. In other words, the most that could be said in favour of a right of rebellion is that it fell outside the prohibition. That makes little sense today for at least two reasons: There is no principled basis on which to separate resort to civil war within states from resort to war between states. In addition, international law is clearly applicable to non-state actors. Principles such as the duty to respect the right to life renders rebellion unlawful in a way nearly equivalent to the prohibition on the use of force.

It once made some sense to consider rebellion a separate category from interstate resort to force. A few of the key scholars of the Just War tradition tolerated military force in an exceptional case to overthrow a government. States attacked each other for different reasons – conquest, revenge, and punishment. When Aquinas wrote, he did not feel that states had the same access to dispute resolution mechanisms as individuals within a domestic legal order. These distinctions have largely fallen away. The interstate system has plenty of courts today and other mechanisms for the

207 Norwegian Nobel Committee, 'The Nobel Peace Prize for 2015', available at www.nobelprize.org/nobel_prizes/peace/laureates/2015/press.html.

peaceful resolution of disputes. States rarely attack other states for conquest. They fight over disputed boundaries, but most conflicts involve intervention in civil war. The line between international and internal conflicts is blurred. The prohibition on the use of force should apply uniformly to prohibit armed conflict regardless of the category.

This understanding of the norm is consistent with the other important principles of international law that transcend the national–international distinction. Human rights law is the most important example. By the time of the Universal Declaration of Human Rights, the idea that governments do not have duties to their own citizens within their own borders directly from international law ended. With the era of international criminal law, it is also indisputable that individuals have duties directly from international law. International law imposes duties directly on non-state actors as to how to wage armed conflict. International law can impose a duty on groups not to resort to armed force within states in the first place. If Kelsen's view that international law is neutral as to rebellion was ever true, it is no longer.

The points just made are affirmative reasons to understand rebellion as banned by the prohibition on the use of force. To the extent writers want to create a right to rebel, by, for example extrapolating from self-defence, they engage in broadening the right to resort to force.[208] Broadening, as argued throughout this book, is derogation, which is not permitted. Moreover, the prohibition on the use of force includes the restrictive principles of necessity and proportionality. Those principles apply fully to any resort to force under the *jus ad bellum*. No detailed discussion is needed here because the same analysis of these principles provided in the context of humanitarian intervention fully apply to the right of rebellion. If the purpose of using force is to end oppression and promote human rights and the conditions of flourishing, civil war is exactly the wrong tool. The cost of civil war is inevitably higher than alternatives. One estimate of the civil war in Congo put the death toll at six million after twenty years of war.[209]

[208] See Hessbruegge, *Human Rights and Personal Self-Defense in International Law* 2017 (n. 14), 332 and *passim*.

[209] I. Sawyer, 'The Congolese Government is at War With Its People', *OpenDemocracy* (13 April 2018), available at www.opendemocracy.net/ida-sawyer/congolese-government-is-at-war-with-its-people.

The decision by rebels to resort to armed conflict with the government must also be measured against the human right to life of those they kill. Prior to engagement in actual fighting when international humanitarian law applies, all government agents are protected by the peacetime right to life. Government opponents may have good reason to suspect that protest and other peaceful anti-government activism may lead to the authorities using excessive force as occurred in Libya. This fear is not a basis, however, for organizing in advance to kill police and members of the armed forces. Individuals who work for the government have human rights, which they do not lose even if they engage in criminal conduct. The most widely applicable positive law version of the right to life is found in Article 6 of the International Covenant on Civil and Political Rights: 'Every human being has the inherent right to life. This right shall be protected by law. No one shall be arbitrarily deprived of his life.'[210] Article 6 renders every first use of military force lacking a Security Council authorization unlawful. The initiator of military force will almost inevitably violate the human right to life. Rebel or insurgent groups who initiate killing to accomplish their objectives are committing murder, a violation of the right to life. Government authorities also commit murder if they intentionally kill with any purpose other than saving a life immediately in situations other than armed conflict.[211] Those who violate the right to life may be charged with a crime but even then are owed due process, which prohibits extra-judicial killing. Any killing that does not conform to the *jus ad bellum*, the *jus in bello*, or peacetime criminal law violates the fundamental right to life, another norm being increasingly discerned as *jus cogens*.[212]

Civil wars are often said to be more brutal than international wars. Ending them can also be more challenging. Peace negotiations

[210] Art. 6 International Covenant on Civil and Political Rights, GA Res. 2200A (XXI) of 16 December 1966. The ICCPR is available at www.ohchr.org/EN/ProfessionalInterest/Pages/CCPR.aspx.

[211] See n. 133.

[212] For evidence of an emerging peremptory norm on the right to life, see, C. Heyns and T. Probert, 'Securing the Right to Life: A Cornerstone of the Human Rights System', *EJIL*: Talk! (11 May 2016), available at www.ejiltalk.org/securing-the-right-to-life-a-cornerstone-of-the-human-rights-system/. *Jus ad bellum* refers to the body of international law governing the resort to military force; the *jus in bello* refers to the body of law regulating the conduct of armed conflict – both the protections afforded persons and the means and methods of warfare.

cannot focus on persuading an invading army to return home across a recognized international border. Enemies in civil war may live side by side. When internal conflicts endure for any amount of time they seem to normalize violence, which then becomes endemic in a community.[213] Congo has been the scene of almost continual armed struggle since its independence. Intense fighting that began in 1994 continues. It is time to stop encouraging these conflicts in the first place through understanding that under the *jus ad bellum* they are unlawful. Governments are restricted from using excessive force against their populations. The parallel principle must be that anti-government opposition groups may not resort to armed conflict against the government. Most states restrict non-state groups from resort to force. International law clearly restricts violating the right to life. States are prohibited from intervening on either side of a civil war. Irregular fighters in civil war remain criminals. Only one principle remains in question today, whether the *jus ad bellum* speaks to the right of rebels to resort to force in the first place. Given the *jus cogens* status of the *jus ad bellum* prohibition on the use of force, the law cannot change to affirmatively provide a new legal right to use armed force. The negative inference, therefore, must be that rebellion is unlawful under international law.

## Conclusion

The prohibition on the use of force incorporates two exceptions, one for self-defence and one for Security Council authorization. States have behaved, however, as though a third excuse exists, a right to use force on another State's territory with the territorial State's consent or invitation. Non-state actors have also persistently taken up arms within the state to fight for various causes. This chapter has shown that invitation is not the solid exception beyond self-defence that some writers believe that it is. Inviting outside military assistance is in tension with the principles of self-determination and non-intervention. It leads to escalation of violence. The traditional principle held that when opposition forces reach the status of belligerency, outside states must withdraw.

[213] V. Lowe, A. Roberts, J. Welsh and D. Zaum, *The United Nations Security Council and War: The Evolution of Thought and Practice Since 1945* (Oxford: Oxford University Press, 2008), 49.

Under the *jus cogens* prohibition on the use of force, restraints on force may not be relaxed.

Governments will have no reason to invite outside military assistance if their opponents do not resort to armed action in the first place. Undoubtedly, governments commit atrocities, and people fear for their lives at the hands of their own state's military. There is equally no question that resort to force in such tragic cases makes the situation worse, not better. The history of the prohibition on force fails to show that it clearly outlawed insurgency. The greatest thinker on the limited justifications for the use of force, Aquinas, seemed to be of two minds about rebellion against tyrannical rulers. Approaching the middle of the twenty-first century, the only answer can be that the prohibition reaches and rejects any right to rebel. Writers who advocate fighting oppressive governments limit the right to situations where no alternative exists. People do have a right of self-defence to defend their lives in the heat of the moment of attack. A right to rebel includes the notion of preparing in advance to take on the state's forces. The prohibition on the use of force cannot be relaxed to encompass rebellion.

Opponents of the right of rebellion base their opposition on the existence of alternatives within the state for dispute resolution. These eliminate the need for resort to force. Such mechanisms are always available. They are not restricted to the well-functioning nation state. Where they have been destroyed in states torn apart by war or ravaged by corruption, they can be rebuilt. Rather than prepare for war, time, talent, and resources can be redirected to peace. The next chapter considers ways to attract the international community back to the mechanisms of dispute resolution.

# 6

# Revitalizing the Process of International Dispute Resolution

In May 2018, China deployed its H-6 K strategic bomber to Woody Island in the South China Sea. Just three years earlier, Chinese President Xi Jinping had solemnly promised China would not 'militarize' islands subject to disputed sovereignty claims. Woody Island is claimed by Taiwan and Vietnam in addition to China. It is also not the only place where, despite the claims of other states, China has or is likely to base missiles, fighter planes, and other sophisticated military weaponry and technology.[1] As problematic as this is, of greater concern is China's creation of artificial islands out of delicate coral reefs as a platform for some of these military bases. To build the islands, it churns up the coral reef with dredgers, then dumps huge quantities of sand and gravel, smothering the reefs to create land. '"The worst issue with the island-building is that the effect is permanent ... Once a portion of coral reef has been buried under tons of sand and gravel, it cannot ever recover."'[2] In addition to the wanton destruction of the natural world, coral reefs are critical to the health of a marine ecosystem that supplies ten per cent of the world's fish for human consumption.[3]

China is taking an increasingly militarist approach to other maritime issues as well. In March 2016, Indonesia detained

[1] R. Beckman, 'The UN Convention on the Law of the Sea and the Maritime Disputes in the South China Sea', *American Journal of International Law*, 107 (2013), 142–63, 144.

[2] H. Beech, 'The Environment is the Silent Casualty of China's Ambitions in the South China Sea', *Time* (1 June 2016), available at http://time.com/4353292/south-china-sea-environment-destruction-coral-giant-clams/.

[3] Ibid.

a Chinese vessel for illegal fishing. Many states are stepping up policing of maritime zones as fish stocks become dangerously depleted.[4] Before Indonesia could bring the suspect fishing vessel into port, however, a 'Chinese coast-guard vessel muscled in to free the Chinese fishing boat from the towline connected to the Indonesian ship'.[5] China took direct, forceful action against Indonesian authorities as part of a policy that includes equipping its nationals with communication devices to call the Navy for assistance should a foreign country attempt to detain them. The policy creates the risk of direct clashes with other states and defies the legal principles governing the oceans.

China's shift to a more militaristist foreign policy in general can be seen in the decision to create military bases in foreign states. In 2017, China established a traditional military base in Djibouti, East Africa. This is China's first ever military base outside territory it claims as its own. Djibouti already hosts US, French, and Japanese bases. The USA pays the tiny former French colony $55 million a year for its base. China will pay $100 million and is reported to be planning a second overseas military base in Pakistan.[6]

These developments in 2018 look like old-fashioned Realist military power projection.[7] They contrast with China's complaints about the heavy-handed American approach to maritime issues, as well as China's critique of the UN's turn to the use of offensive military force in peacekeeping.[8] In the past, China has avoided debilitating armed conflicts like those pursued by the United States, United Kingdom, France, and Russia in Afghanistan, Iraq, Syria, Mali, Ukraine, Yemen, and other places. China, by contrast, has pursued its economic interests in the very places where the other permanent Security Council members have pursued a military strategy.[9] Increasingly, as China has

[4] L. Chow, 'Global Fish Stocks Depleted to "Alarming Levels"', *EcoWatch* (8 July 2016), available at www.ecowatch.com/one-third-of-commercial-fish-stocks-fished-at-unsustainable-levels-1910593830.html.

[5] Beech, 'The Environment is the Silent Casualty of China's Ambitions' 2016 (n. 2).

[6] J. Goldkorn, 'After Djibouti, China To Build Second Overseas Military Base In Pakistan', *supchina.com* (5 January 2018), available at https://supchina.com/2018/01/05/djibouti-china-build-second-overseas-military-base-pakistan/.

[7] See, e.g., H. Kissinger, *Diplomacy* (New York: Simon & Schuster, 1994).

[8] See Chapters 3 and 5.

[9] China has, for example, established a near-monopoly worldwide of raw materials essential to high-tech manufacturing known as 'rare earth minerals'. See

acquired resources and development contracts abroad, it has also increasingly engaged with international law and institutions. It notably joined the 1982 United Nations Convention on the Law of the Sea (UNCLOS) while the USA remained a non-party. Chinese President Xi Jinping declared that China would fill the leadership vacuum in combating climate destruction when the USA announced its intention to withdraw from the 2015 Paris Agreement on Climate Change.[10] Chinese leaders have also declared the intention to be a defender of the World Trade Organization's (WTO) rules for global trade.[11] When US President Donald Trump imposed steep tariffs on China and other trading partners, China swiftly brought a case against the US at the WTO.[12] There is an 'emerging consensus among Chinese international lawyers that forward-leaning engagement will on balance be a positive for China, and the best protection of its national interests'.[13]

As China rises – some say becoming the second pole to the United States in a new bipolar world[14] – the question becomes whether it will take the 'cafeteria' approach to international law or an integral one. China could follow the lead of other powers, picking what it likes of international law, failing to see it as an integrated system of

M. Hughes, 'US Looks to Afghanistan to Counter China's Rare Earths Monopoly', *Globe Post* (2 August 2017), available at www.theglobepost.com/2017/08/02/afghanistan-rare-earth-china/. (An adviser to the US government referred to the effort as China's 'brilliant long-term strategy to monopolize rare earth materials'.)

[10] J. Worland, 'It Didn't Take Long for China to Fill America's Shoes on Climate Change', *Time* (8 June 2017), available at http://time.com/4810846/china-energy-climate-change-paris-agreement/.

[11] T. Eder, 'China Leans In On International Adjudication: Why Beijing's Answer to Defeat Will Be More Forceful Engagement', *EJIL*: Talk! (2 May 2018), available at www.ejiltalk.org/?s=China+Leans.

[12] Associated Press, 'China Files WTO Challenge to Trump's $200 Billion Tariff Plan', *Los Angeles Times* (16 July 2018), available at www.latimes.com/business/la-fi-china-wto-challenge-20180716-story.html.

[13] Ibid.

[14] See, e.g., Ø. Tunsjø, *The Return of Bipolarity in World Politics, China, the United States, and Geostructural Realism* (New York: Columbia University Press, 2018), 1. 'An era of unprecedented unipolarity has come to an end as China's rise has changed the underlying distribution of power in the international system. While China is not equal to the United States in power aggregate, it has narrowed the power gap significantly and vaulted into top ranking. Equally important, no other state is strong enough to serve as a competitor to these two. Since the top two states are now much more powerful than any third state, the structure of the international system has changed from unipolarity to bipolarity.' Ibid.

interconnected rights, duties, and processes. China's military and economic strength may tempt its leaders toward just such an exceptionalist stance. It already displays interest in leading at the WTO and with respect to climate but not on the law of the sea, human rights, or international dispute resolution. China has shown willingness to comply with WTO decisions against it.[15] Yet, when the Philippines instituted arbitral proceedings for Chinese violations of UNCLOS obligations,[16] China refused to participate.[17] China claimed the tribunal had no jurisdiction. The tribunal determined both that it had jurisdiction and that China was in serious breach of duties under UNCLOS; China denounced the tribunal. The award was particularly clear respecting China's violations of its duties to preserve and protect the marine environment:

> ... China's artificial island-building activities on the seven reefs in the Spratly Islands have caused devastating and long-lasting damage to the marine environment. ... China has breached its obligation under Article 192 to protect and preserve the marine environment, has conducted dredging in such a way as to pollute the marine environment with sediment in breach of Article 194(1), and has violated its duty under Article 194(5) to take measures necessary to protect and preserve rare or fragile ecosystems as well as the habitat of depleted, threatened or endangered species and other forms of marine life.[18]

China's attitude toward the tribunal and the award are reminiscent of the American and French attitudes toward the International Court of Justice when the ICJ took cases that overlapped with

[15] In an otherwise highly critical report on China's compliance with WTO requirements, the US Trade Representative omitted mention of failure to comply with Dispute Settlement Body decisions. United States Trade Representative, 2017 Report to Congress on China's WTO Compliance (January 2018), available at https://ustr.gov/sites/default/files/files/Press/Reports/China%202017%20WTO%20Report.pdf. See also J. Bacchus, 'How the World Trade Organization Can Curb China's Intellectual Property Transgressions', *CATO*, (22 March 2018), available at www.cato.org/blog/how-world-trade-organization-can-curb-chinas-intellectual-property-transgressions.

[16] Permanent Court of Arbitration, In the Matter of the South China Sea Arbitration, (PCA Case No. 2013–19), Arbitral Tribunal Constituted Under Annex VII to the 1982 UN Convention on the Law of the Sea (The Republic of the Philippines and The People's Republic of China), 12 July 2016.

[17] F. Ying, 'Why China Says No to the Arbitration on the South China Sea', *Foreign Policy* (10 July 2016), available at https://foreignpolicy.com/2016/07/10/why-china-says-no-to-the-arbitration-on-the-south-china-sea/.

[18] PCA, In the Matter of the South China Sea Arbitration (n. 16), para. 983.

national security.[19] Both states refused to participate in cases brought against them. When the ICJ found it had jurisdiction, both renounced the decisions, then withdrew altogether from the ICJ's compulsory jurisdiction.[20] The indications are that China will not withdraw from UNCLOS, but it has gone on the offensive to undermine the validity of the award.[21] In a move not without irony, the United States called on China to comply with the tribunal's decision.[22]

China wants the advantages of UNCLOS membership without bearing the burdens. It 'needs UNCLOS to protect its interests and gain influence on maritime governance'.[23] It plans to be part of the deep-sea bed 'mining bonanza' on a privileged basis as a member of the treaty and to have a role in 'Arctic governance issues', even though it is not an Arctic nation.[24] China seeks these benefits while rejecting UNCLOS obligations from complying with the arbitral

[19] See ICJ, *Military and Paramilitary Activities in and against Nicaragua* (*Nicaragua* v. *United States*), Merits, Judgment of 27 June 1986, ICJ Reports 1986, 14; ICJ, *Nuclear Tests Case* (*Australia* v. *France*), Judgment of 20 December 1974, ICJ Reports 1974, 253; and ICJ, *Nuclear Tests Case* (*New Zealand* v. *France*), Judgment of 20 December 1974, ICJ Reports 1974, 457.

[20] ICJ, *Nuclear Tests Case* (*Australia* v. *France*), (n. 19), 253, 457; United States Department of State, 'US Withdrawal from the Proceedings Initiated by Nicaragua in the ICJ, 18 January 1985', *United States Department of State Bulletin*, 85 (March 1985), 64.

[21] Eder, 'China Leans In' 2018 (n. 11). One tangible indication that China is pursuing such a strategy is a 500-page special issue of the *Chinese Journal of International Law* linked to the Chinese Foreign Ministry to which seventy authors contributed criticizing the South China Sea Award. See, Chinese Society of International Law, 'The South China Sea Arbitration Awards: A Critical Study', *Chinese Journal of International Law*, 17 (2018), 207–748. The Study is discussed by Douglas Guilfoyle in two online posts. See D. Guilfoyle, 'A New Twist in the South China Sea Arbitration: The Chinese Society of International Law's "Critical Study"', *EJIL*: Talk! (25 May 2018), available at www.ejiltalk.org/a-new-twist-in-the-south-china-sea-arbitration-the-chinese-society-of-international-laws-critical-study/; and D. Guilfoyle, 'Taking the Party Line on the South China Sea Arbitration', *EJIL*: Talk! (28 May 2018), available at www.ejiltalk.org/taking-the-party-line-on-the-south-china-sea-arbitration/, citing B. Ling, 'This Critical Study is not some spontaneous work by individual academics, but clearly a government-orchestrated project produced in the name of a learned society ... [It] was carried out under the supervision of the Foreign Ministry.'

[22] F.-S. Gady, 'South China Sea Verdict: US Reactions', *Diplomat* (15 July 2016), available at https://thediplomat.com/2016/07/south-china-sea-verdict-us-reactions/.

[23] Eder, 'China Leans In' 2018 (n. 11). [24] Ibid.

award protecting the maritime environment. This attitude reflects a misunderstanding of the fact that gaining the benefits of the world's legal order is related to bearing its burdens. Particular respect is required for the law's *jus cogens* norms. States seeking to gain must forego the use of force and turn to alternatives to force for the settlement of disputes. These alternatives are flexible, optional, effective, and open to creativity.

Indeed, alternatives for peaceful settlement once captured the imagination of broad swaths of the public around the world. From the audiences of thousands that came to hear Jane Addams of Chicago, USA, to the millions who followed Mahatma Gandhi of Gujarat, India, ideas about negotiation, mediation, and judicial process inspired action.[25] Reigniting that excitement will require looking beyond the usual ideas about carrots and sticks that motivate human behaviour.[26] This chapter returns to the third motivator, the conviction of doing the right thing based on reasons that attract without appealing to self-interest.

A shift in metaphor reveals the idea. The dominant metaphor of dispute resolution is as a contest, such as a sports competition or a military battle, with winners and losers. Dispute resolution, however, has as much or more in common with the performance arts, especially theatre, than a sports competition or war. Like legal process, theatre involves performance, participation, and language. Since the days of ancient Greece, the law and legal process have been explored in plays, but ideas inspired by theatre have only rarely been applied to legal theory. International law advisers to the Chinese government have convinced officials that with respect to the WTO, 'showing up is half the battle'.[27] Showing up *is* the important part, but not of a battle. Participation is a show of support for the rule of law in the world, regardless of outcome.

Hersch Lauterpacht would likely be unimpressed by an argument promoting mere participation. He wrote that 'obligatory arbitration is a *conditio sine qua non* of the normal machinery of peace . . .'.[28] He considered that it is not enough to have substantive principles

[25] For a sampling of their views, see J. Addams, *Newer Ideals of Peace* (New York: Macmillan, 1907); and M. K. Gandhi, *An Autobiography* (Boston: Beacon Press, 1957).

[26] Chapter 1. [27] Eder, 'China Leans In' 2018 (n. 11).

[28] H. Lauterpacht, *The Function of Law in the International Community* (Oxford: Clarendon Press, 1933), 437–8.

prohibiting the use of force. Compulsory dispute resolution is also required.[29] To eventually reach his vision, however, the re-creation of enthusiasm for courts and tribunals of general jurisdiction is needed. In 1945, the International Court of Justice took over from the Permanent Court of International Justice (PCIJ) as the court with general jurisdiction over states and their disputes under international law. The PCIJ's option for compulsory jurisdiction was also transferred, but that was also the last major international step toward an obligation to adjudicate general disputes.[30] Moreover, two of the five Permanent Members of the UN Security Council, China and Russia, have never accepted the ICJ's optional compulsory jurisdiction. Two more, France and the United States, terminated their acceptance, leaving only the United Kingdom with an acceptance, but one that is highly restricted by reservations. While these states that should lead the way in respect for international law are notable for failing to support compulsory jurisdiction, many other states also strenuously resist ICJ jurisdiction. Enthusiasm for international courts of all kinds was in clear decline by the first decade of the twenty-first century. Such attitudes can change, however, when the prestige of participating outweighs the reasons for resisting.

The chapter begins in Part I with the concept of peaceful settlement in international law.[31] Part II looks at the long struggle to create international law and institutions to substitute for war. Courts and tribunals for the peaceful settlement of disputes once had immense popular appeal. That appeal peaked, however, in the years between World Wars I and II and has yet to recover. Part III turns to the arts for an approach aimed at recapturing the commitment of that earlier time. A norm supporting the duty to settle disputes peacefully, like legal authority, the topic of Chapter 1, is not easily explained by the dominant legal theory of positivism. Legal process theory, appearing in the 1930s, has been a useful

[29] Ibid.

[30] M. E. O'Connell and L. VanderZee, 'The History of International Adjudication', in C. J. Romano, K. J. Alter, and Y. Shany (eds.), *The Handbook of International Adjudication* (Oxford: Oxford University Press, 2014), 40–62; and C. J. Tams, 'World Courts as Guardians of Peace?' *Global Cooperation Research Papers 15* (Käte Hamburg Kolleg/Centre for Global Cooperation Research, 2016), 26–7.

[31] See notes 33–59 and accompanying text.

addition, but more can be done to again encourage the international community to favour peaceful settlement over military force.[32]

## I The Prohibition on Force and Peaceful Settlement

In his engaging analysis of the classical Greek trilogy *The Oresteia* by Aeschylus, Paul Gewirtz writes that the plays are about the 'emergence of law'.[33] In his telling, they are more precisely about the fair application of the law through public, orderly, impartial process and reasoned discussion at a consecrated site.[34] The story moves from the private resolution of disputes within the family, involving 'uncontrolled violence' to 'wise resolution' through legal process.[35] The type of process with the characteristics found in the play has all the hallmarks of law. As long as international law has existed, it has included such process mechanisms in combination with the restrictions on the use of force. As Lauterpacht argues, prohibiting resort to force in substantive law requires the pairing of means for the peaceful settlement of disputes.[36]

The prohibition on force is part of the most fundamental principle of international legal dispute resolution: if parties to a dispute attempt to settle it, they must do so peacefully.[37] A positive law version of the principle is found in United Nations Charter Article 2(3): 'All Members shall settle their international disputes by peaceful means in such a manner that international peace and security, and justice, are not endangered.'[38] It precedes Article 2(4), the prohibition on the use of force.[39] The two articles are interconnected and complementary to each other. The next section discusses the breadth of Article 2(3) – whether it extends today to an obligation to take affirmative steps to attempt settlement in all

[32] See notes 123–69 and accompanying text.

[33] Paul Gewirtz, 'Aeschylus' Law', *Harvard Law Review,* 101 (1988), 1043–55, 1044. The trilogy consists of *Agamemnon, The Libation Bearers,* and *The Eumenides.*

[34] Ibid., 1045. [35] Ibid., 1046. [36] See, e.g., Chapters 4 and 5.

[37] Wide consensus exists as to this basic duty under international law respecting dispute resolution. Cf. R. B. Bilder, 'An Overview of International Dispute Resolution', *Emory Journal of International Dispute Resolution,* 1 (1986), 1–32 and M. O. Hudson, *By Pacific Means: The Implementation of Article Two of the Pact of Paris* (New Haven: Yale University Press, 1935). For evidence of a more expansive duty, see notes 82–116 and accompanying text.

[38] Art. 2(3) United Nations Charter. [39] Art. 2(4) United Nations Charter.

disputes. At the least, 'it is clear that states must attempt to settle their most serious controversies by peaceful means'.[40] The most serious controversies tend to involve the threat or use of armed force.

The means accepted as peaceful are listed in Chapter VI, Article 33(1) of the Charter: 'negotiation, enquiry, mediation, conciliation, arbitration, judicial settlement, resort to regional agencies or arrangements, or other peaceful means of their own choice'.[41] The methods listed in Article 33 will be referred to here collectively as either 'dispute resolution' or 'dispute settlement', using the terms synonymously.[42] The list does not include mechanisms for international criminal responsibility. Certain writers believe it should, but international criminal tribunals are not direct substitutes for war in the settlement of disputes and are omitted here because the link to peace is indirect.[43] The drafters of the UN Charter considered the mechanisms in Article 33 to be direct substitutes for war.[44] With the strict prohibition on the use of force in

[40] C. F. Murphy, 'The Obligation of States to Settle Disputes by Peaceful Means', *Virginia Journal of International Law*, 14 (1973), 57–74, 57.

[41] Art. 33(1) UN Charter. There is a large literature on this general topic, see, e.g., J. H. W. Verzijl, *International Law in Historical Perspective: Inter-State Disputes and Their Settlement* 8 (Leyden: A.W. Sijthoff, 1976); I. Diaconu, 'Peaceful Settlement of Disputes Between States: History and Prospects', in R. St J. Macdonald and D. M. Johnston (eds.), *The Structure and Process of International Law: Essays in Legal Philosophy Doctrine and Theory* (Dordrecht: Martinus Nijhof, 1983), 1095–119, 1096–7; J. Collier and V. Lowe, *The Settlement of Disputes in International Law: Institutions and Procedures* (Oxford: Oxford University Press, 1999); J. G. Merrills, *International Dispute Settlement* (Cambridge: Cambridge University Press, 2011); C. M. Bailliet and K. M. Larsen, *Promoting Peace Through International Law* (Oxford: Oxford University Press, 2015); and J. G. Merrills, 'The Means of International Dispute Settlement', in M. Evans (ed.), *International Law* 5th edn (Oxford: Oxford University Press, 2018), chap. 18.

[42] Vaughan Lowe and John Collier believe that international law is more centrally concerned with 'settlement', rather than 'resolution' of disputes as resolution connotes for them solving the root of the problem that gave rise to the dispute. While they have a point, the more common practice in international law seems to be the one adopted here, to treat the terms synonymously. See Collier and Lowe, *The Settlement of Disputes in International Law* 1999 (n. 41).

[43] See, e.g., L. Condorelli and S. Villalpando, 'Can the Security Council Extend the ICC's Jurisdiction?', in A. Cassese, P. Gaeta and J. R. W. D. Jones (eds.), *The Rome Statute of the International Criminal Court: A Commentary* (Oxford: Oxford University Press, 2002), 571–82, 571–2.

[44] L. B. Sohn, 'The Future of Dispute Resolution', in Macdonald and Johnston (eds.), *The Structure and Process of International Law* 1983 (n. 41), 1121–46, 1121.

Article 2(4), international lawyers and government officials understood that alternatives would be needed.[45] The means of peaceful settlement together with the prohibition on the use of force form a unit. International criminal law processes may well be supportive of the goal of global order but not as a direct substitute for armed force.[46]

Even without international criminal courts, the Article 33(1) list from negotiation through 'other peaceful means' of the parties' choice is lengthy and open-ended. It is not clear what other means exist beyond the list. If there are any, they are not well known. In fact, the list gives the impression of more options than exist as truly distinctive means. Mediation, conciliation, and resort to agencies are variations on third-party, non-binding processes. Arbitration and judicial settlement are variations of binding ones. The methods with distinctive substantive aspects are negotiation, fact-finding, mediation, and adjudication.[47] In negotiation, parties to a dispute meet directly without third-party intervention. It is governed by few, if any, rules beyond good faith.[48] Fact-finding (inquiry) introduces a third party for one purpose, reporting on a disputed fact or question.[49] Mediation also brings a third party into the process but to facilitate negotiation.[50] The outcomes of these processes are not binding. The mechanisms that produce binding outcomes consist of proceedings before courts and arbitral tribunals. These are governed by more detailed rules found in general international law and the specific rules of the court or tribunal.[51]

Sometimes governments will complain about the 'aggressive' use of these mechanisms or otherwise infer that their use is coercive, illicit, or inappropriate.[52] A theme of this chapter is to support

[45] Ibid.

[46] Condorelli and Villalpando, 'Can the Security Council Extend the ICC's Jurisdiction?' 2002 (n. 43).

[47] See generally United Nations Office of Legal Affairs, Codification Division, *Handbook on the Peaceful Settlement of Disputes Between States* (New York: United Nations, 1992), UN Doc. OLA/COD/2394, available at http://legal.un.org/cod/books/HandbookOnPSD.pdf; and M. E. O'Connell, *Cases and Materials on International Dispute Resolution* 2nd edn (Durham, NC: Carolina Academic Press, 2006).

[48] United Nations, *Handbook on the Peaceful Settlement of Disputes* 1992 (n. 47), 21–73.

[49] Ibid., 74–100. [50] Ibid., 123–39. [51] Ibid., 168–229.

[52] China's reaction to the Philippines' claims under UNCLOS and the US reaction to Nicaragua's case against it in the 1980s at the International Court of Justice are two examples. Regarding China, see notes 1–24 and accompanying text.

a pro-participation ethos of international law. International law encourages resort to the peaceful mechanisms. The coercive means in international law are the use of force and countermeasures. The use of force has already been discussed extensively. As for countermeasures, international law permits a state to violate a rule benefitting another state if that state has first violated a duty owed to the state taking the measure.[53] If a state refuses to comply with an arbitral award in favour of another state, for example, the state seeking compliance may refuse to fulfil a duty of its own to the defaulting state.[54] The rules governing countermeasures are strict, requiring a request for compliance, respect for the principles of necessity and proportionality, and the exclusion of measures that violate human rights, diplomatic privileges, the environment, and, of course, *jus cogens* norms.[55]

In contrast to this restrictive approach to countermeasures and the use of military force, the dispute settlement regime is in many respects flexible and unrestrictive. Designers of dispute resolution mechanisms have always sought to make the options attractive to win the voluntary participation of sovereign states. The dispute resolution section of UNCLOS, Part XV, for example, begins with these provisions:

> Article 279
>
> Obligation to settle disputes by peaceful means
>
> States Parties shall settle any dispute between them concerning the interpretation or application of this Convention by peaceful means in accordance with Article 2, paragraph 3, of the Charter of the United

Regarding the USA, see, United States Department of State, 'US Withdrawal from the Proceedings Initiated by Nicaragua in the ICJ, 18 January 1985', *United States Department of State Bulletin* 85 (March 1985), 64.

53 International Law Commission, *Responsibility of States for Internationally Wrongful Acts*, UNGA, 55th Sess, Supp No. 10, UN Doc A/56/10; United Nations General Assembly, *Responsibility of States for Internationally Wrongful Acts*, UNGAOR, 56th Sess, Agenda Item 162, UN Doc. A/RES/56/83 (12 December 2001), Arts. 22, 49–54.

54 See Mexico's withholding of payments due following the Pious Fund arbitration with the USA to induce the USA to comply with the award of territory to Mexico in the El Chamizal arbitration recounted in P. C. Jessup, 'El Chamizal', *American Journal of International Law*, 67 (1973), 423–45, 440.

55 ILC, *Responsibility of States for Internationally Wrongful Acts* (n. 53), Arts. 49–54; see also, Air Services Agreement (*US* v. *France*), 18 *Report of International Arbitral Awards* 417, 444 (1978).

> Nations and, to this end, shall seek a solution by the means indicated in Article 33, paragraph 1, of the Charter.
> Article 280
> Settlement of disputes by any peaceful means chosen by the parties.
> Nothing in this Part impairs the right of any States Parties to agree at any time to settle a dispute between them concerning the interpretation or application of this Convention by any peaceful means of their own choice.[56]

Once a state commits to a binding mechanism, however, it is obligated to comply with the outcome of the process. One of the bedrock principles of adjudication is that the court or tribunal determines its own jurisdiction.[57] National legal systems and the international one need to continually reinforce this principle. The efficacy of the legal process and, therefore, of legal systems in general depends on the deference of subjects. Defiance of courts indicates the breakdown of the rule of law within societies. Conversely, participation in legal processes internalizes principles such as respect of legal process. Participation also builds the 'law habit',[58] and can counter the inclination to avoid dispute settlement.[59]

As just restated, international law's traditional principle of dispute resolution is paired with the prohibition on the use of force.[60] The Charter's pairing of Article 2(3) and Article 2(4) is the legacy of a more than a century of passionate campaigning for peace through law. By the early twentieth century, the effort had evolved into a more technical attempt to build positive law, including institutions and mechanisms to substitute for war. Following two world wars in the twentieth century and disappointment in international law's capacity combined with growing confidence in military force, interest in dispute resolution has been declining.[61] During the

[56] UN Convention on the Law of the Sea, opened for signature Dec. 10, 1982, 1833 UNTS 397, Part XV.

[57] The principle is known as known as 'competence de la competence' or 'Kompetenz-Kompetenz'.

[58] See Chapter 1.

[59] The United States went to great lengths to avoid jurisdiction in the Nicaragua case, including attempting to amend its acceptance of the ICJ's compulsory jurisdiction three days before Nicaragua applied to the court. A. Chayes, 'Nicaragua, the United States, and the World Court', *Columbia Law Review*, 85 (1985), 1445–82.

[60] Murphy, 'The Obligation of States to Settle Disputes' 1973 (n. 40), 57.

[61] See note 30 and accompanying text.

drafting of the Charter, those still committed to peace through law made bold proposals to move beyond the League of Nations system.[62] Those efforts failed. Not only are the Charter provisions on dispute resolution weaker than those of the League Covenant, interest in peaceful settlement has faded, too, while interest in the use of force has grown.[63] 'This is unfortunate, because adequate comprehension of Charter principles is possible only when the complementary character of Article 2(3) and 2(4) is understood.'[64]

## A *The Charter*

The United Nations Charter begins in Chapter I, Article 1 with a statement of the UN's purposes, which are to

> maintain international peace and security, and to that end: to take effective collective measures for the prevention and removal of threats to the peace, and for the suppression of acts of aggression or other breaches of the peace . . . and to bring about by peaceful means, and in conformity with the principles of justice and international law, adjustment or settlement of international disputes or situations which might lead to a breach of the peace.[65]

Article 1(1) places an affirmative duty on the UN as an organization to bring about peaceful settlement – it is an obligation that requires continuing efforts, certainly to end ongoing armed conflict. The Article 2(3) duty on member states is more equivocal: 'All Members shall settle their international disputes by peaceful means in such a manner that international peace and security, and justice, are not endangered.' The provision's emphasis could be on 'shall settle' or on 'by peaceful means'. The ambiguity is carried forward in Chapter VI of the Charter. Chapter VI Article 33(1) refers to disputes that are 'likely' to threaten the peace and provides that States 'shall seek' peaceful settlement: 'The parties to any dispute, the continuance of which is likely to endanger the

[62] R. B. Russell, *A History of the United Nations Charter* (Washington, DC: Brookings Institution, 1958), 884–90.

[63] 'While . . . Article 2(4) [. . .] has been the subject of considerable scholarship, very little attention has been directed towards the meaning and significance of the positive duty of peaceful settlement.' Murphy, 'The Obligation of States to Settle Disputes' 1973 (n. 40), 57.

[64] Ibid. [65] Art. 1 UN Charter.

maintenance of international peace and security, shall, first of all, seek a solution by . . . peaceful means . . . '.[66]

The understanding of these provisions appears to have passed through three phases of scholarly interpretation. The earlier writers, such as Hans Kelsen, held that states must seek to settle all disputes.[67] Josef Kunz, somewhat later, saw the obligation as one to settle disputes that might endanger peace and security.[68] The third view, held by Richard Bilder, and apparently the currently prevailing one, holds 'that in the absence of special agreement, states are under no international legal obligation to settle, or even to try to settle, their disputes'.[69]

The negotiating history of the Charter is mixed as well. The drafters considered Chapter VI an important, if not the most important, set of rules in the Charter. They proposed ambitious provisions, including that the International Court of Justice be given compulsory jurisdiction. They proposed that the Security Council itself sit as a court in cases involving international security. It was to be given authority to 'prescribe the terms of settlement of a dispute within its jurisdiction and institute measures for the enforcement of its decisions'.[70] The United States and the Soviet Union strongly objected to the proposals, and they were dropped.[71] The result was a Charter with many references to dispute resolution but few firm obligations. Still, Louis Sohn saw the Charter dispute resolution obligations as 'parallel' to the prohibition on the use of force.[72] That conviction suggests moving to a more robust understanding of Article 2(3) than the one that prevails among scholars today, which is the topic of Part III below.

One key to understanding the decline in popular perception of the relative importance of Article 2(3) compared with 2(4) is seen in the decision to give the Security Council greater discretion respecting dispute resolution than its predecessor, the League Council. Article 33(2) provides that the Security Council shall,

66 Art. 33 UN Charter.

67 H. Kelsen, *The Law of the United Nations: A Critical Analysis of Its Fundamental Problems* (New York: Frederick A. Praeger, 1950), 359.

68 J. L. Kunz, *The Changing Law of Nations* (Columbus: Ohio State University Press, 1968), 588.

69 Bilder, 'An Overview of International Dispute Resolution' 1986 (n. 37), (1).

70 Russell, *A History of the United Nations Charter* 1958 (n. 62), 991–3.

71 Ibid., 884–93.

72 Sohn, 'The Future of Dispute Resolution' 1983 (n. 44), 1121.

when it deems necessary, call upon the parties to a dispute to settle it. US State Department officials drafting early versions of the Charter proposed that the Security Council be required to direct states to take disputes to the International Court of Justice, the PCIJ's successor.[73] The PCIJ was considered a success, and there had been no doubt that a world court would continue when the new UN was established.[74] President Franklin Roosevelt, however, wanted the Security Council to be free to act. He shared the view that the League of Nations had failed in part because the Council of the League was too constrained.[75] Under Article 13(4), the League Council was obligated to enforce international judicial and arbitral awards.[76] In the event of any failure by a member of the League to carry out a judicial decision or arbitral award, 'the Council shall propose what steps should be taken to give effect thereto'.[77]

The proposal to require the new Council to refer cases to the ICJ was rejected.[78] The Security Council has wide discretion and could mandate that parties take a case to the International Court.[79] It has never done so. It has never even taken steps to enforce ICJ judgments despite the specific terms of Charter Article 94 giving it discretion to do so. The Charter has no reference to Security

[73] For more on the ICJ, see Introduction, n. 28.

[74] Russell, *A History of the United Nations Charter* 1958 (n. 62), 289.

[75] The League Covenant already showed signs of waning interest in promoting peace through international law and the international institutions for peaceful dispute resolution. The peak in general interest was apparently just prior to the outbreak of World War I. S. Wertheim, 'The League of Nations: A Retreat from International Law', *Journal of Global History*, 7 (2012), 210–32.

[76] Article 13(4): 'The Members of the League agree that they will carry out in full good faith any award or decision that may be rendered, and that they will not resort to war against a Member of the League which complies therewith. In the event of any failure to carry out such an award or decision, the Council shall propose what steps should be taken to give effect thereto.' Covenant of the League of Nations (1919), available at http://avalon.law.yale.edu/20th_century/leagcov.asp. The League Council interpreted Article 13(4) as giving it discretion not to enforce in the Hungarian-Rumanian Optants Case, *League of Nations Official Journal*, 8 (1927), 1379.

[77] Covenant of the League of Nations (1919), available at http://avalon.law.yale.edu/20th_century/leagcov.asp.

[78] Russell, *A History of the United Nations Charter* 1958 (n. 62), 289.

[79] The Council is considered to have wide powers in the area of peace and security, see, Condorelli and Villalpando, 'Can the Security Council Extend the ICC's Jurisdiction?' 2002 (n. 43).

Council enforcement of arbitral awards, another change from the League. Indeed, beyond encouraging parties to negotiate or to engage with a mediator, the Security Council has done almost nothing to promote dispute resolution. The Security Council orders states to undertake a variety of burdensome, unwelcome obligations, such as giving up nuclear programmes, withdrawing from territory, handing nationals over to international criminal courts, and participating in sanctions regimes. By comparison, mandating fair and impartial dispute resolution should seem attractive.

The Charter is also weaker than the League Covenant with respect to the powers of the UN General Assembly respecting dispute resolution. UN Charter Chapter IV, which is devoted to the General Assembly, does not mention dispute settlement directly, nor is the Assembly mentioned in Chapter VI. Still, in 1970, the General Assembly adopted the Declaration on Friendly Relations to fill out the details of the Charter's duties on states. The Declaration again pairs the prohibition on force and dispute resolution, reversing the order in the Charter. The Declaration's Principle 1 restates in detailed form the Article 2(4) prohibition on the use of force. Principle 2 restates Article 2(3). Principle 2, paragraph 2 supports Kelsen's view that states are obligated to generally seek resolution of outstanding disputes, but the more robust duty is in paragraph 3, which requires states to continue seeking a settlement but only once attempts have begun:

2) States shall accordingly seek early and just settlement of their international disputes by negotiation, inquiry, mediation, conciliation, arbitration, judicial settlement, resort to regional agencies or arrangements or other peaceful means of their choice. In seeking such a settlement, the parties shall agree upon such peaceful means as may be appropriate to the circumstances and nature of the dispute.
3) The parties to a dispute have the duty, in the event of failure to reach a solution by any one of the above peaceful means, to continue to seek a settlement of the dispute by other peaceful means agreed upon by them.[80]

[80] UN General Assembly Declaration on Principles of International Law concerning Friendly Relations and Cooperation among States, UN GOAR, 6th Committee, 25th Sess, Agenda Item 85, UN Doc. A/RES/25/2625 (24 October 1970), Principle 2(2) and 2(3). See also S. O'Connor and

The General Assembly has undertaken a variety of initiatives to promote international law and the peaceful resolution of disputes. It has sought to promote a human right to peace. Yet, one effort, partially under the terms of Chapter VI, stands out beyond all others, UN Peacekeeping. Brian Urquhart, the 'father' of UN Peacekeeping, explains that peacekeeping relies on 'Chapter VI and a half' because it is a use of troops.[81] Troops are not mentioned in Chapter VI but are mentioned in Chapter VII. In the ICJ advisory opinion *Certain Expenses*, the court found that the General Assembly could lawfully organize peacekeeping and pay for it out of member state dues because of the Assembly's secondary role in promoting peace and security.[82] Since the end of the Cold War, the Security Council has taken over peacekeeping, moving it firmly out of Chapter VI and into Chapter VII. The history of peacekeeping exemplifies the general trend favouring military force in the Charter era, as described in Chapters 3 and 4.

### *B The Complementary Principles Pre-Charter*

The pairing of Articles 2(3) and 2(4) follow a long, intertwined history of prohibiting force and providing peaceful methods of dispute resolution. The ancient Greeks were known to use arbitration as an alternative to war.[83] Hugo Grotius supported the use of arbitration by quoting the historian of ancient Greece, Thucydides, whose famous work was an account of the Peloponnesian Wars. Thucydides was a military commander and later in his life a historian who wrote that 'it is not lawful to proceed against one who offers arbitration just as against a wrongdoer'.[84] Grotius's direct

C. M. Bailliet, 'The Good Faith Obligation to Maintain International Peace and Security and the Pacific Settlement of Disputes', in C. M. Bailliet and K. M. Larsen (eds.), *Promoting Peace Through International Law* (Oxford: Oxford University Press, 2015), 66–85, 70.

[81] Chapter 3.

[82] ICJ, *Certain Expenses of the United Nations (Article 17, paragraph 2 of the Charter)* Advisory Opinion of 20 July 1962, ICJ Reports 1962, 151.

[83] D. Bederman, *International Law in Antiquity* (Cambridge: Cambridge University Press, 2001), 82. See also C. G. Roelofsen, 'International Arbitration and Courts', in B. Fassbender and A. Peters (eds.), *The Oxford Handbook of The History of International Law* (Oxford: Oxford University Press, 2012), 145–69.

[84] H. Grotius, *De Jure Belli ac Pacis Libri Tres* 1, F. W. Kelsey (trans.) (1964), 560–2.

predecessors, the Spanish Scholastics, proposed the use of arbitration as a substitute for papal determinations of compliance with the restrictions of the Just War Doctrine.[85]

Participants in the infamous Thirty Years' War (1618–38) used mediation to finally bring the war to an end. 'Among the most famous instances of mediation I cite that of Venice and the Pope between France and the Empire ... and of Denmark between the Empire and Sweden ... prior to and during the Congress of Westphalia of 1648.'[86] The treaties that followed prohibited military intervention and the use of force. They also called for dispute resolution by 'amicable settlement of legal discussion'.[87] A century later, Emmerich de Vattel advocated arbitration, citing various examples of successful cases to persuade his readers.[88]

The American Founding Fathers were among those readers. In the peace agreement with Britain following their war of independence, the Jay Treaty of 1794, the two states agreed to use arbitration to settle the remaining issues between them.[89] From 1794 to 1804, the United States and Britain participated in 536 arbitrations under the Jay Treaty, beginning with the St. Croix River Arbitration of 1798, which delineated much of the Canada–United States boundary.[90] This successful example of dispute resolution in lieu of war helped galvanize the religiously based anti-war movement in the USA, which began among the Quakers, Mennonites, and Anabaptists who had fled persecution in Europe levelled against

[85] M. E. O'Connell, 'Arbitration and the Avoidance of War: The Nineteenth-Century American Vision', in C. Romano (ed.), *The United States and International Courts and Tribunals* (Cambridge: Cambridge University Press, 2009), 24–25.

[86] Verzijl, *International Law in Historical Perspective* 1976 (n. 41), 52.

[87] The Articles of the Treaty of Peace, signed and sealed at Münster, in Westphalia, 24 October 1648, Art. 73, *Parry's Consolidated Treaty Series* 319; Treaty of Peace between the Empires and Sweden, concluded and signed at Osnabrück, 24 October 1648, *Parry's Consolidated Treaty Series* 198. See also A. Nussbaum, *A Concise History of the Law of Nations* (rev. ed. 1954).

[88] E. de Vattel, *The Law of Nations or the Principles of Natural Law*, C. G. Fenwick trans. of 1758 edn (Washington, DC: Carnegie Institution of Washington, 1916) 189–92; see also C. Gray and B. Kingsbury, 'Developments in Dispute Settlement: Inter-State Arbitration Since 1945', *British Yearbook of International Law*, 63 (1992), 97–134.

[89] International Court of Justice, 'History', available at icj-cij.org/court/index/php?p1=1&p2=1.

[90] A. M. Stuyt (ed.), *Survey of International Arbitration, 1794–1989* (Dordrecht: Martinus Nijhof, 1990), 1–4.

them, in part owing to their pacifist beliefs.[91] The first secular organization for peace was established in the USA in 1815, the New York Peace Society.[92] More peace societies followed in North America and throughout Europe. These organizations focused on the reasons to oppose military force and to use international law and dispute settlement mechanisms it its place. The 1872 *Alabama Claims* arbitration between the USA and Britain arising out of events of the American Civil War was a sensation in the pro-peace community.[93] In 1873, the Russian tsar acted as sole arbitrator in a dispute between Peru and Japan, the *Maria Luz* case. The decision helped demonstrate the universality of international law and the rise of internationally protected human rights.[94] The 'peace through law' movement was gaining political, intellectual, and artistic support.[95] Their main message was that the world had effective alternatives to war.[96]

With the nineteenth-century move away from natural law to positivism, those advocating courts saw them as a way to develop material evidence of international law through decisions – as the United States Supreme Court had done. The 'science of international law' required courts. Leonidas Kamarowsky proposed a voluntary court of international justice, which would not only settle international disputes but would aid in the codification and promulgation of international law.[97] Proposals such as Kamarowsky's were topics at the

[91] L. S. Wittner, *Rebels Against War: The American Peace Movement* (Philadelphia: Temple University Press, 1984).
[92] Ibid.
[93] See E. C. Bruggink, 'The Alabama Claims', *Alabama Law Review*, 57 (1996), 339.
[94] Stuyt, *Survey of International Arbitrations* 1990 (n. 90), 107.
[95] Influential writers, visual artists, and composers took up the cause of peace. One of the best known of the late nineteenth and early twentieth centuries was the writer and activist Bertha von Sutner, who won the Nobel Peace Prize. The website for the Nobel Prize describes her most acclaimed book on the subject of peace, *Die Waffen Nieder* (*Lay Down Your Weapons*), as making a 'tremendous' impact on the reading public. https://www.nobelprize.org/nobel_prizes/peace/laureates/1905/suttner-bio.html. See also, S. Peter, 'Bertha von Suttner (1843–1914)', in B. Fassbender and A. Peters (eds.), *The Oxford Handbook of the History of International Law* (Oxford: Oxford University Press, 2012), chap. 58.
[96] See Y. Shany, 'No Longer a Weak Department of Power? Reflections on the Emergence of a New International Judiciary,' *European Journal of International Law*, 20 (2009), 73–92.
[97] Discussed in J. H. Ralston, *International Arbitration, from Athens to Locarno* (Stanford: Stanford University Press, 1929), 125–6.

First Hague Peace Conference of 1899. The US delegation attended the conference with instructions to propose the establishment of a permanent international court.[98]

The Americans failed in their mission, to the disappointment of the peace movement, but the delegates did agree to establish the Permanent Court of Arbitration (PCA), consisting of a registry, a Permanent Administrative Council made up of diplomatic representatives from state parties, and a list of arbitrators from which states could select should they voluntarily submit a dispute to arbitration. At the Second Hague Peace Conference in 1907, another attempt was made to create a court, as well as to establish compulsory jurisdiction for the PCA. Germany, however, blocked the proposals, arguing that dispute settlement commitments should be created through bilateral treaties, not a multilateral one.[99] The delegates did succeed in adding a limited form of compulsory dispute settlement to the new Convention of 1907 Respecting the Limitation of the Employment of Force for the Recovery of Contract Debts.[100] The treaty prohibited the use of force to coerce debt payments and provided that where parties had agreed to resolve disputes by arbitration but failed to specify further details, the Permanent Court of Arbitration would become the default forum.[101]

The next year, the US Secretary of State, Elihu Root, joined with Central American states to create the Central American Court of Justice in 1908.[102] The Central American Court was the first permanent court for the settlement of interstate disputes.[103] The Court sat

[98] R. P. Anand, *Studies in International Adjudication* (Dobbs Ferry, NY: Oceana Publications, 1969) 2, citing E. Root, *Instructions to the American Delegates to the Hague Peace Conferences*, J. B. Scott (ed.) (Oxford: Oxford University Press, 1916), 79–80.

[99] W. E. Butler, 'The Hague Permanent Court of Arbitration', in M. W. Janis (ed.), *International Courts for the Twenty-First Century* (Dordrecht: Martinus Nijhoff, 1992), 43–53, 44.

[100] Hague Convention Respecting the Limitation of the Employment of Force for the Recovery of Contract Debts, 18 October 1907, 36 Stat. 2241.

[101] Hague Convention for the Pacific Settlement of International Disputes of 1907 (I), Art. 53.2.

[102] F. L. Grieves, *Supranational and International Adjudication* (Champaign, IL: University of Illinois Press, 1969), 22.

[103] H. M. Hill, 'Central American Court of Justice,' in R. Bernhardt (ed.), *Max Planck Encyclopedia of Public International Law* 1 (Oxford: Oxford University Press, 1992), 41–4.

in a villa in San José, Costa Rica, and lasted ten years when agreement was reached to create the Permanent Court of International Justice. The Central American court, interestingly, had broad jurisdiction that included a right of individuals to bring cases against states, including states of which they were not nationals. Of the ten cases heard by the CACJ, individuals brought five.

The devastation of the First World War provided the impetus to move forward toward prohibiting war and creating a court to resolve disputes. Kelsen argued in favour of a court being at the heart of the new organization and blamed the eventual demise of the League on this 'fatal' design flaw.[104] Kelsen believed that a world organization needed to begin with a competent court empowered with compulsory jurisdiction and featuring expert and impartial judges.[105] Kelsen also argued that the most important aspect of the judicial system at the centre of a successful world organization is compulsory jurisdiction. Without it, the world court would be unable to prevent the escalation of conflicts.[106] Kelsen was well aware of the opposition to compulsory jurisdiction. Some scholars again raised concerns about whether international law was adequate to answer the range of issues arising in interstate disputes. Kelsen foresaw that the future world court would be just as capable as national courts in finding legal answers to the unlimited questions that confronted them.[107]

Only in 1920 did the Council of the League organize a commission of ten prominent jurists to draft a statute for the new court. It would not be at the centre of global organization for peace then or in the hundred years that followed. The committee was chaired by Belgium's Baron Descamps and the draft adopted in December 1920. It entered into force in 1921, and the Permanent Court of International Justice began work on its first

[104] H. Kelsen, *Law and Peace in International Relations* (first published 1942, New York: William S. Hein & Co., Inc, 1997), 151–2. For more on Kelsen's view on international law and tribunals, see H. Kelsen, *Peace Through Law* (Chapel Hill: University of North Carolina Press, 1944); H. Kelsen, *General Theory of Law and State* (A. Wedberg (trans.) Cambridge, MA: Harvard University Press, 1945).

[105] See J. von Bernstorff, *The Public International Law Theory of Hans Kelsen: Believing in Universal Law* (Cambridge: Cambridge University Press, 2010), 201.

[106] Ibid., 159.

[107] Ibid., 164. On this point, see also, Lauterpacht, *The Function of Law* 1933, (n. 28).

cases in 1922.[108] The UK member of the drafting commission, Lord Phillimore, wanted the new court to be a 'Court of Justice in the true sense of the word, a court before which it should be possible to call States having broken the law of Nations, without having to obtain their consent in advance'.[109] The Dutch jurist Bernard C. J. Loder echoed this sentiment, arguing that compulsory jurisdiction was a crucial step forward from arbitral jurisdiction.[110]

Other members, however, doubted that the time was right for compulsory jurisdiction or were opposed to it altogether. The USA's Root counselled delay.[111] Mineichiro Adatci of Japan feared the premature adoption of compulsory jurisdiction at the outset of the League of Nations experiment could be risky for the future of dispute settlement.[112] Eventually the commission reached a compromise, known as the Root-Phillimore plan, that allowed states to accept compulsory jurisdiction at their option on the basis of reciprocity with other states accepting the same commitment. Twenty-nine states accepted the optional compulsory jurisdiction of the PCIJ.[113] This was to be the high-water mark of general compulsory jurisdiction – in the century that followed, the international community made no advance on the Root-Phillimore plan.

It came close in 1924 when all forty-seven members of the League of Nations approved the Geneva Protocol for the Pacific Settlement of Disputes. Article 3 of the Protocol committed all parties to the compulsory jurisdiction of the PCIJ. The UK had spearheaded the effort but after a change of government, it changed positions, and the Protocol never came into force. In 1928, states made another attempt, this time removing the compulsory dispute resolution provisions to make it more acceptable. The General Act for the Pacific Settlement of Disputes did enter into force, in 1929, but with no real impact.[114] In the same year, the USA and France drafted the Kellogg-Briand Pact to generally renounce war as an instrument of

[108] International Court of Justice, 'Permanent Court of International Justice', available at www.icj-cij.org/en/pcij.

[109] Permanent Court of International Justice, Advisory Committee of Jurists, *Procès-Verbaux of the Proceedings of the Committee June 16 to July 24, 1920* (The Hague: Van Langenhuysen Brothers 1920; The Lawbook Exchange, 2005), 104.

[110] Ibid., 224. [111] Ibid., 308. [112] Ibid., 651–2.

[113] J. Allain, *A Century of International Adjudication: The Rule of Law and its Limits* (The Hague: TMC Asser Press, 2000), 13.

[114] *League of Nations Treaty Series*, vol. 93 (344–63).

foreign policy.[115] Article 2 of the Pact committed parties to resolve conflicts through peaceful means but without any commitment to compulsory jurisdiction.

With the looming crisis of another world war, proponents of the new ideology of Realism began to attack the efforts at world peace through law and institutions. The British academic E. H. Carr, in his book *The Twenty Years' Crisis 1919–1939*, argued directly against Kelsen's vision of world order. For Carr, 'the view of international law as a legal system that was institutionally completed by compulsory jurisdiction was another "distinguished international lawyer's dream of an international community whose center of gravity is in the administration of international justice"'.[116] For Carr, the legal process is fundamentally different from the political process because it blocks out the importance of power in international relations. The idea that nations are equal before the law, regardless of the asymmetries of material power, was a 'fiction [which] contradicted the inherent logic of international politics, where the strength of the individual states had to be considered a crucial factor in the solution of conflicts of interest'.[117] This critique of Kelsen's theory gained adherents in the United States as it amassed its own material power.

The drafting of the UN Charter should have been the moment to move the world finally to a positive law prohibition on force with obligatory compulsory dispute resolution. It did not happen.

### C *Beyond the Charter*

After the adoption of the Charter, states and organizations turned away from a focus on peace to specialized topics of international law.[118] The human rights era had dawned with the adoption of the Universal Declaration of Human Rights in 1948. In the years that followed, dozens of human rights treaties were adopted, and courts

[115] Reprinted at http://www.yale.edu/lawweb/avalon/imt/kbpact.htm. See also Chapters 2 and 4.

[116] Von Bernstorff, *The Public International Law Theory of Hans Kelsen* 2010 (n. 105), 220 (citing E. H. Carr, *The Twenty Years' Crisis 1919–1939* (New York: Macmillan & Co, 1939), 186).

[117] Ibid., 221 (citing Carr, 188).

[118] See, generally, W. A. Schabas and S. Murphy (eds.), *Research Handbook on International Courts and Tribunals* (Cheltenham: Edward Elgar, 2017).

and other bodies were established to interpret and implement them. In the 1970s, with the rise of international environmental concerns, negotiations began for the 1982 United Nations Convention on the Law of the Sea and its comprehensive and compulsory system of dispute resolution. States developed a similar system in 1994 for world trade disputes.[119] The Security Council instituted the first international criminal tribunal since the Nuremberg and Tokyo Tribunals, also in 1994. Soon after, States and organizations adopted the Rome Statute of the International Criminal Court.[120]

The International Court of Justice and various arbitral tribunals continued to decide cases involving violations of the prohibition on force. Yet, it is difficult to find real advances in dispute resolution duties relative to the prohibition on force. At most, it is possible to see an emerging obligation to enter into good faith negotiations upon the request of one state to another. Anne Peters has discerned a 'duty at least to negotiate'.[121] In the important *Abyei* arbitration, a non-state actor, the South Sudan People's Liberation Movement, received the status of a sovereign state in a boundary dispute with Sudan.[122] In the course of a century, these are tiny steps.

Peace through law and legal institutions no longer captures the imagination of statesmen or even peace activists. Well before the United States withdrew from the ICJ's compulsory jurisdiction, American interest in general compulsory jurisdiction had waned. In the dominant ideology of Realism, international courts are 'ultimately embedded in an international system characterized by unequal distribution of power, and powerful states retain the right

[119] WTO.org. See also, R. Z. Lawrence, 'The United States and the WTO Dispute Settlement System', Council on Foreign Relations CSR No. 25, March 2007.

[120] The negotiators of the Rome Statute agreed to delay inclusion of the crime of aggression until a later review conference. The ICC now has jurisdiction over the crime of aggression, but aggression does not have the same meaning as within the *jus ad bellum*. To that extent, the ICC may contribute to the weakened perception of the prohibition on the use of force. See M. E. O'Connell and M. Niyazmatov, 'What is Aggression? Comparing the *Jus Ad Bellum* and the ICC Statute', *Journal of International Criminal Justice*, 10 (2012), 189–207, 191–2.

[121] A. Peters, 'International Dispute Settlement: A Network of Cooperational Duties', *European Journal of International Law*, 14 (2003), 1–34, 29.

[122] Permanent Court of Arbitration, Abyei Arbitration (Sudan/Sudan People's Liberation Movement/Army) (22 July 2008), www.pca-cpa.org/showpage.asp?ac=print&pag_id=1306.

to sanction or ignore any international court that rules against its vital interests. Hence, in the long run, "interpretation replicates power."'[123] Given this perception that the powerful need not respect the decisions of international courts and tribunals, it is irrational for China, the USA, Russia, the UK, or France to bother with courts. It is that perception that can be modified taking an approach inspired by the world of theatre.

## II International Legal Process and Theatre

Realism has had an impressively long run as the dominant ideology of foreign policy,[124] a fact that proves the old aphorism 'ideas matter'. Still, it is an idea with little to show for its long tenure. It has led to a world wracked by armed conflict and flooded with weapons of every imaginable kind. Other ideas promise far better outcomes, including an idea for revitalizing international legal processes for the peaceful settlement of disputes. Revitalizing the idea of peace through legal process builds on current process theory by looking to the world of theatre. The arts fascinate, and among the arts, the theatre arts have features in common with legal process. The commonality is strong enough to warrant borrowing for purposes of attracting new interest, even passion, for alternatives to war.

### *A International Legal Process*

Judges and lawyers involved in the practice of law tend to hold a set of common concepts about the legal process. These were identified a century ago by two Harvard law professors, Henry Hart and Albert Sacks. They labelled them 'Legal Process'.[125] Hart and Sacks were

123 M. Pollack, 'Political Science and International Adjudication', in C. P. R. Romano, K. J. Alter, and Y. Shany (eds.), *The Oxford Handbook of International Adjudication* (Oxford: Oxford University Press, 2014), 358–87, 362. See also notes 115–16 and accompanying text.

124 N. Guilhot, *After the Enlightenment: Political Realism and International Relations in the Mid-Twentieth Century* (Cambridge: Cambridge University Press, 2017), and see Introduction, this Volume.

125 W. N. Eskridge, Jr and P. P. Frickey, 'An Historical and Critical Introduction to the Legal Process', in H. M. Hart, Jr and A. M. Sacks, *The Legal Process: Basic Problems in the Making and Application of Law*, W. N. Eskridge, Jr and P. P. Frickey (eds.) (Egan, MN: Foundation Press, 1994).

responding to another set of ideas also labeled 'Realism' that had emerged in the late nineteenth century to challenge the formalist view that judges could objectively apply the law, irrespective of personal views.[126] The Realists recognized that a judge is influenced by many things besides the words of a statute or an earlier judgment. They counselled using the newly emerging social sciences to reach the most advantageous decisions for society, but they had no real arguments to justify as a matter of law why any judge should do so. US Supreme Court Justice Oliver Wendell Holmes decreed famously in answer to the question, 'What constitutes the law?', 'what is decided by the courts ...'.[127] Most legal systems provide review of sole judicial decisions, and courts of last instance tend to have multiple judges, requiring a majority. At the least, the judge will have to persuade a higher court or a fellow judge of what the law is beyond her own view, unless she does not care about being overruled. Hart and Sacks found in the law multiple methods of ensuring the law was not simply a judge's personal view. They argued that requiring publicly available reasons, or, in their words the 'reasoned elaboration' of decisions, served as the best restraint.[128]

Hart and Sacks based this central provision of Legal Process on their understanding of the purpose of law. They taught that law and its institutions exist to settle 'by authority of the group various types of questions of concern to the group'.[129] Hart argued further that a 'court in making law is bound to base its action not on free judgment of relative social advantage, but on a process of reasoned development of authoritative starting points (i.e., statutes, prior judicial decisions, etc. etc.)'.[130] These starting points tether decisions to the wider community beyond the courtroom and to the law made on behalf of that community. Hart and Sacks urged the continuing study of legal process and 'consideration of legal doctrine in light of law's purposes and the polity's underlying

126 Ibid., lviii.

127 O. W. Holmes, Jr, 'The Path of the Law', *Harvard Law Review,* 10 (1897), 457–78, 460.

128 Eskridge and Frickey, 'An Historical and Critical Introduction to the Legal Process' 1994 (n. 125), xci.

129 Ibid., lxxxiii (quoting H. M. Hart, Jr, 'Notes and Other Materials for the Study of Legislation' (1950)).

130 Ibid., lxxix-lxxx (quoting Hart's Legislation Notes (1946–47), Oct. 29, 1946, at 8–9).

principles'.[131] By the 1950s, Legal Process thinking became the background assumption of legal method in general with its simple but elegant approach, one quite similar to that extolled in *The Oresteia.* Reformers have sought to infuse the Legal Process approach with more inclusive perspectives[132] while continuing to support the need to respect 'formal authorities' as law's most distinctive feature.[133] Certain attempts have also been made to adapt Legal Process for application to international law, but the method already applies to law in general. It needs no adaptation to fit international legal process.[134]

Hart and Sacks looked beyond courts and judicial decisionmaking in teaching the legal process. Negotiation in lawyers' offices, hearings before agencies, and the like are also legal process. Looking at the deficits in international legal process, the problem of attitude is plain. The lack of progress toward compulsory dispute resolution, the failure to appear before courts and tribunals, the refusal to comply with decisions, all speak to a shortcoming in international legal process to inspire respect, let alone enthusiasm. In 2007, Martti Koskenniemi wrote: 'It is high time that "international adjudication" were made the object of critical analysis instead

[131] Ibid.

[132] See W. N. Eskridge, Jr and G. Peller, 'The New Public Law Movement: Moderation as a Postmodern Cultural Form', *Michigan Law Review*, 89 (1991), 707–91; and D. B. Rodriguez, 'The Substance of the New Legal Process', *California Law Review*, 77 (1989) 919–53.

[133] Eskridge and Frickey, 'An Historical and Critical Introduction to the Legal Process' 1994 (n. 125), cxxvi.

[134] See A. Chayes/T. Ehrlichand A. F. Lowenfeld, *International Legal Process: Materials for an Introductory Course* (Boston: Little, Brown, & Co, 1968); and H. H. Koh, 'Transnational Legal Process', *Nebraska Law Review*, 75 (1996), 181–207. See also support for formalism in International Law Commission, 'Fragmentation of International Law: Difficulties Arising from the Diversification and Expansion of International Law – Report of the Study Group of the International Law Commission', UN Doc. A/CN.4/L.682 (Apr. 13, 2006), as corrected UN Doc. A/CN.4/L.682/Corr.1 (Aug. 11, 2006) (finalized by Martti Koskenniemi), 251:

> The growing body of courts and tribunals can help ensure universality by employing certain approaches to decision-making. Formalism, for example, is a legal method that strives for objective analysis of law, minimizing reliance on personal opinion, personal moral views, or the personal policy of the one analyzing the law. Formal analysis of a treaty is based on strict adherence to the treaty text as opposed to the reader interpreting words to reach personal objectives. Formal analysis of customary law is based on careful assessment of practice and *opinio juris.*

of religious faith.'[135] Critical analysis is a proven method of information gathering as to problems. Critical analysis does not, however, generate solutions. In the case of the ICJ and other international courts, poor adherence is a well-known problem. The need is for a response, one that can stimulate new faith in courts.

In the past, the campaigners for peace through law were motivated by the horrors of war. Jane Addams wrote passionately and poetically of the widows and orphans who struggled to reach safety in America because husbands and fathers had died fighting Europe's wars. She wrote:

> [W]e will no longer endure without protest that added burden of maimed and invalid men and poverty-stricken women and orphans which war places on us.
>
> ... [W]e will no longer endure that hoary evil which in an hour destroys, or tolerate that denial of the sovereignty of reason and justice by which war and all that makes for war today render impotent the idealism of the race.[136]

Addams pleaded for a 'moral substitute for war' on podiums across Europe and North America.[137]

Aeschylus and the later proponents of international legal process also used the horror of violence and military conflict as the principal reason to argue for alternatives. They contrasted the orderly, impartial, and reasoned methods of law with chaotic and destructive physical force. Yet, violence no longer seems to horrify. Global culture is inundated with entertainment that features killing, news media that constantly streams scenes of devastation, and the Realist message that using force to pursue goals is righteous. Describing a teenager blown apart by an unlawful drone strike or the statistics of hundreds of children dying in similar ways seem to make no impact on leaders.[138] Drone attacks beyond armed conflict zones

[135] M. Koskenniemi, 'The Ideology of International Adjudication and the 1907 Hague Conference', in Y. Daudet (ed.), *Topicality of the 1907 Hague Conference, The Second Hague Peace Conference: Proceedings of the Workshop held in The Hague on 6–7 September 2007* (Leiden: Martinus Nijhoff, 2008), 127–152, 152.

[136] Quotation in J. C. Farrell, *Beloved Lady: A History of Jane Addams' Ideas on Reform and Peace* (Baltimore: Johns Hopkins Press, 1967), 140 (quoting Jane Addams, 1915).

[137] Ibid., 144.

[138] For a graphic and detailed description of the killing of an al-Qaeda propagandist, Anwar Al Awlaki, as well as his teenage son and nephew, see J. Scahill, *Dirty Wars: The World is a Battlefield* (New York: Nation Books, 2013).

continue in increasing numbers by ever more attackers.[139] Drones lower the political cost of killing by completely protecting the operator from kinetic counter-attack. The next step is removing human beings altogether from the killing process.[140] Computers have the capacity to select and execute human targets.

The latest weapons developments indicate the high acceptance of violence, as does the discussion to this point on militarized peace-keeping, attenuated self-defence, violent rebellion, and armed intervention. This acceptance of violence is paired with the attitude of scepticism for the world's alternatives to killing. Parties to conflict fear giving up to a third party the power to decide. They often show more confidence in their ability to use military force than engage in direct negotiation. The attitude is irrational. In case after case, from Afghanistan to Zimbabwe, the facts of history and military science direct parties away from the use of armed force. Rational facts are plainly not enough to overcome what Andrew Bacevich has called 'infatuation' with the military.[141] The acceptance of violence is

139 In 2003, Asma Jahangir reported to the UN Human Rights Committee that the US use of an unmanned aerial vehicle or drone to target an individual and five people in a vehicle with him in Yemen in 2002 was extra-judicial, unlawful killing. Special Rapporteur on Extrajudicial, Summary, or Arbitrary Executions, 'Report of the Special Rapporteur, Asma Jahangir, Civil and Political Rights, Including the Questions of Disappearances and Summary Executions', UN Doc. E/CN.4/2003/3 (13 January 2003), paras. 37–39. Her report failed to slow the US killing for one moment: '... the drone wars implemented by Obama, mean [Trump's] Democratic predecessor still has a considerable amount of blood on his hands. After all, drones were Obama's default weapon, and he significantly expanded their use during his own administration. If the previous Democratic president had cared more about innocent life and gone out of his way to protect it, perhaps his co-partisans would be willing to hold Trump accountable on this issue.' M. Rozsa, 'Why Aren't Americans Outraged Over Trump's Escalation of Drone Strikes?' *Salon* (4 February 2018), available at www.salon.com/2018/02/04/why-arent-americans-outraged-over-trumps-escalation-of-drone-strikes/.

140 See, e.g., N. Bhuta, S. Beck, R. Geiss, H.-Y. Liu, and C. Kress, *Autonomous Weapons Systems, Law, Ethics, & Policy* (Cambridge: Cambridge University Press, 2016); R. Sparrow, 'Robots and Respect: Assessing the Case Against Autonomous Weapons', *Ethics & International Affairs*, 30 (2016), 93–116; International Committee of the Red Cross, 'Autonomous Weapon Systems: Implications of Increasing Autonomy in the Critical Functions of Weapons' (1 September 2016); and C. Heyns, 'Report of the Special Rapporteur on Extrajudicial, Summary or Arbitrary Executions, UN Office of the High Commissioner on Human Rights', UN Doc. A/HRC/23/47 (9 April 2013).

141 A. J. Bacevich, *The Limits of Power: The End of American Exceptionalism* (New York: Henry Holt & Co, 2008), 160.

linked to the rejection of ever losing. Part of the Realist world view sees a party to a conflict that can undertake an armed attack as superior to one losing a case in an international forum on the basis of international law. France, the USA, and China have all demonstrated this attitude in walking away from the ICJ and PCA upon receiving adverse decisions.[142] The attitude has spread. Nigeria has failed to respect the boundary found by the ICJ in 2002 in a case with Cameroon.[143] Colombia rejected out-of-hand the ICJ's decision in an island and maritime boundary case with Nicaragua.[144] Colombia did well in the case – yet, because the ICJ did not accept all of Colombia's arguments, Colombia refused to comply. Colombia refused, despite the reality that good relations with Nicaragua will pay dividends far beyond the resources of the ocean space the ICJ found belongs legally to Nicaragua.[145]

While it is important never to give up on reason, supplementing pure reason could attract the world to see things differently, to build on developments such as the resistance within the tech community toward having their work used for military purposes.[146] In 2018, Ethiopia announced the intention to finally comply after eighteen years with an arbitral award on title to territory found to belong to Eritrea.[147] The idea of calm order in the chaos of the present may well have mass appeal, disseminated through a new vocabulary.

[142] See notes 16–20 and accompanying text.

[143] ICJ, *Land and Maritime Boundary Between Cameroon and Nigeria* (*Cameroon* v. *Nigeria*, Equatorial Guinea intervening), Judgment of 10 October 2002, ICJ Reports 2002.

[144] ICJ, *Territorial and Maritime Dispute* (*Nicaragua* v. *Colombia*), Judgment of 19 November 2012, ICJ Reports 2012.

[145] See, e.g., P. Holley, 'Tech Leaders Say Killer Robots Would be "Dangerously Destabilizing" Force in the World', *Chicago Tribune* (20 July 2018), available at www.chicagotribune.com/business/ct-biz-killer-robots-danger-20180720-story .html.

[146] A. Huneeus, 'Compliance with Judgments and Decisions', in C. P. R. Romano and K. J. Alter and Y. Shany, *The Oxford Handbook of International Adjudication*, (Oxford: Oxford University Press, 2014), 437–63, 455.

[147] P. Schemm, 'Ethiopia Says It is Ready to Implement Eritrea Peace Deal and Privatize Parts of the Economy', *Washington Post* (5 June 2018), available at www .washingtonpost.com/world/africa/ethiopia-says-its-ready-to-implement-eri trea-peace-deal-and-privatize-parts-of-the-economy/2018/06/05/f5813936-68e4-11e8-9e38-24e693b38637_story.html?utm_term=.3a28e938a135.

### *B Legal Drama*

People attend the theatre to be part of something – part of a community brought together by a literary work performed by actors who interact with a live audience. Theatre is an art form of participation. It compares with participation in law and government, institutions that promote popular perception of their legitimacy. For Jürgen Habermas, law is a functional response to potential conflicts in the absence of shared religious belief. Law has substituted for religion, providing a way to common life without the need for common answers to fundamental questions. Law does, however, require participation to serve this role. It is through common action, including communication, that leads to shared belief in process in the absence of common belief in substantive answers.[148]

Habermas' conception is comparable to Joseph Raz's insight that the basis of legal authority lies in the common coordination it allows members of society in responding to shared problems.[149] Both Habermas and Raz see law not unlike law and economics scholars, as an instrument for problem solving. The difference is that they also see in the coordination or interaction that law requires the simultaneous development of bonds among individuals and groups, leading to a sense of community.[150] This community sense gained through participation in legal responses to social challenges also creates an appreciation or acceptance of law. Raz has identified participation as an explanation for social acceptance of law that underlies Hart's basis of legal authority in that same social acceptance.[151]

[148] See generally J. Habermas, *Between Facts and Norms: Contributions to a Discourse Theory of Law and Democracy*, W. Rehg (trans.), (Cambridge, MA: MIT Press, 1996). See also J. Bohman and W. Rehg, 'Jürgen Habermas', in E. N. Zalta (ed.), *Stanford Encyclopedia of Philosophy* (Fall 2017), 1–59, 37.

[149] J. Raz, *The Authority of Law: Essays on Law and Morality* (Oxford: Clarendon Press, 1979). See also J. Waldron, 'Authority for Officials', in L. Meyer, S. Paulson, T. Pogge (eds.), *Rights, Culture and the Law: Themes from the Legal and Political Philosophy of Joseph Raz* (2003), 45; and S. Besson, 'The Authority of International Law – Lifting the Veil', *Sydney Law Review*, 31 (2009), 343–80, 344, 345 note 2.

[150] See, e.g., J. Brunnée and S. Toope, *Legitimacy and Legality in International Law: An Interactional Account* (Cambridge: Cambridge University Press, 2010). More specifically on the effect of participation in international courts and tribunals, see, e.g., A. S. Sweet, 'Judicialization and the Construction of Governance', *Comparative Political Studies*, 32 (1999), 147–84.

[151] See Chapter 1.

The attitude of acceptance of law and legal institutions that Hart, Raz, and Habermas observe, born of participation (inspired by tradition), is the opposite of the attitude of domination, force, and coercion in problem solving. It is an attitude that not only supports law within states but international law as well.

Students of theatre understand why participation in public, orderly, and literary events has positive impact. Paul Woodruff writes in *The Necessity of Theater: The Art of Watching and Being Watched,* that '[t]heater is most theater . . . when the arts of watching and being watched merge and give way to shared action, shared experience, a shared moment of transcendence, beyond theater'.[152] Howard Stein, commenting on Woodruff's book, explains that human beings become 'aware of what it is to be human . . . by watching and being watched'.[153] Woodruff highlights how watching together leads to shared meaning, and how this founds community, both on the level of interpersonal relationships, and on the level of culture and society. 'Theater is immediate, its actions are present to participants and audience.'[154] As everyone is a participant in the theatre, however, the better terms are 'performers' and 'audience'. Theatre is only possible with engaged participants – on stage and off. In film or literature, the action may be present to the watcher, but one cannot participate in its art as in the theatre. Peter Brook's *The Empty Space* sees the 'immediate theater' as theatre in its fullest.[155]

As with the visual arts and music, the experience of theatre links us to each other. Indeed, it would seem the theatre in bringing people physically together may more directly open us to the other. Theatre provides tangible evidence of humanity's social side, exposing the need for law that harmonizes life in society through the pursuit of justice. Art attracts without the spectacle of actual violence or the nihilism of zero-sum outcomes. It involves an aspect of human nature that does not involve striving for advantage.

152 P. Woodruff, *The Necessity of Theater: The Art of Watching and Being Watched* (Oxford: Oxford University Press, 2008), 229.

153 H. Stein, 'Theater as a Humanizing Force', *Arion* 16.3 (Winter 2009), available at www.bu.edu/arion/files/2010/03/Stein-Theater-as-Humanizing.pdf. (The article summarizes key aspects of Woodruff's book, n. 152.)

154 Woodruff, *The Necessity of Theater* 2008 (n. 152), 17.

155 P. Brook, *The Empty Space* (New York: Touchstone Books, 1996), 98.

One of the best-known dramatists of the twentieth century, Bertolt Brecht, wanted audiences to watch his plays with a critical eye. He presented a show for what it was, an illusion. He wanted theatregoers to engage with the action but not to become completely absorbed by it. He wanted audiences to maintain a critical stance. Brecht taught that plays are illusory but so is life. Theatre and society are both reliant on constructed concepts and representations. Those concepts can be flawed, contradictory, unsettling, or comforting – and they can be changed. Brecht sought just this – new attitudes, new awareness, new impetus to action.

In Brecht's play *Mother Courage*, the central character is a woman trying to steer herself and her children through the Thirty Years' War – the very same horrific war that drove Grotius to write *The Law of War and Peace.*[156] She makes many mistakes, but constantly strives to save her children. Despite her striving, the children perish. Brecht did not want audiences to identify or sympathize with Mother Courage, though many do despite her serious shortcomings – more proof of people's innate empathetic capacity. Brecht wanted the play to provoke people to action by seeing Mother Courage's care, but also her complicity in the social upheaval around her. He wanted audience participants to act to prevent such complicity in evil in their own lives.[157]

People do not leave the theatre as winners or losers. They may leave transformed, depending on the quality of the play, the performers, the staging, the scenery, the space and their own commitment to engage. Participants in international legal process need not be designated 'winners' or 'losers' either. They may be assessed for the quality of their performances, their ability to communicate. Transforming attitudes to favour international settlement of disputes might begin with new terminology.[158] The use of certain vocabulary can have transformative effect.[159]

156 B. Brecht, *Mother Courage and Her Children*, E. Bentley (trans.), (New York: Grove Press, 1955).
157 See B. Brecht, 'The Modern Theatre is the Epic Theatre', in J. Willett (ed./trans.), *Brecht on Theater: The Development of an Aesthetic* (London: Methuen, 1964), 33–42.
158 J. J. A. Shaw, 'Introduction to the Special Issue on Reimagining Justice: Aesthetics and Law', *Liverpool Law Review*, 38 (2017), 1–10, 1.
159 M. P. Hitt and K. Searles, 'Media Coverage and Public Approval of the US Supreme Court', *Political Communication* 35 (2018), 1–21.

In discussing law, lawyers, government officials, scholars, and the media use the terms of competition commonly from sports and the military. They refer to 'winners and losers', 'victory and defeat', 'failed and effective strategies', the 'so-called game-frame', which emphasizes strategy rather than principle.[160] Analogies, terminology, and metaphors drawn from competition have clearly corrosive effects on regard for law and legal institutions. Empirical evidence has demonstrated what scholars of language and aesthetics have long observed, the terminology used matters. Terms from games and military engagement are often the same in English, the metaphor 'game plan' is interchangeable with 'war plan'. Such terms undermine regard for courts and their decisions. The public perceives judicial decisions as unprincipled, nothing more than 'partisan wins, losses, and competition'.[161] Exposure to such terminology has 'deleterious' effects on respect for courts.[162] The decision-makers themselves, judges and commissioners, are also likely to be impacted, ruling in favour of their team.

War, sport, and theatre share the characteristics of attracting mass participation. The distinction between theatre and war, however, is the creative productivity of an art form. Art is generative of the new. Sun Tzu's title, *The Art of War*, links to the performative and creative aspects of designing a war plan and conducting armed conflict. The result is not, however, a new creation; it is destruction. Theatre combines another artistic form – literature – and transforms it into a production.

International legal process and theatre have much in common – far more than battle and games. Terms from the performance arts are highly transferable. Legal process requires a space,[163] presenters, audience, and words. It is more generative than destructive. It requires vigilance and critical observation to prevent it becoming a tool of oppression. Today, law requires creative analysis to prevent it becoming irrelevant, a sideshow. New terminology of participation and new outreach to the mass audience reachable through new media is possible. Practitioners and advocates before courts already use many of the techniques of theatre. They know to characterize

[160] Ibid., 1, 6. [161] Ibid., 1. [162] Ibid., 15.

[163] On the importance of space for legal process, see J. Resnik and D. E. Curtis, 'Representing Justice: From Renaissance to 21st Century Courthouses', *Yale Law School Faculty Scholarship* (2007), available at http://digitalcommons.law.yale.edu/cgi/viewcontent.cgi?article=1692&context=fss_papers.

their clients as real communities and individuals to convince judges and the public gallery that they deserve empathy. This knowledge can be incorporated into theory and education about international law more generally. The goal can be equipping an international law-trained adviser to a government, for example, with the vocabulary and theory that provide political leaders with a more complete understanding of the options.

Legal educators, especially educator-advocates who have a long history at the International Court of Justice, can see their role as more than the few hours in the courtroom. As Hart and Sacks taught, the legal process extends to client counselling. It extends to persuading clients not only to enter into dispute resolution but to comply with outcomes. Chapter 1 provided a new perspective on compliance. It is for the good of the community, even when not directly in the material interest of a party. One of the profound lessons of *The Oresteia* is how to speak of the party that failed to persuade the judge on all points. Athena, the judge, offers the Furies, who are angered by her decision and are threatening death and destruction, 'an honored place within the community'.[164] This offer is for accepting the judgment, not winning it.

Derek Bowett was a prominent educator-advocate. He was the Whewell Professor of Public International Law in Cambridge and one of the most sought-after advocates before the International Court of Justice in the 1970s–1990s.[165] He represented Libya under Colonel Ghaddafi in several boundary disputes at the court. He returned to Cambridge after meeting in Tripoli with the infamously mercurial and authoritarian leader. The ICJ had just ruled more favourably in a case for one of Libya's neighbours than Libya. Bowett described to the students of his general international law class how he had persuaded Ghaddafi to comply with the judgment. He recounted how it was one of his most challenging performances. He succeeded by explaining the honour that accompanies a demonstration of respect for the law. It was a real success for peace in the region.[166]

[164] Gewirtz, 'Aeschylus's Law' 1988 (n. 33), 1046.

[165] Ian Brownlie, James Crawford, Vaughan Lowe, and Allain Pellet are other examples.

[166] The author was a student in Bowett's class and recalls the day he returned from Libya to recount this event. Compare Bowett's writing in apology for the British role in the Suez Crisis described in Chapter 4.

Legal process is not the pure art of theatre. Law requires that the substance of the legal process is found in the sources of the law. This understanding limits the open, more fully creative essence of theatre, distinguishing the two areas of human endeavour but allowing them to respond to different human needs. Still, the metaphor of theatre can open thinking to new persuasive reasons to prefer law to war.

Woodruff also speaks to the theatre/law connection referencing the ancient Greeks' association of a jury with the chorus found commonly in classical Greek drama. In *Antigone*, a woman buries her brother in defiance of the legal authority's command and faces death. Her fiancé tries to dissuade the authority from carrying out the sentence. A vigorous debate ensues, nearly erupting in violence. The chorus, listening like the jury on behalf of the community, implores them to listen to one another: 'Both sides spoke well.'[167] The chorus/jury values and benefits from both performances, regardless of how they finally decide. The makers of theatre regularly borrow the metaphor of law and the modes of legal process. In a perceptive essay on post-9/11 British theatre, Ian Ward writes of a group of authors all looking to uncover gross miscarriages of justice. 'Theater … is the "best court society has", whilst "Judgement" is "the heart of theater"'. '[T]he theater is the one "place where society can go to take a sober account of itself, and see itself more truly"'.[168]

Borrowing in the other direction from theatre to law is also occurring but can expand, replacing the terms and the thinking drawn from competition. Borrowing from the theatre arts may well reignite something so patently missing from popular attitudes toward international dispute resolution since World War I: passionate commitment. In *The Oresteia*, Gewirtz observes that 'passion is seen as a central, necessary element of law …'.[169] Passion/emotion *is* an essential element of law; it is not simply cold reason. Reason alone does not rule the world of law. Different terminology leading to different perception has a chance to rebalance attitudes toward law from something appealing only to the weak to a new ground of prestige.[170]

[167] *Antigone*, Line 725. [168] Ibid.
[169] Gewirtz, 'Aeschylus's Law' 1988 (n. 33), 1047–8.
[170] For additional analysis aimed at improving the effectiveness of international courts, see K. J. Alter, L. R. Helfer, and M. R. Madsen (eds.), *International Court Authority* (Oxford: Oxford University Press, 2018).

## Conclusion

International law's principles of dispute resolution are paired with the prohibition on the use of force.[171] The most important dispute resolution principle obligates states involved in violent conflict or the threat of violent conflict to seek peaceful resolution. This restatement of the principle is not widely appreciated. It is more common to hear that if a party decides to resolve a dispute, peaceful means must be used. The obligation, however, as shown in this chapter, is more robust, requiring action. This conclusion contrasts with the history of declining interest in the peaceful resolution of international conflict, a cause that once engaged wide segments of popular opinion. In contrast, the irrational belief in the efficacy of military force has grown.

Well before France left the ICJ's compulsory jurisdiction in 1974, enthusiasm for peace through law had faded. Indeed, the clear turn away from popular support for a world court occurred with World War I. The champions of alternatives lost their audiences and faded into obscurity.[172] Militaristic ideologies followed, including Realism, which continues to drive spending, research, and policy toward the use of military force. Under Realism, the use of international courts and tribunals is perceived as a place of unnecessary risk to be avoided by the self-perceived powerful.

A reversal of such a durable way of thinking requires a bold approach. Scanning the world for what attracts – what fascinates the way war does – leads to the arts. The arts hold the secret of attracting humanity. If war fascinates, so does art. What attracts people to the theatre can attract them to courtroom. The ancient Greeks developed institutions of legal process through drama. That approach offers a way to reignite popular interest in peaceful settlement. Using the language of participation and performance, rather than that of war and games, can help resurrect respect for legal process and new interest in process theory.[173] Actors who refuse to perform out of hubris are rightly criticized. Good performances, even if not the staring or award-winning role, are praised, appreciated, and lead to new opportunities. Every performance helps build a community of non-violent, shared culture.

[171] Murphy, 'The Obligation of States to Settle Disputes' 1973 (n. 40), 57.
[172] Farrell, *Beloved Lady* 1967 (n. 136).
[173] Gewirtz, 'Aeschylus's Law' 1988 (n. 33), 1043.

# Conclusion

Reigning political ideologies that ignore international law have helped to deliver a world in which armed conflicts drag on for decades and vast resources are diverted to war.[1] In Sisyphean fashion, holders of these perspectives persevere in advocating for military force in the face of the most obvious military failures.[2] The use of armed force is popular seemingly because populations lack awareness of alternatives.[3] During and immediately after World War II, when a similar logic of violence threatened to overwhelm resort to law and legal process,[4] Hersch Lauterpacht published his article 'The Grotian Tradition'. He challenged the confidence of Realists in military force. When Lauterpacht wrote, however, he could still rely on his readers' knowledge of natural law and the

1 For just two examples, see C. J. Chivers, 'Wars Without End', *New York Times* (8 August 2018), available at www.nytimes.com/2018/08/08/magazine/war-afghanistan-iraq-soldiers.html ('The Pentagon's failed campaigns in Iraq and Afghanistan left a generation of soldiers with little to fight for but one another.' Ibid.) And, 'Democratic Republic of Congo Profile – Timeline', *BBC* (1 August 2018), available at www.bbc.com/news/world-africa-13286306. The conflict in the Democratic Republic of the Congo (formerly Zaire), ongoing in 2018 at the time of writing, began in 1996.

2 Ibid.

3 See, e.g., M. Zenko, 'America's First Reality TV War', *Foreign Policy* (16 April 2018) (on Trump's decision to attack Syria in April 2018 being about little more than a dramatic political gesture), available at http://foreignpolicy.com/2018/04/16/americas-first-reality-tv-war/.

4 See, e.g., E. H. Carr, *The Twenty Years' Crisis 1919–1939* (New York: Macmillan & Co, 1939); H. J. Morgenthau, 'Positivism, Functionalism, and International Law', *American Journal of International Law*, 34 (1940), 260–84; G. Kennan, *American Diplomacy 1900–1950* (New York: Mentor, 1951); and the Introduction to this Volume.

passion for peace through law that lingered in the popular imagination. *The Art of Law in the International Community* has returned to those ideas, seeking to re-elevate them with three propositions on the theory, substance, and practice of law for peace.

~ The first proposition is that a persuasive theory of international law for peace includes natural law, positive law, and process law components. Positivism, the theory that consent accounts for the legally binding quality of rules, is a sufficient explanation for most substantive legal content. Positivism does not explain, however, why consent binds. An explanation from outside positivism, specifically outside the theory of consent, is needed. The only other available theory is natural law. Natural law explains why consent-based positive law binds, what the moral limits of positive rules are, and how the general principles needed to maintain fairness function. Process theory aids in understanding and improving the effective and just operation of the positive law. Yet, as discussed throughout the book, knowledge of natural law and process theory have declined for decades, weakening understanding of and respect for law. Chapter 1 investigated the reasons for this decline, finding that the religious aspects of natural law have lost meaning for many in a diverse, post-Enlightenment world. As Onora O'Neill explains, loss of faith has led to a tendency is to assert the law's authority without any deeper justification.[5]

The belief that obedience to law is a divine command has faded, so that while the tradition of law compliance continues, it lacks a rationale beyond self-interest. Chapter 1 described a revitalized natural law based on a secular justification for complying when wholly for the good of others. Parallel to divine command, the universal pleasure in the contemplation of beauty provides the starting point for an argument for law compliance as altruism. Renewing natural law from this aesthetic perspective opens a way to shifting the balance of persuasion from Realism to peace through law.

*The Art of Law* supports a return to natural law through aesthetic philosophy, the study of beauty. The international community is a community of diversity.[6] The law of such a community must be

[5] O. O'Neill, 'Accountable Institutions, Trustworthy Cultures', *Second Annual TMC Asser Lecture* (The Hague: Asser Press, 2017), 4–5.

[6] A. Adeno, 'Imagining the International Community', *Human Rights Quarterly*, 31 (2009), 129–62.

accessible to people of all faiths and none. Aesthetic philosophy reveals that contemplation of beauty and the experience of pleasure it generates is a universal experience. It is an experience that provides a philosophical basis for honouring law even in the absence of personal advantage or disadvantage. The insight provided by beauty is comparable to the insight of theologians in discerning divine law. These are two closely related paths to the same principles of natural law. The secular path is especially well suited to revitalizing the natural law component of contemporary international law. Revitalized natural law supports the authority of international law to command compliance and underpins the international community's most important norms: the prohibitions on the use of force, genocide, torture, slavery, apartheid, and attacking civilians in armed conflict. Natural law further explains inherent general principles such as equality, fairness, attribution, necessity, and proportionality.

If, for the religious person, divine command explains the reason to obey the law for the good of others, beauty conveys the same insight. Compliance with the positive law is understandable when it is set in a frame of natural law that uses reason, observation of the natural world, and transcendent inspiration as the ground for accepting the good of law compliance, regardless of personal benefit or detriment. Aesthetic philosophy, thus, provides reasons for participation and compliance with law designed to support flourishing everywhere.

~ *The Art of Law*'s second proposition is that the core provision of the international legal regime of peace is the prohibition on the use of force. It is a *jus cogens*, natural law norm, which is no empty label. *Jus cogens* norms permit no derogation. The no-derogation point is well accepted respecting other *jus cogens* norms on genocide, slavery, torture, and apartheid, for example. Yet, owing to the influence of Realism and other causes, commentators resist the implications of not derogating from the prohibition on the use of force.[7] Instead, the tendency is to champion new exceptions to the prohibition, responding to changing security concerns or subjective views of moral imperative. Chapter 2 shows that in the history of international law, prohibiting force has been associated with the natural

[7] J. A. Green, 'Questioning the Peremptory Status of the Prohibition of the Use of Force', *Michigan Journal of International Law*, 39 (2011), 215–57.

law and the natural law's normative goal of leading women and men to virtue. The prohibition on the use of force is part of the essence of law in controlling violence and of supporting the conditions of social harmony. Law exists as an alternative to force and violence. In all legal systems, as in the international one, resort to force is exceptional. It is typically permitted in self-defence and to the authorities. These principles reflect the international community's understanding of what promotes security and morality.

Over the long history of the prohibition on force, different versions of the principle have evolved. In 1945, in adopting the United Nations Charter the international community agreed to the version found today in Article 2(4). That is the version from which no derogation is permitted. Indisputably, no derogation means that no new treaty rule may alter the substance of Article 2(4).[8] Less well known is the fact that no derogation also means Article 2(4) may not be diluted or weakened through interpretation. Article 2(4) may be discerned in the future, for example, as clearly prohibiting all external intervention in civil war or resort to force by non-state actors in rebellion against a government.[9]

Realist belief in armed force has militated against this version of Article 2(4). Extraordinary levels of spending have been devoted to the promise of greater personal security through resort to force. Studies have shown, however, that violence begets violence. Security purchased at the price of obedience to law often leads to greater insecurity.[10] Almost inexplicably, the confidence in killing has moved beyond the security realm to humanitarianism. Since the end of the Cold War, attempts have been made to weaken the prohibition using moral arguments in favour of so-called 'humanitarian intervention', also known at times as 'Responsibility to Protect'. These arguments have provided a particularly strong challenge to the *jus cogens* prohibition on force. They invoke the

[8] United Nations Convention on the Law of Treaties, 23 May 1969, 1155 UNTS 331, *reprinted in* 8 ILM 679 (1969), arts. 53 and 64.

[9] See Chapter 5.

[10] See, e.g., the American Civil Liberties Union (ACLU) study of the link between excessive use of force by police in the United States and the country's continual involvement in armed conflict abroad. American Civil Liberties Union, *War Comes Home, The Excessive Militarization of American Policing* (June 2014), https://www.aclu.org/report/war-comes-home-excessive-militarization-american-police.

venerable idea of civil disobedience – that if the law undermines or restricts the accomplishment of a moral good, the law is immoral and has no binding quality. Since NATO's intervention in Kosovo in 1999, the moral good of protecting human rights has been used to justify the use of military force for human rights. The logic omits the fact that military force is never itself a moral good. Killing may be justified in situations of extremis but is always a tragedy. As Chapter 2 demonstrated, moral reasoning leads to a different conclusion, that Article 2(4) is a good. When human rights are violated or other humanitarian concerns are raised, the moral answer is not to resort to military force and inevitable death, injury, and destruction.[11] The answer is to turn to legal alternatives to unlawful violence, the topic of Chapter 6.

The legal alternatives to using force have been relatively neglected in contrast to the interest in weakening the prohibition on force. In recent decades, the arguments for justifying armed measures have reached beyond Article 2(4) to self-defence (UN Charter Article 51) and UN Security Council authorization.[12] Chapters 3 and 4 dealt with these topics, reviewing the large literature that approaches them from the perspective of positivism. The proper interpretation of self-defence and Security Council authorization, however, begins with the fact that the prohibition on force is *jus cogens*. Self-defence and Security Council authorization are exceptions built into the prohibition so that like the prohibition itself they may not be diluted to permit greater resort to armed force. Proposals to justify more force for arms control, against terrorists, or for humanitarian purposes conflict with the prohibition. It is impossible for new rules of customary law to develop that conflict with an established peremptory norm. New contrary state practice violates these norms; it does not change them. Equally, *jus cogens* norms must be interpreted strictly to

11 F. Paddeu, 'Excusing Humanitarian Intervention: A Reply to Jure Vidmar', *EJIL* Talk!, (27 April 2017), available at www.ejiltalk.org/excusing-humanitarian-intervention-a-reply-to-jure-vidmar/.

12 See, e.g., efforts to dilute the prohibition described in V. Kattan, 'Furthering the "War on Terrorism" Through International Law: How the United States and the United Kingdom Resurrected the Bush Doctrine on Using Preventive Military Force to Combat Terrorism', *Journal on the Use of Force and International Law*, 23 (2017), 1–48; and J. Brunnée and S. J. Toope, 'Self-Defence Against Non-State Actors: Are Powerful States Willing but Unable to Change International Law?', *International and Comparative Law Quarterly*, 67 (2017), 263–86.

avoid derogation. Courts and other interpreters may discern over time that peremptory norms reach more conduct; they may not be interpreted to reach less.[13]

No derogation is permitted from the prohibition as it was adopted in 1945 in the United Nations Charter. The Charter version was intended to be all-encompassing and, thus, possibly broader than previous interpretations. It cannot be narrowed regardless of the level of practice in violation of it. These features of the prohibition on the use of force have implications for the use of force in self-defence and for force with the authorization of the Security Council. As part and parcel of the prohibition, interpretation of these exceptions may also in the future be narrower, never broader. The energy that goes into arguments to broaden the right to resort to force is better turned to advancing peaceful legal process.[14]

In any case of uncertainty, the logic of *jus cogens* requires adherence to peacetime law. The whole body of international law is structured to move toward eliminating war. The exceptions to the prohibition of force are designed to apply in narrowly defined emergencies. It is the body of human rights law that applies normally, as a matter of presumption. In any case of doubt, international law requires erring on the side of peace and peacetime law. This restatement of the prohibition likely sounds restrictive, even unduly so. The drafters of the UN Charter, however, clearly designed the Security Council for the maintenance of peace, not the promotion of war.

The Council can fulfil that role in multiple ways, including by becoming a positive force for the rule of law. Under the law governing the Council, resort to force is reserved for use as a last resort in preserving the peace. Unlike amending the veto power or other politically difficult reforms, standing for the law can be accomplished through changing mindsets. Reining in claims of justified force in self-defence should be yet easier still. The Charter's allowance for self-defence is for protection in the moment of attack, not to exact revenge, to send a message, to punish, or to secure longer-term protection through deterrence and the like. 'In essence, then, the right of self-defence ... is severely circumscribed.'[15] Ideas that

[13] Chapter 2. [14] Chapter 2.
[15] M. A. Weightman, 'Self-Defense in International Law', *Virginia Law Review*, 37 (1951), 1095–115, 1095.

recapture the imagination for peace can help support this understanding. It took two catastrophes in the twentieth century to build the law of today. It should not take a third world war to return to humanity's higher ideals.

Those ideals indicate it is right to restrict intervention by invitation and the resort to force in rebellion, the topics of Chapter 5. Invitation is not the solid exception beyond self-defence that some writers indicate that it is.[16] Inviting outside military assistance is in tension with the principles of self-determination and non-intervention. It also leads to escalation of violence. The traditional principle on intervention by invitation held that when opposition forces reach the status of belligerency, outside states must withdraw. Under the *jus cogens* prohibition on the use of force, at the very least, this restraint may not be relaxed. Arguments to do so have spread to arguing for a right to intervene on the side of government opposition fighters. The logical deduction is now being made that if intervention on the side of rebels is lawful, so is the rebellion. This erosion of the prohibition on force conflicts with the ancient moral opprobrium for war. It distracts from the moral and legal alternatives. Martin Luther King, Jr adopted non-violent resistance as the way to transform a widely segregated society. He came to non-violence through Christianity and the teaching of peace advocates, including Mahatma Gandhi. When King received the Nobel Peace Prize in 1964, he said the Prize was 'profound recognition that nonviolence is the answer to the crucial political and moral question of our time – the need for man to overcome oppression and violence without resorting to violence and oppression'.[17]

~ The third proposition turns to alternatives to violence. It is through the legal process that disputes may be resolved effectively. The hope in military force is misplaced when compared with the mechanisms of peaceful settlement. A further implication of the peremptory status of the prohibition on the use of force is to confirm the importance of the legal substitutes for war, the methods of peaceful dispute settlement. Chapter 6 linked *jus cogens* status to the obligation to proactively seek to settle disputes risking or

[16] L. Doswald-Beck, 'The Legal Validity of Military Intervention by Invitation of the Government', *British Yearbook of International Law*, 56 (1985), 189–252.

[17] Dr Martin Luther King, Jr, Acceptance Speech for the 1964 Nobel Peace Prize (10 Dec. 1964) (transcript available at: www.nobelprize.org/nobel_prizes/peace/laureates/1964/king-acceptance_en.html).

resulting in violence. As Lauterpacht taught, the most critical method for the international community is courts with compulsory jurisdiction.[18] The performance arts reveal that shifting metaphors of legal process from battle to performance could well capture the popular imagination and move the international community more fully toward Lauterpacht's vision. Empirical data reviewed in Chapter 6 supports the old truism that words matter.[19] They matter for shaping attitudes, for inspiring resort to courts, and for preferring law to war.

Reversing the hardened thinking of decades that favours military force and the scepticism towards dispute resolution requires a bold approach. Scanning the world for what attracts – what fascinates the way war does – leads to the arts. The arts hold the secret of attracting people. If war fascinates, so does art. What attracts people to the theatre can attract them to the courtroom. The ancient Greeks developed institutions of legal process through drama. Their approach offers a way to reignite interest in the peaceful settlement of international disputes. Using the language of participation and performance, rather than that of games, can steadily resurrect respect for legal process and new interest in process theory. Good performances, even if not the starring or award-winning role, are praised, appreciated, and lead to new opportunities. Every performance helps build a community of non-violent, shared culture.

Viewing international law as more art than science, more ideal than material, is to associate it once again with doing the right thing. It is not enough, to have means of enforcing international law or to point to the benefits of law compliance.[20] In today's world, militarily powerful states and wealthy states require an argument that appeals to social solidarity. Such states can always use force instead of complying with the law. The challenge is to persuade the leaders and citizens of such states to value law compliance because it

[18] Sir Hersch Lauterpacht, *The Function of Law in the International Community* (Oxford: Oxford University Press, 1933), 437–8.

[19] M. P. Hitt/Kathleen Searles, 'Media Coverage and Public Approval of the U.S. Supreme Court', *Political Communication* 35 (2018), 1–21.

[20] On the enforcement mechanisms, see M. E. O'Connell, *The Power and Purpose of International Law, Insights from the Theory and Practice of Enforcement* (New York: Oxford University Press, 2008); and on the advantages of compliance with international law see L. Henkin, *How Nations Behave* 2nd edn (New York: Columbia University Press, 1974.)

is the right thing to do, regardless of gain or pain. The study of beauty reveals the human attraction to social harmony, order, equality, and proportion over disharmony, privilege, asymmetry, and violence. It teaches law compliance as a virtue and a pleasure. These insights revitalize natural law with its higher norms and principles of fairness. They support a robust rule against the use of force.

Clarifying the peremptory status of the prohibition on force should have immediate beneficial consequences. Not only does the prohibition on the use of force support the use of alternatives, actors on the world stage can be drawn to them through a new vocabulary inspired by the performance arts. Legal educators, scholars, and legal advisers can disseminate these ideas that promise to challenge the nihilism of current ideologies.

Lauterpacht wrote to encourage these preferences:

> For peace is not only a moral idea ... Peace is pre-eminently a legal postulate. Juridically it is a metaphor for the postulate of the unity of the legal system. Juridical logic inevitably leads to condemnation, as a matter of law, of anarchy and private force. ... [M]odern international law ... has neglected to find a legal foundation for the so-called pacifism which it has relegated to the domain of morals and sociology. Just as positivism in the domain of international law has become unscientific by being driven, through its own exaggerations, to disregard the very practice of States which it professes to regard as the only source of law, so the desire of generations of international lawyers to confine their activity to a registration of the practice of States has discouraged any determined attempt at relating it to higher legal principle, or to the conception of international law as a whole.[21]

No mere critic, Lauterpacht proposed a way out of this cul-de-sac through the building of compulsory adjudication. This book has sought to update his analysis with the added evidence of the Cold War and the piecemeal World War III that has followed. In one of the great paradoxes of history, the ideas of Realism and militarism have profited from this state of constant armed conflict, rather than being defeated by it. Over-confidence in military force and the extraordinary commitment of resources committed to it continue. Attracting humanity away from the false promises of security anchored by the visible materiality of war is a daunting prospect.

[21] Lauterpacht, *The Function of Law in the International Community* 1933 (n. 18), 438.

Lauterpacht, however, retained his confidence in international law and in humanity, despite his own devastating personal losses to the madness of war.[22]

Returning to Lauterpacht's teaching, *The Art of Law* has proposed revitalizing natural law through aesthetic philosophy, deepening comprehension of what *jus cogens* status means with respect to the prohibition on the use of force – and, finally, taking a creative approach to the legal process through the inspiration of the performance arts. All three propositions incorporate Lauterpacht's understanding that international law is a space for transcendent vision. Martti Koskenniemi observed that the international community looks to international law for just such a 'horizon of transcendence'.[23] Philip Allott has sought to impart courage to generations since Lauterpacht to see the transcendent vision Lauterpacht saw.[24] That is also the goal of *The Art of Law.*

[22] Sir Hersch Lauterpacht, 'The Grotian Tradition in International Law,' *British Yearbook of International Law*, 23 (1946), 1–53.

[23] M. Koskenniemi, 'The Fate of Public International Law: Between Technique and Politics', *Modern Law Review*, 70 (2007), 1–30 (30).

[24] P. Allott, 'Europe and the Idea of the Transcendental, Human Rights and Other Imagined Entities', Conference on *The Crisis of Eurocentrism and the Future of the European Humanism: Historical, Cultural, Religious, Legal and Socio-Economic Perspectives*, Università Cattolica del Sacro Cuore, Milan (16 April 2016).

# Index

Graham Cambridge · Orla Lynch ·
James Windle

# The Desistance Journey

## Into Recovery and Out of Chaos

palgrave
macmillan